Wheels of Creation

A Guide to Life After Death, Reincarnation & the Journey of Your Soul

Wheels of Creation

A Guide to Life After Death, Reincarnation & the Journey of Your Soul

E. M. Nicolay and H. L. Jang

Forethought Publishing

Forethought Publishing
P.O. Box 7023, La Quinta, CA 92248

"Dedicated to those who have gone ahead to light the way"

Contents

Contents

Contents

Related Books in the EssencePath Series

*The Samuel Sessions: A Collection of Sessions, Essays, Transcripts
and Revelations for Achieving Higher Spiritual Guidance, Understanding the Nature of the Multi-Dimensional Universe and Discovering your EssencePath*
A Guide that brings unique insights to awaken us to our full potential and provide the keys needed to unlock vast mysteries, including a truer vision of the
Universe, the real story behind a Soul's extraordinary journey through the
Twelve Universal Dimensions and a look into your own relationship to your
Higher Self and your guides.

Contents

 **INTRODUCTION**

There is no greater knowledge you can have than to understand the origins, mechanics and reality of your own journey – or the journey of your Soul through the multidimensional Universe. And perhaps the most significant aspect of that journey as your Soul makes its way through the twelve Universal Dimensions in order to rejoin its original Source, is the process of Reincarnation, Transmigration and Ascension.

Unfortunately, within the physical plane of the Third Universal Dimension where you are focused currently, over time the concept of Reincarnation, the Soul's simultaneous incarnation in physical forms at different points on the dimensional timeline, has been misinterpreted, misunderstood and in many cases wiped clear from your various dogmas, spiritual teachings and general awareness. In a sense, a complete understanding of the journey of your Soul has become nearly impossible to pin point, let alone comprehend.

Some consider themselves to be under the sole and utter sway of a personified omnipotent Being, or God, who doles out favors to those he has pre-selected, or provides them with Free Will and then chastises and persecutes them for exercising it via the choices they make. Others add an additional layer to this concept and believe that this same omnipotent, father-like God Being grants them one single physical lifetime during the course of which he tempts and cajoles them through an array of tests before passing final judgment on them after it is all over. In an imagined celestial proceeding after physical life, many believe that this omnipotent force determines if they deserve eternal damnation or everlasting disembodiment in a cloud-based, magical realm. And all of this is based on just one physical lifetime and the random choices made based on the experiences encountered, most of which are perceived as life or death situations where the individual makes rash, momentary choices exercising their Free Will. As a result of all this, an everlasting, no-appeals judgment is then passed upon them.

Hopefully you have sensed an ironic tone as we describe these notoriously simplistic notions of what truly is one of the most complex, multidimensional and mysterious processes known in the Universe. If you have ever wondered if the primitive notions of God and your Soul's journey you have been taught are true, let us assure you that your Soul is far more complex and, as a result, much more divine in its nature than any God-like figure you currently imagine or are guided to believe in based on the religions and cultural standards of the Earth at the present time.

In fact, we would suggest that your Soul, and the complicated multidimensional journey it undertakes through the Universe using the processes of Reincarnation, Transmigration and Ascension, is more divine, mysterious and breathtaking than any of the mythologies you have heard or been led to espouse. In this book, we intend to assist you to rediscover the vast complexity and exciting mystery of whom you really are as we unveil, layer by layer, the truth about your own journey and the journey of your Soul. In doing so, we hope to increase your understanding and knowledge of how Soul progression is achieved. Soul growth that enables it to rejoin its Source is the goal of each and every Soul, and the lifetimes a Soul creates, one of which may be you, travel through physical and non-corporeal planes of existence in order to do so. That journey takes place against the backdrop of an expanding multidimensional Universe, which is the Soul's schoolroom.

Our expedition will take us from the origins of your Soul as it is cast out by All That Is (original Source) and created with a particular energetic polarity and spiritual orientation, to how it undertakes and inhabits the many varied lifetimes and physical incarnations it takes on. We will follow the Soul's journey of reincarnations within a Universal Dimension, through the Dimension's Astral planes (the twelve Sublevels found in every Universal Dimension) after physical death and finally Ascension as your Soul transmigrates from one Universal Dimension to the next. We shall examine how the Soul utilizes its experiences in order to master the process of Soul growth, and through this process perfect its energetic "spin," a vibrational frequency and resonant signature that is the essence of its propulsion and creative expression that carries it from Dimension to Dimension, through time and space and throughout the Universe.

It is through the evolutionary process of growth known as Ascension, that every Soul ultimately comes to full comprehension, completion and reunification with "All That Is" — the Universal Consciousness, or "God." As a Soul grows in consciousness, awareness and ability, this process of growth culminates with the Soul ultimately reaching and returning to its place of origin, the highest Universal Dimensions, which we have often referred to as the true "Realms of God." The Trinity of Universal Dimensions, from which religious mythology concerning a God "Trinity" is derived and from where the number three draws its mystical connection, consists of the Tenth, Eleventh and Twelfth Universal Dimensions. These highest dimensional realms are the primordial Source from which all universal creation can be said to originate.

It is the definitive goal of each Soul to reunify with these realms after journeying through all Universal Dimensions. This is accomplished through consciousness growth arrived at through Reincarnation and Transmigration, in union with a Universal Ascension process that propels each Soul through the Universal Dimensions in a manner that is uniquely multidimensional, creative, miraculous and divine.

This process of growth through creative endeavor enables a Soul to not only transmigrate through the various dimensional realities using vehicles of both physical and spiritual incarnation, but ultimately allows the Soul to rejoin its original source, bringing with it all that it has achieved. This occurs in a metaphysical and metaphoric manner, in much the same way a family member might go into the world and bring back their personal successes in the form of who they have become to benefit their family and friends. It could also be likened to the manner by which a citizen's personal accomplishments and endeavors out in the world might one day be incorporated into mass consciousness for the benefit of the individual's community, culture, race, nation or world, whether it was the intention of the individual to do so or not.

This never-ending expansion of "All That Is" – God – continues without end, forever. In effect, the process represents universal expansion, the Universe breathing in and out, as it constantly casts out new Souls and Soul groups beginning their journey, while at the same time reintegrating the Soul entities that have completed, through the process of Reincarnation, Transmigration and Ascension, their long multidimensional journey home. It is for this very reason that scientific observation has often described the Universe as a living entity, continually in a state of magnificent expansion that appears to be without end.

Within the process of Soul Ascension, it is unfortunate that the concept of Reincarnation has come to mean a linear progression of physical lifetimes in only one Dimension. It is also unfortunate that the concept of transmigration through the various levels of physical and spiritual planes has become divorced from the multidimensional nature of the Universe and the Soul. Not only does the Soul itself journey through the Twelve Universal Dimensions, it also journeys through the Twelve Dimensional Sublevels, or Astral realms, of each Universal Dimension.

For those with an inclination towards symbolic numbers who recognize this as 144 potential steps to reintegration with Source (God), we would suggest that certain religious beliefs related to the numbers 144 or 144,000, including the idea that 144,000 Souls are all that were ever created or all that will ever reach the "kingdom" of God, are gross misinterpretations of this Truth. This belief has been altered through time and misunderstood, yet it remains a dominant belief interpreted through various layers of esoteric and religious thought.

This is yet another indication of why you should carefully ponder religious and spiritual writing or teachings, particularly those passed down through many generations. Unfortunately, the vast majority of these are only quaint reminiscences that were already loosely based on gross misinterpretations of the "Truth" when first created. Such teachings should never be confused with "Truth" itself. Individuals using such misinterpretations to justify their goals or agendas, be they applicable to individual or societal norms, do so as a result of their young Soul age, as well as their Soul's desire to generate karma for themselves and for others around them, another subject we shall explore herein.

As we have explained in the past, you currently find yourself focused in the Third Sublevel of the Third Universal Dimension on a planet known in that Dimension as Earth, in a particular Solar System and Galaxy in a specific sector of the Third Dimensional Universe. The Third Sublevel of the Third Universal Dimension contains the physical reality you are familiar with and your current incarnation in a physical body takes part daily on a point on the timeline in that particular reality.

However, it should be understood that you have also already journeyed through the First and Second Universal Dimensions, and the Twelve Dimensional Sublevels inherent in those Universal Dimensions in order to arrive at your current positioning. Though you are living cycles of physical lifetime experiences at the Third Sublevel of the Third Universal Dimension, when your current physical body becomes too cumbersome or exhausted, the essence of "You" will pass into the higher Sublevels of the Third Universal Dimension. These Sublevels are commonly known as the Lower and Higher Astral planes of Earth, despite the fact that they are not visible due to vibrational and dimensional physics. However, we assure you these Dimensional Sublevels and Astral realms are as full of life and as "real" as any environment you currently know.

So as you may be aware, the higher Sublevels of the Third Universal Dimension are less physically dense and are unseen by you due to the nature of your perception and the vibrational frequency of your

Essence when in physical form. An analogy we have used often is the fact that you are surrounded daily by frequencies you do not actually see or experience without specific technologies, but these frequencies are ever-present nonetheless.

In other words, the thousand-plus television or radio stations that are broadcasting and available to you are always broadcasting, even if for the most part you can only visually tune into one broadcasting frequency on your television at a time. Expand this concept to a multidimensional Universe where you are programmed to only visually experience one frequency or reality at a time, and you begin to understand that even though you are not necessarily equipped to "see" beyond your current range of perception at a given point, other realities exist simultaneously nevertheless.

In addition, you should know that once your Soul has accomplished all its incarnations within the Third Universal Dimension (those happening simultaneously and otherwise) and has reintegrated these reincarnations at the highest Sublevels of that Universal Dimension, your Soul, together with you, is poised to ascend to higher Universal Dimensions. Indeed, hopefully you have come to understand by now that you are actually a spiritual Being journeying through a myriad of physical as well as not-so-physical environments, adapting to a variety of incarnational or energetic forms along the way. You do so while subject to dimensional vibrational frequencies, a reality's physics and geometric constitution and the related inherent universal space-time laws. Some Universal Dimensions, like most higher Dimensional Sublevels, or Astral planes, are substantially less dense or physical in nature. Others, like the First, Second and Third Dimensional Sublevels of the Universal Dimension are actually much more dense and physically anchored.

Most of those who have either heard about or have been taught about Reincarnation probably believe that additional lifetimes are an outward extension of their current life and self. This is far from the case and another misunderstanding concerning Reincarnation. In actuality, you are only one lifetime and a small fraction of your divine Soul's total experience in any particular time-space continuum, even though you retain your own focus and remain a vital, aware and enduring aspect of your multidimensional Soul as you journey through the Universal Dimension towards reintegration with your Soul.

It is important however, for you to realize that you are one extension of a much larger family – a cell within the greater body of your Soul – in much the same way that your Soul in its entirety (with you included) is a cell within the body of the Universe, or the Universal God force if you prefer. Seeing yourself as the center of this composition, convenient though it might be, is egocentric at best and actually rather limiting. Such an outlook is usually reserved for younger Souls, and it is reinforced by religious teachings that are mostly formulated by younger Souls seeking commonality and the curtailing of your personal creative reach by dwindling a real understanding of your multidimensional nature and the true magnificence of your Soul.

In this book we will help you dispel these notions and begin to see how the origins of your Soul, and your creation as one lifetime on a Wheel of Creation of your Soul, is a divine process that connects you with your Essence as well as other cycles of reincarnations that your Soul is choosing to experience. In addition, we wish to demonstrate how your life has purpose that originates from the desire of your Soul for growth and places you on a specific EssencePath that is part of your Soul's journey. We shall try to help you discover how your Soul is responsible for actually animating life force simultaneously on different points of the dimensional timeline and within different Astral realms of the Universal Dimension. We shall investigate how your Soul – and You – chart this course together and make progress by virtue of your growth, as you transmigrate from one Dimensional Sublevel to the next, and as your Soul transmigrates through the process of Universal Ascension from one Universal Dimension to the next.

We shall explore with you the purpose behind your exploration and the nature of your energetic origins in terms of how this is applicable to your life missions and goals as you progress through the Universe. We will demonstrate how this applies to not only the Human Angelic Soul species in this sector of the Galaxy, but also to the infinite number of cultural and divergent life forms existent in other sectors of the Third Universal Dimension. We hope to explore the interplay between all the lifetimes that are connected to You. And, we will look at how these many reincarnation lifetimes are related and orchestrated by your Soul through karmic balancing and other cycles that form the basis for what has been described in esoteric literature as the "Wheels of Reincarnation."

We have termed these reincarnation cycles "Wheels of Creation," since all the Soul's lifetimes connect to each other via these energetic interconnected wheels, which are essential to the true creative expression of your Soul. We shall see how energy imprints originating from your lifetimes form the basis of the interdimensional Akashic Records, the Eighth Dimensional energetic logs imprinted from each of a Soul's many lifetimes. We will discuss how karma comes into play as an energetic balancing of the Wheels the Soul creates in much the same way weights are placed on a tire in order to balance its spin. We will see how energetic balancing of the spokes, or lifetimes, found on each Wheel is required in order to provide a Soul with the vibrational resonance and consciousness necessary as a prerequisite to Transmigration and Ascension.

We wish to explore with you the close relationship you have with the many varied lifetimes related to you on your Soul's Wheels of Creation as you experience different Dimensional Sublevels, and we shall see how each lifetime on a Wheel of Creation contributes as a cellular component that is ultimately the body of your Soul. We will guide you through a typical journey of a Soul through the various Universal Dimensions, and most importantly take a look at how you shapeshift through the various Dimensional Sublevels and Astral planes as part of your journey through a Universal Dimension.

We shall examine the typical experience one goes through transitioning from life on the physical plane to life as an Etheric Body in the Astral planes after experiencing the condition known to you as "death." More importantly, we will guide you through what happens as your Etheric body rises through the various Astral planes, making its way through the Healing arenas, through the realms known as Perceived Heaven, the realm known as True Celestial Heaven and beyond that to the staging realms where reintegration with your Soul begins in order to allow for Ascension to the next Universal Dimension.

We will look with you at the interfaces and connections you have with other Souls, Soul Mates, Task Mates and Soul Guardians, as well as the lifetimes that are simultaneous to your own that may or may not be connected to you on Wheels of Creation or as a part of your Soul group. We shall investigate the concept of Soul Cadres, Soul Groups, and how your Soul is related to other Souls that are cast out either with the same mission or the same spiritual orientation.

We will take a look at the interface available to you with families, communities, organizations, cultures, ethnicities and other groupings that have similar or dissimilar lessons and goals, and look at how and why you participate with these and with others for the purpose of Soul growth. Most importantly, we shall examine how the interconnectedness of all things offers your Soul maximum opportunities to grow, especially within Dimensions where polarity or karmic energetic interchange is prevalent, such as in your current physical reality.

Finally, we shall explore the nature of higher Dimensional Guardian and Master Guide energies, the Sons of God, the Celestial Guides, the Akashic Guides and those high Guardians known as System Lords that have achieved higher levels of consciousness, which enables them to return and incarnate physically in lower Universal Dimensions to act as Guides or Avatars for Beings such as you. We will look in and see how your own Spirit Guides are related to you and how some of these are reincarnations of your own Soul or members of your own Soul Group that have risen to higher levels of Astral consciousness and returned to assist you, in much the same way an older sibling might return to assist its younger family members. And we will investigate with you the ability to transmigrate and ascend in the effort to grow your consciousness and master Universal Truth on behalf of your Soul and, through Ascension, on behalf of All That Is, or God if you prefer.

As always, we are pleased to offer this level of understanding to those who have discovered that there is far more to existence than the simplistic notions touted by younger Souls who hold that physical life is either merely an endless series of negative experiences or a prerequisite required by some omnipotent figure that may or may not allow you access to mythical rewards. When you understand the power and the magnificence of your place in the Universe, when you see how your consciousness and the growth of your Soul firmly empower you as a co-creator with God, childish notions presented to you by well meaning religious leaders and scholars of outmoded spiritual belief systems will make you chuckle as one might on hearing a child describe their vision of a Heaven.

We offer this to those who seek a higher level of Universal and spiritual understanding through the knowledge that their personal journey is a journey charted by their immortal Soul. It is a miraculous journey that you experience and enjoy through all eternity, one that will ultimately reunite who you are with your Essence, return you to your Source and confirm forever that you are now, and have always been, a vital part of the Universe and All-That-Is, at one with all creation.

 CHAPTER 1

REINCARNATION AND THE MULTIDIMENSIONAL TRANSMIGRATION OF THE SOUL

First, let us begin by refining our use of the terms Reincarnation and Transmigration of the Soul. We take Reincarnation to mean the ability of a Soul to incarnate in physical form in a cyclical nature and numerous times at particular points on the timeline of a specific Universal Dimension. Generally, reincarnation within a specific dimensional timeline is well planned by the Soul and cycles of related lifetimes are orchestrated in order to achieve maximum growth and balance depending upon the needs and goals of the Soul.

Like its brother Reincarnation, Transmigration of the Soul is the ability of a Soul, together with the personalities and experiences derived from its many incarnations, to migrate from a Sublevel of a Universal Dimension to another Sublevel of that Universal Dimension. In addition, transmigration can mean the ability of a Soul to migrate from one Universal Dimension to another, or similarly from a Universal Dimension to the corresponding Sublevel of other Universal Dimension. Thus as an example, a Being from the Twelfth Universal Dimension is able to transmigrate at will to the Twelfth Sublevel of any Universal Dimension, which is considered a corresponding Dimension. In general, this only occurs from higher dimensional levels.

Transmigration is most often accomplished through the process of Ascension according to the Ascension timeframe of the Galaxy of which your Solar System is part. For those seeking a more profound understanding of the process of Universal Ascension, we have discussed this extensively in our book *The System Lords and the Twelve Dimensions.*

According to these definitions then, a Soul reincarnates when it transmigrates to and physically incarnates in a specific Universal Dimension. The many lifetimes a Soul develops within that dimensional space-time wave are grouped into associative lifetimes that occur in a cyclical nature. These associative lifetimes are grouped on what we term a Soul's "Wheels of Creation" (See Page 447, Figure 1 of Diagrams in the Appendix.), and the Soul manifests literally hundreds of lifetimes on numerous Wheels that can consist, on an average, of seven to twenty life entities each, as preferred by the Soul with no prerequisite or mandated number of lives on any given Wheel of Creation. (See Page 448, Figure 2 of Diagrams in the Appendix.)

Although not all lifetimes cast into physical reality by the Soul are associated, for the most part groupings of lifetimes are formed based on the Soul's particular focus around karmic endeavors, goals and other associated links. In other words, a Soul plans many groupings of lifetimes that are linked together and organized according to specific goals for growth, as well as karmic bonds and Soul Agreements it has made that unconsciously bleed through energetically from one lifetime to another within the specific Wheel and group cycles.

When a specific life incarnation "passes" from one Sublevel of the Universal Dimension to another, exemplified most often through the process you know as physical death, it can be said to have transmigrated. Therefore, it can be said that the various life incarnations (reincarnations) of the Soul, each of which is an aspect of the Soul's energy, will move from the physical Sublevel of a Dimension to a different vibrational Sublevel of the Dimension when the Soul's goals for that physical lifetime have been served. The process of moving from one vibrational Sublevel to another is transmigration.

In simplified terms, when one has contact with a conscious physical being one is in contact with a Soul's reincarnated self at a specific vibrational density. When one has contact with that same consciousness in an Astral state, one is connecting with an aspect of the Soul's transmigrating self. It is little wonder that the issue of immigration and "migration" has dominated your world news of late, since not only is this a metaphor for the actual current and coming state of you and your Soul, it is related to the mass transmigration happening through the process of Ascension as Souls leave physical life in preparation for Ascension from the Third Universal Dimension to Fifth Universal Dimension. In effect, every incarnated physical Being in your world today could be considered a "migrant." Individual, cultural and mass conscious karma is being played out and generated before your eyes as a result.

We shall discover more about the process of Reincarnation and transmigration shortly, but first let's continue our definition of Reincarnation and transmigration. When speaking of the journey of your Soul and the concept of Reincarnation from one lifetime to another and the transmigration of the Soul from one Dimension to another, it is perhaps easiest to first delve into what Reincarnation and Transmigration are not.

First and foremost, Reincarnation is not a punishment. Some cultural and spiritual beliefs equate Reincarnation of the Soul with punishment for deeds that have occurred or have been perpetrated during a physical lifetime. This is a simplistic and somewhat erroneous understanding of the concept in much the same way karma should not be considered punishment and is simply a balancing of individual Soul energy. Whether it is emotionally or physically derived, energy in almost every form will strive to find its counterpoint in order to achieve homeostasis, harmony and balance.

Thus Reincarnation, like karma, can be connected to energy balancing through the use of the various physical lifetimes the Soul creates, but experiencing physical lifetimes again and again through Reincarnation is not something forced on a Soul, and additional lifetimes are certainly not punishment for the deeds being transacted. Those who understand the concept that outside of the linear measurement you know as time there is actually no time, or at best there is simultaneous time, will understand that all the lifetimes a Soul creates happen simultaneously. In such a case, what happens in one lifetime has an immediate and direct correlation on what happens in every other lifetime of the Soul, particularly those incarnations that are connected within the same cycle or wheel. Understanding this allows the concept of energy balancing from one lifetime to another to become apparent.

In addition, although you might find individuals and even entire cultures and religions that believe that reincarnation or transmigration can take place across animal or insect species, Reincarnation is never cross-species in this way. It is not part of the process of either Reincarnation or Transmigration for a Soul to incarnate in a species other than the species designed to physically contain and house the nature and energy of a specific Soul group. Human Angelic Souls are the Soul group destined to incarnate in human physical form on Earth, and this Soul group is closely associated with your Solar System and your particular sector of the Universe.

To be clear, at higher levels of awareness and Soul age, there can be incarnations in various physical forms if there is a correlation based on sentience or consciousness. This can be the case when, as an example, an alien sentient, conscious Soul species attempts to incarnate in human form. Similarly, this is the case when a Human Angelic Soul at a higher dimensional level wishes to incarnate in what you would consider an "alien" sentient body or form.

For the most part these are rare occurrences, and we only bring this to your attention based on the experience of your planet in the current timeline where there is a profound attempt to colonize your sector of the Universe through an "alien" Soul bio-invasion, where an alien Soul race is incarnating in human physical bodies as we detailed for you in *The System Lords and the Twelve Dimensions.* As we also pointed out in our subsequent book, *Timeline Collapse and Universal Ascension*, because Earth is intended as the home planet of Human Angelic Souls, among other Earth-based species, the planet will reset itself with the help of your Solar System once this phenomenon of hybrid physical human beings has reached a tipping point.

But with respect to Soul groups such as the Human Angelic Soul group, what is important to understand is that it is not possible for a Human Angelic Soul to incarnate as a cow or as an insect, for example, as some cultures or religions might believe. This is not to imply that some Soul groups incarnated along side you are less important or that hive Soul groups (where one common Soul is shared amongst a large group of Beings) that incarnate as different animal, plant and insect species are not sacred, for indeed they are.

We are suggesting only that an erroneous understanding of this matter may be related to the fact that all life is precious, and when you kill or take life from any species you are potentially removing a portion of an entity or Soul group's initiative, its purpose for entering into physical form. We say potentially because this is a general rule, and it must be considered that in rare cases the taking of life is a result of Soul agreements among the participants for a higher purpose or good. This, however, is rare, and any spiritual edict that mandates the respect of life in all forms must be foremost, and should be considered across all species.

This does not mean to imply that there are not Soul groups, particularly animal hive Soul groups that are incarnating as part of an agreement with Human Angelics or with other Soul groups for the purpose of assisting their growth by means of nourishing their physical biological bodies in what can be called the chain of physical life. As an example, the hive Soul groups, that pertain to certain animals that you have cultivated for millennia as sustenance are most probably participating in a broader Soul group arrangement that ensures your Soul group's physical survival, thereby allowing the passive hive Soul groups important universal growth.

It is based on this that some of your religious teachings seem to place the husbandry of various hive Soul groups (animal), if not all of nature, in your hands. Many arrogant religious leaders however, have wrongly taken this to mean a God-given dominance over the Earth and have used it to justify their desire to do whatever they want in the face of nature. This is an incorrect understanding of such Soul group participation, and it is for this reason that the mistreatment of nature – plants, insects and animals in your care – in any form -- is a grave karmic misstep. As a prime example, the inhumane treatment or slaughter of animals currently employed, or the unthinking treatment and poisoning of the Earth's resources, including water, plants and animals, has tremendous karmic implications for the Human Angelic Soul group of which you should be aware.

Suffice it to say that what we wish to explain here is the fact that Human Angelic Souls do not incarnate as animals, insects or other species, and certainly are not forced into such incarnations as a punishment for deeds committed during one's human physical incarnation. We shall delve into this further later, but in the meantime it should be understood that this does not mitigate the fact that balancing energy and karma generated by those relationships and associative deeds carries with it universal laws concerning how the energies generated come to be balanced.

Next there is the misunderstanding that Reincarnation and Transmigration occur on a linear timeline. As we have discussed extensively, this is not the case. The nature of time and space is such that essentially within a specific Universal Dimension, all space-time waves occur simultaneously in a spiral where each has the potential for direct relationship and can have close proximity to other points on the timeline that seem distant when seen in a linear fashion.

In that respect it can be ascertained that in a broader sense all of a Soul's lifetimes within a given Universal Dimensional timeline are occurring simultaneously. Taking this further, a lifetime you are currently living in, say the 21st Century, might have a correlation with a lifetime that your Soul is about to begin in the 17th Century, and both of these might have relationship to a lifetime that is just ending somewhere in the distant future. If you envision the timeline as a spiral, with chronological dates represented on the spiral, you begin to see the possible close relationships and proximities of various points on the timeline, regardless of their chronological lineup or linear progression. (See Page 449, Figure 3 of Diagrams in the Appendix.)

This brings us to another erroneous concept, which pertains to the fact that because you see time as linear in nature, individuals tend to believe that they are the purveyors of their Soul and that all lifetimes must therefore project forward from them and from their current position. Thus, there is the belief that Reincarnation is also linear in nature, and as a result must originate with the personality of the current lifetime. Moreover, the belief is that an individual is their Soul, and they are the originator of any and all future lifetimes. In other words, the future and all other lifetimes generated exist as a direct result of, or in effect are a reincarnation of "them."

This is then further applied to transmigration, and one concludes that who you are today is *also* your Soul, and vice versa. Though a difficult concept to master, both in the case of Reincarnation and Transmigration, you are in fact an indispensable cell existing within the body of your Soul. Your Soul projects its energy throughout the time-space continuum in your Universal Dimension into many different lifetimes simultaneously, drawing experiences and growth from all the reincarnations it manifests on the Wheels of Creation it creates. You are part of a much greater schematic that is the comprehensive creative endeavor of your Soul, and the group of lifetimes of which your life is a part, all of which are all happening concurrently, are indirectly connected to you since they are all a manifestation, in various forms of your Soul.

Much could be said about the conflation in esoteric literature of the term Soul with the term God. In fact, the creative God force of the Universe is reflected through the Souls it creates in much the same way that you, as an embodiment and creation of your Soul, are a reflection of its creative endeavors. There is a reason why the religious literature you know of speaks of God and his creations as having a "father and son/daughter" relationship, as well as identifying all humans as brothers and sisters. We would suggest that these relationships are reflective and applicable to the Soul as well. It is reflected through the many lifetimes your Soul manifests and empowers through each Universal Dimension.

It is also reflected in your potential relationships with other entities and Beings in all corners of the world that are known to your Soul, not to mention the close connection you may have to other entities living simultaneously at different points on the dimensional timeline. These relationships are genetic, energetic and spiritual in nature. Although they are hinted at occasionally and should be used as a connecting point for the entire Human Angelic species, sadly dimensional mass consciousness has not yet arrived at the real Truth behind these relationships.

We emphasize that the Soul is projecting through lifetimes that are all independent, and in some cases happening concurrently. This means that you may possibly have a Soul Twin or Task Mate that is incarnated in another part of your world or even down the street living at the same point of the timeline that you are currently existing at. Whether you know them or not, they are directly related to you by virtue of the connection you both have to your Soul. Such Twin entities may or may not have any interaction or connection with you the entire time you/they exist in physical form, since they have their own purpose, life mission and karmic endeavors. But on occasion, Soul twins are planned by the Soul in order to facilitate growth, and they tend to meet up in one way or another in order to bring or share opportunities for growth intrinsic to the Soul from which they both spring.

If we are detailing this background for you, it is to impress upon you your connection to a greater and higher self. Hopefully, this will pre-empt any misunderstanding that leads you to believe that you personally are the originator of the current lifetime, or that you are the originator of other lifetimes or reincarnations that you envision coming from you based on your current perspective.

We have explained many times in the past that the Universe is multidimensional in nature. This is also true in any discussion concerning Reincarnation or Transmigration. To better understand this concept and how it applies to Reincarnation or Transmigration we need to first provide a brief summary of the Universal Dimensions and universal structure as we have described it in the past.

The known Universe is segmented into what we have called Twelve Universal Dimensions. (See Page 450, Figure 4 of Diagrams in the Appendix.) Each of these Universal Dimensions is separated by its unique vibrational frequency and resonance, and each Universal Dimension is further segmented into Twelve Sublevels of that Universal Dimension. (See Pages 451 & 452, Figures 5 & 6 of Diagrams in the Appendix.)

At any given point these Universal Dimensions, including the Sublevels, overlap and generate a specific time-wave continuum. These timelines are vibrational in nature and this is essentially the most significant defining factor of any given Dimension. Dimensions and the dimensional time-wave that defines them, reside in close proximity one to the other in much the same way the waves in the ocean are distinct but can be seen to be closely related and move in unison. One wave ultimately moves into the position of its predecessor, and takes its place at predefined intervals based on motion and resonance in much the same way one Universal Dimension evolves into the next.

That evolution of a Universal Dimension is the concept we know as Ascension. The importance of this universal process cannot be understated in as much as it represents the evolutionary progress of not only every Universal Dimension but all Beings contained within the Universal Dimension or any of its Dimensional Sublevels. The evolutionary process whereby entire Universal Dimensions evolve to ultimately become the next Universal Dimension during specific universal and galactic periods takes place eternally without end.

Furthermore, as we have discussed in the past, Universal Dimensions overlap and due to frequency, consciousness and vibration, the universal rule of thumb is that higher Dimensions (and Dimensional Beings) can "see" into lower Dimensions and are aware of their existence, but lower Dimensions cannot necessarily see or become aware of higher ones. In many cases, lower Dimensions are actually comprised of and part of higher universal dimensionality, even if the higher Dimensions are aware of the lower energy without necessarily participating in its reality. A simple analogy would be your ability to "see" or be aware of the mineral kingdom, but not necessarily participate in the "life" and destiny of a rock or crystal, other than to move it around, modify or change its appearance. And for its part, a boulder, crystal or mountain range cannot truly be said to be aware of your world or share in the life you are living all around it.

The same premise is applicable to the Sublevels or Astral planes of a Universal Dimension. Again, higher has an awareness of the existence of lower, but lower cannot necessarily see higher. So if, as an example, your physical lifetime is being lived at the Third Sublevel of the Third Universal Dimension, and the Astral planes where you might reside following the passage out of the physical body is in the Fourth or higher Sublevel of the Third Universal Dimension, it reasons that you might not necessarily be aware of the entities, including friends and loved ones, who have transmigrated out of physical bodies into higher Dimensional Sublevels, but they might be aware of you.

Again, higher can see lower (if it chooses to) but lower cannot generally see higher. For the purpose of our conversation however, what becomes significant here is the concept of varying dimensional levels where existence is not curtailed and is even enhanced. In fact, it is the realm of highest Dimensionality that originates life, from where what some might consider the God force emanates.

It is best to envision Universal dimensional structure in much the same way you would envision nesting dolls, but allowing transparency and visibility between each layer and from level to level. The dimensional point of view is positioned inward coming from the inner most doll and, as a result as we have said, each can see the lower levels and layers beneath it, but the lower levels may not be able to see the higher dimensional layers.

As we have told you in the past, the three highest Dimensions, also the biggest in actual size since these encompass all other Dimensions, are the Tenth, Eleventh and Twelfth Universal Dimensions. These three dimensional layers contain and house all the other dimensional layers within them, and in many ways act as the glue or skin that binds the whole in place. It is for this reason that these dimensional realms are known as the God Source, and it is not by accident that the Trinity of your Mythical and religious thought, the very essence of "God" as it were, is considered three distinct Beings that are separate, but unified in their divinity. Much of the religious mythology surrounding the idea of a God "Trinity" is a simplification and an-thropomorphization of this dimensional concept rendered in terms that were more understandable to ancient cultures. (See Page 453, Figure 7 of Diagrams in the Appendix.)

Similarly, the concept that life's sole purpose is to rejoin "God" is an-other simplification of the Soul's true journey. In fact, via the Ascen-sion process, all consciousness, or energy, strives to return to its original Source. We would even explain that the concept that you "climb" to heaven is indicative of the fact that you "ascend" from lower Dimensions through various Sublevels and into higher Dimen-sions, until ultimately you reach the "realm of All That Is" or the God Source. This would be a metaphor for the reintegration of your Soul that occurs in the Tenth, Eleventh and Twelfth Universal Dimensions.

As you may know, physics permit the constant reconfiguration and evo-lution of energy into an abundance of forms. The process of transmi-gration facilitates energy's growth and transformation into new forms. So when your Soul's energy is transformed, either through Reincarna-tion, Transmigration or Ascension, it is this natural energetic process that drives the Soul into higher and higher levels of consciousness.

The electromagnetic transfer of Soul energy through these evolu-tionary processes aside, suffice to say that it is the goal of your Soul's energy, including you as part of your Soul's energy, to reconfigure, consolidate and rejoin at the highest realms of creation. This process of reintegration of the many lifetimes of the Soul within a Universal Dimension takes place at the highest Sublevels of that Universal Di-mension. This reintegration, when complete, allows the Soul to as-cend to the next Universal Dimension until it has traversed the Twelve Universal Dimensions. In a way, the fact that each Universal

Dimension has twelve Dimensional Sublevels, mirrors Universal Dimensional structure and provides the Soul with a direct link to the highest Twelve Universal Dimensions, reflected within in every Universal Dimension.

In other words, when all of the Soul's various incarnations that take place on a Soul's Wheels of Creation in a specific Universal Dimension have passed through all the Sublevels of that Universal Dimension, these lifetimes, of which your life may be one, are reintegrated into the Soul's energy. This reintegration retains the individuality of each entity as it maximizes the Soul's consciousness growth. Reintegration occurs at the Tenth, Eleventh and Twelfth Dimensional Sublevels of a Universal Dimension.

Similarly, when your Soul has passed through the nine Universal Dimensions, in one form or another, it begins reintegration with Source in the Tenth, Eleventh and Twelfth Universal Dimensions. The Soul's energy, now carrying with it the consciousness of each and every lifetime it has created and experienced in every Universal Dimension, begins its reintegration with Source – God. This process of regeneration, reunification and reintegration, at each level, is a constant and fundamental basis of Universal structure.

On the other side of this equation is what we shall term the "casting" of Souls from Source. Reintegration and casting-out of Souls from the Twelfth Universal Dimension is spontaneous, and the entire process could be likened to the Universe breathing in, and breathing out where breathing in is the reintegration of Souls (energy-consciousness) and breathing out is the casting of Souls into the Universal process of creation. It is for this reason that Shamans consider the breath to be scared, and breathing is indeed not only vital to physical life it is metaphorically representative of life and creation in the Universe. It is also why spiritual breathing techniques are practiced in various forms, and why proper physical breathing is health inducing, a fact recognized by most Gurus and in a wide range of spiritual practices.

Akin to this is the idea that breath creates the spoken "word." The myths of creation all consider the "word" to be the most powerful act, and indeed there is power in sound and the spoken word but it is mute without the energy inherent in the act of breathing. In effect, with the combination of breath energy and the spoken word you witness the true act and meaning of creation. In a metaphorical sense the act of creation that is birthed from the breathing out of the Creative God force in the twelfth Universal Dimension is part and parcel of the casting out of Souls, which begins a Soul's journey through the Dimensions. (See Page 454, Figure 8 of Diagrams in the Appendix.) That journey, and the energy that precedes it, is expanded exponentially as many entities and personalities are reincarnated and spawned in every Dimension. If you will, the Soul evolves itself by carrying forth the creative breath of "All That Is."

However, it should be understood that when Souls are first cast out with this breath of creation, they are in a sense primitive energies that may not be related to your current understanding of the Soul. To see this, one need look no further than the birth and growth of children in physical life. Babies in the Third Dimension are not born with a complete understanding or awareness of who or what they are, and in fact they may be quite primitive as they are raised, schooled and nurtured, and open through new experiences and growth that comes as a result of their choices and deeds. Similarly, Souls, depending upon their Soul group, purpose and spiritual orientation, originate as primal energies suited to begin their journey of growth and consciousness elevation at the lowest Universal dimensional levels.

As an example, a newly cast out Human Angelic Soul might spend at least one Ascension period in First and Second Dimensional incarnations on Earth when it is first cast out. Such newly cast Souls will incarnate in group forms and generally prefer to incarnate as the "essence" of dense First Dimensional beings, such as a rock in a mountain range or wind in a global weather system. While each Soul is different and it really is not possible to generalize, even a Human Angelic Soul passes through many incarnations at lower, denser dimensional levels until it has ascended to the Third Universal Dimension, where incarnations as an independent physical human being (whatever form that might be depending upon the timeline involved) becomes possible. (See Page 452, Figure 6 of Diagrams in the Appendix.)

Many assume that Human Angelic Souls are cast out fully assembled, sophisticated and ready to take on incarnations as physical humans, but this is not the case. All Souls pass through the multidimensional structure we have described, and in your case, a Human Angelic Soul is subject to begin its journey of incarnation, physical and otherwise, at dimensional levels lower than the Third Universal Dimension of which you are currently part. (See Page 453, Figure 7 of Diagrams in the Appendix.)

For this reason it is important to understand that although we have said that Human Angelic Souls and other Souls are always cast within their own Soul species and destined to live their incarnations within a specific sector of the Universe relevant to the species, it is not to say that individual Souls do not ascend and progress from a starting point. Although for the most part a Human Angelic Soul is always destined to one-day experience individual lives through incarnations as human entities, it should not be assumed that in its earliest renditions it does not incarnate in Soul groups within lower Universal Dimensions.

In this way it is highly probable that a Human Angelic Soul will join with other Souls, within the First and Second Universal Dimensions, to grow through joint experiences. For example, it is not uncommon for a Human Angelic Soul in the First or Second Universal Dimension to join with other Souls to "experience" life as a mountain range, a north wind or a sea, in the lower and denser physical reality that you know.

This should be recognized as the basis for many of the spiritual traditions that imbue seemingly non-human elements on Earth, like a mountain range or a river, with divine and often human characteristics. This anthropomorphizing of the surroundings carries a primitive Truth in that sometimes a mountain range or a river or a forest actually does have a connection to the Human Angelic Soul species as we have now described for you.

To be sure, there are other aspects of the casting out and creation of Souls, some of which are beyond your current level of understanding and pertain to higher dimensional levels of which you can barely conceive. For the purpose of our discussion however, we will include a few additional aspects here. First and foremost, the Universe's casting of Souls can take place in significant numbers. Therefore, the terminology you know as Soul Twins and Soul Mates does indeed have certain validity. Similarly, there are Soul groups within a Soul species, and in this respect Soul families are formed. We prefer to term these as Cadres or Soul Units, but it would not be incorrect to consider them to be Soul Families.

Additionally it should be noted that all Souls progress, transmigrate and ascend at their own speed, and therefore it is always possible that a Soul may choose not to transmigrate or ascend together with its Cadre or Twins. This is especially true during periods of Universal Ascension, where Soul Ascension from one Universal Dimension to another is possible. This leads to the varied nature and Soul's age of Souls incarnating at any given period. This phenomenon allows Souls of various Soul ages to be present and incarnating together within the same time-wave or Dimension. We have discussed this fact often, since it is the basis of the current Ascension period where you have older Souls preparing to cycle off to a higher Universal Dimension finishing lifetimes side-by-side with Younger and even Baby Souls who are just beginning Third Universal Dimension incarnations. The growing disparity seen in the consciousness levels of individuals in your world now is highly reflective of this.

At the Twelfth Universal Dimension, the Universal life force, God or All That Is, will cast out a significant number of individualized Soul energies that become an infinite variety of Soul species, in varying Cadres, Orientations and Groups, and all of these Souls will go on to join the complex process of Reincarnation, Transmigration and Ascension that will ultimately bring them to their rightful place in creation and the Universe. For our purposes here, let us begin at the beginning by discussing how Human Angelic Souls, in unison and individually, enter and become part of creation at the level of the First Universal Dimension, later graduating through the Dimensional Sublevels and from Universal Dimension to Universal Dimension, ascending through incarnations at ever higher Universal Dimensions before returning to Source.

 # Chapter 2
The Casting of a Human Angelic Soul and its Physical Incarnations in the First and Second Universal Dimensions

We have spoken often in the past about the concept of polarity. Polarity or its facsimile exists throughout all universal structures in numerous and various forms. As we have said before, there are many possible polar conditions, some of which Third Dimensional physics may not be aware of simply because they are not readily visible in your Universal Dimension.

For example, at higher dimensional levels several forms of polarity that are not dual or are not duality-based exist in nature. Polarity at higher dimensional levels can expand to include three, four, five, six and even seven polar relationships creating universal "spin" within these Dimensions that defy your dualistic interpretations of what is necessary to create polar dynamics and electromagnetic spin. For our purposes here as it regards the Soul's transmigration and the breathing of energy and life into physical form, the most basic polarity is dual in nature.

Duality of some kind is the basis of spin and a precursor to physical creation. The properties of dual polarity, then, are most prevalent from the First Universal Dimension up to and including the Third Universal Dimension. In these Dimensions, duality and energy are fundamental parts of manifestation, and the electromagnetic spin that results from this relationship is the primary force that draws energetic particles into "creative" physical form. (See Page 455, Figure 9 of Diagrams in the Appendix.)

We say "creative" here in the sense that drawing energetic particles together into physical form is a process guided by electromagnetic thought forms and not a random occurrence, as you might think. Although electromagnetic "spin" is required to pull energy into physical formation, the actual physical form energy takes is based on principles of attraction. The creative input guiding energy into formation comes from a wide range of factors, most prominently the guidance of your Soul in conjunction with You based on your current "now" position on the timeline. This vibrational guidance may include unconscious goals for Soul growth, karmic endeavors and individual thought forms you originate during the course of your physical incarnation. Secondarily, but equally important, it also includes the personal beliefs and fears affecting your vibrational state in the "Now" as well as the relativity and reactivity of the mass consciousness backdrop or physical environment against which your personal reality is projected.

To begin at the beginning, it is important to understand first of all that when Souls are initially cast out, and this is universally true, they are cast into one of two basic orientations that serve as the fundamental basis of spiritual polarity. The first orientation, as we have discussed in the past, is related to the Soul orientation that we describe as "Service-to-Others." Most if not all Human Angelic Souls are cast with the Service-to-Others orientation. This orientation pushes a Soul's primal expression, even more basic than the Soul's principal archetypal expression throughout all lifetimes that we will discuss, to achieve Soul growth through the discovery of service to other Souls, Beings or entities. The Soul's orientation is relevant to each of the Soul's many lifetimes and it is relevant whether in physical incarnation, such as the one you know, or the transmigrating Soul entity passing through less physical layers of the Astral planes or related realms.

Service-to-Others Soul orientation does not necessarily mean however, that the entity is endlessly volunteering for suitable needy causes, nor is it reflective of someone who is perpetually altruistic, kind or charitable. In fact, to the contrary, a Service-to-Others orientation relates mostly to the Soul's Universal thrust, but when it comes to individual lifetimes, a Soul with this orientation can create a good many lives that are neither service-oriented, charitable nor kind. This includes treatment of Soul Mates and Soul Twins. Often these Soul relationships are paradoxical and not what one would expect based on the designation. Service-to-Others orientation does mean however, that the primary driving force behind a Soul, a Soul group or a Soul species is based on a universal drive to make manifest realities out of a desire to provide service and growth to all other Beings.

As an example, we have said in the past that often an entity in a lifetime will take on specific hardships during the course of an incarnation. Such hardships, which can take many forms, are taken on by the Soul not only for its own growth potential, but also to benefit the Soul growth of others. A terminally ill or handicapped child, something always felt initially as a tragic or sad occurrence, is often representative of a Soul providing opportunities for growth to others around them, usually through close relationships like parenthood that may require specific bonds to be maintained. The Soul taking on a lifetime of hardship such as this is usually a reflection of a Soul demonstrating, at least initially, a basic Service-to-Others orientation.

Similarly, an entire Soul group that chooses to come to the rescue of another group of entities because of what it considers to be a "good cause" is probably an act based on an orientation of Service-to-Others. This is inevitably seen during disasters or periods of persecution as individuals come together for the purpose of helping their fellow Beings. It is also relevant in instances of war where one group comes to the rescue of another that has been subjugated or repressed, an occurrence witnessed extensively throughout modern history and particularly exemplified during the period known as World War II in the mid 20th Century. The same will be witnessed during the period of a coming war that will be designated as World War III.

Service-to-Others orientation is also on view when you see various societal groups try to highlight or bring to the attention of others important cultural or consciousness events such as climate alteration, environmental pollution, the torture of humans or the inhumane treatment of other Beings, such as what occurs with animal cruelty. All of these initiatives are, at their core, expressions that originate in Service-to-Others orientation.

To be sure, although Service-to-Others orientation might serve as a primal motivating factor, particularly when it is group-related it is always accompanied by each individual Soul's intentions and goals for growth in a specific lifetime. In fact, it could be said that the basic Soul orientation works to prime the pump that is then fueled further (or not) by a Soul's specific growth plans for the lifetime. In such a case then, the child who is born handicapped in some way may be demonstrating Service-to-Others orientation, but sometimes, more importantly, might also be working on its own personal Soul growth or on balancing karma, which caused the Soul to take on the handicap in the first place.

Suffice to say that in all cases Service-to-Others is an underlying

motivation basic to every Soul cast with this particular orientation.
This is also important with respect to the electromagnetic polarity
of a Soul and its subsequent energetic "spin" that serves to manifest
the Soul's astral "vehicle," sometimes called the Lightbody or Merkaba, which it projects outward in holographic form and uses to
travel through all the many incarnations it imbues, as well as to facilitate its Transmigration through Universal Dimensions and Dimensional Sublevels.

The second principal polar orientation of a Soul or a Soul group is
termed the "Service-to-Self" orientation. These Souls are rarely
Human Angelic in that the complex emotional body and nervous system networks necessary for achieving compassion in a Human Angelic Soul, as well as the lifetimes it creates, is unnecessary for Souls
that do not have a Service-to-Others orientation. For the most part,
Souls cast out from Source with a Service-to-Self orientation tend
to be what Human Angelics would consider "alien" or extraterrestrial species generally. Some of these, though not all, are also comprised of hive Soul groups, which implies a lack of individuality or the
accompanying emotional body needed for growth derived from Service-to-Others orientation.

This may seem a paradox in that one would assume Service-to-Others Souls might be interested in the Soul growth of the group based
on their orientation, but the orientation actually means that the individual Soul obtains individual growth through the indirect compassionate assistance of other entities and Beings. On the other hand,
Service-to-Self Souls obtain Soul growth through the growth of the
Soul group as a whole, and therefore in serving themselves they are
contributing to the growth of their Soul group rather than to their
own individual Soul.

Based on this, Service-to-Self Souls are focused mainly on themselves and their personal advancements or achievements, since this is the most direct route to growth of the entire Soul group or hive. In contrast, Service-to-Others Souls center around lifetimes that focus on assisting other entities in order to derive personal Soul growth and evolve their own individual Soul as it progresses in its evolution through the Universal Dimensions.

As we have said many times, these definitions do not have a better, worse, good or bad connotation. Each Soul orientation has its merits and each has its distractions. In this case, most Human Angelics would consider Service-to-Others orientation to be a higher standard and goal, just as they would consider their own personal evolution and the enlightenment obtained through altruistic services rendered to other Beings as an ideal. Service-to-Self Souls however, would consider their personal self-aggrandizement to be of primary importance in life (something seemingly selfish to a Human Angelic Soul), but ultimately their Self-focused efforts are part of the advancement of their Soul group or hive, and not the growth of their own individual Soul.

Service-to-Self Souls tend to have difficulty exhibiting compassion or understanding anyone who thinks of others before themselves, and as we mentioned most do not have highly evolved emotional bodies or empathetic abilities since they are oriented towards serving their own needs and desires. It is for this reason that incarnating into Human Angelic physical bodies, where a complex emotional body and nervous system is usually present, can be problematic for them. Service-to-Self Souls that do so anyway will tend to be aloof and cold natured, exclusively using the background of mass consciousness as a stepping-stone for self-aggrandizement and their own purposes. These individuals are noticeably self-centered and selfish, and at the minimum will seem unconcerned with the wellbeing or betterment of others.

In extreme cases, they can take on psychopathic tendencies, and it is unfortunate that your current period has elevated these traits to high status in your society, where many political and business leaders are Service-to-Self extraterrestrial Soul species incarnated in physical human bodies. Shrewd and cunning, since their game plan is essentially without boundaries, in certain cases such individuals might appear or even pretend to be serving or acting to benefit others. This is usually however, only if their service somehow achieves a measure of personal benefit.

Such individuals are easily recognized by the fact that on the exterior they exclaim that they are harboring goodwill towards all when in fact their hidden purpose is their own enrichment or achievement of power, typically for the benefit of a distinct or small group of followers (their hive, or those related to them by virtue of their Soul group). Whatever the particular distinction, Service-to-Self entities will always be primarily concerned with the advancement of themselves. They can be self-possessed and often are overly critical and suspicious of others, since they usually see everyone as being cast in their own mode, which makes them see the world as a field of competition where the motto to live by is always, "Me first, and then Me again."

We would caution again however, against subjective judgments of Service-to-Self Souls or the belief that any orientation is more desirable or better than another. Add to this the understanding that polar orientations are Soul originated and therefore intrinsic to the nature of the Soul as well as the lifetimes it manifests. Soul orientation is not a choice and does not change throughout the entire journey of a Soul, regardless of the Dimension or other Souls with whom they come into contact.

As we have touched upon, we would also like to insert a note here explaining, as we have in the past, that not all Souls incarnated in physical human form within your particular sector of the Galaxy (that of Human Angelics), including Earth, are necessarily Human Angelic Souls. This will become more and more clear as your future unfolds, although it is already becoming clear to many now taking note of a world where the attitudes and motives of people within your proximity are becoming markedly different, sometimes shockingly so.

Through this realization you may also become aware that recently more and more Alien Soul species are incarnating within physical human form, and though these Souls are not Human Angelic in origination, the bodies they inhabit are human bodies. These human beings are unaware of their Soul affiliation in much the same way that not all of you are aware of your actual Soul origination or orientation. Again, this is not to say that these particular individuals are better or worse than you, but thought should be given as to why Alien Souls would now choose to incarnate in physical bodies not completely comfortable or akin to them.

The human form has evolved over great spans of the timeline on Earth, as we will discuss later in this book, for the purpose of providing Human Angelic Souls with the perfect physical vehicle for reincarnation purposes. In general, Soul species tend to incarnate in designated sectors of the Universe that are reserved for a particular Soul species. Physical forms (bodies) for incarnation are evolved to maximize a particular Soul group's orientation, desires and goals as well as the life missions of individual Souls within that Soul group.

Service-to-Self Soul orientations have difficulty manifesting an emotional and etheric body energetically, and since these bodies are integral to the physical body evolved for Human Angelics these individuals will be emotionally withdrawn and unable to interact on a compassionate or emotional level with others, particularly other Human Angelic Souls. Lack of real empathy or understanding for fellow beings can make their actions seem psychopathic in nature since there is no real energetic alignment between the physical, emotional and etheric body. Incarnations of such a nature tend to be an isolated occurrence for a specific purpose related to the Soul or a purpose that has been requested through agreement between various Soul groups.

In some cases however, such incarnations can amount to the effort of an alien Soul group to infiltrate a universal sector or planet by using the physical body of a corresponding Soul group. The Alien Soul bio-invasion we have alluded to that is currently taking place on Earth using the Human Angelic physical body is such a case. As we have mentioned in the past, many of your global political and business leaders originate as a direct result of this Soul invasion. Some of the American leadership at the time of this writing is a demonstration of such Souls in action, and it is not by accident that these entities will always choose to consort and interact with others who possess similar world outlooks, since essentially they are related to each other by virtue of their (alien) Soul group or Soul species. Neither is it a coincidence that the vast majority of true Human Angelic Souls will invariably prefer to walk away than argue when hearing about particularly disturbing and unconscionable deeds performed by these entities, since the decisions being made are unfathomable to them and defy every standard and norm they might hold.

Even though it is possible for a Soul to incarnate in a physical or etheric form that is different from the one developed for its Soul species, such incarnations can still be problematic and are often difficult to manage or maintain. Their physical body will inevitably look and feel awkward to others, and they tend to stand out based on either their unique appearance and stature or their unusual gangly appearance, physical disproportions and anomalies as well as their somewhat nonsensical reactions or deeds. In a society where individuals who stand out based on their unique appearance, difference, reactive attitudes and even strangeness are singled out and elevated for admiration, this can tend to catapult these Souls to positions of high influence and power.

Unfortunately, the incarnation of alien Soul species in physical human forms intended for Human Angelic Soul groups will not only cause substantial physical reality conflicts going forward, in fact it will lead to Earth's "reset" in the 26th Century as we have also outlined for you previously. Because of this, at a minimum it is important to understand that Soul/Body hybridization of this nature is possible and being used, including Alien Soul groups incarnating in physical human forms that were designed for the Human Angelic Soul species, just as we have detailed in our book *The System Lords and the Twelve Dimensions*.

Whether they are "Service-to-Others" or "Service-to-Self" orientation, Souls are cast out from the Twelfth Universal Dimension by the God source and this begins the process of creation that unfolds in an infinite and timeless manner. Souls are cast out via a natural process of energetic "breath" and in some ways are cast in what could be considered "batches" or groups where orientation as well as their placement in the Universe has already been determined by this organic process.

This happens in much the same way a woman on Earth might give birth to either a male or female child, and based on the parents' circumstances will usually start life in a specific place or location. Like

the human child being born, even though a Soul can be considered a
blank slate where its experiences are concerned, intrinsic attributes
such as Soul orientation, Soul species, Soul group and, hence, the
Soul's starting point and location in the Universe – the Galaxy, star
system or constellation where they begin their journey -- are inherent and already present at the time the Soul is cast.

So, as a general rule the Soul's species and orientation determine
where in the Universe it begins its journey and where it is destined
to incarnate in physical form for the first time. Later however, it is
possible for this to be altered by the Soul as it advances in consciousness. Transmigration, particularly through Ascension from one Universal Dimension to another, is possible once a Soul augments its
vibrational integrity. Transmigration such as this becomes the decision
of the Soul itself and may be unrelated to the Soul's orientation,
species or location in the Universe. Whenever a Soul of this or that
orientation, group or species incarnates in physical form outside of
its standard, it is usually based on that Soul's individual mission,
growth experiences and specific choices.

Human Angelic Souls when first cast out, with by nature a Service-
to-Others orientation, will generally desire and be destined for physical incarnation in the First Universal Dimension in that sector of the
Universe you know as your own Solar System and Galaxy. There are
those Soul species in various sectors of your Galaxy that have similar,
if not nearly identical, physical appearances and forms, but although
they may be distant cousins, they are not Human Angelic Souls. In
some cases, these populations outnumber the Soul incarnations on
your world. For our purposes here, we will limit our discussion to
Human Angelic Souls that have incarnations and experiences in the
location you know as Earth in your present day Solar System.

It is important to recall that Earth is the designation given for the Third Universal Dimension planet where you are located. However, the planet also exists in varying forms and vibrational frequencies in other Universal Dimensions, each Dimension superimposed as it is one upon the other. Similarly, we remind you that physical Dimensions tend to be grouped into three's. Even though all Dimensions super-impose one upon the other, be aware that higher Dimensions can see lower Dimensions, but lower Dimensions cannot see higher ones.

Following through on this idea of three visible, physical dimensional levels being grouped together, you can understand that the First through Third Universal Dimensions contain the world you know as Earth. The Fourth through Sixth Universal Dimensional levels contain the planet where it is known as Terra, and in the Seventh through Ninth Universal Dimension levels the same planet you know as Earth at those dimensional levels, existing at a higher vibrational resonance, is known as Gaia. (See Page 453, Figure 7 of Diagrams in the Appendix.)

Life incarnations in physical form begin in the First Universal Dimen-sion of the planet that your Soul gravitates towards based on its Soul orientation, group and species. Reincarnation through a Soul's Wheels of Creation is the process that allows physical incarnations to take place at any dimensional level. In turn, Transmigration is the process that allows a Soul to graduate through dimensional realms, and As-cension further allows for the Soul's evolution and passage to the next Universal Dimension.

Human Angelic Souls are by no means the only group of Souls or entities that originate from a "Service-to-Others" orientation. In other sectors of the Galaxy and Universe, there are Souls and Soul groups incarnating with both orientations. Some incarnate in close proximity and others do not. In some sectors, such as your own,

Service-to-Others orientation predominates, but in some, quite the opposite is true and Service-to-Self orientation is the norm.

Regardless of orientation, these Souls all begin with incarnations projected into the First Universal Dimension of their particular solar system, Galaxy or sector, just as all Souls, through Transmigration, will traverse the Sublevels or Astral planes within each Universal Dimension. (See Page 454, Figure 8 of Diagrams in the Appendix.) Similarly, when they have completed their cycles of incarnation within any given Universal Dimension, all of them will have the opportunity, through the process of Ascension, to evolve to higher Universal Dimensions and begin life incarnations there. Some of these will be densely physical and some will be ethereal, depending on the Universal Dimension.

Incarnations in higher Universal Dimensions are always more etheric and ethereal in nature, whereas incarnations in lower Universal Dimensions are far more physical, since the nature of the lower Universal Dimensions is that they are chock full of dense physical elements and matter. For our purposes, we will limit our discussion principally to how Service-to-Others Human Angelic Soul groups striving for individualization and physical incarnation begin their progress in the First Universal Dimension of the Solar System and sector known as Earth.

This process of incarnation in the First Universal Dimension on Earth, then, is not unlike the progress made when a baby, by way of physical birth, is born into a family in your Third Universal Dimension. The child becomes a member of a unit, family or otherwise, and grows to develop a conscious understanding of its position within the unit it is born into. As the baby grows and develops, it becomes aware of itself first; then a distinction between itself and its environment is made and finally, the relationship it has with others within its physical surroundings is established. Consciousness, and cellular light absorption (en-light-en-ment) is augmented as the baby grows and becomes a child, then an adolescent and finally an adult. Throughout the process, growth, enlightenment and individualization are driving factors.

Similar to the newborn, a Soul that is newly cast out will first need to become accustomed to the rigors of dense physical incarnation as it experiences itself, its environment and its relationship to other incarnates in the physical world that surrounds it. In this sense, we use the term "incarnations" to not only signify incarnation in human form, but in all forms of life whether you perceive these as "living" or not, from rocks to mountain ranges, forests, rivers, sands and clouds, just to name a few. All of these are possible incarnates and incarnations into dense physical matter and form beginning with the initial incarnations of a Soul in the First Universal Dimension.

A newly cast Human Angelic Soul, for example, will participate as a basic element of the First Dimensional structure. In doing so, an infant Soul becomes aware of the scope and magnitude of the physical Dimension it is experiencing while also learning the principles behind physical structure manifestation and existence. These Souls often spend whatever period of time they like, according to their own needs, desires and goals, incarnated as basic and primal First Dimensional physical beings. (See Page 454, Figure 8 of Diagrams in the Appendix.)

In the Third Universal Dimension, without realizing it, you exist side by side with First and Second Dimensional beings. You will recall that higher can see lower, but lower cannot see higher, a universal precept, and as a result, although you are vaguely aware of these First and Second Dimensional beings and can "See" them, they tend to seem like background for you. In other words, minerals, rocks, water and clouds are primal First Dimensional Beings. You see them and place them in whatever category your science defines, but you do not actually understand that there is an energetic consciousness that drives them. Nor do you imagine that each grain of sand, each crystal, each cloud or water droplet may represent an entity, the incarnation of a baby from the Human Angelic Soul species that is, for the first time taking on the experience of life through a form in a physical density or world.

Granted, as consciousness improves and you gain more enlightenment and vibrational integrity there are those that begin to have a certain understanding that every physical element and being in your world – seen and not seen -- is made manifest from energy and may have an inherent "Soul," which it does. But for the most part, you see the world around you as ornamental and something that either acts as a backdrop or serves a particular need of your species.

Thus you are not necessarily aware of a rock or a tree as an energetic projection of a Soul experiencing physical life. And in keeping with the universal precept that higher can see lower but lower cannot see higher dimensionally speaking, the rock, grain of sand and the cloud are fairly oblivious if not completely blind to you. True as that might be, a newly cast infant Human Angelic Soul in the First Universal Dimension of Earth will generally choose to solidify and unify itself with typical First Dimensional elements and beings that are occupying a place, sometimes for very short periods and other times for eons of linear time, within the physical world you know. The next time you find yourself present with a rock, a crystal, a mountain range, a grain of sand, a cloud, a breeze, a drop of water, a drop of rain, a river or an ocean, consider its relationship to you and to the world from your Soul's perspective, and perhaps you will gain new insight into how all things are truly related and unified. In effect, all things are just like you expressing themselves in unique dimensional, sometimes physical and sometimes ethereal formats.

As that baby Soul develops in the First Universal Dimension, it finds individualization through its cycles of incarnation, and this leads to its understanding of the relationship it has energetically with both its physical structure, its ability to manipulate its physical structure and the world at large within a specific Universal Dimension. As that occurs and the Soul begins the process of distinction and individualization, its vibrational resonance and consciousness increases so that it will be prepared to evolve, through Ascension, at the appropriate time, to higher levels of physical incarnation. The ultimate aim: Incarnation in physical human form starting in the Third Universal Dimension.

But before we discuss the Human Angelic Soul's cycles of incarnation further, let's discuss for a moment, in simplified manner, the fundamental process of a Soul's journey through the Universal Dimensions and into physical incarnation. First of all, as we have explained it must be understood that the process of physical manifestation is related to the principle of spin, polarity and ultimately the electromagnetic impulses that interface to pull particles into manifestation. In a sense, at its core energetic spin is the true spark of life. That is to say, polarity, electromagnetic spin, scalar energy and the resulting interactions are what draw particles into formalized composition, or matter. Together with specific rules governed by the prevailing dimensional physics and assisted by fractal geometrics, these properties combine to slow down and pull energy particles together to create substance.

Thought and creative impulse on your part and the part of your Soul further contribute to this, defining matter into form and the consequential physical results that provide you with physical reality, which includes the physical being, that you witness and experience.

Naturally, as we have explained, the initial creative energetic spark originates from the God Source in the Twelfth Universal Dimension, and this spark is breathed into existence via the casting of your Soul. Once originated and emitted, the Soul has both orientation and, indirectly, an archetypal expression that it carries with it and expresses throughout the many entities that the Soul further creates. The Soul does so in much the same way, metaphorically, that you might emit a breath if you were to do so mindfully, as in the practice of Yoga.

As in Yoga, purposeful breath harnesses life-giving force that can be directed in a particular fashion for a specific purpose. In much the same way, at the highest dimensional levels, the God source or All-That-Is casts out Souls. Similarly, your Soul breaths life into the numerous lifetimes it is experiencing, all simultaneously within a specific Universal Dimension. This is with the understanding, of course, that all the lifetimes of your Soul within the Dimension are subject to the mechanics of time-wave motion within that Universal Dimension according to its alignment with Galactic Ascension principles.

In order to fully understand how such a spark evolves, we remind you of past discussions in prior books concerning the method by which energy progresses and evolves through the Universe from one Universal Dimension to the next. For now, let us merely remind you that all energy is derived and emitted through the Galaxy's solar source, and generally that energy can be defined. It might be helpful to envision the solar entity, your Sun for example, as a primary energy portal into each system. Although there are many examples of such energetic portals within a system, the Sun of a particular Solar System serves as the preeminent channel and predominant dimensional pass-through for the influx of energy into a system.

As the planets, Sun, Galaxy and other celestial bodies travel within a particular time-wave and space that defines the Dimension, the photonic energy is "slowed" or magnetized into form and physical elements are created. As this occurs, energy particles are magnetized by a variety of factors, including spin, thought forms and like-attraction. Ultimately the energy is rendered into either ethereal or physical substance depending on the sub-dimensional overlay that attracts it.

As these molecular particles continue to pass through the system and are slowed down further and magnetized into form, they continually evolve and are transformed through various stages of substance as they unify, then disintegrate and deconstruct in much the same manner as they are created, formed and constructed, only in reverse. In due course, they pass through the system entirely, having lived complete life cycles themselves, pulled through by subtle but powerful gravitational waves emanating throughout the system from what you know as Black Holes. Like Solar bodies, but much more powerful in a certain manner of speaking, Black Holes are the interdimensional portals that draw energy through the system, deconstructing, recycling and recouping it, then transferring it back to the God Source. (See Page 456, Figure 10 of Diagrams in the Appendix.)

In a very similar way that this process of matter materialization and dematerialization unfolds, this is also what happens with the evolution and journey of the energy that is your "Soul" as it makes its way through physical incarnations within the Universal Dimensions. The only difference is that as the physical matter that was your physical being is deconstructed and returned to Source, the energy that is you is recouped, returned and rejoined with your Soul, which is then able to continue its interdimensional journey intact and, as part of the process, augmented.

So as a Soul's energy is cast out and "breathed" by Life Source from the Twelfth Universal Dimension, the realm of God, that energy is channeled through the Solar portal and Transmigrates via the corresponding Sublevel of the Universal Dimension where the Soul is destined to incarnate. Thus, as an example, the Soul, cast out as it is from the Twelfth Universal Dimension, is first cast into the Twelfth Sublevel of the First Universal Dimension. As it transmigrates and is drawn through that portal, the Soul is placed within the highest realms of the Dimension where it will incarnate lifetimes in close proximity to all the components that are necessary for it to begin its journey of creation into various physical and ethereal incarnations and life forms.

This includes incarnations into the First Universal Dimension and subsequent journeys through all the Dimensional Sublevels of that Universal Dimension. These Sublevels act as overlapping waves or frequency fields within the Universal Dimension. Many of these Sublevel Dimensions are identified or described in your ancient Mythology, and, though the descriptions and designations are not precise, you might recognize some of them as Heaven, Hell, Nirvana, Valhalla, the Underworld, the dream state, the subconscious, and the like.

As a Soul transmigrates via the highest dimensional Sublevels and the Solar portal of the Solar System in question, it projects itself casting out lifetimes in the initial dimensional system at the lowest frequencies. It is through the Soul's vibrational signature that it is magnetized to the First Universal Dimension, and prior to actually materializing and manifesting physical entities, whatever form they may be, from the Twelfth Astral plane of the Universal Dimension, the Soul finds itself planning incarnations, or Wheels of Creation, for experiences within the lower Sublevels of the Universal Dimension. It is at this particular point that Soul energy now individualized, distinctive and becoming Self-conscious through the entities it is creating in the lower Sublevels of the Dimension, will, assisted by Master and Celestial Guides from the Seventh, Eighth, Ninth, Tenth and Eleventh Astral Sublevels of the Dimension, begin lifetimes in dense physical structures.

There is no specific formula for such incarnations, and there is similarly no particular time frame that must be adhered to. A Soul in the process of individualization and primary incarnations in the First Universal Dimension awaits its own directive and its own awareness by scanning the potential that is inherent for it within that Dimension. At a particular juncture, again assessing the potential from the highest, non-physical Dimensional Sublevel of the Universal Dimension, the Soul will decide ultimately when and how to participate in the act of creation. It will then invest its energy by becoming part of the physical forms in that universal structure. In a sense, the Soul is "born" into actual physical reality and manifestation at that time.

Longing to create and to be created, the Soul will choose a particular association or specialty, and the thought form projected by the Soul will then become magnetized into some physical form. In the First Sublevel of the First Universal Dimension, this usually takes place within the elemental Kingdom. The mythology you know related to the personification of rivers, streams, mountains, valleys, sky, wind and the like, is in great part related to the inner understanding that a Human Angelic Soul originally beginning incarnations in the First

Universal Dimension will have a tendency towards participating in the physical realm as minerals or dense physical elements related to the First Dimension. This becomes the launching pad so to speak for their progression and the start of their journey through higher and higher levels of incarnation and dimensional transmigration.

For this reason, the act of creation can be said to be universal and each Soul can be called a Creator or, at a minimum, a Co-creator with God. In a sense each individualized Soul cast out from the Twelfth Universal Dimension shares in the creative process and becomes a creator itself. In this way, it is completely accurate to conclude that this is the essential unity shared with God the Creator force, and it is also the link that each Soul maintains universally and throughout its existence with the Twelfth Universal Dimension, the realm of the God Source or, as we prefer to say, the Dimension of All That Is.

At the beginning of a Soul's creation journey, it does not necessarily choose any "specialty," just as a baby does not choose the profession it will pursue as an adult. However, by virtue of what the Soul chooses as its primary incarnations in the physical world, it can be said that the Soul sometimes becomes predisposed to certain specialties and affiliations with respect to the elemental entity it chooses as its Avatar in physical reality. The Soul will usually carry this forward into the many lifetimes it creates, and most of the reincarnations on its numerous Wheels of Creation will have a deep attraction to traits related to its first incarnations in the First Universal Dimension.

As an example, later entities on the Soul's Wheels of Creation in the Third Universal Dimension might have natural tendencies to see the world in a certain manner, or use the elements of the physical substance that once represented them in their first incarnation. An entity with an Artisan as its chief energetic expression, whose first incarnation was as a hill of marble, might well become a renowned sculptor of marble statues. It is not by accident when such Artisans tell patrons that they merely "pull" from the marble what they see inside it. Similarly a woodworker might have spent eons as a Redwood Tree in the Second Universal Dimension, and an IT professional might have an unending fascination for how quartz crystal can store data or hold resonance based on its molecular composition. The list goes on and on.

It must be understood that at this point in the early cycles of physical manifestation, an individual Soul does not, in and of itself, become a mountain, a river, the sea, a cloud or the wind. Instead, it becomes a part of the many entities that constitute such a manifestation, in much the same way a cell in the physical body that is you participates in the formulation and function of your physical body. In a manner of speaking, one might literally say that although a baby Soul manifesting in the First Universal Dimension for the first time is not necessarily the mountain, that Soul could possibly be referred to metaphorically speaking as a particular rock or even a mineral formation that is part of the mountain entity. In this way the Soul contributes to the creation, spirit and life mission of the entire mountain range. Many entities with an affinity or innate understanding of the use of crystals and gemstones in higher dimensional incarnations may well have spent their beginning incarnations in the First Universal Dimension as part of just such a mountain range.

This becomes especially apparent once a Soul has evolved and ascended from the Fist Universal Dimension to the Second, where a Soul's incarnations are more individualized, and able to manifest readily into independent forms. These incarnations also have specific, individualized life missions, personality traits and levels of awareness.

Naturally, the Second Universal Dimension is more highly evolved than the First, and individualized Souls at this level separate from the kind of unified consciousness and physical manifestation that generally occurs in the First Universal Dimension. A genre of incarnation for Human Angelic Souls that you might recognize in the Second Universal Dimension can be found in personifications and entities such as gnomes, fairies, tree spirits and the like, to name a few possibilities. A Soul choosing such incarnations in the Second Universal Dimension will almost always form associations and will be close to determining an understanding of itself, or a "specialty" as it were, based on the composite of its First and Second Universal Dimension incarnations.

Despite the fact that the Soul is an individualized entity unto itself, for the most part, in the First Universal Dimension, incarnations are generally regarded as dense physical life structures where the Soul is more of a "cooperating" entity forming large, dense manifestations. Each Soul always remains independent but, in such a case, is also unified in creative cooperation as it learns the ropes, so to speak, of physical creation, manifestation and existence. As the Soul becomes more and more distinctive and individualized over the course of its long process of existence in the First Universal Dimension, it evolves towards the Second Universal Dimensions where this independence will eventually lead it to experience physical incarnations that are housed in distinctly separate physical bodies and states.

It is not by accident that incarnations in the First Universal Dimension are exceedingly long as a Soul learns the continual process of physical manifestation and reality co-creation. Lifetimes in the First and Second Universal Dimension last longer and are therefore fewer in number, as can be seen in the fact that the apparent "life" span of a mountain range, a river or a sea, per our example, usually far exceeds the life span of almost all other creations and Beings in the natural world. Karmic balancing is not a major consideration on these early Wheels of Creation, but is experienced more and more as individualization takes place in the late stages of Second Universal Dimension lifetimes and, naturally, once Third Universal Dimension lifetimes are the norm.

Ascension permits this universal evolution and growth, and this same process allows a Soul to progress through particular energetic stages and junctions in order to reach higher realms of existence when the Soul has achieved the necessary consciousness and resonance. When each individualized Soul is ready, experienced maximum growth through its incarnations in a particular Universal Dimension, then during the Ascension period windows, ascending into higher levels of consciousness and forms of reincarnation are possible.

Ultimately, after ascending from the Second Universal Dimension, the Soul reaches what you know as the Third Universal Dimension, and this in turn leads to the particular lifetimes you currently experience at various points on the dimensional timeline. In the Third Universal Dimension, physical incarnations in human form begin at the Third Sublevel of the Dimension. We will discuss in greater depth shortly the various life entry points in a Universal Dimension, as well as the incarnations and cycles you experience in the Third Universal Dimension. For now, please understand that Ascension, whether it be for a Soul, a Planetary Body, a Galaxy or an entire Universal Dimension (or Space-time wave) is something to cherish as the natural progression of a Soul as it makes the long journey back to its originating Source. This is understood to be the journey a Soul makes through all Twelve Universal Dimensions as well as all Twelve Sub-levels of each of those Universal Dimensions.

It is a strange irony that most entities incarnated at the Third Sublevel of the Third Universal Dimension in physical reality on Earth believe consciousness to be an extension of their physical body or mind, and there is, therefore, a close attachment to the physical body and that particular physical reality. This is far from the case. Consciousness, which could also be referred to as the Soul, is the real creator, mover and motivator of not only the physical body you inhabit, but is also the external reality you experience as a whole.

Therefore, since consciousness -- the Soul -- comes first, you must also conclude that it does not terminate with the extinction of the physical body or the physical reality. It has often been said that you are essentially spiritual beings creating and enjoying a physical experience. You are not physical beings that sprout a spiritual nature or who have a spiritual side projected out from you as a result of your physical state, your condition or your environment. In fact, we would suggest that far too often your spiritual nature is experienced as an afterthought of your physical being, and it is precisely this pattern that predisposes you to think of the physical body first and the spiritual side of you as being secondary, or, at best, along for the ride.

Thus it is important to understand that consciousness, as a component of your Soul, transcends the physical Dimensions in which you may be currently attuned. Bodies, whether they are physical, ethereal, Astral or some composite thereof, serve merely as vehicles for the Soul. The point here is that your consciousness does not cease to exist when the physical housing it temporarily inhabits is no longer viable.

For the Soul, having a physical or Astral body is not unlike the individual that has many houses all over the world, which it owns but visits only for a short period. Realizing this, you begin to understand the scope of the Soul's complexity as well as the concept that it is never physically bound by the structures it owns or visits, wherever in the world or whenever they may exist. What is perhaps more complex, but important to understand, is the idea that the Soul may also live in all its houses simultaneously. Indeed, it can simultaneously procure, dispose of, design, renovate or build new ones within a specific Universal Dimension, as needed, for any and all purposes of growth. In planning all these, the Soul can also incorporate any attribute or specific need it might like the physical structure to have, not to mention the diversity of the environment in which it might be constructed or maintained.

It is also interesting to note that your Soul or ethereal consciousness, your energetic self as it were, has the ability not only to transcend the physical incarnations it inhabits, but each incarnation is fully automated and a living entity, which has the ability to exist and act completely independent of its far-off owner.

It is especially important to note here that "Source," meaning the God force in the Twelfth Universal Dimension from which all entities originate, in no way directs, instructs, cajoles or in any way causes or has direct input into the physical reality that you traverse or create. The irony here is that what the majority of people in your world today envision as "God," i.e., an anthropomorphic Being directing every movement and event in your world, is actually more closely related to the functioning of the Soul. The actual God Source, All That Is, is a far more complex state of being than most give it credit for, and that Source is exceedingly removed from lower dimensional activities, if involved in them at all.

In fact, as a Co-Creator of you and your reality, your Soul, which comprises the major part of your consciousness, creates physical incarnations in a divine way completely in accord with its own process, plan for growth and path to Ascension. Naturally, this all occurs within the scope of universal laws, the physics of the particular reality and the parameters of the Universal Dimension where the Soul resides and currently incarnates into living entities.

In general, it is the process of Transmigration through all the Sublevels of a Dimension and all the Universal Dimensions, transacted through the interdimensional process of Ascension that is the primordial guide for each Soul. This also directs and impacts how a Soul plans its cycles of lifetimes on Wheels of Creation within a Dimension. In some measure this is also responsible for what actually happens to all reincarnations, as well as how the energy of consciousness from each lifetime is reintegrated with the Soul at the highest levels of a Universal Dimension.

Returning to our topic concerning the incarnation of the Soul in physical form in the First Universal Dimension, let us recap what we have discussed thus far. As we mentioned, once a Soul has been cast out from the Twelfth Universal Dimension it travels by way of the Dimensional Sublevels through the solar source of the Solar System in question. Establishing itself in the Twelfth Dimensional Sublevel of the First Universal Dimension, the Soul is ready to begin physical incarnations in the lower Sublevels of that Universal Dimension. First Dimensional physical incarnations are the starting point of a Soul's journey through all the Universal Dimensions based on that Dimension's low resonance, high density and the tendency for the creative process to be shared by Soul groups that bind together to manifest physicality and a mass conscious reality.

Most Souls choose to have limited First Dimensional incarnations of this nature in striving for quality over quantity, and for this reason such incarnations can be in one physical state that lasts millennia, if the Soul chooses. First Dimensional incarnations are longer lasting when seen from a linear timeline perspective, and as the Soul progresses to higher dimensional levels life incarnations become more individualized and limited in length.

Once the Soul has transmigrated to higher dimensional levels from the First and Second Universal Dimensions, Souls have substantially more individuality and plan much higher numbers of lifetimes since longevity of experience is no longer necessary. However, it is important to note that this changes when the Soul begins Fifth Universal Dimension lifetimes. Lifetimes in the Fifth Universal Dimension increase in length since there is greater awareness of the Soul's purpose in those incarnations and less of a need to balance karmic energy as there is when experiencing a myriad of shorter lifetimes.

Despite the fact that the First Universal Dimension comprises a trinity that consists of the First, Second and Third Universal Dimensions, First Universal Dimension incarnations offer distinct growth experiences related to the environment in which the Soul will later incarnate as an individual human entity. This experience allows the Soul to understand the principles of duality, density and substance manifestation, which also prepare it for Ascension to higher realities where the principles of creation and manifestation become more individualized and, in many ways, more important as a result of separate lifetime incarnations.

We remind you that each Universal Dimension is segmented into twelve Dimensional Sublevels. As an example, if your Soul entered your Galaxy and Solar System and began dimensional incarnations, it would first participate as part of a greater entity, say a mountain or a stream or a grain of sand on a beach, at the First Sublevel of the First Universal Dimension. Over time and with experience, the incarnation would advance to the Second Sublevel of the First Universal Dimension, still existing as a physical entity within the First Universal Dimension.

This process would continue into the Third Sublevel of the First Universal Dimension, and the entity would still exist in physical form within the First Universal Dimension. Once the entity had raised its consciousness enough, it would then pass into the etheric realms, and the entity would travel through the remaining Astral realms of the First Universal Dimension. Beginning with the Fourth Dimensional Sublevel, the Astral realms or higher Dimensional Sublevels of the First and Second Universal Dimensions are similar in constitution to those found in the Third Universal Dimension, which we will discuss in greater detail momentarily.

For our purposes here, understand that in the First Universal Dimension, the entity journeys through three stages of physical reality and then transmigrates to the higher Astral planes. Once each of the incarnations or lifetimes is completed in both the physical and non-physical Dimensional Sublevels, the energy and personality of each entity the Soul has created in the Universal Dimension passes through the higher Astral realms and reintegrates with the Soul in the Twelfth Dimensional Sublevel of the First Universal Dimension.

Much transpires in these Astral Sublevels as the various lifetimes carry on in non-corporeal Astral existence until reconsolidation with the Soul in the highest Dimensional Sublevels is achieved. We will cover the rise through these Sublevels in great detail as we explore your own physical reincarnations in the Third Universal Dimension. For now, understand that at the highest Sublevels of the Universal Dimension the Soul is reunified with the many lifetimes it has inspired, and this includes whatever form or substance life takes in the First and Second Universal Dimension. Ascension carries the Soul forward into the next Universal Dimension once all lifetimes have completed their journey through the Astral planes, and rejoined the Soul in the Twelfth Astral realm.

Like incarnations in the First Universal Dimension, incarnations in the Second Universal Dimension are physical and visibly existent to you in the Third Universal Dimension. However, generally you are not aware that the physical entities and incarnations you are seeing are actually Second Dimensional Beings. Again, this is true in much the same manner as viewers in the Third Universal Dimension are not necessarily aware that a mountain range, an ocean or a wind is actually a First Universal Dimension Being.

In the Second Universal Dimension, various Human Angelic Soul groups incarnate as entities from what is termed the "Elemental" or Devic Kingdom. Since you highly focused on your own perspective in the Third Universal Dimension, which limits your sensitivity to them, Beings of the Devic Kingdom are not "seen" by you in their true form or in a form you would easily recognize. What you see instead is a physical Being that appears static and immovable in your world. The truth is that these Beings have one side to them rendered invisible and one side rendered visible to you. One side you interact with daily, and the other you cannot see or experience as a tangible reality.

Thus in the Second Universal Dimension, living physical creatures such as plants, insects, and, in some cases, certain animals, exist in the forms you see and know very well. You see them, interact with them and know them as part of your world. But you do not actually share in their true Soul or life experiences. We say in some cases because most animals are actually Third Universal Dimension Beings, which we will save for a later discussion. In general however, most Beings from the natural kingdoms, in particular the plant or insect kingdoms, and especially those creatures that are members of a hive Soul group, are Beings going through Second Universal Dimension incarnations.

More importantly, these Beings are an integral part of what is termed the "Devic" kingdoms, and we will leave you to explore this further on your own. For our purposes here as it relates to Second Dimensional incarnations, the definition we employ of an Elemental is derived from the phenomenon you may recognize as Nature Spirits, including Earth Spirits, Fire Spirits, Wind and Air Spirits and Water Spirits. There are many sub groups of these Beings under various Elemental categories, including, among others, Devas, Brownies, Faeries, Elves, Trolls, Gnomes, Satyrs, Pans, Water Nymphs, Tree Spirits, Sprites and the like.

Elementals operate in unison with the natural elements – fire, air, earth and water – and express themselves primarily through their mental or ethereal bodies. Elementals are not considered immortals, although their lifetimes can span thousands of linear years, and though they seem fantastical, invisible and ethereal to you, they have quasi-human, semi-individualized lives where they raise families and, though limited, may even have attributes and life missions that your Soul might later choose in Third Dimensional incarnation. In a sense, they have miniaturized versions of the societal structures you know, however, they are not fully individualized Beings, so they straddle the boundaries between group co-existence and individual creation, as we saw with First Universal Dimensional Beings. Full individualization of Self in the form of human existence is a later hallmark restricted to Third Universal Dimension incarnations.

Elementals communicate telepathically, and they are experts at transforming Second Dimensional thought-forms into physical manifestation. It is the practice of transforming thought-forms into physical reality representations that is important here, since this is a principal way in which Baby and Younger Souls incarnating as Elementals learn the ropes, so to speak, of physical reality creation and manifestation. Their dominion is over the First as well as over the Second Universal Dimension.

The fact that you do not see their true nature and instead see a physical representation of who and what they are, as expressed in Third Dimensional reality, is a matter of much confusion, so let us explain. As we just detailed, using the plant kingdom as our example, when focused in Third Dimensional reality you might see a tree. In other words, the "tree" is a physical representation of a Being from the plant kingdom that you know well.

What you do not see is the actual "consciousness" that is really the essence of that "tree." True to our universal law that higher Dimensions can see lower, but lower does not see higher (dimensionally), you rightfully see a physical tree but you are not aware of the tree's consciousness and form, which is orchestrated and represented by a specific spirit of Nature-- a faerie, gnome, elf or other being.

In this way, Second Dimensional Beings are physically an integral part of your world and you see a physical representation of them (the tree), but you are not able to truly see them as they really exist, nor are you able to participate in their experiences. In addition, you are not able to communicate with their consciousness, unless you have a unique talent chosen as a personality attribute for you by your Soul for the current lifetime. Such attributes are rare and we would add that usually such talents stem from an individual's lifetimes as a member of these Beings, or someone with a similar personal affiliation with the Elemental kingdom that was experienced during an incarnation in either the First or Second Universal Dimension.

What is interesting here is the answer you find when you ask yourself who and what Soul group is responsible for these Beings. If you answer that these Beings represent the life cycles and incarnations of Human Angelic Souls journeying through the Second Universal Dimension as part of the Elemental world, you would be correct. Prior to their incarnations in the Third Universal Dimension, where they take on the physical human bodies that you know well, Human Angelic Souls are actually the Elementals of your mythology experiencing incarnations in the Second Universal Dimension.

Now, it is important to understand two things here. First, though Human Angelic Souls may incarnate in the Elemental world as faeries, trolls, gnomes, nymphs or sprites, or whatever, and, although they are seen to you as plants or insects, this does not necessarily mean that Human Angelic Souls are incarnating as the plants, insects or animals you see. This is important to understand since contrary to some popular beliefs about Reincarnation, Human Angelic Souls do not incarnate as plants, insects or animals.

However, they do incarnate as Elemental Beings associated with the physical representations you see, and we would tell you that the current misunderstanding concerning Human Angelic Souls incarnating in these forms is most likely derived from seeing the physical appearance of say, a tree, and not being able to see the true spirit or consciousness of that tree – the faerie, gnome or etheric Being that is actually responsible for the physical manifestation that you see.

Secondly, please understand, in addition to this, that after a Human Angelic Soul has evolved to incarnations in the Third Universal Dimension that Soul will never again incarnate in a lower dimensional form such as a plant, insect or animal and, in conjunction with this, will never incarnate as an Elemental Being again. This is not to say, however, that the experience of a Being in a Second Dimensional incarnation does not prepare you for incarnations and transmigration into higher consciousness. Rather it is to say that higher consciousness will never recede into lower consciousness forms due to "bad" karmic debts or as a punishment from God, as many religious or spiritual dogmas will have you believe.

This misunderstanding concerning Reincarnation and Transmigration will become apparent as we continue to examine the journey of the Soul. Suffice to say that this concept likely comes from the deep inner knowledge you may have that some of you, if not most of you, have at some point spent Second Dimensional life incarnations as Elementals caring for and responsible for the physical environment or a specific aspect of the natural world prior to your Ascension to the Third Universal Dimension. As an added note, we would point to incarnations by Human Angelic Souls in the Elemental Kingdom as an important precursor to learning to care for your physical environment.

We would suggest, therefore, that this is also a way to distinguish a

Human Angelic Soul from one that is an alien hybrid Soul incarnated in a physical human body. Human Angelics will almost always have a deep measure of love, respect and wonder for the planet and will always look to care for, in some manner or another, the natural elements and Earth's environment. Non-Human Angelic Souls do not have such experiences or empathy for the physical environment.

Different Soul groups, as well as different Soul orientations (Service-to-Self or Service-to-Others as the basis of our examples), prefer certain types of incarnations in every Universal Dimension. In this regard, Elemental and Devic incarnations of a Human Angelic Soul in the Second Universal Dimension represent an important stepping stone and valuable growth experience that precedes incarnations in human bodies in the Third Universal Dimension.

The relevance and impact of this cannot be underestimated. By experiencing Second Dimensional life as quasi-human entities, learning important lessons on how to transform thought-form into substance and matter, and subsequently physical reality, is an important prerequisite for experiencing Third Dimensional life. Essentially, reincarnation cycles as Elemental Beings in the Second Universal Dimension prepares the Human Angelic Soul for Third Dimensional incarnations as humans when ascended.

Returning to the subject of Transmigration and a Soul's journey, just as we have described concerning lifetimes in the First Universal Dimension and lifetimes experienced in the Second Universal Dimension, energy is never lost. The Soul's energy is merely projected and transmuted from one dimensional environment to the next, after which it is recaptured in the highest Astral planes in preparation for the Soul's continuing journey into the next Universal Dimension.

Once reintegration is accomplished, the Soul's consciousness has reached the point where Ascension from the Second Universal Dimension is possible, and at that point, the Soul is poised to ascend and begin its incarnations in the Third Universal Dimension.

The Third Universal Dimension heralds a significant change in the Reincarnation and Transmigration process in much the same manner that within your current school systems, graduation from certain levels of education to more advanced levels of education is an accomplishment that signals progress has been made. Such progress carries with it significant changes and new responsibilities.

While this is true, each time an entity evolves and ascends from one Universal Dimension to incarnations in the next, it is particularly true when entities ascend after lifetimes in the Second Universal Dimension and begin physical life incarnations in the Third Universal Dimension. Here, the real story of Human Angelic Soul progression starts. So let us now begin an exploration of the Soul's journey once it has evolved and ascended to the vast potential found in the life cycle incarnations such as the ones you are experiencing in the Third Universal Dimension.

 CHAPTER 3
THE FUNDAMENTALS OF PHYSICAL REINCARNATION IN THE THIRD UNIVERSAL DIMENSION

Before we begin our journey into Third Dimensional incarnations and reincarnation in the Earth realm, let's first review a few basic assumptions that are important to understand. First and foremost, as we have discussed already, when Souls are cast out from the Twelfth Universal Dimension by Source, they are by nature imbued with specific energetic orientations. These orientations have polarity, which is to say this forms the basis for polarity within a Soul's sacred energy. Polarity then provides the origin of an underlying electromagnetic "spin" that has scalar and vector properties. Those properties not only embody the Soul, they propel it, together with any fragments the Soul itself may cast out within a specific Dimension, and act as the energetic vehicle of the Soul through all spheres of time and space.

Though there are significant changes in these scalar and vector properties dependent upon the dimensional physics that are in play, all sentient Beings possess some form of inherent polarity or scalar motion that ultimately expands its nature (dual, tertiary, quaternary, and so forth as the case may be depending upon the Dimension) as consciousness increases and Ascension occurs. Followers of biology will be interested to note that physical bodies alter to accommodate the scalar nature of your energetic body and not the other way around based upon the properties of the Dimension where you reside.

For this reason, as an example, in your particular Dimension physical bodies have dual hemispheres of the brain as well as a dual system of blood flow that generates its own scalar energy field reflective of the duality (dual polarity) you experience. Scalar motion therefore, can be seen as a fundamental factor of a Soul's polar orientation.

Polar orientations are not wholly random, but vary according to dimensional space-time wave physics and specifics related to the universal sector for which they are initially bound. Since we are dealing principally with the Third Universal Dimensional here, and because physical polarity is almost always one-dimensional aspect lower than the Universal Dimension you inhabit, we will primarily discuss the dual polarities represented within your physical reality that we have highlighted for you already.

The first orientation we have discussed is the orientation of Service-to-Others. This orientation is an orientation that predisposes a particular Soul or Soul group (through the course of development) to obtain Soul growth through the offer of service to the Universe at large and to other Beings with whom they come in contact. It is interesting to note here that Souls from the Service-to-Others orientation tend to predominate within particular Soul groups, particularly in your sector of the Galaxy. It could be noted that more than half of Human Angelic Souls on Earth tend to originate from Service-to-Others orientation. Regardless of this, it does not mean that all Human Angelic or that all Souls in your Galaxy are Service-to-Others oriented. In general, there tends to be an equal number of Souls in the Universe from each orientation.

That said, most Human Angelic Souls are in fact oriented towards Service-to-Others. Soul groups within this orientation will find that their growth in every Dimension ultimately stems from service to other Beings. In fact, it could be said that this Soul orientation at higher Dimensional levels, such as from the Seventh, Eighth and Ninth Universal Dimensions, is responsible for what you would term "Spirit Guides." By choice these Souls assist Beings in lower dimensional realms such as your own by either physically incarnating in lower Dimensions, or energetically and telepathically assisting other Beings in the form you commonly know as "Spirit Guides" or "Angels."

In most cases, these entities telepathically communicate with those who, through their Souls, have agreed prior to the lifetime to utilize such guidance as a matter of Soul and consciousness growth generally. Further explanations of this and the greater purpose these Souls achieve by serving as Spirit Guides, Avatars or even as System Lords within the space-time wave, can be found in our book *The System Lords and the Twelve Dimensions* for those interested in these particular Soul specialties.

In direct contrast to the Service-to-Others Soul orientation is the Service-to-Self Soul orientation. As we explained, for the most part this orientation tends to be Soul groups that are outside of the Human Angelic experience. However, we must remind you that being from a different Soul group or species does not mean that these Souls cannot incarnate into physical human bodies. Indeed, although there are important caveats we will discuss, it is quite possible for those who are not from either the Human Angelic Soul group or from a Service-to-Others orientation to incarnate as human beings within your realm.

Understanding this, you begin to see that living with you in your world, simultaneously and along side you (if you are Human Angelic,) are Soul groups, and therefore individuals, who may have Service-to-Self orientation. This creates an interesting dynamic universally, and also adds to the polarity or duality that you may be aware of that is living with you on Third Dimensional Earth. This duality can become quite pronounced when Ascension energies peak, such as those currently passing through your sector influencing you and your world. Again, we caution against thinking of this in terms of worse, better or best, since every Being is created equally. However, it may help shed some light on the basis of the extreme dichotomies found worldwide, especially some of those that are currently being experienced in terms of political, religious, cultural or ethnic structures and their accompanying belief systems.

Although Soul group orientation can originate from either Service-to-Others or Service-to-Self orientation, Soul species tend to be more from one orientation than the other. Thus, while the majority of Human Angelic Souls may tend to lean more towards Service-to-Others orientation, there are nonetheless some Human Angelic Souls that are cast out with Service-to-Self orientation. On the other hand, many "alien" (to you) Soul species might have the opposite tendency, and the majority of Souls within those species are from the Service-to-Self orientation. In this way a Soul species, as well as particular Soul groups within a Soul species, can be said to have a particular "leaning" in terms of orientation and, accordingly, energetic expressions.

In discussing this we would add another point that is not outwardly related but in fact is an important consideration, which is also relevant. That point revolves around the fact that the human physical structure, and its accompanying physiology and psyche, is not necessarily amenable to all alien Soul species. Incarnation for alien Soul species into a human physical body designed and intended for the Human Angelic Soul race can be problematic at best. Despite this, the current evolution of the physical human structure does permit limited alien Soul incarnation. This is particularly true should the "alien" Souls in question have a purpose or a mission related to or derived from experiences that can only be had within the Earth sphere where Human Angelic Souls predominate.

Though for the most part this would be related to a mission that benefits all Beings existing within the Earth sphere, it can also be true for Soul groups that are orchestrating inroads into a realm that is not native to them and is dominated by another Soul species. You might go as far as to consider this as a kind of bio-invasion, and there are such incidents occurring now on Third Dimensional Earth.

Regardless of this, and less you become alarmed at the suggestion, there are specific safeguards put in place by higher dimensional and planetary guardians that prevent interference at this level before it becomes overwhelming to a Solar System or planet. Such safeguards are applicable to Third Dimensional Earth at the present time. Should the need arise, circumstances will always be created to end any attempt to commandeer a planet or Galaxy by any alien Soul group or species other than the one for which the Solar System or planet is intended.

This is exactly what occurred when Draconians, a Reptilian Soul species from the Draco Constellation, attempted colonization of your Solar System from a higher Universal Dimension in the distant past. An effort was made by that species to evolve physical Beings that could ultimately be used to incarnate their own Soul species and groups on Earth during the Mesozoic Era and particularly at its height in the Jurassic period. Earth's higher dimensional guardians ultimately intervened to eliminate that budding domination long before Ascension allowed consciousness to evolve to the point where the physical bodies of that species could accommodate sentient incarnations of the Draco Soul group.

Planetary colonization is very misunderstood by you based on your concept of conquering a region that is not native to you by taking it over using force. On the contrary, inter-Galaxy or inter-planetary colonization is almost always done on an interdimensional and evolutionary basis through various forms of solar, planetary and bioengineering by or in cooperation with a specific Soul species. This is usually carried out in conjunction with the Soul group intended to inhabit the realm as well as the solar and planetary system Beings involved. Higher Dimensional Guardians work with these participants as progenitors in any particular Universal sector.

Indeed, the Guardians and Avatars of Earth, or System Lords as we prefer to call them, are the true protectors of your realm. Entering your world from the highest Universal Dimensions and considered to be "Sons" of God by virtue of their Dimensional status (a symbolism still found expressed in many of your more recent religions) it is they who have always worked to perfect human physical existence and forms on Earth in order to create an environment conducive to consciousness growth for the Soul species designated.

They have done so from the beginnings of creation in your Galaxy, and do so even when the life forms of a particular Solar System are not yet viable and are still in genetic experimentation or have reached a point where they are poised for dimensional advancement at times of universal Ascension. Many, though not all, of the (Soul) species that are currently disappearing from your realm are doing so via the process of Ascension and not necessarily as a result of being forced into extinction. They are however, certainly extinct within your particular Dimension once Ascension energies are maximized and the species has transmigrated and ascended to higher dimensional levels.

Many of you attribute the creation of man on Earth to extraterrestrial visitors, but we would suggest that the natural evolution of the physical human structure is being constantly overseen by Earth's higher Dimensional Guardians in conjunction with the Human Angelic and other interdimensional Soul entities, who have had a significant hand in the perfection of physical bodies on Earth. This is particularly true at the earliest introductions of a human physical structure to serve as the vehicle for incarnations of Human Angelic Souls.

Though many may attribute these mysteries to this or that particular God force, and while parallels may exists, you should know that it is neither a singular God nor a singular alien Soul race that is responsible for creation. Rather it is higher Dimensional Guardians working within specific universal sectors and Dimensions together with Soul races relevant to the Solar System or Galaxy in question that have guided the evolution of physical life within a planetary system. This evolution is conducted in conjunction with Ascension during specific Ascension cycles. The process does so in accordance with what is of most use and benefit to the Soul growth of all Beings, Soul species and Soul groups developed within that sector.

Apropos, but changing this narrative slightly, understand also that when Souls are first cast from the Twelfth Dimensional Universal God Source they are generally cast out in groups. Though each Soul within the group is individualized when cast out, as it transmigrates to a new Universal Dimension the Soul becomes a co-creator in its own right. As such, it has the ability to "cast" out numerous energetic extensions of itself into the physical incarnations or reincarnations experienced within that Universal Dimension.

To be clear, these various energetic extensions of a Soul, or life incarnations, are each independent from the originating Soul, just as the Soul itself becomes independent of the God force once it is cast out. However, a Soul is an independent extension of the Twelfth Dimensional creative God force, having its own mission, experiences and consciousness, and it is ultimately destined to rejoin its original creator at some point. In the same way, life extensions of itself that the Soul has cast out are independent with a degree of autonomy, unique experiences and independent consciousness. This independence permits the Soul's reincarnations to create the experiences the Soul desires in order to grow and prepare for its own consciousness growth and evolution.

Ultimately, these versions or fragments of itself that are cast out by the Soul – of which you are likely one -- are destined to reconcile and reintegrate with the originating Soul at the highest levels of the Dimension. Once reconciliation and reintegration of all Soul fragments is accomplished, the Soul continues its progression through Ascension to the next Universal Dimension. Eventually, once the Soul completes its Ascension through all the Universal Dimensions, that Soul, which now includes the compilation of every lifetime and all of its Soul fragments, reintegrates and rejoins the originating God force at the level of the Twelfth Universal Dimension, from where it was originally cast out.

Now, not only does a Soul cast out various pieces of itself into independent incarnations and life cycles in a Universal Dimension, these fragments or incarnations all take place and "live" simultaneously since linear time as you experience it does not truly exist. Souls tend to be cast out by the God force in groups, or cadres, and the same is true of the independent fragments being cast out by Souls within the Dimension. In fact, we would say that similar to the way in which

Souls themselves maintain relationships as they progress through the Dimensions, energetic fragments created by the Soul as reincarnation lifetimes within the Universal Dimension tend to do the same. In effect, Souls within specific groups, as well as the fragments they cast into lifetimes within a Universal Dimension, are natural siblings that gravitate towards each other in physical and non-physical life.

Though they remain independent to be sure, Souls and the fragments of themselves they cast for incarnational experiences within a dimensional realm retain relationship and are naturally a part of their group at every level of existence. In this way, all Souls in a specific Soul group or cadre are familiar with each other based on their shared Soul origination. It is for this reason that Soul fragments created for incarnational purposes usually share physical and non-physical life experiences with Soul relatives. They are in fact related in much the same way you would envision a family tree with extensive branches and inter-dynamic sets of relationships.

Although many lives further down the family tree would seem to have no connection at all to the originating Soul group, in fact they are very much tied to the group via their originating Soul. This becomes important from the standpoint of Soul guidance as well as the actual experiences that Souls will plan, which leads us to our next precept.

Souls known to each other from their cadre or originating group will create physical life experiences and relationships based on what you might term "contracts" or agreements with each other for any number of purposes related to the specific growth of that particular individual fragment and, ultimately, the desire or need of the Soul in planning the fragment's lifetime. Often guidance is offered from behind the scenes and comes in the form of what you have termed

Spirit Guides, and at other times such guidance is orchestrated through experiential encounters and opportunities.

Whatever the case, incarnational lifetimes are never without a mission or purpose that is derived from the purpose of the Soul. It follows then that a Soul casts out fragments of itself into physical incarnation for specific purposes of growth through physical encounter and experience. In order to further facilitate the creation of circumstances and opportunities necessary to the Soul's growth, it "contracts" with Souls within its group or cadre so that a dynamic is created and the conditions become ripe for opportunities related to the Soul's mission or purpose for that particular Soul fragment or incarnation.

This does not, however, represent an override of an entity's "Free Will" since the Soul's fragments or physical incarnations always have the ability to make their own choices during the course of physical reality. An entity's Free Will is employed as opportunities and experiences are generated around them and as other Soul fragments appear within the context of daily life. In order to ensure that a particular opportunity for growth appears, depending upon its importance in terms of the Soul's chosen mission for that particular lifetime, it is not unheard of for a Soul to have pre-arranged many semi-loose agreements with other Souls all related to the same purpose. In this way, should the fragment or physical incarnation choose not to pursue it's "contract" at any given time through the use of Free Will, there is ample time for it to have the possibility of coming across the situation again in another context, usually with someone new at a different point on the timeline.

Sometimes, if it is an issue of central importance to the Soul's mission for the lifetime, such choices or contracts can appear in your life again and again in different forms, almost like a revolving door. While many of you ponder such things as simply coincidental repetition of what you have already experienced, the fact is this is usually an important indication that the issue or circumstances are of central importance to your lifetime and your life lesson.

It is also indicative of the fact that the Soul makes many such possible "agreements" for you to encounter and experience throughout the lifetime. Often, if one such contract or encounter fails to materialize at a designated point on the timeline, or if through Free Will you move past it before its appearance or resolution, there are others that will potentially provide nearly the same opportunities for growth that your Soul intended. We say "potentially" in that Free Will and choice are always present and possible. This provides you with the ability to not only consciously recognize and push aside any experience planned for you by your Soul, it also allows you a possible glimpse into your life mission.

Many assume that a life mission planned by the Soul must be related to their profession or a particular path they need to take while in physical incarnation. Nothing could be further from the truth, and these misconceptions are based strictly on societal or cultural standards and norms that are irrelevant to your Soul. A life mission as planned by your Soul is generally much more esoteric in nature, and is usually more related to navigating deeper emotional or spiritual perspectives, such as learning lessons of acceptance through love, learning how to navigate through disadvantages or learning the difference between a life controlled by others and a life that you control through your own Free Will.

Becoming conscious of this through your life's learning experiences and choices, as well as discovering how to navigate the rewards or challenges of those choices successfully is the true intention of the Soul. It is also the most important step towards growth and Ascension that you can take. This is the reason that although it is neither positive nor negative, and perfectly acceptable to do so if one chooses, those chasing elusive physical rewards through career, position, power or money in the belief that success in these areas are related to their life "mission" will be sorely disappointed. Generally, these individuals quickly discover after physical life in the Third Sublevel of the Third Universal Dimension that a true life-purpose, from the Soul's perspective, is not even remotely related to such things. At a minimum, the central adage that the pursuit of worldly riches is not the means to happiness remains buried in most spiritual or religious teaching, despite the fact that so many erroneous and misleading misconceptions have clouded this thinking in the modern age.

Furthermore, as you may be aware, your experiences are attracted to you electromagnetically based on the scalar energy produced through your emotions, thoughts, fears, desires and your cellular vibrational resonance related to your life goals and mission. Many of these are subconsciously generated and derived from your inner core beliefs and the personality parameters created by your childhood environment, which was chosen by you and your Soul in order to create those personality features and belief structures. The environment you grow up in, including your parents, is never accidental and is always a prime factor in creating the inner belief systems and personality features your Soul wishes to explore and navigate with throughout life.

The laws of attraction are ever present in creating your reality and this in turn ensures that your mission and the "contracts" your Soul has arranged for you prior to the lifetime with your Soul Mates and Soul Cousins are in some manner vibrationally attracted to you at some point during the lifetime. This occurs through your energetic expression and the dynamic energetic interface you have with your physical reality. In many cases, the timeline and mass consciousness will also serve as a backdrop against which your experiences and events are played out, and these can interject an important variant as well. The intersection of your life mission, your Soul's expression, the contracts you have with Soul Cousins, your conscious and subconscious desires, the scalar energy of your emotions based on your core beliefs and personality features and the energetic intensity with which these things are propelled into the physical realm are the true "Secret" to the creation of reality.

As we have said many times, a lifetime is not planned by your Soul to get "over" anything. Knowing that your Soul has planned the lifetime with a particular mission or goal in mind, and realizing that time is an allusion and the entire lifetime is designated for the purpose of accomplishing that mission, your Soul is not expecting that you get "over" it. Rather, it is intended that you experientially augment your awareness, your consciousness and consequently your growth through your interaction and the choices you make concerning usually one, or rarely, two central themes.

It is therefore not unusual to bump into the same issue, sometimes in the form of a challenge and sometimes not, again and again throughout life. It is also not unusual to encounter individuals in your life who, ultimately at the core, generate and present you with similar or identical life situations, with new choices related to the same issue you have experienced over and over again. This is not because you have done something badly or incorrectly, as many assume. It is simply assurance, or insurance from the perspective of your Soul, that the life purpose is understood, being met and even reinforced via the contracts and agreements made by your Soul with other members of its Soul group or cadre. Moreover, since the lifetime was intended with mastery of this as a central goal, the same or similar situations will crop up throughout the lifetime. It is merely your job to be aware of it and understand how to consciously meet and deal with whatever format it has taken during the current round.

Instead of admonishing yourself for such repetitive situations, it might be preferable to adopt the attitude of having "been here, done that." Conscious understanding and mindfulness not only makes the repeated experience easier to explore, navigate and pass through, it neutralizes and dissipates its energy. This has a subsequent effect on how the issue affects your consciousness, as well as your own energetic levels as monitored in your emotional output. In some cases, such repeat life occurrences could be seen as a test, or the Universe examining you to see if you are now truly conscious on how to deal with all possibilities in a particular issue or experience. Or, just as easily it might be a need to explore many different aspects of that issue in greater depth, or in a more elaborate manner.

Similarly, you will most likely encounter a wide variety of Soul mates, or Soul cousins, during the course of your lifetime. Some encounters will continue throughout life or for decades, and some will only be nameless and fleeting. Though you will certainly also encounter individuals not related to you at a Soul level, for the most part those with whom you have longevity or important life-changing interactions, whether good or challenging, are usually derived from some form of Soul connection.

Contrary to the subjective belief that everything is either good or bad, right or wrong, which is not applicable to the Soul's desire for experiential growth, experiences you may have with your Soul associations are not always cheerful, happy or carefree. In fact, we would suggest that since most life associations are organized by your Soul to maximize growth within a particular lifetime, and because such experiences and interactions can be fraught with complexity, in many cases they create harrowing experiences for an individual to navigate.

That said, it is just as likely that your Soul has organized for you to meet and happily marry a "mate" from within your Soul cadre who brings you fulfillment and satisfaction as it is likely that you meet and marry someone who presents you with endless difficulty and regret. A Soul mate might be someone who assists you on your career path and offers you your first real progress in life, or just as likely might be the one that abuses you and treats you abominably creating choices that either doom you to inaction or oblige you through endless challenges to break out and pursue an entirely different life course. As you can see then, it is just as likely that a Soul mate might be the one that admires and assists you as the one who abuses you, accuses you, imprisons you, tortures you and, in extraordinary instances, is responsible for your demise.

Understanding these precepts leads us to discussions concerning the Soul's planning of physical life cycles in the Third Universal Dimensional. We remind you that the Universe is comprised of twelve Universal Dimensions, each of which is further segmented into twelve Dimensional Sublevels. The lower Sublevels of a Universal Dimension are those that are vibrationally denser and therefore more physical in nature. Physical reality within a Universal Dimension tends to reside in the lower Dimensional Sublevels.

Higher Sublevels of a Universal Dimension consist of the Astral or etheric planes, which are energetic, ethereal and, generally, non-corporeal in nature. All Dimensional Sublevels are superimposed one upon the other, thinly divided by frequency and vibrational resonance. Nonetheless, the Sublevels represent distinct Dimensions and in some cases distinct realities. The physical reality you are familiar with on Earth from day to day is focused within the first three Sublevels of the Third Universal Dimension, whereas the Fourth through Twelfth Dimensional Sublevels are non-corporeal and etheric in nature, as we shall discuss shortly.

For our purposes in this book, we are going to focus primarily on reincarnations and life cycles in the various Sublevels, physical and etheric, as they relate to the Third Universal Dimension on Earth. This is most applicable to your own lifetimes and also most applicable to the majority of Human Angelic Souls. As we have mentioned, Human Angelic Souls are generally orientated towards Service-to-Others and in the Third Universal Dimension, principally incarnate and inhabit your Solar System in the Milky Way Galaxy.

We will confine our discussion to Human Angelic Soul incarnations in the Third Universal Dimension on Earth, and will only touch upon extraterrestrial Soul incarnations elsewhere if necessary to our conversations. Although we are limiting our discussion to the physical reincarnations and life cycles of Human Angelic Souls, we reiterate that it is possible for extraterrestrial Soul groups to incarnate in human physical form on Third Dimensional Earth.

In fact, there is some measure of concern related to the genetic creation and experimentation with hybrid human physical bodies suited for incarnations from alien Souls, which is secretly underway on Earth at the present time. The creation of hybrid humans being orchestrated by scientists in various countries with the implied purpose of creating master races or superior warriors, should not be scoffed at or taken lightly. This work is being done in concert with extraterrestrial technology offered by these alien races to certain governments that, unbeknownst to them or the scientists working with them, have put into motion one genre of bio invasion. We will discuss other such potential bio-invasions momentarily, and will return to this subject periodically based on its importance in your world at the present time.

As we have discussed already with respect to Human Angelic Souls in the Third Universal Dimension, once cast out from the Twelfth Universal Dimension Source, these Souls begin their universal journey through incarnations they project into the First and then the Second Universal Dimensions. As Universal Dimension environments, these are visible to you in your world but they are not accurately represented to you based on the differences in the vibrational resonances and dimensional timelines.

Beings incarnated into First and Second Dimensional physical incarnations are infinitely slower in their development when measured by your Third Dimensional linear timeline concepts. It is for this reason, as you well know, that a rock, a chain of mountains, a grain of sand, a forest of trees or a body of water can have incarnations that span generations, even thousands and tens of thousands of years measured by your time constructs.

It is within each Universal Dimension that space and time, or the space-time wave, is managed and constructed. In a way, the space-time wave actually defines the Dimension and that wave frequency is always a factor of the Universal Dimension and its Sublevels. Biological or physical longevity, together with the lifetimes created therein, are aligned with the specific space-time wave of the Universal Dimension.

Your perspective of time, or the timeline generated by your Dimension that you perceive as linear, is in fact notably spiral or curled in nature. One might envision this as one envisions the motion of an ocean wave, cresting in its momentum, and then curling in on itself before breaking towards the shore. This is an important analogy as it also pertains to life incarnations and reincarnation cycles planned by your Soul, as we shall see.

When you begin to see that time is not linear but instead is more spiral or curled in nature, and when you understand that time as you measure it is not at all the way it is perceived or measured by your Soul, you can begin to envision and understand the relationship that exists between all Soul fragments and their prospective lifetimes, unfolding as they do in unison on the dimensional timeline. As this becomes clearer you see that time is not linear as you expect. The lifetimes that your Soul creates, all of which have a relationship to you and are occurring simultaneously, allow associations that are closely formed by the proximity of their position on what is a spiral timeline. This is despite the fact that the lifetimes may seem to be removed by great distances when measured chronologically using a linear "time" sequence model.

This becomes an important observation. Lifetimes that are lived within a specific Universal Dimension are at the mercy of the biological, physical and sacred geometrical properties of that Dimension. For the most part they appear to not necessarily have any connection to each other when they are viewed as lifetimes happening one after another on a linear trajectory. But since the space-time wave is spiral or curved and not linear as you envision, it is not only possible for all lifetimes to be realized simultaneously, it is possible for them to have proximity and close association. This is possible on a spiral timeline even if the actual point or historical time periods are vastly different and do not seem remotely related.

Picture a spiral or curve as you find it in nature, and place number points on the spiral as it progresses and wraps around its inner core. Counting upwards, as an example, you would see that on the spiral timeline a lifetime that occurs in 1750 CE can have close association by virtue of the timeline's curvature with a lifetime taking place in 2021 CE. Similarly, the same lifetime in 1750 CE can have proximity to a lifetime lived historically in 2350 CE, or even in 25,000 BCE. These close relationships exist simply by virtue of the spirals...etc. (See Page 449, Figure 3 of Diagrams in the Appendix)

Now to be sure, we are using quantitative numbering here for distinction only, and not to indicate any exact number of lifetimes or particular order on the timeline of the reincarnation lived by the Soul. If you examine this closely, you begin to see a pattern emerging where lifetimes can be lived in close proximity on a spiral timeline, regardless of the historical period or the distance represented by the passage of linear time. Now add an additional factor that allows the Soul to live each of these lifetimes simultaneously because the timeline is expanding and all time is happening at once.

Furthermore, imagine that the Soul is able to imbue each of these lifetimes with its own mission and attributes, and organizes them so that those in close proximity will have a relationship that causes them to be tightly intertwined, despite the time period separations. Finally, because the system is fluid and dynamic, imagine that what happens in one has a direct effect on one or all of the other lifetimes related to it, with the ability to balance each other and effectuate karmic balancing as these related lives unfold in real time.

We consider the groupings of lifetimes that demonstrate such relationship, positioned as they are in close and unique positions on the spiral timeline, to be cycles of reincarnation. When seen on that timeline, these groupings of reincarnated selves appear to circle around each other, connected like the spokes of a Wheel through the Soul. Dynamic and always in a state of motion and change, the circular groupings of lifetimes are known to us as a Soul's "Wheel of Creation." (See Page 447, Figure 1 of Diagrams in the Appendix)

Understanding that groupings of lifetimes may be related through close proximity on a spiral timeline, allows you a glimpse into the relationships created by the vast and almost molecular interface of the lifetimes on a Soul's Wheels of Creation. And when you realize that a Soul might potentially manifest thousands of fragments of itself into physical incarnation on various Wheels within a Universal Dimension during the course of one Ascension space-time wave (the Galactic Ascension cycle of about 260,000 years), you begin to see the magnitude of the Soul's experience and reach. Since a typical Wheel of Creation can consist of anywhere from 6 to 18 lifetimes (dependent upon the Soul's mission, growth goals and learning desires for that particular Wheel of lifetimes), you further see how, based on the spiral nature of the timeline, there are Wheels, within Wheels, within Wheels. This is much more a norm than an exception.

It is not by accident that ancient spiritual texts dealing with the subject of Reincarnation present you with a simplified concept of incarnations taking place within cycles, and some even represent the process of Reincarnation symbolically as wheels when visualized. This is an ancient metaphor for identifying specific lifetimes of a Soul that have relationship, one to another. It should be noted that not all lifetimes experienced by a Soul are within the same "Wheels" or cycles, but hopefully the image presented allows you to understand that Soul incarnations, though far too many to note within a typical Galactic Ascension period of 260,000 years, are not all directly related to each other. This is despite the fact that they originate and are made manifest by the same Soul.

It becomes clear, however, that lifetimes in close proximity on the spiral timeline form such groupings naturally. So taking this a step further, if certain lifetimes have association, if the Soul is planning each with a specific mission and goal in mind and if, additionally, lifetimes are dynamic and happening simultaneously, it reasons that each lifetime must have some influence on others within a specific grouping or on a particular Wheel of Creation. It is important to understand that if we agree there is a relationship between the lifetimes on a Wheel of Creation then those associations must have an influence. What befalls one lifetime on the Wheel can be said to have an effect on other lifetimes linked to that particular Wheel.

We have talked in the past about Karma as an energetic balancing of Soul energy from lifetime to lifetime, and nowhere is this more apparent than in the Reincarnation model. In fact, we would say this is the true basis of Karma as it transcends and impacts you as well as all other lifetimes associated with you. What is less apparent is the fact that Karma, as a subsequent energy balancing mechanism, can have immediate impact or effect from one lifetime into another in a system where all lifetimes are happening simultaneously.

In fact, it is quite possible that other lifetimes on your own Wheel of Creation are influencing you in the now just as your choices are influencing other selves on the same Wheel. Therefore, the choices you make and the energy and emotions you express in the here and now, which have energetic reverberation, can echo through into all the other lifetimes connected to you within your Wheel of Creation.

Similarly, the choices made by you and by other Selves on the same Wheel have dynamic resonance and energetic consequences (karma) that reverberate into your own life, as well as their life, in a dynamic manner. This energetic exchange is concurrent and immediate, whether it is felt consciously or not.

Also clear in this model, as the diagram confirms, is the fact that lifetimes on a given Wheel of Creation do not necessarily have to be chronologically related, although they may be if they are close enough in location. As an example of this, a lifetime taking place BCE or even in the prehistory period may have inference and direct relationship with a lifetime taking place in the 21st Century.

Despite a seeming disparity in chronology, by virtue of the fact that they are on the same Wheel of Creation, these lifetimes can be closely interfaced through karmic energy balancing as well as other considerations, including possible genetic ties, however distant the linear time position may be. It is important to understand that the karma generated on one spoke of the Wheel by a lifetime being lived in a different now, but simultaneously, has an immediate and important impact on other lifetimes on the same Wheel. In many cases, particularly if the energetic balancing is significant, what happens in one can actually push through to not only emotionally change a related lifetime, but even physically alter its circumstances.

As an example, the physical loss of an arm or a leg in one lifetime can come through at the time of the occurrence and cause cellular response in another lifetime on the same Wheel. This might then translate into arm or leg "issues" for the individual experiencing a

completely different lifetime. The old adage, "I must have done something in a past life," is not too far off the mark with one important
distinction – the events are happening in real time, not in a life from
the "past" as it is assumed.

What has happened in another lifetime on the particular Wheel of
which you are a part is simply bleeding through into your current
experience either as a matter of a new choice being perpetrated by
another Self, or as a matter of karmic balancing. This becomes more
complex when it is also looked at in light of other participating Souls
who have contracted with your Soul to assist growth for one lifetime
on the Wheel that naturally permeates through to all lifetimes on
the Wheel. Such a viewpoint makes it clear that others are also involved in this endeavor. It is quite possible to have such energetic
bleed-through involve other Souls, who are also present with lifetimes in your current now, and who could arise and participate in
some way with you in order to balance the karma created.

Following our original example one step further, what if your arm
or leg were purposely cut off by someone in that related lifetime?
Now not only are the issues that impact your own life energetically
focused on a actual physical handicap that was received, including
whatever growth can be obtained by this event, they are also focused
on a person or persons perpetrating the loss of your limb. And
should these Souls have lifetimes present on your point on the timeline, suddenly there is a karmic balancing in need of being effectuated
by one or maybe every lifetime on multiple Wheels of Creation.

This interaction makes it easy to understand why the choices you
make are important and how what you do in any given current incarnation affects not only you personally, but also will befall other
lifetimes related to you and your Soul on your Wheel of Creation.

And the inverse is true as well. Choices made by other reincarnations of your Soul on the Wheel of Creation have direct effect on you. Becoming conscious of this is an important step towards Soul growth and awareness, for you and for each reincarnated self on your Soul's Wheel of Creation.

It is important to see that the concept you currently have of experiencing karma as something that occurs in a chronological order in some future time-scape when you are some future self, is an erroneous one that exonerates you personally and defers the energetic balancing. The true system of karmic balance is far more dynamic and immediate. Once you have realized you may be affecting the quality of life and experiences of many other selves, and that they may be affecting you, currently and in the eternal now, the stakes become much greater. Your responsibility to yourself, other reincarnational selves and your Soul takes on immediate mindfulness and consideration.

Learning this responsibility is seen as a Universal Truth. It is for this reason that the saying, "as you sow, so shall you reap," is a notable aspect of all real growth that should be carefully weighed. You are contributing not only to your overall consciousness growth but also to the growth of all the lifetimes related to you on your Soul's Wheel of Creation. Reaching a higher vibrational integrity as a result of that growth is not only responsible for raising your own awareness and resonance, it is responsible for augmenting your Soul's energetic fingerprint in the Universe, a prerequisite for achieving Ascension for you and your Soul.

As you will come to see, understanding the Soul's cyclical planning and intra-grouping of lifetimes is much easier when one takes into consideration the fact that the measurement of time that you know, as a linear occurrence consisting of a past, a present and a future, does not exist. However accurate it might seem, realizing that the concept of time is fabricated for convenience sake based on the succession of "Now's" you experience, one begins to see how easy it is for the Soul to plan lifetimes in groupings that are closely related to each other on a spiral space-time wave around a Wheel of Creation, as we have described. It is also easy to see that not all lifetimes on the spiral space-time wave have proximity, or are necessarily associated.

Although this does not mean that any given lifetime cannot be energetically linked with another anywhere on the timeline, including one outside its proximity, the grouping method facilitates the dispersion of energy. This is particularly important as it relates to karmic balancing that is accomplished within the lifetimes on a given Wheel. Karmic balancing is always energetic in nature directly affecting one or more lifetimes, and close proximity on the space-time spiral means direct access for each lifetime on the Wheel of Creation. Of course, karmic balance and the ability for a Soul to have far reaching lifetimes on the timeline is also a factor of the Soul's vibrational frequency, higher consciousness, Soul age and related abilities.

Since the Soul is outside and peripheral to the actual historic time segment within which a particular lifetime unfolds, it makes it easier to understand the relationships formed between Souls that come together by agreement to provide individual lifetimes or reincarnations with opportunities and events for the purposes of growth. Hopefully, this also assists you to understand how exactly you come to meet and have relationships with the individuals that you do, most of whom are either known to you at a Soul level, are Soul or Task mates or are related to you as a member of your particular Soul cadre or group.

Within this, there is an additional factor that we have not yet discussed but is somewhat important to mention here. We have already examined the concept of Soul origination and orientation, related either to Service-to-Self or Service-to-Others. In conjunction with this however, a Soul can also be said to have what we would call a specific energetic expression. Like Service-to-Self or Service-to-Others orientation, the Soul's specific energetic expression is also present at the time it is cast out by Source, and it is therefore something present and expressed in all of a Soul's life incarnations.

These energetic expressions, though not a singular component of the Soul's complete expression and influence, are nonetheless a strong influence that is unchanging throughout the life of the Soul as well as the many reincarnations and lifetimes it creates on its Wheels of Creation. Energetic expression is best described as an archetypal energy a particular Soul is learning to encompass and express through exploration of various incarnations in every realm, both physical and etheric in nature. These archetypal expressions depend upon the Soul and its origins, but it is generally safe to identify seven principal energetic expressions that Souls, particularly Human Angelic Souls, can have. These energetic expressions are: the Leader expression; the Soldier expression; the Giver expression; the Guardian expression; the Speaker expression; the Creator/Healer expression; and the Academic expression.

The energetic expression of a Soul forms the basis of its intrinsic makeup, affecting the composition, desires and temperament of the Soul, as well as each and every incarnation it has as it navigates through the Universal Dimension. We mention this here in order to assist you to understand that, in many cases, your preferences, talents and traits, as well as many of your basic goals and relationships in life, are naturally formed as a result of the particular archetypal energetic expression you share with your Soul.

In particular, the way in which relationships and interactions develop for you, as well as your preferences and interests, can have a great deal to do with your Soul's archetypal energetic expression. These can also have much to do with the energetic expression of the individuals with whom you come into contact. Energetic expression, or what you are ultimately seeking to express in your life, your relationships and at large in the world, generally forms the basis of your "modus operandi," how you act and how you perceive life, if you will.

This is why you will often find, especially as you age and reach independence or adulthood, that there are individuals around you with similar talents, focuses, wants and ambitions. Those with the same or similar energetic expressions will find themselves in the same organizations, often seeking related goals and objectives. In other words, like-minded individuals will seem to naturally find others who are like-minded. Often, since organizations, companies, cultures and even nations can have an energetic expression, the Soul's energetic expression is compatible with these organizations so that even if the individuals display different energy expressions, they may be highly compatible or attracted to the energetic expression of specific fields, careers or companies that are related thereto.

Despite this, diversity of energetic expression is also a relevant and important means towards Soul growth. It should be clear that were you to exist in a world where all individuals originated from one particular Soul energetic expression or archetype, too much sameness and lack of energetic diversity would quickly become tiresome and, more importantly, lead to a lack of rewarding exchange, the basis for creating opportunities for growth. This would be a mindset as boring as it might be useless, and the different points of view that energetic expressions naturally have, even those leading to conflict, are an important catalyst for Soul growth. For this reason, family, work and social as well as other circles consist of interactions with people of varied archetypal energetic expressions, even though those with similar energetic expressions to you will lead you into a field of desire.

In general, Souls that are cast out in particular cadres are endowed with similar if not highly compatible archetypal energetic expressions. This should be easy to understand in that Souls with certain energetic expressions, different though they may be, tend to enjoy each other's company. You can confirm this by taking a second look at our list of archetypal expressions in order to determine which might have compatibility and which does not. The same holds true for all of a Soul's life incarnations or Soul fragments, and this can be the basis for many Soul contracts and agreements. Different cadres and groups agree to meet up with each other when in physical incarnation in order to organize growth situations and opportunities. This is particularly the norm when there are already relationships existing at the Soul level among cadres and groups.

The greatest learning and growth experiences a Soul can have while in physical incarnation generally come through interactions with a wide variety of Soul archetypal energetic expressions. Although those who share the same energetic expression might serve as ideal work or pub mates, the best growth opportunities, whether they be rewarding or frustrating, are generated by lifetime interactions between those of different Soul energetic expressions.

As we progress in these conversations, we need to also touch momentarily upon related information that concerns the "mission" a Soul identifies for each lifetime that it casts out. An individual life goal or mission is chosen specifically for each lifetime the a Soul creates, and that mission exists independent of either the Soul's orientation or its energetic expression. Energetic expression is consistent throughout the Soul's existence and in all lifetimes of the Soul. However, life missions are specific to the independent lifetime that is cast out by the Soul, and it is always chosen for purposes of growth or in order to balance or expand the karmic or other endeavors of another lifetime on the Soul's Wheel of Creation.

In other words, looking at all the lifetimes the Soul creates on a particular Wheel of Creation can be seen to have some relationship or interface with other lifetimes, and all link together as it regards the Soul's growth in general. In this way, life missions are complimentary and are woven together by the Soul to generate maximum potential opportunities through specific life events that are planned. Although Free Will of each independent lifetime of a Soul has precedence over such planned life events, certain situations, environments, backdrops and the like are nevertheless planned in order to provide specific possibilities that the Soul desires for growth through its life incarnations.

Understanding that the Soul's energetic expression and orientation do not change from lifetime to lifetime the way an individual life mission does is important in that the energetic expression and orientation of a Soul are part of the Soul's fundamental vibrational signature throughout its journey, through all ages and in all Universal Dimensions. Life missions on the other hand are specific to one lifetime on the Soul's Wheels of Creation in one Universal Dimension, and these do not transcend the Dimension, other than to be part of the Soul's overall learning and growth process in a particular Universal Dimension. The life mission of a particular lifetime in a Dimension remains with the individual Soul fragment or lifetime, and it remains specific to that lifetime. The mission does not transcend the lifetime, other than to become part of the Soul's learning and growth process, once reintegration has occurred prior to Ascension.

To explain this in a more colloquial manner, consider the Soul's expression and orientation as being akin to a family or surname in your current culture, carried as an identifier and used by each family member throughout the course of their life. A life mission on the other hand, or the learning of a specific subject matter through one course being taken during that lifetime, is equivalent to an individual family member's first name. As you are aware, the family or surname continues on through other lifetimes even when the individual family member is no longer present.

Even so, although the Soul's archetypal energy expression is of primal vibrational importance, the role of each Soul fragment's individual life mission should not be underestimated. Every life that is lived in physical incarnation, as well as through its continuation in semi or post-physical Astral states, is imbued with a specific mission that has fundamental purpose, both for the lifetime and for the Soul. This fact cannot be understated, and no one should in any way think that a particular lifetime, such as the one you are currently invested in, is in any way disconnected from or without impact and consequence on the development and growth of your Soul.

Understanding this also makes it clear that accomplishing one's life mission in a particular lifetime is of importance to the Soul. In fact, the successful navigation of one's individual life mission greatly enhances the Soul's ability to express its archetypal energy, both within the lifetime as well as at the highest levels of the Soul. Naturally, there are other contributing factors as well, such as the specific attributes and personality features a Soul will pick for each individual lifetime it creates. These personality attributes, formed in no small way by a combination of your genetics, your early relationships and the environment in which you grow up, create the way in which you see the world and consequently the personality parameters of the lifetime.

It is vital to note that many life situations are not as haphazard as you may think. This includes the parents you have and the childhood circumstances and environments you encounter. Many of these are carefully chosen and orchestrated by your Soul through agreements with other Souls in order to create the lenses through which you will ultimately see the world. Such features temper the way in which you see yourself, your world and those around you, creating predispositions that together with your thoughts and emotions, energetically attract to you individuals, circumstances and events that you must learn to navigate through Free Will and choice.

Such events, of which many possibilities are planned and will emerge over the course of life, tend to be directly connected to your life mission, and therefore the choices you make have real consequence. At the very least, the stage has been set for the choices you will be obliged to make in the future, particularly once childhood has passed and you are an adult. Learning to consciously be aware of your particular way of seeing things and analyzing its relevance and truth, or lack of truth more notably, are important steps to recognizing your real mission, understand your life's purpose and become conscious of who you really are. It is, of course, equally important to allowing a true expression of yourself during the lifetime, empowering you to express your energetic nature and, in doing so, express your Soul's energy in the world.

Every lifetime, therefore, is not only related to the specific growth objectives identified for you by your Soul but also related to the Soul's ability to learn and understand the true and purest expression of its archetypal energy in that Universal Dimension. In fact, one could say that through all the various missions in all the numerous lifetimes the Soul plans and lives, most will have at their core providing the Soul with a complete understanding of its energetic archetype and, secondarily, its Soul orientation (Service-to-Others or Service-to-Self).

Together with Soul orientation, archetypal Soul energy, as an originating expression of each Soul that is cast out from the God Source, finds its origins at the very depths of a Soul's creation. It is for this reason we consider it to be of prime importance, and, as it relates to our discussion of Reincarnation and the Wheels of Creation, expressing this energy is a primal urge for every lifetime in the Soul's Universal journey. This is true no matter what Universal Dimension we are considering, from the First Universal Dimension up to the "Trinity" Dimensions (Tenth, Eleventh and Twelfth Universal Dimensions), which, as we have said, are considered the realm of the Arch Angels, the Sons of "God" and the God-Source itself, or as we prefer, the Dimension of All-That-Is.

Life missions become more and more delineated and highly specialized as Souls ascend from lower to higher Universal Dimensions. This is true of the Soul's Wheels of Creation as well. As a Soul ascends to higher Dimensional frequencies and Universal Dimensions, Wheels of Creation, and their associations, missions and interactions, become highly sophisticated and more complex. In the First and Second Universal Dimensions as an example, even though the archetypal energy is always being expressed underneath, the nature of the physical incarnations in those Dimensions lends itself towards group or "hive" incarnations. Therefore, individual missions, even if present, are not as defined and are certainly not as singular as they can be starting with the Third Universal Dimension. This distinction is clear if you realize that a Soul's incarnations in the First or Second Universal Dimension might be as a grain of sand that joins with others to create a vast stretch of beach, a drop of water that with others forms an ocean itself or a single mineral or rock that forms part of a mountain range, as we have explained.

However, once a Soul ascends to Third Universal Dimension incarnations, the missions become more independent, focused and distinctive for each lifetime cast out and planned by the Soul. Again, this is not to say that a lifetime in the First and Second Universal Dimension, or any lifetime for that matter, is without merit, meaning or purpose. On the contrary, they form the root basis of a Soul's creative endeavors as it casts pieces of itself into incarnation and reincarnation cycles.

First and Second Universal Dimension life incarnations tend to be more group or hive oriented, and certainly they are denser physically. The space-time wave itself in these Dimensions is much longer in chronological or linear terms. Following our example, the lifetime of an ocean or mountain range is usually of much greater length than the lifetime of a human being. It becomes clear that the Soul's purpose takes longer in those Dimensions as well, assuming you allow for the belief that every physical object in creation – from a grain of sand to a drop of water -- has a purpose, as indeed it does.

Frankly, First and Second Universal Dimensional lifetimes are integral to a Soul's early understanding of how to cast out fragments of itself, incarnate, maintain a physical "body" and create existence through physical matter and structure. These incarnations act as a sort of primer for the Soul on how physical life is constructed, takes place and unfolds. Once a Soul has garnered the understanding of how physical structure is created, contributes to reality manifestation and is properly maintained, it is then prepared to ascend to the individual lifetimes you know in the Third Universal Dimension.

It is also at this particular point of experience that an infant or baby Soul is ready to move into further and more complex awareness of itself. This is accomplished not only in terms of the manifestation and maintenance of a physical structure and body, but also in terms of generating Wheels of Creation where specific life missions, lifetime personality attributes and Soul-contracted events and relationships, as well as techniques for energy balancing through the process of Karma, become standard endeavors.

As we have often said, life missions are never built around or de-pendent upon careers, professions, feats or any other physical ac-complishment that you might feel are a measure of success based on societal or cultural standards. In fact, although many or all of those things might play a part in achieving a life mission, the Soul's mission for particular lifetimes tend to be far more metaphysical, esoteric and philosophical in nature.

For the most part, it is not possible to delineate an individual life mis-sion because they are not based on the standards of success that you acknowledge as important during a lifetime, and they are always highly subjective. Life missions are planned according to the needs of the Soul for growth, both as it relates to the Soul overall and as it relates to karmic balancing in conjunction with other lifetimes asso-ciated with it on a particular cycle or Wheel of Creation.

Though it is not possible to identify a life mission because of their unique and individual nature, it is possible to identify seven general categories within which life missions are usually planned by the Soul.

These include Soul growth through: 1) Lessons of Love, Acceptance and Rejection; 2) Lessons of Abundance and Lack; 3) Lessons in Leadership and Control; 4) Lessons in Energetic Life Rhythms and the Expression of the Soul's archetypal energy; 5) Lessons in Mastering Adversity or Extraordinary Circumstances; 6) Lessons in Judgment, Discernment and how to assert the expression of individual Desire and Will; and 7) Lessons in Service and Sacrifice.

It is within these archetypal categories that a Soul will generally learn to master particular aspects of itself as it grows by using physical events, environments, relationships and other situations meted out in varying stages or degrees during the course of a physical life incarnation in the Third Universal Dimension. This diversity is a main reason a Soul orchestrates the vast number of lifetimes it does while in a Universal Dimension. Rather than one continuous life where all life missions are explored together, life missions are segregated into smaller related groupings or Wheels where each lifetime essentially specializes in a particular mission in order to maximize an in-depth, hands-on learning experience. This is the primary reason Reincarnation exists as a process that is organized through the manifestation of a Soul's dimensional Wheels of Creation.

Life missions are therefore individual, singular and specific in nature. However, the experiences from one lifetime can be further developed over and over or explored in greater depth through the associated Wheel of Creation. Reincarnation in this regard, from the Soul's perspective, becomes the ability for a Soul to better explore a mission or lesson from every perspective. In fact, the lifetimes on an entire Wheel of Creation can be closely related to each other in terms of identical or similar life missions that unfold from many different angles or points of view, with each correlating to another.

As an example, in the case of a Wheel of lifetimes with the same mission built around abundance or lack, one lifetime on the Wheel might be planned with the possibility of having an abundance of everything. An associated lifetime on the same Wheel of Creation with the same mission might be planned with the possibility of never having enough and a lack of all energetic things, such as love, health or money. A third lifetime with the same mission on the same Wheel might deal with having things flow and ebb into the lifetime, forcing one to deal with issues around having everything come easily, and then losing it all in varying degrees and at various intervals.

On the other hand, lifetimes on a Wheel of Creation can each have different life missions that still demonstrate a close relationship and have a strong correlation. In such a case using our same model, one lifetime might be blessed with abundance, while another (mission) deals with learning lessons around control and domination of others. Such a relationship could be based on the fact that the lifetime dealing with abundance causes the first individual, through their prosperity, to arrogantly attempt to control others by virtue of their ample situation, power and financial means. The second lifetime then balances the karmic implications, by teaching the individual what it is like to be controlled and dominated by others through no fault of their own. Yet another lifetime on the same Wheel might have a mission of service and sacrifice, and this lifetime might further be based on the karmic balancing needed in either of the other two lifetimes.

The possibilities and interactions can be endless, but the real point here is a demonstration of the interaction of lifetimes, based on life missions, within a Soul's reincarnations and the lifetimes planed on its Wheels of Creation. It becomes easy to see how complex the associations are, and even more so when one takes into consideration the Free Will interactions, associations and dynamics of live action interfaces, that may or may not take place during any given lifetime or incarnation.

Even so, it must be understood that there is no specific outline or model a Soul must follow and therefore no real generalization can be made as to how a Soul plans its many lifetimes or Wheels of Creation within a Universal Dimension. Each lifetime becomes an independent act of creation following the Will of the Soul and a Soul can have numerous objectives in planning these Wheels of Reincarnation. As a result, it is not really possible to talk about the specifics of a Soul's journey through various Dimensions, particularly since the process is dynamic, always changing and unfolding in new ways at every turn and in every instance.

To recap what we have learned thus far, newly cast out Baby Souls begin physical incarnations in the First Universal Dimension. We have already described how First Dimensional incarnations are extremely physical and dense, and for this reason they tend to be limited to solid, natural elements that you are familiar with, despite the fact that you do not currently see them as individual incarnations of a Baby Soul.

Yet, creating lifetimes in First Dimensional reality, as minerals in a mountain range or as drops of water in the ocean, is not unheard of depending upon the desires, goals and preferences of a Soul. For many, it is just such lifetimes that represent the very first incarnations a Soul experiences until ascending to higher Universal Dimensions, where more complex and independent incarnations are possible.

Like the lifetimes of all Souls in every Dimension, incarnations cast out by a Soul run in Wheels or cycles and generally will encompass the span of an Ascension period or cycle. In other words, the Soul is present through its incarnations until the timeline shifts and evolves itself, which is the end of the Ascension period. When the Soul's growth in a particular Universal Dimension has been achieved, at the next appropriate time of Ascension, which occurs as a result of universal laws that ultimately evolve a Universal Dimension, and everything within it, into the next Universal Dimension, the Soul is carried on the Ascension wave of the Dimension. It will then begin to cast out lifetimes in the next Universal Dimension.

Lifetimes in the Second Universal Dimension are more independent than in the First Universal Dimension, but like lifetimes in the First Universal Dimension, they tend to have hive Soul similarities. In other words, Lifetimes on Wheels of Creation within the Second Universal Dimension are more individualized and independent, but also usually find unity by having common life purposes or missions. This is what makes them more hive-like seeming. However, make no mistake that personality, individuality and independence does begin to emerge and develop in Second Universal Dimension incarnations.

For Human Angelic Souls, typical lifetimes in the Second Universal Dimension generally include incarnations as members of the Devic Kingdom, the realm of devas, nature spirits and other Beings. Although plants, insects and certain lower animal species are also Second Universal Dimension Beings, Human Angelics act as guardians for these creatures in that Dimension, and this is why there is a link identified in ancient Vedic and other nature mythologies between those species and the Devic world.

We would say that one of the greatest misinterpretations of Reincarnation – that you can be human and then incarnate, due to karma, backwards into the form of an insect or an animal – is directly related to this. While it is true that Human Angelic Baby Souls may begin incarnations in many dense forms, Human Angelic Souls do not incarnate in these species in the First or Second Universal Dimensions. Furthermore, once they have ascended to Third Universal Dimension incarnations they *never* descend evolutionally or incarnate as First or Second Dimensional Beings life forms or Beings again. In this way, although a Baby Soul may have numerous lifetimes in the First and Second Dimension as crystals, minerals, trees, nature or Devic entities, once they have graduated to higher Dimensions they strictly incarnate in life forms that are applicable and hold higher dimensional frequencies.

Before we dive into the fundamentals of how a Soul plans life cycles in the Third Universal Dimension, a few additional background points may be helpful. First of all, transmigration of the Soul is never static either in its journey through the many Sublevels of a Universal Dimension or in the manner in which lifetimes are planned and completed. This is to say that throughout the entirety of a Universal Dimension, lifetimes remain independent and dynamic, and this means that they do not disappear in the absence of a physical body after their lives in the physical reality you know. In other words, the many lifetimes that are interconnected fragments cast out by the Soul in the Universal Dimension exist as creations unto themselves once created, and continue on through all aspects and levels of the Dimension.

These fragments, of which you are most probably one, travel the breadth of a Dimension, including through all its non-corporeal Sublevels or Astral planes. Whether in dense physical form or in an Etheric Astral body, each lifetime remains individual, active and relevant until it's final reunification with the Soul itself. This reunification happens once that individual entity has journeyed through all the Astral realms, and it is complete when reunification of all lifetimes the Soul has created is accomplished. This accomplishment then forms the basis of a Soul's Ascension to the next Universal Dimension.

Until the time of that reunification, each lifetime or entity remains conscious, independent and vital. When you or a loved one has passed into an Etheric body after physical death, you live on and transmigrate through the lower and higher Astral planes with much the same consciousness and in much the same way you did in the physical world, minus the physical density you are accustom to, of course. Therefore, when in physical reality you feel that you have achieved some form of communication with a loved one who has passed into their spirit body to a higher Sublevel of the Universal Dimension, you are indeed communicating with the personality and consciousness of that loved one who is continuing their journey towards reunification with the Soul. Suffice to say that reunification with the Soul is a lengthy process that requires each entity complete their individual journey through all Sublevels of the Universal Dimension, physical body or not.

Secondarily, since each individual lifetime or entity has independent consciousness, existence and Free Will, they are considered a co-creator with their Soul, able to direct, through choice, their continuing destiny. Other lifetimes within the same Wheel of Creation remain constantly affected by an entity's choices and actions, even after the entity is no longer in a physical body and has passed into the Astral Sublevels. This is perhaps one of the most important aspects of life after death and Reincarnation to grasp. An entity continues to enjoy Free Will and to make life choices that have impact on other entities on its Wheel of Creation even long after physical death has occurred.

In addition to this, every lifetime continues to have an impact on the growth and vibrational elevation of its Soul until after it has rejoined it at the Twelfth Sublevel of the Universal Dimension.

We shall detail in depth the cyclical nature of Reincarnation and the associations possible shortly. For our current purpose what is most relevant to understand is that each lifetime focuses on a mission identified by its Soul, and that mission is in some way crucial to all the lifetimes on the Soul's Wheel of Creation. Usually, the life missions on a Wheel of Creation, different thought they might be, have some kind of interface or connection.

Additionally, all of these missions and lifetimes can be linked to a single grander mission identified by the Soul. As an example, one lifetime on a Wheel might be related to learning the lessons of providing selfless service, while another is related to learning lessons related to the flow of love in and out of life. A third might have a mission of learning how to discern what one wants in life. Yet the Soul might in some way be using the combination of all these lifetime missions, as well as many others that are also linked to it, to provide an overriding lesson related to the learning of pride and how to arrive at acceptance without passing judgment. Again, the possibilities are nearly infinite, and are only restricted by the vibration, level of consciousness and age of the creator Soul at that point within that Universal Dimension.

This is also where our metaphor of a Wheel of Creation is derived, since if the lifetimes and life missions in the cycle are the spokes of a Wheel of Creation, then the Soul and its overall mission becomes the hub of the Wheel itself. Taking this metaphor one step further, you might see the Soul's overriding grand mission (the hub) as the actual impetus that generates motion and the turning of the Wheel, moving the Soul forward constantly. In this manner once again, "spin" is achieved and the Soul's advancement through the universal structure is accomplished.

In a certain sense, karma, which as we explained is strictly a balancing of energy, and not the simplistic eye-for-an-eye, tooth-for-a-tooth version that you have been taught, is also based on the particular "turning" of the Soul's Wheel. The many lifetimes on the Wheel balance each other out energetically as the Wheel itself spins, in much the same manner that certain spokes of a wagon wheel carry the weight of other spokes in the Wheel depending upon their positioning in the radius at any given time.

Metaphors aside, every lifetime on a Wheel of Creation presents implications for other lifetimes on the Wheel, and those implications relate to the overall growth of the Soul. There are even occasions where what is occurring in one lifetime on a Wheel directly impacts the actual outcome of an associated lifetime, or where what transpires in a lifetime can help ease the burdens or challenges being experienced by a different and related lifetime on the same Wheel.

As an example, many of you are acquainted with, or have seen, how suddenly a physical ailment or other experience can arise in one's life seemingly out of nowhere. This is often related to the same concept that what happens in one lifetime can impact another. The impact from entity to entity on a Wheel can even appear as the same approximate physical ailment or in the same area or body-part. Sudden blindness in one eye could be related to having an eye put out in another lifetime on the Wheel; The sudden development of carpal tunnel in one's hand might be a hand that was cut off or severely injured in an associated lifetime; Arthritis in the current lifetime might arise from the overworked physical body in a related lifetime as a slave; An unexpected bout of severe gastrointestinal distress or even the development of colon cancer could originate in an associated lifetime where the entity has been impaled and put to death. The list goes on and on.

To be clear, such situations do not have to always have roots in another lifetime or associated entity on your Soul's Wheel of Creation. However, many do, and a good many physical as well as emotional ailments can have direct association with another lifetime on the same Wheel of Creation. This is especially true where the energy from that entity's experience is so intense it literally bleeds through to other entities and lifetimes on the same Wheel.

Often, when the energetic balancing is complete, the physical or emotional ailment that it registered can disappear or be "healed" as abruptly as it arrived. In other cases, the balancing of very intense energies can be felt for an entire lifetime. This is not meant to negate any experiences that happen during a lifetime or pass off personal responsibility for them, regardless of their origin. Every happening during the course of a lifetime is real, wholly felt and can, at times, prove challenging. But it is important to note that such energetic balancing and sharing of experiences between entities has a higher purpose that is of benefit to all parties, even if it does not truly originate as a result of the actions of a particular entity. In that regard, think of these experiences as a sacrifice you make by agreement with your Soul in exchange for being created. This occurs for the purpose of balancing energetic trauma, whether it is emotional, physical or both, for a sibling entity on the same Wheel of Creation as you.

A good point to make here is that despite the fact a Soul sets a specific life mission or goal together with any number of parameters in each lifetime, this is not to be confused with any concept of predestination, which does not exist. Each entity is able, through Free Will, to make its own life choices while in physical incarnation, albeit within the parameters of certain events, relationships and other situations that arise and are attracted to the entity in any number of ways.

A Soul's planning of a lifetime should be seen as the Soul creating parameters and guidelines for growth surrounding the entity and creating the entity's attraction to them within the context of a particular incarnation. Once an entity is created, the Soul willingly allows that entity, as a co-creator, to experience and explore creation, including how it approaches and views the many situations and other entities it encounters.

Each entity has the ability to make decisions through Free Will, even though the generated personality features and Soul energy will generally tend to provide a subconscious impetus that the entity follows in real time as the lifetime unfolds. None of this, however, should imply that the Soul does not create a life mission or an ideal "EssencePath" for experiencing that mission during the lifetime.

In fact, consciously discovering and becoming aware of that path can be essential to a joyful and successful life experience. Moreover, since one's mission or EssencePath can be lived through either the positive or the negative polarity, becoming aware of this and knowing your Soul's Path allows an individual to learn how to experience life from the positive polarity rather than the negative one. This is instrumental to finding joy, peace and ease in life, as opposed to experiencing life through the negative perspective, which is more apt to bring challenge, hardship and endless difficulties.

Ultimately, you will learn your life's lessons in either case and from either polarity. Your Soul is not concerned with whether your experience is good, bad, right or wrong, which are subjective viewpoints that are not relevant to your Soul growth. As you can surmise however, learning your life lessons from the positive pole is far easier and exceedingly more productive while experiencing physical reality in the world that you share.

There is no law, written or unwritten, stating that an entity must complete their lifetime in any particular way or even as originally outlined by their Soul. Indeed, this is where balancing on the Wheel of Creation is invaluable and acts as a relief valve for any lifetime that is not able to follow their EssencePath as originally intended. Since the outcome is never considered good, bad, right or wrong, the only real objective is overall consciousness growth and increased vibrational frequency for the entity and, ultimately, the Soul.

This is true whether the growth is derived from the positive or the negative pole, or from joyful or from challenging experiences. In this way, there truly are no positive or negative experiences in life (even if you consider them in the moment to be extremely difficult or detrimental). Experiences of any kind enable growth. How each individual entity chooses to experience and manage these situations, by consciously pushing them into positive outcomes or by dealing with them through negative ones, is entirely up to the entity by virtue of their own Free Will, their perspective and the choices they make based on the events and relationships that arise.

The idea that a life lived is negative or positive, good or bad, tends to be a misconception derived from standards and norms an individual is taught, usually by those who would wish to control your actions by providing you with dogma or rules, which they intend you to live by. Naturally, this does not excuse individual bad behavior, in particular behavior that is in anyway harmful to you or others. In general though, it is an important aspect of personal growth to realize that you are not better, best or more worthwhile because you have adhered to someone else's standards.

Equally, it is vital to understand that there is no anthropomorphic Godhead, mysterious force or metaphysical judge directing you or demanding specific actions and deeds from you. Nor are you any better or worse because you follow some particular dogma or form of worship. Although you are free to do so, these things do not offer some mythical preference or mystical success in life, other than to allow you to be controlled by an overseer in an effort to curtail any primitive natural instincts you might exhibit through Free Will, if and when they arise.

What *is* important to understand, however, is our premise that the choices you make in life have direct correlation and consequence in other lifetimes on your own Wheel of Creation, just as what other lifetimes choose and do has impact on your own. Ultimately all of this allows growth for your Soul, but we would suggest that being aware of these consequences within every lifetime allows you to assist the vibrational elevation of yourself and your Soul. This will allow your Soul (and you) to continually raise its consciousness and energetic signature in a manner that prepares it (and you with it) for Ascension to higher and higher Universal Dimensions.

Let us add to this that a Soul's life incarnations, and its Wheels of Creation overall, are quite numerous and in many cases far too many to really count. It should be remembered that the average dimensional space time-wave is immense and therefore the time span for a Soul's journey through one Universal Dimension, measured in your linear time, is a Galactic Ascension cycle or approximately 260,000 years. Though one Wheel of Creation can have as few as six or as many as twenty-four (or more) lifetimes on it, a Soul can literally manifest thousands of Wheels of Creation during the course of a dimensional timeline.

The number 144,000 has been used in the past to represent the number of lifetimes manifested by a Soul during one Galactic Ascension era. Its geometric and numerological value aside, this is essentially an arbitrary number, since a Soul can manifest any number of lifetimes it chooses on a dimensional timeline. This exact number has been called a Soul number by various religious or spiritual mythologies, but this is inaccurate, and any idea that there are only 144,000 legitimate Souls in creation is not correct. We mention it here as a demonstration of the many lifetimes a Soul can energetically cast out and manifest simultaneously, and suggest that the amount is actually more representative of an ideal number of lifetimes that a Soul will create over the course of its journey through one space-time wave, in one Universal Dimension.

Considering the average Galactic Ascension period is approximately 260,000 years as we have said (intersected by lesser Ascension periods of 26,000 years known as Solar Ascension periods), hopefully this further demonstrates the enormous complexity of a Soul's journey within a Universal Dimension. It also demonstrates how expansive and fluid a Soul's energy actually is in order to be invested in so many physical and non-physical incarnations, all taking place simultaneously during one Galactic Ascension space-time wave.

Related to the number of lifetimes made manifest by a Soul in a Universal Dimension is the age of a Soul. In a way, Soul age is almost completely dependent upon Ascension periods and progression of a

Soul through a typical Galactic Ascension cycle in a Universal Dimension. When a Soul invests its energy in any given number of lifetimes or Wheels of Creation, it is Soul age (the level of consciousness and vibrational resonance) that is the truest measure of how complex and interconnected those lifetimes will be, as well as the degree of complexity of the events and relationships the individual entity the Soul creates experiences. Soul age is the determining factor also in the kinds of experiences met during the lifetimes of that Soul, and has much to do with the level of consciousness and inner awareness expressed by each entity during the course of its own lifetime. In this way it becomes the most significant determining factor with respect to the complexity of associations and the kind of events that emerge in an individual's lifetime.

To be more precise, Soul age and consciousness level in each individual entity are always represented in the interconnectedness, or lack of connectedness, experienced during the lifetime, as well as with other associated lifetimes on the Wheel of Creation. This is especially true where it concerns karmic events and karmic balancing. Younger Souls have vast karmic associations and interconnectedness on their Wheels of Creation and tend to have larger quantities of lifetimes created on one Wheel. On the other hand, Older Souls, whose lifetimes are mostly focused on Self or inner karmic balancing (more emotionally centered), tend to have fewer lifetimes on a Wheel of Creation and less interconnectedness of the lifetimes on that Wheel, since there is not as much need for karmic balancing.

As an example of how Soul age comes through into each lifetime created on a given Wheel of Creation, take the individual in a small village within a primitive society, who never moves further than five miles from their original birthplace. Such a lifetime is inherently less complex than the life of an individual born into an advanced society, where choice, structure, diversity, travel, complicated relationships and life responsibilities provide proportional complexity. Again, Soul age becomes a determining factor in the creation of such lifetimes, with the experiences therein being a measure of the Soul's level of consciousness and, therefore, Soul age.

Generally, a Soul works in concert with others in the same Soul group or cadre to organize things such as parentage and genetics (meaning that parents and environment are always a consideration for the Soul in order to accomplish the goals of the entity in that particular lifetime). Children tend to be of the same Soul age as their parents, although often children can represent a slightly older Soul age.

Indigos are an example of Young Soul age parents nurturing much Older Soul individuals, who have come into the lifetime with specific missions related to growth for society or even for that particular genetic line. However, this is usually rare and, as stated, there is always a higher purpose related to the specific Souls and entities that are involved.

It is even more rare for progeny to be a Younger Soul age than their parents. Usually this is done, if at all, explicitly as a matter of Soul growth, such as in the case of handicapped, ill or challenged children. In most of these cases however, the child is actually an Older Soul wishing to contribute to the Soul growth of the Younger Soul age parents through the rigors they may face as a result of their association and love for the child. What is important here is to know that Soul age of an individual, and consequently the life events and complexity of experiences made manifest for that individual, is usually closely related for all entities that have a relationship. This is true unless there are specific reasons related to the growth of one or all parties, in which case an Older Soul will create a lifetime that may have close association with Younger Soul entities.

Soul age in no way implies better or worse. Nor should it imply that Older Souls have easier lifetimes than Younger Souls, or vice versa. It is simply a measure of consciousness, vibrational resonance and awareness, which is reflected in the kinds of growth opportunities that may or may not be attracted to a particular individual. Remembering that the purpose of life is Soul growth, every Soul will invest the lifetimes it manifest with every chance possible to generate growth, and as we have always said, that growth can come through various means, seen as both positive and negative.

Suffice to say that most events that take place from one lifetime to another will have complexity directly related to Soul age. In fact, Older Souls can have far more complex experiences and inter-relationships. In addition, as a Soul graduates to higher Universal Dimensions through Ascension, life complexity increases for the individuals created on the Soul's Wheels of Creation. Since a Soul's age and therefore the lifetimes generated within a Universal Dimension are closely related in terms of consciousness level and awareness in any given Dimension, the events experienced by all individuals in that Dimension will have similarity.

In other words, the life of individuals within a given family, culture, society or timeframe will generally seem consistent and standardized from one person to the next. It should be recognized that this is due in large part to an individual's Soul age, and it is only when there are large gaps in Soul ages that familial, societal or cultural discord is experienced and becomes noticeable.

It is said that higher consciousness brings with it greater responsibility, and this adage holds truth, importance and consequence. We would add that higher levels of awareness also bring fuller range and complexity as well. The intensity of an individual's life experiences and choices, whether they are physical, emotional or otherwise, as well as the interconnectedness and depth of relationships formed with others, is a real means of evaluating not only the individual's personal level of consciousness, but their Soul age.

All the lifetimes created by a Soul within the confines of a Universal Dimension cumulatively contribute to the vibrational frequency of that Soul itself. In a way, you could describe Ascension as the result of the crescendo of energy reached by a Soul at the culmination of an Ascension cycle. In effect, it is the integration of the Soul's lifetimes within a Dimension that creates the vibrational momentum needed to propel a Soul into higher consciousness, and as a result vibrational resonance compatible with a higher Dimension is achieved. Once this occurs, a reinvigorated, re-integrated Soul (the sum of its many lifetimes in the Dimension) is ready to begin new Wheels of life at higher dimensional vibration.

To be clear, as universal as it is, the process is also highly individual and dependent on the Soul itself. If the Soul does not reach the level of consciousness or energetic resonance necessary to propel it into the next higher Dimension at the time of Ascension, then it simply remains within the same Dimension and continues on until all lifetimes are properly reintegrated. During the next Ascension cycle, which can be the Solar cycle of 26,000 years, as proper resonance is achieved, the Soul will simply ascend at that particular point.

Because it is such an individualized process, it reasons that Souls of different Soul Ages can all have lifetimes projected on the timeline along side one another. This generally occurs at the beginning and end of every Ascension cycle, when Older Souls are cycling off and preparing to ascend just as Younger Souls that have just ascended from a lower Dimension are beginning to incarnate. This means that although optimally, especially during the middle of a dimensional timeline, the majority of lifetimes cast by Souls in that Dimension will be of similar Soul age, young Souls can physically incarnate alongside Mature Souls or Older Souls.

This can create turmoil, since perspective can be quite different depending upon Soul age. Furthermore, as we have said many times, Older Souls tend to seek refuge and peace whereas Younger Souls look for karmic adventures at every turn. Younger Souls seek out growth through environmental conflicts, soured relationships and endless disagreements based on personal, cultural or political views.

This is akin to what you see occurring firsthand in your world today. Many of the differences in philosophical outlook you are witnessing, such as a Young Souls' attraction to fundamentalist views, evangelical religions or conservative ideas contrast sharply with Mature or Older Souls' desires for progressive, more inclusive life experiences. This is highly representative of this struggle. At times of Universal Ascension, especially Galactic Ascension as you now have, major conflicts and even upheaval is more the norm than the exception. Errant and discordant vibrations created from such disharmony can further unleash new and strange Earth energy patterns that are seemingly out of control, including intense global weather changes and other natural cataclysm.

The extreme polarity you see in your world will continue and deepen until such time as almost all Older Souls have left physical incarnation on the current timeline, and begin the process of journeying through the Astral environments to rejoin their Soul. The well-known phrase "...the meek shall inherit the Earth," does not foretell a time when individuals of a gentle, kinder nature will dominate, as you are taught. Rather, although the term was translated as meek it was originally intended to describe inheritance of the Dimension by younger, inexperienced Souls -- the Baby and Young Souls emerging amongst you -- who are destined to incarnate and remain in the Dimension for the next Galactic Ascension cycle. These Younger Souls have recently ascended from lower Dimensions, just as Older Souls will soon cycle off and begin incarnations in higher Universal Dimensions.

Our point here is to help you understand that the concept of Reincarnation you know, which suggests that one lifetime follows another endlessly, is erroneous at best. In truth, Wheels or cycles of lifetimes, all happening simultaneously, are interwoven to generate experiences that lead to overall growth for the Soul in a non-linear fashion until such time as a critical energetic wave has been achieved. At that point the Soul, rejoined with all the lifetimes it has created -- one of which may be you -- is ready to ascend to a higher Universal Dimension.

You will forgive us if we quickly move into our next discussion concerning physical Reincarnation and the Wheels of Creation created by your Soul in a realm that you are familiar with, the Third Universal Dimension, instead of lingering on the life cycles your Soul creates in the First or Second Universal Dimensions. However interesting that discussion might be to some, the fact that you are currently experiencing a lifetime at the Third Sublevel of the Third Universal Dimension makes a detailed look at these Reincarnation Wheels far more pertinent to the understanding of who you are truly. If we have skipped ahead precipitously, it is simply to afford you an in-depth understanding that applies directly to you now, and a look forward after the current physical life to your journey in the lower and higher Astral planes.

Thus far, we have attempted to provide the necessary basic facts and concepts, including the origins of the Soul and Soul groups, how lifetimes are planned through Wheels of Reincarnation cycles; how each individual lifetime in a Soul's Wheel of Creation has a mission; how these lifetimes are interconnected and how they may be called upon to balance energy from one lifetime to another based on karmic interaction. In doing so, hopefully we have also demonstrated how Transmigration of the Soul from Dimensional Sublevel to Dimensional Sublevel and from Universal Dimension to Universal Dimension is the basis for all Soul growth and Ascension.

What may be difficult for some to fully grasp as we move forward is the fact that even though an individual lifetime is reintegrated into its Soul, ultimately the consciousness that is that individual lifetime is never destroyed or forgotten. The reason this might be a difficult concept to understand is because of the generally centric view that your current physical lifetime is the originator of all other lifetimes, and even, as some might think, the originator of your Soul.

The idea that you are actually a fragment and continuing part of a multidimensional Being -- a spiritual entity temporarily focused within a physical experience -- can be difficult to accept. Understanding this however, will assist you to see how one essentially discards a physical body, transcends death and, through an etheric body, survives and continually journeys, raising vibrational integrity throughout the process. In much the same way that your Soul is forever part of All-

That-Is (or God, depending upon your perspective), once you have been cast out and created as a fragment of your Soul you exist and are part of it for all eternity. This then becomes the TRUE meaning of a Soul "group," despite the fact the Soul itself is a member of a group of Souls originally cast out from Source.

A true analogy we would make is one where you recognize the cells of your body as independent from you, but also integral and dependent upon you. Those cells make up who you are in totality and every cell is forever a valuable part of who you have been, who you are and who you will one day become. In much the same way you are part of your Soul and, like your Soul, who is Co-Creator with "God," you are a Co-Creator in this Universal Dimension with your Soul. This association is retained throughout the Soul's journey through the Twelve Universal Dimensions until such time that you, as a cell in the body of your Soul, return together with it to the original Source. The inclusion of your consciousness and the augmented consciousness of your Soul, together with all Souls that rejoin Source, fuels the continuous expansion of the Universe and the God Force at large.

Next, we shall explore your multidimensionality by taking you through the actual process of physical birth and death in the Third Universal Dimension. Doing so we will look not only at the planning of your lifetime as an independent entity on your Soul's Wheel of Creation, but also investigate the non-corporeal after-life journey each of you will one day make through the lower and higher Astral environments or Dimensional Sublevels. This process moves you ever closer in your goal to reunite with your Soul and achieve Universal Ascension.

Stories from a Soul's Wheel of Creation
The Story of Aaron and Regina

The first time Aaron and Regina met, both became unnerved just as if they had been hit by something so powerful, it was beyond anyone's understanding. The attraction was irresistible and they were drawn to each other with a passion that neither had ever experienced before or could fathom. After a volatile whirlwind courtship, they became engaged.

Originally from Ohio, Regina's dream of one day having a romantic destination wedding somewhere in Europe was something about which she had long fantasized. Despite the fact that she had never been to Ireland, when Aaron proposed and they looked at a location on the Southwestern coast for their wedding, she jumped at the idea with an enthusiasm that even surprised her. They married within six months of meeting in a beautiful outdoor ceremony on the coast of Southern Ireland, near the ruins of a 6th Century monastery.

Minor "episodes" of tension underlying their passion had been present before the wedding, but each blissfully ignored and forgot them almost as soon as they happened. The make-up sessions always removed any doubt for both of them that there was anything but an extraordinary emotional and physical attraction.

Endless skirmishes followed by glorious make up sessions con-

tinued however, until the battles became so intense and frequent that they couldn't be ignored any longer. Their marriage became the ideal definition of a love-hate relationship.

Counseling revealed that Regina had developed deep feelings of insecurity and victimhood, with vague and unexpressed resentment towards Aaron. She began to oppose him at every turn, and soon became afraid of the very things that had first attracted her. Though he had never been physically violent, now she would shiver unexplainably with fright whenever he was near her. She became hopelessly depressed convinced that her life would follow some inevitable, uncharted and inescapable fate, which her orthodox religious upbringing taught was possible when God had abandoned you.

In truth, few could ignore Aaron's overly confident domineering nature, which he wielded through his flaming red hair and his fit, Saturnian 6'5" masculine physique. A consummate athlete, since childhood he turned heads when he walked into a room. As an adult, his imposing authoritative personality and dominant figure were described as impressive and inspiring by some, and called frightening and arrogant by others.

For his part, as a younger man Aaron had seen this happen before in no less than two previous relationships. As with each relationship prior, he was dismayed at his partners' sudden fear of him and refusal to submit to his views about how to act, what to do and when to do it. He was particularly shocked by *any refusal to comply with what he wanted however simple the request happened to be.*

Aaron chalked it up to Regina's new friends whom he thought were instigating in her the inability to think clearly about the true order of things or, from his perspective, how things should be handled based on gender and strength. They were telling Regina to leave Aaron as soon as possible, which she adamantly insisted was not possible without offering any real excuse why she felt that way.

Meanwhile, Aaron continued to feel betrayed by her attitude, and as a male, the breadwinner, the more athletic and the better educated of the two, he felt Regina should readily submit to his will. Moreover, because he had not changed or altered his behavior in any way from before the time they were married, he was mystified as to why Regina should suddenly see him so differently and why she would be so resistant to him seemingly overnight.

Things continued unhappily this way, until one day a friend somewhat jokingly suggested that Aaron and Regina must be experiencing "karma" potentially derived from a past life experience. Somehow the suggestion resonated with them both and lingered, until finally they decided to seek out further answers by finding someone who could delve into their personal information concerning "reincarnation."

During their first session, Regina was made aware that in examining other lifetimes on the Wheels of Creation of her Soul, one lifetime stood out, which was a lifetime in Southwestern Ireland taking place in the mid 8th Century. In that life, she was a young male who was a novitiate Monk residing at a monastery not far from the ruins where the current couple's wedding had taken place three years earlier.

During that reincarnation as a Monk in Ireland, hard work and devotion consumed daily life until one-day things were altered dramatically forever. A Viking raid burnt down the monastery, and while his friends and fellow Monks were tortured and killed in front of him, the young Monk was saved from death by one of the Viking raiders, who, recognizing his youth and vigor, took him captive and enslaved him. The Monk's Viking captor was a reincarnation of Aaron's Soul.

The life as a Monk was a counterpart lifetime of Regina, existing as it did on the same Wheel of Creation as her own life. Clearly, the Monk's difficult experiences together with the karmic imbalances created through the severe fear and loathing festering deep inside the enslaved Monk was now bleeding through into Regina's life circumstances, requiring energetic balance.

As for Aaron, the Viking lifetime that had enslaved the Monk and others in the past had formed tremendous energetic blockages and imbalances that were now bleeding into Aaron's life relationships. As the counter balance lifetime to Aaron's life on his Soul's same Wheel of Creation, the karma generated by the Viking demanded correction and cure through Aaron.

It soon became clear that Aaron and Regina's Souls had pre-arranged their meeting and marriage in order to assist each to balance and cure the tremendous karmic imbalances generated in both of their related lifetimes. In truth, Aaron had been given the chance to balance his karma with two other Viking lifetime victims, but circumstances combined with Free Will had prematurely ended those relationships before karmic balance could occur.

In those two cases, Aaron had refused to be empathetic, patient and understanding and resisted delving further into what he was doing to cause his partners' dramatic attitude shifts. He ended both relationships before karmic balancing, an important basis of Aaron's life mission, could occur.

Now his marriage to Regina had changed the equation for an older and wiser Aaron, obliging him to remain in the relationship and dig deeper into the emotional and psychological implications, particularly his role in what his partners were feeling. Suddenly he was forced to ponder the freedom that each individual possesses in life as well as their right to explore and find their own personal expression without domination from another.

On the other side of the equation, the enslaved Monk had died not soon after being captured when he had his throat slit by another Viking following a dispute concerning willful disobedience. That particular karmic interaction (leading to the enslaved Monk's death) was being addressed in another unrelated lifetime on the same Wheel of Creation. Curiously however, about the same age as the death of the Monk in his lifetime, Regina had her thyroid surgically removed when a growth was found in that organ.

In real terms, enslavement had led to the prior lifetime's demise, not only creating important energy around being dominated by others but also fostering a severe weakness in the throat chakra that reached through energetically into Regina's physical body. The Monk's disobedience had literally meant his death, creating an overwhelming energetic blockage around issues of enslavement and domination for Regina. These issues were now in need of balancing in her lifetime, since Aaron was not only a constant subconscious reminder of the Monk's ordeal, he was closely associated with the original offense that had led to the Monk's demise.

Having knowledge of this information to work with, both Regina and Aaron were able to reflect deeply on their roles and the reason each reacted to and faced the emotions they did had towards the other. Overtime, their energy cleared and balanced, and their relationship changed dramatically, almost as if beginning anew. Aaron was less demanding and careful to allow

Regina to have her own expression and a high degree of freedom in the current lifetime. Regina was able to waylay any fears she had that she was being dominated or controlled, and she was able to assert herself without needing to deceive or resist Aaron any longer.

Successful in balancing the hidden karmic energies that bound them initially, the passion that had first attracted them waned, and their relationship turned into a new and solid friendship based on trust and understanding. The karma from their Souls' Wheels of Creation now balanced however, meant that over time each mutually lost interest in the other. Eventually, without fanfare or argument, and with full amicable agreement, they separated.

They consciously mused that the karmic energies that had attracted and bound them together before, were no longer present. Therefore, their purpose in being together was now fulfilled leaving them free to decide what they wanted their future paths to be. Shortly afterwards, both Aaron and Regina met and married individuals they later described to each other as the "love" of their life. Their new relationships showed no remnant whatsoever of the issues that had always plagued them in the past. Today, Aaron and Regina are the closest of friends.

 ## CHAPTER 4
WHEELS OF CREATION AND THE PHYSICAL BIRTH AND DEATH PROCESS IN THIRD DIMENSIONAL REALITY

Let us begin our discussion of the physical life and death process in Third Dimensional reality by looking into the manner in which a Soul transmigrates to the Dimension and then fragments itself into the many physical life incarnations, that become your "reincarnated" selves. In doing so, we hope to shed light on how a Soul is able to inhabit a physical body, animate that physical Being and carry out life against the backdrop of physical reality you know.

Additionally, it becomes important to understand how that same physical life is lived until either the individual's mission is accomplished or the physical body has exhausted its usefulness and ability. Generally, life "exit strategies" are predetermined by the Soul prior to the particular lifetime, and the Soul allows for several different scenarios or opportunities to depart the lifetime. In addition, Free Will allows the entity to choose spontaneous opportunities that arise at specific points during the course of the lifetime as well. This is usually the case if the entity has fully accomplished its "life mission," or if the life mission is considered by the Soul or the entity to be unobtainable in that lifetime based on unfolding circumstances, or should external events no longer be useful to the Soul and the lifetime's growth.

Please note that we are not referring to suicide or any form of conscious death by choice. Rather, we are referring to the unconscious energetic ability of the individual entity, in conjunction with its Soul, to subconsciously choose circumstances such as illness or accidents in order to terminate a lifetime that has either been successfully accomplished, or one that is no longer able to accomplish its life mission.

The discussion of suicide is another one completely. Although it does not have the condemnation in the "afterlife" that is allocated to it presently by your religions and culture, the fact that every life has a specific mission and also has the ability to self extinguish by a vast many other subconscious means, should the entity's mission be accomplished or no longer tenable, makes the decision of suicide a misguided effort. In addition, more often than not it is the result of profound psychological or biological imbalances, which in itself can be a mechanism of Soul growth. Then again, for those extremely sensitive or intuitive, it can sometimes even be the result of the bleed through of tragic events from other lifetimes close to the entity on the Soul's Wheel of Creation.

All this is assuming it is not an event pre-planned as part of the Soul's desire for growth within the lifetime. Though it is sometimes sadly a choice made by an individual based on fear and suffering, more often than not suicide is self-karmic in nature. In most cases however, it is the undertaking of a Soul who for karmic reasons or by agreement prior to the lifetime is offering parents, friends and family members other than itself special opportunities for growth based on the personal interactions and profound emotions felt around the loss of that loved one. These tend to be Soul lessons that endure throughout the lifetime of those affected.

How the Soul retires its energy when a physical lifetime is accomplished is of fundamental importance in understanding how it passes from physical life into ethereal life at higher Sublevels of the current Dimension. In that regard, when the entity, who is essentially still part and parcel of the Soul, "passes" on from the Third Sublevel of the Dimension through the act of definitively separating from the physical body, it passes into the Astral planes where it begins its transmigration through those planes of reality.

The Astral realms, starting with the Fourth Astral Sublevel, are essentially Sublevels of the Universal Dimension that carry varying and different frequencies and are less physical than the reality you are accustomed to at the Third Sublevel. Because these Sublevels exist at higher vibrational resonances, as per the Universal plan they are not normally visible to you from your dimensional vantage point.

For the most part, the separation of the Soul from a particular physical lifetime is accomplished through the union of energetic momentum contained in the act of passing from the physical vehicle joined together with the Soul's energetic ability to withdraw its animating life force. This allows consciousness to recede from the physical body. The process unfolds principally by funneling life energy out of the physical body into the etheric or energetic body, which surrounds and is attached to the physical body throughout physical existence. That energetic body is always present and in fact serves as an energy container that is more or less the transitional vehicle that interfaces between the physical biological body and the Soul. Once the Soul's life force energies have completely drained from the physical body into the etheric body, the etheric detaches from the physical container permanently.

Many of you have been taught that the Astral realms contain "Heaven" or some other final destination extolled in spiritual or religious mythology, and you are told this represents a final endpoint of your Soul's journey. This is not true. While there may be minor,

incomplete elements of truth found in some of the paradise concepts, for the most part heavenly realms, rewards for good behavior,
damnation for bad behavior, and the concept that there is some final
place or ideal location ready made for you where you reside forever
after physical life, is completely fictitious.

This is not to imply however, that there is finality and "nothingness"
after life, as others may believe, or that one's spirit floats aimlessly in
an unstructured limbo after physical death. Detached from the physical body after death, the energetic body continues to operate by
housing your consciousness and remains ever-present acting as the
primary vehicle for your experiences in the Astral realms after demise of the physical self. This energetic body, which resonates at a
higher vibrational frequency and is less dense to match higher dimensional resonance, is just as real, even if not as dense, as the physical body you perceive right now in your Third Dimensional reality.

The same goes for whatever (seemingly) structured environment or
surroundings you find yourself in following the physical departure.
The environment in the Fourth Astral plane is created by you, for
you, depending upon the consciousness developed in the lifetime
from which you have just departed. Reality in the Fourth Astral Plane
is manifested based on the beliefs, ideas, sentiments and nature of
the objects you are familiar with from the physical reality just departed. You create these surroundings through the thought forms,
desires and emotions that you project forth within the Astral realm.

Since there is no physical time lag for the creation of reality in that
Dimensional Sublevel, your reality there materializes around you immediately in the eternal "Now," in much the same way dream reality
materializes spontaneously when you are dreaming. If there is one
most important technique that should be mastered and worked on

during the lifetime, it is practicing control of your thoughts and being constantly conscious of your feelings, desires and the thought forms you send forth at all times. This prepares you for control of the Astral environment and the surroundings you will create for yourself after departing the physical body.

Based on this, the Astral environment is almost always an expression of whatever you desire it to be at any given moment, and this may well be where the confusion concerning the concept of "paradise" stems. Upon passing, some see loved ones or religious figures blissfully known to them. Others may envision devils or have Hellish experiences (particularly if shame and guilt are prevalent in their consciousness repertoire at the time of death). This is particularly true if your thoughts are haphazard and random, or if fear predominates them after departure from the physical body.

It is for this reason that carrying with you into the Astral state a conscious remembrance of the power you possess and who you are is so very important following physical death. The consciousness that represents who you are remains with you at your passing, and you are in charge of the environment you create there, at least in the early stages of transition and transmigration in the lower Astral realm. This remembrance is only available to you however, if you understand and have awareness of what is happening as you pass into the Astral state. And this is only possible if you have been schooled in the process of death, dying and the transition that takes place following the departure from the physical body. Hopefully, this information will assist you when needed in that transition.

In the distant past, this was the reason Shamans or mystics, like midwives assisting birth, were always called to the side of the dying, and their mission was to assist them to remember and remain lucid once they departed the body in order to retain awareness that their consciousness was in full charge of creating their surroundings immediately following death. Such efforts have been drummed out of your modern religious and spiritual practices where death and the process of dying is kept hidden from you, and your power in this has been turned over to a religious or institutionalized format. While it is all fine and good to call on an officiant to offer words of comfort and blessing to anyone undergoing the process of transition, this is a far cry from truly assisting them to take control of their coming journey through conscious lucidity. Such acts may provide momentary solace but they can also confuse the individual further by burying them deeper in obscure, fairly unhelpful dogma that will need to be discarded before real progress can be made at the next level of reality.

As Dimensional Sublevels found within every Universal Dimension, the Astral planes are in fact transitional realms of varying and different densities that facilitate the journey of the individual entity's consciousness in its processing and eventual reintegration with its own Soul. These planes are usually the Sublevel planes that are above whatever Sublevel "physical" reality (in quotes please, since physical reality varies from Dimension to Dimension, and is not the same as you are familiar with necessarily) in a particular Universal Dimension where you are focused. For the Third Universal Dimension, the Astral planes begin at the Fourth and continue through the Twelfth Dimensional Sublevel.

Reintegration with all of its lifetimes and entities must be accomplished before a Soul graduates and ascends from one particular Universal Dimension to the next. All created individual entities and lifetimes that the Soul has created must pass through the various Sublevel Dimensions in a subtle but deliberate process of reintegration with the Soul. Thus, the mythology of "heaven" as you may know it, is only a minor experience in the entire journey. Simplification of its understanding over time has become a confusing, limiting and erroneous interpretation of the entire process.

It is this concept, first and foremost, that we wish to correct, along with any notion that there is one specific location, dead-end or final arrival point after physical life. That limiting concept is not at all in keeping with the magnanimity, multidimensionality and majesty of your Soul. Neither is it compatible with the complexity that is the Universal God force.

As we have said many times, you are essentially a spiritual being having a localized physical experience, and this continues to be a core truth for all those within your reality. You are currently focused vibrationally in a body living a lifetime in a physical reality within the Third Sublevel of the Third Universal Dimension. Similarly, in the Third Universal Dimension, the physical incarnations of all Human Angelic and Sentient Soul species, those you are aware of and those you are not, exist at the Third Sublevel of the Universal Dimension.

In any Universal Dimension, after the current physical lifetime's completion all entities leave the physical bonds of the particular Sublevel and pass into higher Sublevels of the Dimension. In the Third Universal Dimension this includes Sublevels Four through Twelve, the Sublevels loosely known as the Astral planes of your Dimension.

Unlike the higher Sublevels of the Third Universal Dimension, the First, Second and Third Sublevels of the Dimension all have some component related to physicality and density. It so happens that the Third Sublevel of the Third Universal Dimension, where you are currently physically incarnated, is the Sublevel that holds the ideal physical attributes for Human Angelic consciousness to be expressed. It is for this reason that Human Angelic Souls incarnate in physical bodies at the Third Sublevel and also incarnate in lifetimes that interconnect with the Dimension's timeline over the course of a given Galactic Ascension cycle (approximately 260,000 Earth years).

Though imperceptible to you, physical density graduates and becomes lighter (both literally and metaphorically) from Universal Dimension to Universal Dimension, as well as from Sublevel to Sublevel of a Universal Dimension. Thus, the Third Dimension and the Third Sublevel of that Dimension are slightly less dense physically than either the First or the Second Universal Dimension or their equivalent Sublevels. Since the ability to carry light is synonymous with higher consciousness (thus the term en-light-en-ment), this graduation of physical density is representative of reality at higher dimensional levels. A crude example of this can be seen in the fact that your personal body, physical though it may seem to you, is less dense and more ethereal as a product of the Third Universal Dimension than say an element like a rock, or mountain range, which are far denser and would be considered typical First or Second Universal Dimension Beings.

While the Fourth through Twelfth Sublevels of the Third Universal Dimension are part of the entire dimensional structure, and cannot be divorced from the Universal Dimension itself, please understand that as Sublevels rise in frequency and vibration they become by their nature less and less physical and more and more ethereal, or energetically formed, in structure. This not only occurs by virtue of the rise in consciousness and vibrational frequency that they experience, but is also what unifies them as part of the entire Dimensional structure.

Sublevels of a Universal Dimension, like the Universal Dimensions they comprise, are organized in vibrational proximity and arranged in groups of three. This stands as a basis of some of your prominent spiritual teachings that consider the number "three" to be important, or groupings of three, a Trilogy, to be divine in nature. The First through Third Universal Dimensions have a close enough vibrational and resonant proximity to have considerable overlap and familiarity, each to the other, and the same is the case for the Fourth through Sixth, the Seventh through Ninth and the Tenth through Twelfth Universal Dimensions. The same can be said for all Sublevels within a Universal Dimension, and the Sublevels are also grouped in much the same way.

Again, this is a general description to help you visualize dimensional structure although, in truth, real separations do not necessarily exist between the various Universal Dimensions (as witnessed in your ability to see and experience a rock, but its inability to see or experience you). Similarly, there can in fact be significant overlap and cohesion from one Sublevel to the next within a Universal Dimension.

In the Third Universal Dimension, physical life as you know it is basically seen from the First to Third Dimension. Therefore the First through Third Dimensional Sublevels of the Third Universal Dimension have a relationship. However, the Fourth through Sixth Dimensional Sublevels begin the Astral environments of the Universal Dimension, and these Sublevels have less physical structure. Thus, the Fourth Dimensional Sublevel, or Astral plane, becomes the one identified as the Dimension that entities pass into following the completion of physical life (as you know it). It is beginning in the Fourth Dimensional Sublevel that entities start their true march towards reintegration with their Soul within the Third Universal Dimension.

It should be noted that here we are describing the Third Dimensional Sublevel of the Third Universal Dimension as a matter of convenience because this is the location where you are currently focused and the one you are physically evolving through. However, physical life (the term must be seen as relative depending upon your perspective) in any Universal Dimension, whatever its nature or attributes, is usually focused in the Sublevel that corresponds to the Universal Dimension itself. Thus, physical life experiences for a Soul of which you are a fragment may be focused at the Third Sublevel of the Third Universal Dimension, but if you were a Fifth Dimensional entity, your physical existence would most likely begin or be focused at the Fifth Dimensional Sublevel, and so on and so forth.

This is because as the Soul graduates to higher Universal dimension levels, its energetic expression, its ability to hold light and, subsequently, its consciousness, is amply augmented to create incarnations within lighter and higher vibrational fields. It is also based on the fact that the entities (lifetimes) a Soul co-creates are of an elevated consciousness in higher Universal Dimensions. Thus there is less need for significant steps to reintegrate with the Soul following physical death for fragments moving through that particular Universal Dimension.

In fact, in higher Universal Dimensions a Soul's life creations do not need the considerable process normally needed by entities in the Astral Sublevels of lower Universal Dimensions. In other words, reintegration with the Soul is easier for lifetimes with higher consciousness in higher Universal Dimensions. Thus, the elevated consciousness and awareness inherently available to say a Fifth or a Seventh Dimensional Soul fragment that has lived its life at the Fifth or Seventh Sublevel of the Universal Dimension requires less "processing" after physical death than an entity completing lifetimes in say the Second or Third Universal Dimension. As a result, less time and, subsequently, fewer Astral Sublevels are necessary to complete the integration process with the Soul.

In this way, the number of Astral planes (the Sublevels above physical reality) is reduced for higher Universal Dimensions. We would add that even beginning with the Fifth Universal Dimension, a life entity or fragment is consciously aware of its Soul connection and even its life mission during and throughout the physical lifetime it lives. This is not available to entities in lower Universal Dimensions, including the Third Universal Dimension, where following completion of the physical lifetime the entity travels through considerably more Astral Sublevels in order to process what has transpired, decipher the success of their physical life mission and, following that, accomplish full reintegration with their Soul.

Before we dive into this any further, it is important to take another look at a few important points related to how the Soul itself transmigrates between Universal Dimensions, once it is cast out from the God Source in the Twelfth Universal Dimension. One would assume that when a Soul is cast out from Source it begins its journey at the beginning, meaning the First Sublevel of the First Universal Dimension. But this is not entirely the case.

While the "fragments" cast-out by a Soul within a Universal Dimension do indeed start their journey in linear fashion this way, the Soul itself enters each Universal Dimension in a different, non-linear way. Remember, if you will, that each Soul as a fragment of the God Source is already vibrating at a resonance that is fairly pure and high. Its main objective is to have experiential growth as a Co-Creator through the experiences of the lifetimes it creates within each Universal Dimension.

Furthermore, the Soul's fundamental goal in creating Wheels of lifetimes within a dimensional structure is to continually raise and augment its own consciousness. When the Soul completes its journey through all Universal Dimensions and finally reintegrates with the God Source, or All That Is, in the Twelfth Universal Dimension, its expanded consciousness also expands the Universe at large. In many ways, one could cite this as the true purpose of all creation.

To do so, and because its energy is such that it can orchestrate and energize numerous lifetimes, and even cycles of lifetimes, when the Soul enters a Universal Dimension it does so at the highest levels of that Dimension. In other words, the Soul begins its journey in each Universal Dimension at the Twelfth Sublevel of that Dimension. This is a somewhat complex concept, but we will attempt to explain.

Dimensional Sublevels have great similarity and vibrational harmony with their Universal Dimension counterpart. As an example, vibrational resonance found in say the Seventh Sublevel of any Universal Dimension is closely aligned with the Seventh Universal Dimension as a whole. Following this line of reasoning then, it is easy to understand that the Twelfth Sublevel of a Universal Dimension is resonant with the Twelfth Universal Dimension, the source of all creation itself.

Since each Soul is originally cast-out from the Twelfth Universal Dimension, it is natural that it finds its greatest compatibility with the Twelfth Sublevel of any given Universal Dimension. And for this reason, when the Soul begins its journey, it enters the Universal Dimension through the Twelfth or highest Sublevel of the Universal Dimension it has entered. Moreover, the Soul remains focused in the Twelfth Sublevel of that Dimension for the duration, and it is usually from that high dimensional Sublevel that it casts out fragments of itself and orchestrates the many Wheels or cycles of lifetimes it does in the lower Sublevels of that Universal Dimension.

On the other hand, the entities and lifetimes a Soul manifests, as well as the Wheels of Creation it puts into motion, start their journey at the Sublevel of that Dimension intended for physical life. The journey of the particular fragment or entity therefore begins in the lower dimensional Sublevel and continues independently graduating through all Sublevels within the Universal Dimension until reunifying with its Soul in the Twelfth Dimensional Sublevel.

It can be a complicated matter to grasp or envision how a Soul that is newly cast-out itself from the God Source and is now residing at the Twelfth Sublevel of a Universal Dimension, can also cast out fragments of itself and create independent reincarnations that journey through the Universal Dimension. No less complex is following that entity as it journeys through the various Sublevels of the Universal Dimension, until such time as the fragment meets up again and reintegrates with the Soul that created it.

Once established in a Universal Dimension, the Soul creates numerous entities or lifetimes simultaneously, and strategically places them in relation to each other on Wheels of Creation that it formulates within the Universal Dimension. Then, increasing this complexity even further, the Soul interfaces the numerous fragments it creates and places them within multiple cycles on the dimensional timeline.

Positioned independently but interlocked on these Wheels of Creation as "reincarnations," each entity has its own lessons, missions, traits, relationships, skill sets, karmic balancing and other growth initiatives -- planned and not planned – providing the Soul with the fullest opportunities for consciousness growth possible. These fragments continue through the Dimensional substructure and when complete bring back their expanded experiential consciousness for reintegration with the Soul. This process represents the Soul's reincarnation and transmigration experience.

When the Soul itself has integrated the consciousness of all its lifetimes back into itself, the Soul is ready to ascend to the next Universal Dimension. At this point it begins the process over again, fragmenting itself once more into numerous lifetimes on that new dimensional timeline. It does this at the end of every migration through a Universal Dimension, until it has completed its journey through the entire Universal dimension structure, and has returned back to its original Source in the Twelfth Universal Dimension.

Once the journey through all the Universal Dimensions is complete, each Soul reintegrates with the God Source in much the same manner as the Soul's fragment lifetimes have reintegrated with it at the end of every Universal Dimension prior to Ascension into a higher Universal Dimension. When this occurs, the Soul is again at one with All-That-Is, which is the creative force that originally cast it out to become a Co-Creator. Envisioning this process, even partially, not only provides a real glimpse into the complexity and multidimensionality of you and your Soul, it also demonstrates in no small way the magnificent structure that is the Universe. This announces what we would consider the Divine Plan.

Now, once a Soul has transmigrated to a Universal Dimension, entering the Dimension through the Twelfth Sublevel as we have discussed, the fragments it casts out begin their journeys through the Dimensions at the Sublevel that corresponds to physical creation for that particular Universal Dimension. For the Third Dimension, that means a Soul's life fragments begin incarnations at the Third Sublevel.

We are purposefully leaving out a full discussion of the lower Sublevels of each Universal Dimension at this point in order to avoid confusion and to prevent any analogy you might identify with religious teachings that use a Hell, a devil or evil in general as a way to create fear and control the actions of followers. Suffice to say however, that Sublevels that are lower than the physical Dimensional Sublevel have a connection in a manner of speaking with higher Sublevels that connect to them in tertiary formation.

For the Third Universal Dimension, this means that the First and Second Sublevel are in close proximity and part of the Trilogy that includes the Third Dimensional Sublevel, which as you know is related to physical incarnations in your Dimension. It is important to understand that these realms do in fact exist, and we will call them balancing realms for the higher physical Sublevels.

Most of what is known of these lower Sublevels is misunderstood, but it would not be totally incorrect to compare them with the mythologies and fables that describe the existence of an "underworld" that acts as a counterpart to your physical reality (thus our desire to not create any religious analogies). As a counterpart and balance that is fed by the complexity of whatever the physical reality might be, using the Third Universal Dimension as our example, we would identify the First and Second Sublevel Dimensions as the realm of pure thought form. These might also be considered realms of the "unconscious" or metaphysical, though we generally reserve the term metaphysical for those unseen experiences that lie above physical reality as opposed to beneath it. Let us explain further.

The First and Second Sublevel of the Third Universal Dimension are not to be confused with the First and Second Universal Dimensions, which are completely different realms. This is where any explanation can become somewhat confusing. That is because there actually are certain comparisons that can be made between say the First Sublevel of the Third Dimension and the First Universal Dimension itself.

Have you ever wondered why the demons and devils of your stories, myths and religions are always pictured in caves or existing underground? This is because in the First Universal Dimension the caves, minerals and mountain ranges that you see, among other things, from your vantage point in the Third Dimension are in fact Beings from that dimension.

However, the First Sublevel of the Third Universal Dimension is the place where what we shall call "dense negative" thought forms (the devils, demons, monsters and other negative imaginings) are created and held. As a result, thought forms from the First Sublevel of your Dimension have become synonymous with the First Universal Dimension's actual physical structures, namely the caves, minerals and mountain ranges that you see around you.

Thus the First Dimensional Sublevel, or "Underworld" as used in ancient mythology, is the realm where thought forms you consider negative linger and exist. Naturally, although this is only a metaphor for a Sublevel reality where negative energies are known to solidify and consolidate, the actual landscape applicable to the First Universal Dimension has over time become the iconography and symbolism you associate with ogres, demons, monsters, dragons or other devils that negative thought forms may conjure as creatures and Beings.

We have explained many times that thoughts are action and, most importantly, that caution should be used in what you think and the thoughts you form. This is because thought forms imbued with enough energy can become real "fragments" or creations projected outward by you that manifest in reality. Though not imbued with the same denser physical existence you enjoy through the auspices of your Soul, given enough intensity, repetition and emotion, these thought forms can take on a type of energetic life that is completely independent from you.

Moreover, thought forms projected outward by groups, cultures, nations, etc., can be powerful indeed. As any child knows, there are indeed "monsters" under the bed. In this case those monsters are the negative thought impulses you singularly or as a group create. As you now can see, thought form Beings are given a life of sorts that takes shape in the First Sublevel of the Third Universal Dimension.

To be clear, the thought forms that exist metaphysically and are associated with actual physical Beings found in the First Universal Dimension that reside under the physical reality you know are what specters are. Indeed, they are the ideas and apparitions that most find frightening, and usually this is a precise definition of what a negative thought form truly is. As we have often said, although there is certainly a negativity attached to such thought forms by virtue of the polarity found in your world, seeing them as "evil" becomes a designation relative to the perceiver. It is, therefore, interesting that in the past most agreed with whatever the relative designation for such a thought form happened to be. More and more now however, the true definition of what constitutes evil, like the definition of what constitutes "Truth," is a matter of debate related to diverging perspectives that are more a reflection of differences in Soul age and level of consciousness than anything else.

Like the dense physical matter they personify, negative thought forms that arise as an undertone of your reality in the First Dimensional Sublevel have no real power unless you choose to allow them to hold power or sway in your life. For this reason, some in your world find them comical while others tremble in fear at their very mention. It is important to understand that higher consciousness always has dominion over lower Sublevels, including negative thought form Beings, unless the higher consciousness entity abdicates its dominion and gives its power over to the Beings that spring from such lower vibrational energies.

Whatever the case, you should be aware that the close proximity these lower thought form Beings have to your Third Sublevel of existence allows them to sometimes transcend, transmigrate the dimensional boundaries and make an appearance, albeit slight, in your reality. This usually occurs within the Dreamscape at the level of the Fourth Astral plane, but at times there can be disembodied energetic forces or shades that are able to stealthily bleed into your world and they can sometimes be seen by those sensitive to such occurrences.

Closer to you in vibrational resonance, and therefore potentially closer in compatibility and understanding, is the Second Dimensional Sublevel. As opposed to what we have just described as the First Dimensional Sublevel, where negative thought forms are made manifest, the Second Sublevel realm could be defined as the place positive thought forms congregate, work and take on energetic physical form and existence. This is the realm of the spirits and metaphysical Beings that you would most likely consider positive, unless your religious dogma has taught you otherwise, as some do in an attempt to mislead, blind and control you.

These positive thought forms and metaphysical entities are most commonly identified as the benevolent spirits and energetic beings of nature and the Earth. They are best described as the Devas, fairies, gnomes, guardians and all similar Beings of the Devic Kingdom, more commonly known to you as "Mother Nature." The planet itself, as a First Universal Dimension Being, has close association with the Natural elements found in the First Universal Dimension, such as the mountain ranges and primal elements. The Second Dimensional Sublevel, which is linked to the Second Universal Dimension, holds what is more commonly known as "nature" and the natural world of Earth.

Thus, there is an important connection also with the Devic Kingdom, which has always had such association, symbolically and otherwise.

Most think angels, as well as nature spirits found in the Devic kingdom, are Beings originating from a somewhat higher Dimension. While there are certainly Spirit Guides, disembodied entities and others, your Soul included, that inhabit higher Dimensional Sublevels and are watching over you, most nature spirits as we have discussed earlier in this book are Souls experiencing lifetimes in the Second Universal Dimension. As a result, these Beings have a strong relationship with your Universal Dimension through the Second Sublevel of that Dimension.

Therefore, despite the fact that they are essentially Second Dimensional Beings, their realm as it is applicable to you is the Second Sublevel of your Third Universal Dimension. Once again this demonstrates the point that the Sublevel of physical reality for a Dimension begins at the Sublevel that is congruent with the Universal Dimension itself. So Second Dimensional Beings are able to transmigrate and be present at the Second Sublevel of the Third Universal Dimension. This further means that they are not all that far removed from where Third Dimensional Beings incarnate physical lifetimes, which, as we have said, is the Third Sublevel of the third Universal Dimension.

You experience Second Universal Dimension Beings physically in your Third Dimensional reality as plants, rivers, streams, certain insects and the like, and you are not usually aware of them as real, personified, energetic or spiritual entities, which indeed they are. In this way, you see and experience their physical but not their energetic representation, in keeping with the Universal rule that higher Dimensions can see lower ones.

We would add to this that not being able to "see" them physically can be more a matter of choice, conditioning and belief (usually drummed out of you in childhood) than anything else. Seeing something or not however is never obligatory and certainly not related to whether it exists or not. Though you may not currently "see" in front of you a close friend or relative, this does not mean they have ceased to exist or are not real somehow.

The overlap of dimensional awareness, visibility and reality, and the added complexity caused by the interface of Dimensional Sublevels and the Universal Dimensions they are connected to, can be confusing and may require some intuitive juggling of your perspective. At the very least however, you should finally be aware that Universal Structure is a multidimensional one based on vibrational resonance and frequency, and the rates of vibrational resonance are a defined and measurable attribute of consciousness, awareness and, as a result, enlightenment.

Returning to our original discussion and as we have discussed in prior chapters, when a Soul is originally cast out, it is cast out from the God Source with certain particulars related to its Soul group or cadre, its orientation (Service-to-Self or Service-to-Others) and its Soul species. These factors all come into play when the Soul transmigrates to specific space-time coordinates in specific regions within the Universal Dimension. The Soul does not float aimlessly through space-time until it finds a home, but rather is attracted by vibrational resonance to the exact location in the Universal Dimension that is akin and magnetic to its own growth process.

Electromagnetically linked via that vibrational frequency, the Soul ultimately takes up residence at specific universal locations within the

Twelfth Sublevel of a particular Universal Dimension, and this begins its co-creative mission. It does so by casting out fragments of itself into lower Sublevels of the Universal Dimension, creating lifetimes that will journey on its behalf and bring back to the Soul the consciousness growth it is seeking.

Thus, as an example, a Human Angelic Soul together with its Soul group or cadre is generally resonant and attracted to that sector of the Third Dimensional Universe that is designated for Human Angelic incarnations. This is not to say that Souls other than Human Angelics are barred or unable to incarnate in these regions of space, and indeed this happens with some frequency especially at higher Dimensions, but for the most part a Soul species, particularly in the earliest stages of its dimensional incarnations, will incarnate in regions of the Universe that are resonant with its cadre where its compatriots are incarnating and exist. In the Third Universal Dimension, this is the planet known as Earth, in the Solar System of your Sun within the Galaxy you know as the Milky Way.

The Universe is vast, and the dimensional timeline is equal in its vastness. For this reason, it is important to note that even though Human Angelics may choose to incarnate on Earth in the Third Universal Dimension, it is naturally possible that a good many other Soul Species are incarnating at varying distances within the Third Universal Dimension as well. In addition, it should be understood that interdimensional contact with Alien Souls from higher Universal Dimensions is possible based on the Universal law that higher can see and participate with lower realities (even if most of the time lower resonant physical realities are completely ignored by higher ones). By virtue of this we are suggesting that the vast majority of "visitations" or UFO sightings experienced in your current reality are actually interdimensional in nature. They are not usually direct visitations from far away star systems or Galaxies from inside the Third Universal Dimension, as you might expect.

All of this is intended to provide you with an understanding that the Soul itself is not lingering somewhere universally disconnected from you (in conjunction with some anthropomorphic God figure) randomly puppeteering fragments of itself in a lower Universal Dimension. The Soul is actually residing within the same Universal Dimension as you, albeit at a higher dimensional Sublevel, participating with you as well as all the lifetimes it creates as they journey through the Dimensional Sublevels and grow in consciousness and vibrational integrity. In many ways, your current notions of "God" are actually more reflective of the relationship you have with your own Soul rather than a true reflection of the much more complex reality surrounding the true Universal God Source (All That Is), of which your Soul is actually a fragment, just as you are a fragment of your Soul.

Now add to this the fact that your Soul, which is cast out as part of a cadre or Soul group, is working in conjunction with other Souls known to it, all of which are residing at the Twelfth Sublevel of the Third Universal Dimension. It becomes clear that as it pertains to the planning of the lifetimes of its various fragments, a Soul will rely on its brethren to plan possible interactions placed along the Dimensional timeline for the purpose of continual growth through these relationships.

It is quite possible and common as an example, that a Soul will plan in conjunction with another Soul the casting out of individual fragments where one Soul's fragment is to be the child and the other Soul's fragment is to be the parent. In doing so, the two Souls plan a karmic exchange for the fragments they have cast out that brings the entities, and ultimately both Souls, growth.

For instance, one Soul plans a lifetime as a child with severe disabilities, while the other plans to be a single parent. The Soul fragment acting as parent may, in another related lifetime, have had the experience of being callous and inhumane and that fragment may have abandoned its children in the related lifetime. Balancing the Karma generated by the callous condition in the related lifetime may be the core purpose of the arrangement, with the mission being to reestablish emotional centering and balance for that entity.

Naturally the scenarios are endless, with the overriding aim of either balancing karma generated by other entities of the Soul or creating opportunities for Soul growth through the choices made around various life events. It is also clear that as a co-creation (or co-creator with your Soul as it were) and as an independent entity, the lifetime created has complete Free Will to make the choices it prefers.

In a manner of speaking, the system of Karma or energetic balancing is a fool proof one, allowing not only full balancing of the Soul's energy but also growth from a 360-degree perspective. Because there is no right or wrong avenue to consciousness growth but merely different means of growth stemming from the choices made, every situation and emotion is completely explored by the Soul. Free will at this level does not alter the full Soul growth inherent in any given life situation from any particular lifetime, and only makes the manner in which the growth is derived different depending upon the individual lifetime.

This system is also dynamic and happening independent of linear time constraints, so the choices made and the experiences undergone reverberate backwards and forwards across the timeline, throughout the Dimensional Sublevels and within the individual lifetimes of a Soul's fragments. Choices made in one lifetime can have consequence for other lifetimes created by the Soul in the linear future as well as in the linear past. Of course these lifetimes are all occurring simultaneously on the dimensional timeline no matter what the linear date measurement is as we have explained. This does not alter the fact that Free Will has an important impact on not only your own growth, but the growth of your sibling lifetimes and ultimately your Soul as well. Similarly, choices made by other lifetimes at any given point on the timeline may have direct impact on your own circumstances and the events attracted into your current life. This becomes an important consideration.

Returning to our example of two Souls creating a lifetime as a parent and a child, once the agreement has been reached, through the act of physical procreation within the Third Sublevel of the Dimension the Soul will inhabit and ultimately animate the physical biological vehicle when it chooses to do so. This happens at a time the Soul alone selects, and it does so by way of an ethereal or energetic body that it forms around and within the cellular structure of the newly formed biological entity.

The Soul does this by fusing its energy into Beingness by means of the scalar waves generated by the biological structure. It is not by accident that your physical body has a heart which pumps in a bi-dynamic way. The bi-polar nature of the flow of blood through the body, and its return back into the heart and lungs, actually creates a scalar energy field -- the true "Chi" (Ki, Qi or Prana) of life -- and the Soul uses this energy field to interface and fuse its ethereal or energetic body into the cellular structure of the physical person.

The Soul also uses DNA to inform the physical body's creation, traits and attributes, not to mention any pre-selected traits it desires that may be needed to provide specific opportunities for growth during the lifetime. It is always possible for the Soul to plan a lifetime based on the physical, inherent genetic traits that your parents or ancestors carry, or based on the environmental factors surrounding the lifetime involved. In some cases these things are specific to the agreements made between Souls.

DNA provides a form of communication between your Soul and your physical body with respect to its physical creation, and it is also a vital means of communication between you and your Soul throughout the lifetime. This is because DNA acts as a two-way antennae providing your physical being with Soul instruction and secondarily creating a method for you to communicate your body's physical and even emotional condition back to your Soul. This is also why DNA can change and evolve over time. In other terms, this is the reason genes can be said to suddenly express themselves at a particular moment during the lifetime, or, just as spontaneously, go dormant again.

Your DNA is constantly messaging your Soul via its vibrational signature with respect to both your emotional and your physical state within the "Now" of reality. It also informs your Soul, and the Universe generally, of any conscious intentions you are creating based on your thoughts, beliefs or emotions that act as general instructions being given by you concerning any alterations, changes or additions you would like to make to your reality via manifestation in your physical state. These "finishing touches" are always based on Free Will initiatives derived from your inner world or from the emerging events taking place in the mass consciousness backdrop of your reality. Finally, DNA can send and receive a vibrational signature to those around you, a signature that not only informs changes in your physical traits and appearance from day-to-day but also subconsciously (or consciously these days when your DNA is mapped) identifies who you are to others.

We understand that the actual moment when a biological structure is fused with Soul energy and becomes a "life" is a matter of much contention and endless conversation in your world. Unfortunately, it is not possible to precisely determine a specific moment when the Soul inhabits what has been physically created since each Soul enters the physical body at its own discretion and when it feels the need or necessity to do so. This can happen at conception but can just as easily happen immediately following physical birth, if at all.

As an example, generally there are times when a Soul that is rambunctious and truly wishing to participate in a particular lifetime with these parents for a specific life mission, will fuse itself almost at conception. However, there are other times when a Soul will hold back and not infuse itself into the fetus until moments before the birth takes place. Sometimes this union is made just after physical birth has occurred.

Usually, the Soul's energetic union with the body is possible as soon as the fetus heartbeat begins about 10 to 15 days after conception, despite the fact that the body's circulatory system is not yet functioning and therefore the energetic scalar waves that we have described are not fully present. Though it is a generalization, the Soul's energy will ebb and flow in and out of the infant's body while in the womb and complete fusion of the two is not one hundred percent complete until at the time of physical birth.

Thus, most Souls choose to come and go prior to actual birth, becoming more and more present as time goes on and actual birth becomes imminent. You may be aware of mothers who when questioned are acutely aware of a presence in the womb almost from conception, while others don't truly feel this until a specific interval sometime during the pregnancy. Still others, if they were honest, would tell you they have no sense of a true presence until the moment of birth or immediately following it. All of this is dependent upon the Soul's choice and the moment it definitively infuses itself into the physical life form.

In general however, it should be noted that unless there is some difficulty with the physical structure of the infant that warrants the Soul to disengage, or if there is some karmic plan for Soul growth of the parent or child being carried out, most Souls are somewhat present within the physical cellular structure fairly early in a pregnancy. And for those that do not, fusion is always within moments of physical birth at the least.

Regarding this, the controversy over what is termed "abortion" arises, and without any judgment intended we would certainly confirm with you that generally sentient life when imbued with the energy of a Soul is sacred and valuable. However, we qualify this by using the phrase "imbued with the energy of a Soul." Because the time at which there is full cellular fusion of a Soul with the biological Being is dependent on the Soul itself, we would also suggest that the Soul is fully aware of these interactions since it has the ability to enter or not enter the fetus at anytime from conception to immediately following birth.

The Soul is also well aware which fetus will come to term and which will not be suitable or viable for its purposes. In other words, the issue of who will parent whom and the purpose of the lifetime is usually well arranged between Souls at the highest levels of the Dimension prior to the lifetime. Therefore, a Soul will not enter or fuse its energy within a physical structure at any point during pregnancy if the physical life of the child is known by the Soul not to be viable. Such would be the case in a parent's voluntary termination of a pregnancy.

Now to be clear, there are instances when, for karmic or growth purposes, a Soul will enter a physical body that will not be physically viable for the long term knowing full well that termination of the pregnancy is expected prior to actual physical birth. This is precisely the case when miscarriage or stillbirth occurs. These situations however, tend to be rare occasions that usually serve the purpose of karmic balance or consciousness growth for either the entity being born, the parents or both. Interestingly enough, almost every such case is in conjunction with a Soul well known to the entities participating, and these miscarried children usually will communicate or meet up again with their parents once all are together again in the higher Astral planes.

For the most part, these cases are karmic or growth scenarios related to the parent, in particular the mother. The degree to which a Soul has fused into the physical body of the child before departing physical existence can be measured in the degree of difficulty the parents experience through such an (seemingly) involuntary event. In rare cases, there are instances where a miscarriage or stillbirth may result even if a Soul has already inhabited the physical body. This occurs if the Soul has determined that the physical body of the child will not be viable for conducting the chosen mission.

An example of this might be the case of a potential parent, through Free Will, taking actions (such as an addicted mother or one given a pharmaceutical causing extreme birth defects) that cause the physical body of the child to become unstable or unusable for the Soul's mission in that lifetime. Again, this is very rare since usually these instances take place with the full knowledge and acceptance of all Souls involved.

Or even more rare but possible is the case where the incoming Soul decides it would prefer to experience its life mission at a different point on the dimensional timeline, or in a different way. This is sometimes the case with someone who has had a miscarriage previously, but successfully carries a child to term thereafter. Such experiences are almost always the original Soul coming through the mother again at a different time interval for specific reasons based on the need to have certain required relationships or environmental events available to it.

Those events may have shifted on the timeline and the Soul will attempt to place the entity within closer proximity to them in order to provide better opportunities for success of the intended mission in that lifetime. An example of this would be a Soul planning on growth through participation as a medical professional in a time of crisis or war. Obviously, it would not be ideal if the war or crisis occurred at a time when the entity was either too old or too young to participate in the opportunities created, should the event have been modified and changed on the probable timeline trajectory. Since dimensional timelines are dynamic and major events that take place on them are subject to shifting sometimes, modification of the Soul's plans are also in order.

As a general rule however, it should be remembered that in all instances, physical procreation generally takes place as a result of a choice by all the Souls involved. There are no real accidents here and although Free Will is important and has merit, your choices, while important, are not as impactful as you may feel they are since many of the circumstances are already known in advance to all Souls involved. This is particularly true pertaining to the overriding plans and mission the Soul wishes to participate in for the purposes of Soul growth within the designated lifetime.

A special note should also be made here in the understanding that generally young children who pass from almost any cause, whether it be disease, genetic consequences or accidents, always do so in order to bring the parents and loved ones substantial opportunities for growth through the loss of that beloved child. This is generally true up to the beginning of the early teenage years, and all young people that depart before adulthood (defined as later teens and beyond) have planned their early departure in conjunction with their Souls prior to birth into the physical reality. These entities are almost always older Souls of the highest consciousness, participating with Souls in their cadre to assist continued consciousness growth of other Souls. Generally, such lifetimes are orchestrated by Souls preparing to cycle off further incarnations on the dimensional timeline, and these Souls choose to create unique and non-karmic growth opportunities for those around them one last time before ascending to the next Universal Dimension.

The process of a Soul manifesting in a newly physical form is a miraculous one and a unique experience. No matter what point of fetal development the Soul chooses to fuse with the entity's physical body however, it cannot be denied that it is a process that can be wrought with difficulty as well. First of all, the condensing of enormous Soul energy into the tiny confined space of a physical body is something of a trial to say the least. As we have said you are spiritual Beings having a physical experience rather than chiefly physical Beings having spiritual moments, and nowhere is this reflected more than in the actual energetic fusing and animating of the physical body at birth.

In truth the departure of the Soul's energy from the body is far easier, and it is for this reason that the information you may have heard brought back from those that have passed from physical form either through what is termed "near-death" or those that have communicated via persons gifted with this ability, describes the great expansiveness that is felt in shedding the physical body. A Soul's energy is greatly diminished and shrunk down during the physical lifetime, and it expands exponentially as soon as the physical limitations of the body are no longer present.

The actual physics of a Soul's energy entering the physical incarnation is something your scientists will someday be able to register and eventually map. In essence, this energetic process can be measured, and the closest facsimile is found in what is experienced when inside an energy vortex. In fact, the ability to measure the precise moment a Soul enters physical form, which will be discovered in the future, will eliminate any discussion about whether or not a fetus is sentient or not.

A physical representation of this energy vortex would appear to you as a tornado around the physical body, where the upper part is wide and the lower part narrows and energetic force is funneled into the crown chakra down into the body to the root chakra. This analogy is a close visual proximity of what you would see if you could witness the Soul's fusion with the physical body that starts at the physical body's crown, funnels life force down through the physical being, and eventually grounds it into the Earth.

As always, this "tornado" of energy is a two way street, and Kundalini energy is energy returned up through the energetic flow allowing the greatest connection to the Soul when activated. Naturally, this is only a crude representation to stress the magnitude of energy being funneled into the physical body. Please be aware that within the body, the energetic flow tends to be more hemispheric in nature, spiraling within the physical structure and through the chakras in a more measured, circular, spinning motion.

Whether or not a Soul has fully inhabited the physical body prior to birth, generally the time of birth is the time when the full energy to be invested by the Soul floods into the physical body of the infant. Sometimes, this energy crescendo actually serves as the catalyst for propulsion that begins contractions, pushes the child into the birth canal and begins labor for the mother. While there is no right or wrong physical birthing process, Caesarean birth and, in certain ways, the administering of overly potent anesthetics, can hinder the ability of the Soul to infuse and complete its energy transfer within the cellular structure of the child.

Although this will always be successfully accomplished by the Soul in the long run, it does cause delay and prolong the process somewhat. It is for this reason that care should be given to the choices selected, and many of these methods should be minimally employed whenever possible.

The same is true in reverse when the Soul's energy departs the physical body at the time of death. While it is indeed humane to prevent excessive suffering, the extreme use of Opioids to prevent pain or panic in those preparing for physical passage in death can prolong the Soul's energetic departure from the physical body's cellular structure immediately just before and following death. This has a dulling effect on the Soul's ability to quickly propel itself out of the physical body into the Astral Sublevel.

It also prevents the entity from retaining the conscious awareness it needs as the death passage proceeds. As we discussed earlier, this dulling effect hinders the ability to remember your true power within the death process or fully understand how to quickly effectuate creating an energetic environment pleasant to the entity as it emerges from physical existence into the Fourth Dimensional Sublevel.

While the physical trauma that is experienced by both the mother and the child during the birthing process is noticeably substantial, it is in fact not as dramatic in some sense as the condensing of a Soul's energy and placement of that energy into the physical being when the Soul fully enters the body and the real spark of life is created. Returning to our analogy, envision the tornado we discussed with its wide energy circulating at the top spiraling down into a pinhole. Elongate this funnel and add a golden or silver cord of light coming from the base of the tornado and connecting it to what appears as a pinhole in the crown of the individual. Now you are envisioning the permanent electromagnetic energetic impulse that communicates with your DNA (and your DNA with it) creating a corded life connection between your Soul and you. Many of you will recognize this life thread as the silver or golden cord from spiritual teachings that is always present linking the physical body with the Soul throughout the lifetime.

While there are many means of communicating with the Soul, via the DNA, via the cellular structure of the body, via your intentions, beliefs and thoughts, particularly as it regards your physical condition, and via your manifestation of events in physical reality, the silver cord that connects the Soul and the physical body comes into full existence at the time of birth and remains intact lifelong. In fact, during times of sleep the cord retains its connection to the physical being but allows an expansive release of the Soul's energy via the ethereal or energetic body into the Astral Sublevels of the Dimension in order to allow you to experiment with various life scenarios and possible events within the Dreamscape.

This cord is only severed in the Third Dimensional Sublevel when the body ceases to function at the time of an individual's physical death. The Soul's energy will recede up the cord pulling with it the ethereal or energetic body until all Soul energy has fully receded from the body and transferred itself to the ethereal body of the individual. This process can be immediate or it can take time depending upon the level or state of the individual's consciousness as well as the individual's physical and emotional condition at the time of death.

Withdrawal of the Soul's energy in unanticipated or traumatic deaths, such as with accidents or unforeseen events, tends to be abrupt and immediate, while those related to illness or age usually allow the Soul to withdraw partially even as the physical body continues to function. Thus, though the departure in these cases is more gradual it is nearly complete by physical death. The consciousness of individuals experiencing dementia or the disease known as Alzheimer's recedes bit by bit over a long period of time, and the loss of awareness and cognition by these individuals is actually the consciousness of that person coming and going at intervals, with it being more gone than not by the end of life.

Some ancient cultures estimated that a minimum three-day period was needed in order to allow the complete withdraw of Soul energy from the physical body. Other cultures and practices estimated that by disposing of the physical body immediately, the ethereal or energetic body (represented to most as spirits, shades or ghosts) would not be able to reenter the physical structure and return, which it was hoped would provide the spirit of those who had passed with the incentive to begin their journey to the next world.

Whatever the cultural belief with regard to the nature or timing of the Soul's energetic departure from the body, what is important to know is that the "cord" detaches from the physical body but always remains attached to the ethereal or energetic body as it leaves the physical structure and transmigrates to the Astral plane (Fourth Dimensional Sublevel). It is precisely in this manner that the link between your consciousness and your Soul is never lost or severed, even when your consciousness has receded completely from physical life and is no longer attached to your physical body.

When the physical lifetime begins, the traits and attributes the Soul chose to experience begin formulation. These psychological parameters are generally put in place by a combination of factors, including parents and the environment of the child. Once fully formed, these parameters will serve as the "glasses" through which the individual sees life, and the beliefs and thought patterns constructed based on them generate a vibrational resonance that is not only the way in which the person sees life, but also the manner in which life events and relationships become magnetic to the individual.

As we have said in the past, there may be alterations but there are very few accidents with respect to the Soul's planned mission in the lifetime. The Soul is always careful to create, usually through childhood or life events, the personal attributes and traits needed by the individual so that specific parameters are in place. This essentially sets the stage, vibrationally speaking, to allow the individual to attract the best growth opportunities during the lifetime that are conducive to the individual and the Soul accomplishing its mission, and, as a consequence, its Soul growth. This is true no matter what effort on the part of the lifetime these events might entail.

Attributes and personality features of an individual lifetime are highly tuned towards generating the vibration that will attract the necessary growth opportunities and life lessons that permit the Soul's mission to be of most success. This is true whether they are related to karmic balancing or the desire for specific events, relationships, lessons or situations that provide continual consciousness growth throughout the lifetime. It is for this reason as well that individuals are almost always vested with the innate desire to discover who they are and, equally, their life purpose. It is also the reason that the ancient admonishment to "know thyself" is such an important concept, even if it is not a prerequisite to the successful accomplishing of one's life or Soul mission.

We would be remiss if we did not add to this conversation a brief reminder of polarity, as we have already discussed, and the understanding that in the Third Universal Dimension, polarity is a fundamental energetic factor. You now understand that a life or Soul mission can be accomplished from either the positive or the negative polarity, and your Soul is not concerned with which way you choose through your consciousness and Free Will to accomplish the mission in the lifetime – be it through related positive events or through negative, challenging ones. As an example of this we have used in the past, if a Soul identifies the mission to learn from lessons of love for a particular lifetime, the nature of polarity means that it is possible to learn about love through involvement in tender and loving situations, or through their polar opposite, hateful, difficult ones.

If you recall that good, bad, right and wrong are subjective perspectives based on cultural or personal standards; these standards have no real meaning for your Soul. Therefore, if your life mission is to learn lessons of love, you are free to have those lessons through whatever polarity suits you, positive or negative, based on your traits, attributes and the level of your consciousness around that particular subject or events. In other words, you are able to learn about love through loving relationships and events just as easily as you can learn about love through hateful, difficult experiences, the opposite pole of the same coin.

What is important here is to recognize the polarity of your experience and "know" thyself in terms of your beliefs and the way in which you see the world. In addition, understanding why you feel a certain way or have inner belief patterns around certain issues and recognizing how to consciously change your vibrational output by changing those thought patterns and beliefs is the means to affecting whether your life lessons are made manifest in your reality from the positive or negative pole. Thus, knowing the traits and thought patterns created in your childhood and confronting them, which allows you to alter those patterns consciously as an adult, will help you to not only understand which issues are related to your life lesson, but also help you better control what events and situations come into your physical reality. This unveils the real reason knowing yourself is a priceless adage of ageless wisdom and a principal means of enlightenment.

Since our present discussion regards the Soul's interaction with the physical birth and death process, we will not here discuss how or why a Soul chooses a specific life mission, or what those missions might be. At best, those discussions are highly individual and though generalities are sometimes possible, for the most part these are particular to the Soul, the karmic interface and the growth needs of the Soul within the lifetime it has planned.

However, you should be aware that a lifetime is structured in such a way that there is commonality with the events and mass consciousness being experienced on the dimensional timeline. We would further add that the manner in which life is generated has a great deal to do with your vibrational resonance and, as a consequence, your vibrational attraction.

Baby and Younger Souls, beginning incarnations in a Universal Dimension that have not had many physical lifetime experiences, as an example, will tend to have more highly charged, emotional, challenging lifetimes that are intricately interwoven with others and are externally karmic in nature. Older Souls on the other hand who are already present in the Universal Dimension and have had numerous life cycles tend to have more neutral and positive experiences based on their consciousness and experience with physical reality.

This is not always the norm, and there are always Baby and Younger Souls whose conscious awareness is higher and who have blissful lifetimes. However, more often than not, Younger and lower levels of consciousness by virtue of physical reality inexperience typically attract events, situations and people into an individual's life that are more problematic and often challenging, operating as they most likely do from the negative polarity of reality manifestation.

This is a good opportunity to clear up any misunderstanding you might have concerning Soul age. We have already discussed that a Soul enters the Twelfth Sublevel of each Dimension in order to generate fragments that go on to experience lifetimes at the physical Sublevel of the Universal Dimension, and informed you that the Soul's vibration is essentially pure and unfettered as a fragment of All That Is. However, the Souls that are cast out, and their corresponding fragments and associated lifetimes, can be said to have an "age" based on their level of consciousness obtained through their experiences and progression through the Universal Dimension.

In other words, not all Soul cadres or groups are cast out at the same time from Source, and therefore their progress through the

Universal Dimensions can vary. Nor do different cadres or Soul groups reach Ascension within a Dimension at the same time. Thus as an example, you might have a Soul that is new to the Third Universal Dimension creating lifetimes on the dimensional timeline that take place at the same time that a Soul that has been in the system for a much longer period and has reintegrated and assimilated many of the lifetimes it created already.

Such assimilation of its lifetimes is always a means for the Soul to grow in consciousness, and Soul Growth then becomes the basis of what we call Soul age within a Universal Dimension. The Soul's consciousness levels are naturally imparted to the consciousness of its fragments, so that in the same way karmic balancing reverberates from lifetime to lifetime within a Wheel of Creation. The Soul's ongoing consciousness growth through assimilation of fragment lifetimes reverberates back through the lifetimes still being explored in physical reality.

Now for the most part, the fragment lifetimes of a newly minted Soul might be leading lives at the same point on the dimensional timeline as the fragment lifetimes of another Soul that has been creating incarnations much longer, and this gap is the basis for Soul age. In this example, the lifetimes of the newly minted Soul could be said to be Baby Souls, whereas the lifetimes of Souls slightly older would be considered Young Souls. Those Souls that have greater experiences and have assimilated more lifetime experiences from their Wheels of Creation could be called Mature Souls. Finally, a Soul that has been in the Universal Dimension longest, and is almost ready to cycle off to a Higher Universal Dimension by the next Solar or Galactic Ascension interval would be referred to as an Old Soul.

To be clear then, Soul age is not something that is applicable to the

Soul from Universal Dimension to Universal Dimension, although it is clear that the more Universal Dimensions a Soul has experienced through its Wheels of Creation, the higher the consciousness and the older that Soul can be said to be. However, because Soul age is more appropriately measured within the dimensional timeline (the Galactic Ascension cycle of approximately 260,000 years) it is experiencing, it is more appropriate to consider a Soul newly arrived in any Dimension as a "Baby" Soul, and the Soul preparing to cycle to the next Universal Dimension as an "Old" Soul. In this way, the Old Soul who cycles from one Dimension to the next becomes the Baby Soul in the next Universal Dimension, and so on and so forth.

A good way to envision this might be to see your reality and current timeline as a one-room School House, where students of all ages are together learning at different speeds and in various ways. In addition, quite appropriately we would add, the students in that School House tend to segregate according to common age and interest, although each is aware at all times that different ages are housed together and have a common bond based on their schooling.

It is for this reason that, as we have discussed often, Baby and Young Souls can be living side by side in physical reality with Mature and Older Souls. These interactions create vast opportunities for growth scenarios relative to all Souls working through physical incarnations. Nowhere is this more obvious than in your world today, where Baby and Young Souls are living along side Older Souls and those younger Souls will most probably remain in Third Dimensional incarnations after the current Galactic Ascension period has concluded.

Similarly, as is often the case, a majority of Mature Souls will choose to continue incarnating within the Dimension after the Ascension cycle is complete in order to be of service and assistance to the younger groups for the purpose of their own Soul growth. Ascension is always a matter of choice, and these Souls will choose to continue creating Wheels of Creation until such time as all lifetimes have been assimilated and the next Galactic Ascension cycle allows Ascension into the next Universal Dimension.

Older Souls however, will usually finish up all lifetimes in their Wheels on the current dimensional timeline and will choose to prepare for Ascension. It is for this reason that currently great numbers are choosing to pass from physical lifetimes through large-scale mass events such as pandemic, natural disaster catastrophe or global war. Preparation for the current Galactic Ascension cycle means that this has already been transpiring for over the past one hundred years and will continue until the Ascension cycle is complete approximately one hundred fifty to two hundred years from now. Once the Ascension of these Older Souls is complete, they will become the next wave of Baby Souls generating cycles of incarnation in a higher Universal Dimension and consciousness level.

Another common misconception that we would like to dispel before moving on is with regard to the manner with which a Soul projects its energy into physical reality through its fragment lifetimes. This misunderstanding is two fold. First it is related to the notion that the Soul has a same or similar look or personality that it simply imbues into every lifetime, or that each lifetime is the exact same reflection of that Soul. Although there are minor similarities between the lifetimes a Soul is creating, just as there are siblings that might share some common traits with each other or their parents, in the end, each lifetime is distinct and has a unique personality.

Certain Soul attributes, such as the orientation of a Soul's origin with regard to Service-to-Others or Service-to-Self are indeed carried over for each lifetime the Soul manifests and this does not change. In addition, there is the energetic archetype of the Soul that is its truest energetic expression derived as part of its origins. The energetic Soul archetype does in fact have an influence on the fragment and is consistent in each lifetime planned by the Soul in every cycle or Wheel of Creation.

However, even with these commonalities each lifetime is a unique combination of traits and attributes -- genetic, emotional, environmental and otherwise -- that the Soul is seeking to compile with the greatest diversity it can in order to provide distinct opportunities for growth as necessitated by the Soul. In much the same way that a child exhibits distinctive personality traits from very early on, so too a Soul fragment may have distinctive characteristics based on vague memories of where it comes from.

Sometimes these memories include other lifetimes of the Soul in the same cycle, and this brings us to the second misconception we are discussing. You have no doubt heard stories concerning children, especially entities connected to Older Souls that have distinct memories of lifetimes other than their own. These generally occur before the child has developed its own personality, and some child psychologists or esoteric teachers are quick to suggest that these are derived from their past life memories.

In fact, these children are having spontaneous flashes or reality bleed-through from other lifetimes related to them and linked to them by virtue of their Souls' cycles of lives within their own Wheel of Creation. The reason we consider this a misconception is the fact that if you believe the child's remembrance to be their own past life you must also believe that time proceeds in a linear fashion and the child is reincarnated from the former lifetime that it is remembering. This egocentric methodology also places the person or child at the center of their journey, and far too often makes the current lifetime the predominate one.

This understanding is not correct. First of all, though you experience the measure of time as linear, time is actually a spiral wave that defines the current Dimension. Thus, having one lifetime followed by another in linear fashion is not possible. Secondly, the memories and impressions being received are impulses coming through to the child from the Soul and the numerous lifetimes from within the Soul's reincarnation Wheel or cycle of which the child is part. Because the current lifetime personality has not become solidified as yet, the child is merely experiencing bleed-through from other lifetimes within its cycle.

The Soul, through the various corded lifetimes that are linked to it, does in fact provide a degree of information to each lifetime in a particular cycle simultaneously despite the fact that it may seem as though the lifetimes are transpiring on a linear timeline. And it is interesting to note that those sensitive adults who have images or impressions of so called "past lives" in either the Dreamscape or under hypnosis, even aches and pains not related to themselves, are actually having the same bleed-through experiences that the child in our example is having. Again these are impressions, memories and karmic interactions coming from other connected lifetimes in the Soul's Wheel of Creation of which you are part. These are all taking place in real time, not in linear fashion, which is also why they can seem so vibrant, real and, at times, emotionally daunting to the perceiver.

For these very reasons, we prefer using the term Wheels of Creation or reincarnated selves instead of perpetuating a definition of Reincarnation that refers to the same individual or personality returning again and again in a linear fashion. This is truly one of the most important misconceptions concerning Reincarnation of the Soul that exists today. Technically, the Soul's Wheels of Creation revolve not so much around the concept of Reincarnation, but around the concept of linked incarnations, or lifetimes created by a Soul in a cyclical manner with the various incarnations energetically connected one to the other to a greater or lesser extent. This is a truer representation of what Reincarnation actually is, which we would further define as the "re-incarnating" of a Soul at many intervals within various interconnected Wheels of Creation during a specific Ascension period within a Universal Dimension.

This also becomes important in terms of understanding death, or more specifically how life energy recedes from the physical body at the time of its passing. Just as a child comes into the world as we have already analyzed by means of the Soul funneling its energy down through the crown chakra into the physical body, so when a person who is ready for passage from physical life the Soul must retire its energy in the opposite direction. In addition, just as the child relied on the Soul's energy to originate it by fusion of itself energetically, and just as the Soul has orchestrated a plan for creating the child's traits, attributes and environment in order to provide the necessary opportunities for growth, the Soul is also responsible and has planned for the lifetime's physical ending.

For the current moment let's simply discuss those occasions when a full lifetime has transpired and the Soul is ready to withdraw from the physical being. In such a case, as opposed to speaking of those instances where a Soul recedes from the physical body unexpectedly or through traumatic events, the individual lifetime comes to a close over a period of time and there are instances towards the end of life that indicate the Soul's energy is preparing to recede and bring about physical death.

It is important to understand that death is never accidental whether it is undertaken at the end of a long life, through illness and disease or even when related to so-called accidental or traumatic events. Prior to generating the lifetime within the Wheels of Creation, a Soul identifies specific opportunities within the dimensional timeline that it may, if it so chooses at any given point, use to exit. Because of the interface with Free Will, these are not to be confused with predestined moments but rather should be considered road signs for the Soul as well as the life fragment that, if desired, this or that event or occurrence is available for use by the individual as a "jumping off" point. Though most will turn a conscious blind eye and prefer not to recognize such signs, particularly since the Ego will always struggle for survival of the physical, biological and mental structure, the Soul, together with the individual, nevertheless has awareness as to how, why and when physical death may be achieved.

We use the term "may be achieved" since, as we mentioned, there are numerous possibilities and options created on the timeline by the Soul in order to do so. Free Will also interacts in these decisions and can come into play. Those who are intuitive, sensitive or have what you term psychic talents have been known to report that individuals seen days to weeks prior to their passing tend to have a reduction of their energetic spark that is particularly noticeable in their energetic or auric fields. Some will describe an absence of energy spiraling around the chakras, a general reduction of light around the individual's physical body and the diminishing or dulling of colors in and around the individual's aura.

With regard to large-scale traumatic incidents such as a plane crash, a building fire or other disaster where many intend to take the opportunity to release from the physical body, that same intuitive can see whole groups of individuals whose auric fields have diminished to the point that they are tinged in a kind of grey cloud. This is so because, as we have stated, for the most part at the Soul level these individuals have been preparing in advance to use the mass event as a means of leaving the physical body behind them. Again while there are numerous opportunities for such separation from physical reality, it should be realized that these are not events orchestrated by a vengeful or inconsiderate God figure as so many believe, but rather chosen at the Soul level by the individuals themselves for their own purposes of growth or, at times, purposes of growth related to loved ones or even the entire community as a whole.

This is a natural part of the withdrawal process as the Soul's energy prepares for departure from the physical body, and is the case whether speaking of traumatic and instantaneous occurrences or following prolonged occurrence such as with disease or illness. Clearly the individual's energetic body is beginning to retire, and life energy is beginning to be pulled back by the Soul's cord in much the same way energy flows in the opposite direction into a child being born into physical reality.

This energy reduction and receding can begin at any time. For those individuals who have planned with their Souls a longer physical life, in some cases the "Chi" will begin to slowly recede from the physical body's energy systems as early as halfway through the lifetime. In such a case, the retiring of energy is gradual overtime and follows the pace of aging of the physical structure. At other times such as with accidental death or traumatic experiences, the energy withdrawal can be immediate. It is also interesting to note that energy withdrawal can even take place just before the moment of death, as in the case of an imminent accident or trauma.

The Soul pulls back its energy completely in these cases so that in some ways it could be said that in case of imminent physical failure the consciousness of the person has already departed just before the actual physical moment of death. There is no need to explain that in this way extreme trauma to the individual and consciousness is lessened by premature departure. This is usually to prevent any additional energetic balancing necessitated from the trauma, particularly if the trauma is not relevant to the Soul's lifetime mission.

Weaning of Soul energy follows the pattern of entry into the body only in reverse, flowing back up through the chakras, releasing itself from the physical body's organs and nervous system, moving up through the Kundalini energy structure, ultimately following the energetic cord as it retires through the crown chakra. As this energy departs, the body's organs and systems fail, with the brain being the last organ to fail as energy exits the crown. The ethereal or energetic body, which remains permanently attached to the Soul's energy cord, follows the flow of energy as it is pulled by the chord up through the chakras, eventually exiting the crown chakra as final death occurs.

This retiring of energy is the very reason that at the moment of death, as retold by those that have had what are described as "near-death" experiences, individuals first experience a sense of exiting and floating or hovering above the physical body, usually in the same body but a much lighter and mobile version. This is the ethereal body.

The experience is usually followed by the sensation that their energy is whooshing through a tunnel of light, as they are pulled forward through a tunnel similar to being pulled through the birthing canal at physical birth. This is in fact based on the actual sensation of the ethereal body being pulled along by the Soul's cord only in the opposite direction from birth. It is also indicative of the ethereal body transmigrating into a higher and lighter vibrational level as the individual's energy consolidates in its new energy body and emerges into the lower Astral plane or the Fourth Sublevel of the Third Universal Dimension.

What is most important to understand here is that even though the physical lifetime has come to an end there is no real ending for the individual's consciousness or its associated personality. By way of the etheric body, the individual's journey and transmigration through the higher levels of the Astral planes will now begin as a healing reintegration process with the Soul's energy. This is accomplished through guidance, at a pace particular to the individual entity in conjunction with all the reintegration of other lifetimes that the Soul has lived in the Universal Dimension.

It is unfortunate that the process of death and dying, particularly as it relates to your journey immediately following death, remains one of the most mysterious and misunderstood experiences known to humanity. In large part this is due to misinterpretations and, in some cases, efforts to mislead individuals outright with respect to the death process. Modern society has chosen to isolate death and the dying process from life, and as a result death has become a fear for most rather than a natural progression and facet of life that can be mapped and understood.

To be fair, your inability to "see" higher Dimensional Sublevels has much to do with the continued mystery surrounding death. In the past however, cultures and societies did at least make genuine attempts to incorporate a conscious effort into the pre-death process, at times making the death and dying process a participatory effort for family, friends and even the community at large. Your memorializing efforts, though well intentioned and many times attended by the Etheric body of the deceased, are of no real assistance to the actual process of dying since they are enacted after the fact. In some ancient cultures, as an example, Shamans, professionals, families, friends and the community helped pave the way for the dying individual through constant prayers, vigil and meditation meant to increase the vibrational resonance and thereby open unseen channels between the Dimensional Sublevels. This opening facilitates the withdrawal of the Soul's energy from the physical body and its passage into the Fourth Dimensional Sublevel.

Of greatest importance here is the understanding that physical death is a process that is completely natural and it *DOES NOT END* the true existence of a created entity. Doubting this even slightly only adds to an individual's general confusion at the time of death. Conscious remembrance of this fact on the other hand will actually aid in the transformation of the entity's energy from one vehicle to another. It should be noted also that the act of physical death heralds the passage into a metaphysical and vibrational state that is far more natural than the one in the physical body and this is applicable to every individual.

In speaking of the moment of death it is important also to understand the makeup of the spiritual vehicle, what we have called the etheric or energetic body, which transcends and transmigrates your consciousness into the higher Sublevels of the Universal Dimension. Healthcare professionals and in particular nurses who are familiar with situations involving the passing from life of individuals know to continue speaking with the deceased for some time even after death.

This is an honorable practice and rightfully so, since the individual who has just passed is in fact still able to hear and understand what is happening even if they are not able to respond. In fact for those who experience confusion at passing, it is actually comforting to the individual and helps them understand and become conscious of what is happening to them, as well as what to do next. Audibly ensuring someone who has just passed away that all is well, and even informing them of what has happened to them and what they should remember is of great service to the deceased individual immediately following physical death.

We have often said that while in physical incarnation various energetic bodies make up the Being you really are. Dissecting the union of these energetic elements, which actually are unified as one, can assist a better understanding of how a Soul animates physical existence. It can also assist in understanding how this same energy is withdrawn from the physical body.

For convenience sake, let us separate these energies with you again into three distinct structures that are part of physical life. First is the Etheric body, which is essentially represented by the central nervous system (the Kundalini), the body's major organs, which are aligned with the energetic chakras, and cellular structure and DNA. All of these have direct link back to the Soul through the Silver or Golden Cord we've described.

Unified with these are two additional energy structures, the Emotional body and the Mental body. The Emotional Structure operates through the Heart and Hormonal components of the body, while the Mental body operates through the Brain and Crown Chakra. Let there be no mistake that these energetic bodies are a unified unit, and separating them in this discussion is a matter of convenience for explaining the process of energetic withdrawal from the body.

At the final moment of physical death, the Etheric body has receded to the point where it has, for all intent and purpose, stepped outside of the physical being. Because it is the central energetic element connected to the Soul, it is considered the main energy body that continues into the higher Sublevels of the Dimension once the individual has passed from physical existence.

However, this is not to diminish the role of either the Emotional or the Mental body. Both the consciousness that you are, including the Ego and personality formed in the lifetime, and the "heartfelt" emotional make-up that defines you are pulled into the Etheric body at the time of death. Though these three bodies could be seen as operating separately during the course of the lifetime, at the time of passing all three become fused into the Etheric as it recedes carrying with it the spark of life as you know it.

Now the actual moment of fusion of these bodies can vary from individual to individual. For this reason sometimes there is a tendency for either the Emotional or the Mental body to "wander" prior to consolidation into the Etheric body and prior to entry into the next Dimensional Sublevel occurs. The bodies will always reunify at some point, and for the vast majority of individuals this happens simultaneously at the time of death.

But if there is considerable trauma at death, if the Ego (Mental body) is overly formed or if other natural physical or other attributes are present, before these energy bodies fuse completely, even if they have been pulled out of the physical body by the same Soul cord, it is possible for the Mental and Emotional body to take on their own momentum or life. This is almost always a temporary situation, although the time needed is different for each entity, and these phantom wandering energies are best known to you as the phenomenon identified as "ghosts."

These bodies can linger attached to their previously known physical environment until such time as actual fusion with the Etheric takes place. Once union is reestablished and the energetic bodies are unified once more, usually in a timely manner and sometimes almost immediately, the natural process of passing energetically into the higher Astral planes can take place. On rare occasions however, a disembodied Mental or Emotional phantom body can remain lodged in between the Third and Fourth Sublevels of the Dimension for some degree of time.

Of course these bodies usually discharge very quickly and rejoin the Etheric, and even though they are not fully situated in the Fourth Sublevel of the Dimension as yet, they have, by virtue of physical death, been placed at its door. For that reason they are considered to be "in" the Fourth Sublevel if not "of" it until they have joined into the Etheric and completely passed into the higher Astral plane. What is interesting to know however is that because the timeline is not linear and because each individual is allotted whatever period it needs to reconsolidate its energetic bodies, some entities can remain situated like this for what, in your measurement of time, may seem like decades to centuries.

The impression that those still living have that they are sensing the continued presence of a deceased person can relate to this, but can also be related to the fact that the individual that has passed is continuing on within a Sublevel Dimension that exists in close proximity to the physical one it has just left behind. With time however, this sensation fades, usually because the deceased individual has graduated to an even higher Sublevel of the Dimension.

This does not preclude the fact that those who have passed on are in fact able to hear and understand you, if they so choose, particularly if they are still present in a lower Sublevel of the Dimension that is closely related to your own. Such connections may be temporary or retained throughout an entire generation, but for the most part they recede as the entity journeys to higher Dimensional Sublevels. Naturally, these connections become less and less intense as the entity continues on towards reintegration with its Soul at higher Dimensional Sublevels.

Equally important concerning physical death is the fact that an individual's Spirit Guides and helpers, those Souls or Spirits who participate with you based on Soul connections and their own growth, work with you in physical life as well as in death. This is particularly true at the time of passage from physical life into the Astral planes, and more often than not these Spirit Guides will assist the dying by taking the form of a particular loved one or family member. Sometimes these guides will also take the form of a religious or other authority figure known and trusted by the individual in order to explain to them what has transpired and assist them with what steps to take next. At other times an actual loved one that has previously left the physical plane, especially one connected to the deceased through their Soul group who is still in close proximity to the lower Sublevels, will be present to assist the loved one in this same manner.

Left to its own devices, the process of dying is one that is natural and in the past was not overly fraught with the side effects you may witness in the contemporary world based on the hefty interference afforded you today by what is termed modern medicine. It must be remembered that for substantial periods prior to the actual passing, usually the Soul readies the physical body for the event despite the fact that the entity is not consciously aware of what is happening. The diminishing of Soul energy usually takes place gradually and well in advance of the actual moment of final departure from physical reality.

Unfortunately fear of the natural death process, the Ego's underlying mandate to protect biological life at all cost and the subsequent attempt to control or counter the onset of death, can lead to unintended complications for the process. The means sometimes used to do so can be jarring and invasive, not only to the physical body but also to the Etheric, Mental and Emotional bodies that may be receding naturally at the time. These methods can actually impede energetic departure from the cellular structure as the Soul transfers from physical life to the higher vibrational Etheric and interdimensional life platform.

It should be understood that while physical pain can be felt in the body up to the time of complete physical death, in most cases consciousness is waning and unless the pain is karmic in nature or offering specific growth to the individual it is generally subdued. The individual is usually not as conscious of the pain's intensity as might be normally felt, and this is augmented by the fact that the individual is actually spending less and less time present in the body proper and more and more time receding from physical life and, therefore, physical sensation.

While this is difficult to understand and runs counter to your current notions of compassion, pain generated in the body up until death is used not only to prepare the spiritual structure for separation from the physical body, but actually provides an energetic momentum for what is transpiring. In many ways therefore, pain of a certain kind hastens the entity's movement towards separation from the physical body.

Compassionate, correct doses of medication can and should be used to lessen pain but overly high doses of pain or opioid type medications to mask physical pain and deaden consciousness can, in many cases, prolong the pain it is attempting to lessen by drawing out passage from the physical body. This can also impede the momentum needed to sever the Etheric body's ties with the physical body, pull Soul energy from the organs and cellular structures and pull back or fuse itself with the Emotional and Mental Bodies, all of which makes it more difficult for an individual to pass.

Again, this is not to imply that some methods should not be administered or relief medications should not be used, particularly in the early stages of the process where pain can be substantial since it is intended to break any resolve for consciousness to remain housed in the body. Indeed, pain in this circumstance wears down organs and shuts down cellular functioning. However, in most cases the drugs and the various mechanical techniques used to prolong life as long as possible actually hinder the natural death process. In some cases the effects of medications, consciousness altering drugs and medical procedures can be so monumental and impactful they can actually keep the Etheric body, meaning the Soul's link, imprisoned in the body even when the physical structure is close to or ceasing to function.

The reason this is problematic is that these techniques interfere with the Etheric body's full retirement, prevent the Mental and Emotional Bodies from fusing with the Etheric, and block the Soul's energy from receding back up the cord and out of the cells, organs and associated chakras of the physical body. You might be surprised to know that often an individual overly drugged has out-of-body experiences, all while remaining closely connected to the physical body, in what could be described as an intoxicated (out-of-body) state. At a moment when being fully aware of what is happening and remaining lucid should be the greatest assets for navigating the death process, an intoxicated physical consciousness often spills over into the Spiritual and Etheric consciousness.

This is important because awareness and the awakening of consciousness in the new Sublevel Dimension at the time of passing is of utmost importance to recognizing quickly what has transpired so that the Soul can proceed to withdraw its life energy from the physical body and the individual consciousness can continue forward. As we mentioned, difficulty integrating the Mental and Emotional Bodies with the Etheric body or pulling these out of the physical structure by the Soul's cord through the crown chakra can mean the difference between these bodies wandering around independently after physical death and a successful entry into a new beginning in the lower Astral planes.

Let us now explore with you the journey immediately following departure from the physical body as one enters the Fourth Dimensional Sublevel of the Third Universal Dimension. That story leads us to the beginning of an individual's continuing non-corporeal transmigration as an entity moves through the Astral planes towards reintegration with their Soul.

Stories from a Soul's Wheel of Creation
The Story of Edward

Before he could even speak, Edward would hide his toys and clothes in every corner of the house so that no one could take them from him. He was so obsessed as a child with the idea that a sibling or some other family member might take his few personal belongings that he would fall into fits of crying that would last for days, much to the dismay and confusion of his parents.

As Edward grew up and became an adult the obsession that people around him were somehow going to "steal" what right-fully belonged to him turned into an outright phobia and mo-tivating force. The fear that he would one day lose everything he possessed preoccupied his every waking thought. That ob-session translated into severe anxiety, which kept him alienated and looking over his shoulder constantly trying to preempt the moves of anyone who got too close.

Since suspicion kept him on his toes it affected all aspects of life. Despite a modicum of success in business, he was con-stantly faced with financial and business losses that always seemed to fulfill his worst fears. As a result, he became ruthless in both personal and professional dealings, which isolated him even further. Both his successes and his failures were based primarily on the fact that he suspected deceit, dishonor and disloyalty from everyone he met, and he was committed to beating them at their own game first, refusing to trust any situation. As he saw it, everyone was secretly working against him, ready to "steal" what was rightfully his.

Becoming more and more guarded, insecure and alone, he remained constantly on edge, believing that the only thing standing between him and a life where he would be destitute and forgotten was his diligence protecting any worldly position he could achieve together with the material things he could accumulate. When he did have success or achievements, he only became more anxious prompting him to become even more obsessed with protecting his possessions. More often than not he would be the victim of scenarios that were the epitome of the deceit he feared. Life became a series of self-fulfilling prophecies.

Then one day Edward met Judith. Judith had grown up in a very wealthy environment, never wanting for anything. As a result, she had faith that the Universe would always provide, trusted everyone she met, had little interest in material things and scoffed at the idea of worldly success or possessions. She was confident and secure, did not want anything from anyone and in many ways was the antithesis of Edward's deepest fears. When he was in her presence, he lost any thoughts or worries related to his lifelong issues of betrayal or distrust, and seeing the kernel of the person he truly wanted to be when he was with her, Edward fell madly in love with Judith.

*Never really noticing his foibles or his paranoia, Judith soon fell
in love with Edward as well since she was able to see parts of
his character that he did not allow anyone else to see. They
were eventually married and their wedding brought two groups
of the most diverse kinds of people possible together. Edward's
friends, family and colleagues were all well-established, mate-
rialistic, somewhat superficial and devious. Judith's friends, family and colleagues were all free spirits and progressive thinkers
who practiced various forms of esoteric healing and led mostly
stress-free lives where creativity, healing and spirituality
trumped success and the material world every time.*

*Immersed in the new world of Judith's friends, Edward's fears
subsided for a time. However, after only seven months of marriage his original demons surfaced again when his mother died
suddenly, leaving a substantial inheritance to him and his sister.
His anxiety levels soared when he discovered that his sister
had secretly maneuvered behind the scenes to have his mother,
who was suffering from undiagnosed dementia, transfer her
entire estate to the sister on her deathbed.*

*Suing after the fact to try to protect his rights, the judge
nonetheless sided with his sister. Her only defense was that
their mother had decided to transfer the entire inheritance to
her based on the fact that she had no job and had always
counted on the mother's financial assistance. The Judge took
her side and even refused to consider the fact that unbeknownst to anyone Edward had been the sole financial support*

of his mother, paying almost all of her bills for nearly the last decade of her life. This he had done to please his mother because, as she explained to him, she wanted to keep the inheritance invested and untouched so that he and his sister could receive the maximum financial benefit when she died.

More anxious and depressed than ever before, Edward had more and more difficulty functioning day to day believing that any time now his life would disintegrate before his eyes. The idea of suicide would pop into his head, and for days at a time he would have an inner argument with himself fighting to push the idea away. Judith tried to assure him that his fears were irrational and completely groundless, but based on his worsening outlook and hopelessness he refused therapy or help of any kind.

Then he began experiencing debilitating nightmares in which he was being persecuted, chased, robbed and beaten. He would wake screaming in terror. Sharing her concerns about this with friends, Judith's circle suggested the couple see a well-known psychologist, intuitive and healer to get to the bottom of Edward's seemingly irrational fears and hopefully banish them forever. Eventually, he succumbed to the pressure all around him, and allowed Judith to make an appointment for the two of them to visit the healer's West Coast abode.

An adept with the psychic ability to check into an individual's Akashic Records, the Therapist asked that she not be given any background concerning the reason for Edward and Judith's visit. She began their session by psychically working with Edward's Spirit Guides and asking them to show her any pertinent information concerning his life mission and his condition.

Accessing Edward's Soul records, she told the couple that Edward's issues stemmed from his Soul's mission for this lifetime, which was related to learning lessons around the fear of loss. Moreover, in the positive polarity the life lesson would be expressed through the ability to conquer fears that he would never have enough of whatever he needed energetically to make life successful. If experienced from the negative polarity however, it would be expressed through living daily with the terrible fear that he would not have whatever he needed to survive and would be constantly haunted by anxiety at the thought of potential loss.

She further explained that this life lesson, or mission if you will, was chosen by his Soul to balance traumatic energy experienced in another lifetime on his Soul's Wheel of Creation that had taken place in the early 13th Century in the Lombardy region of Italy. As a young man there, his father, who was the ruling aristocrat of the locale, was poisoned and had died leaving the inexperienced youth as de facto ruler of a small principality. His father had been assassinated by an Uncle working with rebel relatives in conjunction with a powerful group of political outsiders. After killing his father, the Uncle quickly moved to steal the young Prince's throne, his inheritance and his rightful *position as well.*

The Prince was imprisoned, and his friends and supporters were all promptly executed. Following a brief sham trial, the usurping Uncle and his powerful associates stripped the prince of his titles, his lands, any claims he had to an inheritance and all of his possessions. Penniless and alone, but no longer viewed as a political threat, the young prince was allowed to live but was banished from his ancestral homeland.

Alone and distraught, the banished Prince lasted less than a fortnight out on his own. Drained of hope due to his loses, he slit his wrists and took his own life on the road leading from his former home. To add insult to injury, as he lay there dying passing bandits stripped him of his clothing and boots as well as the few remaining possessions he still had on him.

Hearing the story, both Edward and Judith burst into tears. Without realizing it, the Therapist had identified and detailed the roots and originating source of his deepest fears in this lifetime. She continued the explanation.

The mission of the young prince's Soul for that lifetime was to learn lessons related to maintaining pride and confidence in oneself through the knowledge that no one can really steal who you are from you. Since he associated who he was so strongly with his position and his possessions, his Free Will choice to take his own life removed any possibility that he could later *turn his tragedy around, with the potential to be a great success in that lifetime through belief in his abilities and his own merit without relying on the assistance of his privilege.*

The current lifetime, which exists on his Soul's same Wheel of Creation, is directly related to the lifetime of the young prince. For that reason, Edward's life was to be a vehicle for his Soul to balance the traumatic karmic energy created around the loss and death that occurred in the 13th Century lifetime. As a result, his Soul had provided experiences around loss in Edward's life and he would be given life choices that might still enable lessons of pride and instill a reliance on himself and his own abilities. This would further provide him with faith in himself and in the Universe, which would offset the blockage of energy and trauma experienced by the young Prince, which had bled through into Edward's life since childhood.

The fact that the young Prince took his own life as a result of losing everything was a choice that had created substantial energetic Soul imbalance that needed to be addressed and Edward's current lifetime issues were the means of his Soul addressing that imbalance. Doing so, allowed him an understanding that the loss of worldly position and material things has no real bearing on life's happiness, success or the growth of who you are at the depths of your Soul.

Facing and walking through the fears that were generated in Edward almost daily, such as had happened in the loss of the inheritance from his mother, was giving him the chance to over-come these feelings of despair and loss. Each situation gave Edward the opportunity to realize that there are things that outweigh material possessions and worldly position and this would counter the feelings of loss and karmic imbalances generated by the suicide of the young prince.

In other words, she continued, life has value above and beyond anything material the world has to offer. Free will can be used to escape one's fate but the imbalance will ultimately need to be discharged by the Soul. Edward had the choice of seeing life as a challenge where his abilities could be used to conquer his situations, or, if he chose, he would come to the same realizations through the negative polarity, in which case life would be a constant struggle with fear and loss.

Edward's experiences would provide opportunities to balance and counter the actions that had caused the young Prince to take his own life. Finally, through the events in both the lifetime of the young Prince and Edward's own current lifetime, karma on his Soul's Wheel of Creation would be balanced and Edward's Soul would be able to achieve harmony through experiential growth.

The Therapist also explained that although not present during the lifetime of the Prince, Judith's Soul was a Task Mate of Edward's Soul. When Edward was ready in this lifetime, by agreement with Edward's Soul she would lead Edward to these realizations and assist him to balance the karmic energies. Their Souls had agreed that this would be accomplished by virtue of the trusting and caring long-term relationship they would form.

As a Soul Task Mate, through the Therapist Judith had helped Edward find the keys to unlock the realizations needed for him to successfully balance these karmic energies. She had fulfilled this task successfully by facilitating this help for Edward, even accompanying him to the visit with the Therapist. The task completed, she would now remain with him for the remainder of their lives to help him always remember his condition, and to walk him through the times when he might relapse or when old fears might resurface. She was fulfilling that mission with Edward for the purposes of her own Soul growth.

After their session, Edward felt an enormous burden had finally been lifted from him. His new understanding of where his deep, seemingly irrational fears came from helped him to consciously subdue them whenever they surfaced. In the process, his anxieties subsided and as they did he was willing to trust whatever the Universe provided, as well as putting his trust and faith in others. The fear that he might lose his worldly position or his material belongings was no longer relevant for him as he became more focused on the emotional and spiritual wellbeing of himself, Judith and their friends and families.

A year after his revelation, Edward furthered his recovery by volunteering at a Suicide Prevention hotline that another friend of Judith's had introduced him to. He became their top volunteer and was praised for assisting even the most distraught individuals through an uncanny compassion and a unique understanding of what the caller was going through. Although he still found himself occasionally purchasing two of everything (just in case, as he would muse) that was the extent of his fear of loss now, and for the most part the depression and anxiety caused by the fear of loss that had been such a large part of his life never returned.

CHAPTER 5

THE FOURTH DIMENSIONAL SUBLEVEL OF THE THIRD UNIVERSAL DIMENSION: THE DREAMSCAPE AND ENTRY INTO THE ASTRAL REALMS

As we have already described, there are many possible occurrences that take place at the moment of passing. Generally, owing to the fusion of all the energetic bodies during the withdrawal from the physical entity, most individuals are aware that they have exited the physical body. In many cases they often will look down from a high, floating position, and often see the body that they have just inhabited beneath them, quickly recognizing that they have passed on from physical life.

It is usually upon the entity's release from the physical body and the euphoric freeing sensation this creates that momentum is generated to continue the death journey. Sometimes this takes place within the individual's own continuing consciousness and sometimes it takes place when those known to the individual or those they trust and believe in appear to greet them and inform them of what is happening or what they need to be aware of and what should be done by them.

It is because of this that stories abound from those just prior to their passage related to seeing loved ones visit them, or having dreams about comforting environments that they usually can't wait to return

184

to. Such thoughts and visions, wherever they are derived from, generate a desire in the individual that not only precedes death but also acts as an energetic impetus that propels them into the final death passage. It could be said that both just before and just after death of the physical body the individual has one foot on each side of the veil, or dimensional divide if you will. This is usually short-lived, and at some point following integration of the energetic structures that surround the physical body, the experience of being pulled into a tunnel of light energy will begin.

Once the proverbial tunnel of light is present, which is essentially a reference to the energy funnel of the Soul's light that is pulling one up into the next Dimensional Sublevel, most entities are more or less compelled and sometimes even forcibly drawn through this dimensional door. For others, particularly those who are stunned or are the victim of a highly traumatic experience just before passing, this takes a bit more time and care as awareness of their state is achieved. Spirit guides related to their specific Soul group are always present to assist these individuals with their passage, and these are more often than not the Angels described as being present at the moment of death.

Whether it is immediate or an occurrence that takes place over a greater period of time, ultimately this is the progression that occurs following the end of physical life. Once the integrated Energetic body has followed into the light, it enters a temporary state that some would consider a place of "limbo." Actually however, this is an environment where the entity is given time to fully regain the consciousness they had in life, while also being instructed as to their current co-creative abilities in forming the backdrop of the Fourth Dimensional Sublevel and the environment they are currently in.

Because the environment found there is derived from the person's

consciousness and beliefs, for some it might be their version of paradise or Heaven. For others, it is the environment they just left, their
family home or their ideal home, town or city where they always
wanted to live. Still others, particularly those harboring extreme
guilt or shame based on the life just lived, may envision that they
are in a version of Hell (literally of their own making). Such creations
change as the individual becomes aware of their power to co-create
the environment they experience and as responsibility for that creation becomes part of their awareness.

Whatever is envisioned, this area is generally a transitory environment and each entity remains focused within it only until such time
as they have explored and fully grasped an understanding of how reality is created within the lower Astral planes. Once that has been
established, the individual is ready to gain a better understanding of
the events, relationships and lessons it has accomplished (or not)
during their physical lifetime in the Third Sublevel of the Universal
Dimension, which has just come to a close.

Now when the Etheric body passes into the first Astral state, or the
Fourth Sublevel of the Third Universal Dimension, it is as close as it
can be to physical incarnation in the physical reality from which it
has just departed. By another name, this lower Astral state is also
known as the "Dreamscape," where by virtue of its close proximity
to physical reality an individual's consciousness, or subconscious as
it is called by you, escapes when sleeping.

Within this Dimensional Sublevel, the physically alive individual ex-
periments in the Dreamscape with possible life scenarios. This is accomplished in a non-physical format. Those events that are desirable

for growth or other purpose can then be definitively decided upon and be brought into physical manifestation. These events then become the most probable events materialized by you, for you, in your Third Dimensional physical reality.

The appellation "Dreamscape" is perhaps a misnomer, since you would naturally consider this to be a realm attached to your physical reality. And you are correct in assuming that there is close affinity to your current physical reality. However, as a Fourth Dimensional Sublevel, not only is this considered a higher dimensional state, it is also the realm or Sublevel that first awaits those who have just passed from physical life.

In this sense, the journey that begins just following passage from the physical body is one that seems "dreamlike" to most, and much could be said about the similarities between dreaming while in a physical body and the sensation of continual dreaming in an out-of-body state where one never awakens. Experienced through the Etheric body, transit into and through the Fourth Dimensional Sublevel can be compared to a lucid dream experience where the more you are aware, the more control you have over the patterns and thought forms being created. On the other hand, the less awareness you have, the more out of control your surroundings may seem.

In short, the more awareness and consciousness you have to draw on through remembrance following death, the more control you have over the experience. Primarily, this leads you to become more conscious of the power you have over what is being created around you, as well as what is happening to you in this new form of reality that you are experiencing.

This is not by accident, and in many ways for most it is even comforting following the transition out of the physical body to feel as though one is merely dreaming. As we mentioned already however, this transitional plane is very much for the purpose of allowing assimilation of all Soul energy out of the physical body and into the Etheric body, as well as provide you with the lessons needed to reawaken your consciousness. This allows you to realize the impact of your thoughts and desires as these relate to the Astral environment you are now creating all around you.

While in physical incarnation, when the consciousness is relaxed through sleep, dreams allow you to work through various life scenarios by exploring your unconscious desires, fears, hurts and accomplishments. In some instances, you are actually experimenting with turning possible realities into probable ones, discovering which events or situations would have the most potential for you to grow from if they were manifest in the structural substance of reality. In this way, inner thoughts, desires and actions can be explored without the burden of physical creation unless they are related to your conscious goals as well as your Soul's life mission.

When transiting through or residing in this particular Sublevel just after passing from physical reality, those now operating through their Etheric body are able to witness, and, in certain instances, even continue to reach out and touch the Third Dimensional physical environment they have left. Thus, an individual's loved one's, family and friends who have passed away remain in close proximity via the somewhat communal Dreamscape, or Fourth Dimensional Sublevel, and in many instances are able to communicate with those known to them that are still residing within physical incarnation. More often than not, this communication is achieved through the communal Dreamscape, and we would say that for the most part, dreams of loved ones that have passed that you might feel are fictitious or "only a dream" are often real visitations from those that have passed from physical life.

As we have detailed for you, the Astral realm can be viewed in two possible ways. First, it serves as a kind of holding chamber for those who are gathering up their Etheric self prior to passing into higher Dimensional Sublevels, such as the Fifth Dimensional Sublevel or higher Astral planes and beyond. Secondarily, it is the place where non-corporeal entities are best able to discover their creative abilities. In doing so they learn to respect and manage their thought forms while also becoming aware of their co-creative abilities and responsibilities.

For many, especially entities from the early life cycles of a Soul, this is where they realize that they have just left the physical body and, more importantly that consciousness is not confined to a physical body and, above all else, exists without end. That realization is one of the most important ones an entity that has passed from physical reality can have, and even if this belief was within the entity's consciousness during the course of the physical lifetime, re-acquaintance with that basic understanding is paramount to moving forward. This awareness hinges on the fact that the first Astral plane is also the place that the entity discovers that what confronts them in this new reality is directly linked to the actual thoughts, desires and feelings they project and create as thought forms.

Naturally, as we have said, time in your Third Dimensional Sublevel may be a linear measure but the actual dimensional time-wave is not a linear construct. Nowhere is this more obvious or true than in the Astral state and this is another important realization that those entities, now in Etheric Bodies and newly arrived in the Astral state, will confront.

Superficial though it may sound, many welcome this awareness wholeheartedly based on the standards and beliefs of their prior consciousness. Ironically, these entities accept the belief by rejoicing at the idea that physical aging is a symptom of the linear time continuum and therefore no longer has any relevance or impact. Almost immediately, most realize that their appearance has reverted to a look associated with their innermost feelings of who they are age wise. Almost every entity will look as they did in a period of the lifetime just passed that was of singular or greatest importance to them, or one that ideally suits their current level of awareness and consciousness.

This brings up another important fact that should be understood. Some believe that entry into higher dimensional venues like the Astral planes provide one with an immediate rise in awareness, knowledge and consciousness. This however is not the case. Although it can be said that there is generally an elevation in an entity's compassion for others after passing from physical existence, physical death and continuation in the Etheric body does not bring an automatic or magical enlightenment to the individual entity. Death does not trigger or equate to epiphany.

If anything, the opposite is sometimes true. As a fragment of the Soul, the individual lifetime is an independent consciousness for all intent and purpose. That consciousness, which is created as a separate entity from the Soul, is above all else taxed with the mission of discovering itself and expanding its consciousness. Ultimately, that consciousness will reintegrate with the Soul that created it, in much the same way that the Soul will ultimately reintegrate with the God Source and expand the magnificence of the Universe and All-That-Is in doing so. Until that happens however each entity, like each Soul, is an independent being, raising its own consciousness while being corded, as we have explained, to its original maker through millennia of experiences in many multidimensional arenas.

After physical death in the Third Dimension, although awareness and consequently consciousness does improve with the continuing experiences of the entity as it raises itself through the Astral Sublevels and becomes closer to its creator, the entity's level of consciousness and awareness at the moment of passing out of the physical body remains intact. In many ways, it remains the same as it was at the moment of physical death. This is yet another reason the awareness and level of consciousness opened up and carried during a lifetime, as well as conscious remembrance of what has been learned at the time of physical death, can be of vital consequence to the entity, and in some ways, to the Universe itself. It can also be problematic, as we will explain.

The belief structure of an individual, whether it is racially, culturally, or socially derived, is ingrained early on in one's physical life. Many of these belief structures are useful in creating the parameters around which opportunities for growth may be easily created. Unfortunately however, while all this might be excellent for growth, many of these beliefs and societal standards are misleading, erroneous or completely incorrect at best.

This is particularly difficult when one enters the Astral plane with their incorrect belief structures in tact and in tow. Though the entity may believe these erroneous things with all their heart based on the learning or teachings of the lifetime just passed, it will now require some time within the Fourth Dimensional Sublevel for these incorrect and, at times, grossly misinformed beliefs to be altered, dispelled and erased.

This is not as simple as it sounds. As an example, an individual believing wholeheartedly in the religious teachings they have learned since childhood is hard pressed to abandon such beliefs. Since the Fourth

Dimensional Sublevel is not a "school" in the sense you know it, these entities must learn on their own how to sort through and relinquish the destructive, unqualified beliefs they have been taught from the beginning of physical life. This is done through inner doubts and ultimately initiatives they undertake when they realize that their beliefs are limiting, incongruous and non-beneficial. They do so in conjunction with their Spirit Guides and other Higher Beings seeking to assist them to do so by acting out scenarios that highlight the inconsistencies between their current environment and their beliefs.

You can well imagine the importance of this before an entity is able to continue their journey. As an example, an entity that believes Jesus, as their God, is the only one that can control their destiny and create their reality, will not easily understand that this is not the case and they are the ones solely responsible for the environment as well as the creations and events happening within it. Such a dilemma can mean that the entity will wait for a visit from Jesus before they continue their consciousness growth or start the trip towards reintegration with their Soul.

To facilitate this, guides will participate and in certain cases act out scenes that assist the individual to see that their beliefs may need altering. Using our example, a guide might appear and take on the form of the religious figure Jesus, and through that trusted figure demonstrate to the entity how the facts differ from their belief system. Such scenarios are always conducted in a way that allows the entity to come to their own conclusion and in a manner best accepted, trusted and utilized by the entity. Some entities require several different scenarios that each demonstrate the error of their belief structure, and a longer period is needed to allow them the ability to alter their beliefs and come to terms with the greater truth that will allow them to proceed on their journey. There is no time limit imposed on this process and each entity learns at their pace.

Once these steps are completely mastered an individual entity is free to continue deeper into Astral awareness. Until it is complete however, each remains within the lower density Fourth Dimensional Sublevel in close proximity to the physical environment, as well as the loved ones they have left behind in physical life. These entities are not to be confused with the disjointed Emotional and Mental body wanderings that we discussed earlier, since entities in the Fourth Sublevel Astral realm are already unified within the Etheric body and now investigating greater Truths (albeit basic ones) through experiential awareness within that new (to them) reality. They are not to be confused with "ghosts" or spirits locked between the Third and Fourth Dimensional Sublevels pending the consolidation of their energetic bodies into one Etheric being.

Fully embodied in the Etheric state and poised in the early stages of the Astral state, these entities are on their way to becoming more and more adept at their new co-creative roles. Many are surprised to learn that not only can they create an environment and see those they wish to see by simply envisioning them they also now have the ability to relive events from the life just passed merely by remembering. Those events become real and available to each entity within the Fourth Dimensional Sublevel, or Dreamscape, in much the same way you can cue up a DVD and watch it over and over again in physical reality.

Such replays however, are immediately created in front of them, and they are far more intense than memories. They also include multiple perspectives, including witnessing scenes from the perspective of others who may have been experiencing the event with you or in relation to you.

Such episodes, experimentation and realizations become very important further on in the Fifth Dimensional Astral Sublevel. In the Fourth Dimensional Sublevel, the events are replayed at will individually, and the entity is only able to see them from various angles and perspectives. Conclusions concerning the purpose and connections to the entity are not readily available at this stage, which is a process that continues in more detail and with greater impact in the Fifth Sublevel. At that Sublevel, consolidation and connection of all life experiences, once analyzed, takes place, and the entity is able to define the associations, consider their true purpose and take stock of all life events in order to uncover the achievements or, sometimes, the missteps taken within Third Sublevel physical reality.

As we will discuss later, healing following that phase in the process is often needed and is made available to entities in the Higher Astral environments. Sometimes physical life and death events, particularly when karmic balancing is necessitated but has not yet occurred, can be traumatic and memorable, and these are relived, adjusted or altered so that the ultimate Soul purpose is readily available to the entity. While reliving the events is an attribute of the Fourth Sublevel Astral realm, adjustments to them and healing are generally made by the entity in the higher Astral realms.

The viewing of events via memory within the Fourth Sublevel Astral environment provide the entity with a better understanding of the life that has just passed, explored at their own pace without the jarring interference or judgment of anyone or anything external to the entity. This will surprise those expecting, based on religious and other dogma, a trial, judgment and reward or punishment. Such expectations are clearly not consistent with Free Will or Truth, and are reserved for the fragments of Baby and Younger Souls who, based on their upbringings and belief structure, prefer that the world strictly mimic and adhere to their own standards and views.

The reliving and understanding of the purpose of the events from the recent lifetime makes the entity more amenable to healing. This is set into motion within the Etheric body once the entity has achieved awareness that there is no good, bad, right or wrong, but only purpose and growth. Much as a wound in physical life needs time to transition to health and harmony, so too the lifetime emotional and mental wounds as well as the misgivings still lodged in the Etheric body need time to surface, be felt fully and be understood in order for the healing process to truly begin.

The healing process begins initially in the Fourth Dimensional Sublevel and tends to be corrected and resolved as the entity progresses through to the Fifth and then the Sixth Astral realm. However, healing only starts by way of the awareness that there is no judgment, reward or punishment by a lofty divine figure. For some, this can be a mammoth step forward that requires, as we have related to you, the assistance of higher guides and various in depth scenarios to dispel the mountain of erroneous beliefs formulated during the lifetime.

Once achieved, this is the starting point of the "enlightening" of one's consciousness. We would note that this is the best definition of enlightenment, which should be defined as a "lightening" of the entity's burden by bringing to "light" a life event's true purpose with respect to the entity's EssencePath and life mission. This definition is applicable to you from day to day in physical reality, as it is also a prerequisite in understanding that all life events lead to growth for the Soul.

It should be recognized at this point that those in physical incarnation that are in some way communicating with loved ones who have passed from the physical sphere, particularly if such communication is immediately or shortly after death, are doing so with the Etheric body of the individual entity's consciousness. As we have described, these entities are, for all intent and purpose, learning the proverbial ropes as they process through the Fourth Dimensional Sublevel. Generally, entities that have just passed through the veil and out of physical life have slightly more difficulty communicating. Or if they are able to communicate at all, they will often have only fleeting insight into the life just lived.

For the most part, entities in the early stages of the Fourth Sublevel are generally preoccupied with the well being of their friends, family and loved ones. Those entities that have progressed slightly further in the Astral realm will inevitably display a more philosophical approach, and will tend towards expressions of understanding and unconditional love. Their messages, brought forth to the recipient from either the Dreamscape or through the assistance of a medium qualified for that purpose, will usually concern actual memorable events derived from their lives. This is a clear indication that the entity is in the stage of viewing and reliving memorable events, in preparation for rectification, healing and understanding of their purpose in a higher Astral state.

In general however, unsolicited visitations in the Dreamscape or, less frequently, within the physical realm, come only when someone still living in physical reality is intensely mourning or generating thought forms of the loved one that has passed over. Usually these visitations, most often conducted through dreaming, come from those entities that have already progressed to the Fifth or Sixth Astral planes.

This does not mean that visitations in the Dreamscape are not possible for those in the early Fourth Astral Sublevel, particularly since this level has the closest proximity to your own Third Dimensional physical reality. But it is to say that contact with loved ones immediately after passing from the physical body is usually reserved for those who have attained a certain understanding of where they are and how their new reality works. It always requires a certain amount of time to learn the ropes as it were, and although some may believe that lack of contact is an indication or proof that consciousness does not survive physical life, this is never the case.

Most true mediums, intuitives and psychics will readily explain that expecting immediate in depth contact with someone who has just passed is not as easy as it might seem, if it is possible at all. Contact, either in the Dreamscape or with the assistance of an intuitive able to facilitate it, is far more productive when the entity that has left physical life has processed what has happened and is aware of their new state in the Fourth Sublevel Dimensional reality. It is then that such contacts are far more fulfilling, realistic and poignant, for both sides.

That said however, as non-corporeal individuals rise through the Astral configurations and become adept at their new environment they become much less preoccupied, aware or even concerned with what is transpiring in the physical Third Dimensional world they have left behind. We have often given an analogy concerning this of an individual, be it a friend, a family member or an acquaintance, that moves out of your neighborhood, your state or even your current country of residence. At first, there is constant contact between you, with frequent post cards, letters and regular phone calls. But as time progresses both individuals, particularly the one that has moved furthest from the old neighborhood, in this case the one who has left the physical body, finds new interests, a new life and new relationships. Often at this point the communications between old friends becomes far less, until one day they are occasional at best until they have ceased entirely.

This does not mean the importance of the past relationship is lessened, nor does it mean that either has forgotten the friendship or connection. In some ways the important moments and memories of the relationship become even more important to each party, and it is for this reason that when meeting up in the Dreamscape, the situation will usually revolve around a past occurrence, an old environment or a variation of some specific event. This does mean however, that as the entity progresses further and continues on its way, especially as it has a new understanding of its life purpose and even the exact reason there was a relationship in the first place, there is a natural tendency for each to find more and more distance placed between them. This is a result of the continuing journey of the individual who has passed into deeper levels of the Dimensional Sublevel and Astral realm where they currently reside.

As we have said, the Dreamscape is an area you can access as you sleep or through your unconscious mind via your conscious intention. Each of you has vast experience exploring the Fourth Dimensional Sublevel and lower Astral plane, which you visit in some way or other every night of your physical life. In a certain sense you could be said to be visiting and experimenting with the very realm you will ultimately find yourself living in when your physical existence ends. So, it should be noted that fear of passing, through physical death, into this realm is a great irony, since this could be equated to having a fear of going to sleep every night. The process and experience is much different to be clear, but it is extremely similar in terms of how the Etheric body processes the Astral environment, and is co-creator of the Dreamscape environment.

In fact we would say that at the current time, the augmented Ascension energies coming through worldwide have meant that many of you are beginning to have the experience of lucid dreaming (the feeling of conscious recognition of yourself while in the dream state) where you realize you are dreaming and may have control over what you wish to envision or experience next. Such experiences are an important awareness to have, and we would suggest expanding this potential for yourself whenever possible through the power of conscious intention and cognitive suggestion just prior to sleep.

None of this is to suggest that physical death is an easy task. Frankly, deterioration of the physical vessel and breakdown of the Soul's physical presence is tedious and can be a disturbing and somewhat disruptive process for many, particularly where illness or aging is concerned. However, we would add to this conversation that even in the most difficult situations the actual departure of the Soul's energy via the Etheric body, whether from age, disease or through accidental, immediate physical death, is not as horrendous an experience as many expect.

This is especially true since there is more often than not a measured and gradual withdrawal of the Soul's energy over time in anticipation of a physical departure. The most dramatic example of this is in the case of a disease such as Alzheimer's. Those experiencing such diseases depart bit by bit over a substantial period until reaching the point where the Soul's consciousness has all but receded from the physical person. While the physical body may retain certain functioning, and although the Ego can remain active and present, even those functions will ultimately end shortly after the Soul's consciousness has completely departed.

Returning to our prior conversation, this is particularly true if you recall that in almost every case the Soul has orchestrated the point of exit and moment of death, and, from a higher perspective, is somewhat prepared for the release of the Etheric body. In fact, in almost every case the individual's Soul begins the process of separation from the physical body early, and even in accidental, immediate death, the Soul will withdraw its energy prior to the physical body's imminent failure. This streamlines the process and makes physical death less traumatic to the individual experiencing it, though this is clearly difficult to see from the perspective of those remaining in physical form that are witnessing the departure of their fellows and projecting onto it their personal perspective.

In fact, this is sometimes very much the entire point since unconsciously a Soul will always naturally seek out important events and issues to provide others with opportunities for growth. The act of dying is perhaps one of the most important of these opportunities, and observing physical death in others is an act that generally has a very important impact on those witnessing the events. This is true whether speaking about the passing of a loved one, or seeing images of those unknown to you that have physically passed, as in the case of seeing reports of casualties of war and violence, or the bodies of immigrants washed up on a shore who passed attempting to find a better life in a distant land, no pun intended.

It should always be remembered that the closest energetic contact you may have with a newly deceased entity, whether it be a loved one or not, is achieved during the period just following their death. While the individual that has passed may not have the wherewithal to understand or communicate with you, you have the greatest single opportunity at that time to consciously reach out to them. As we have detailed, since they are still within "hearing" range at this very early point while their energetic bodies are consolidating, the recently deceased are very aware of thoughts and words you express about them. In fact, they can be drawn to your prayers, kind words and other energetic displays of affection, and these are important in assisting them to understand what is transpiring. It is not by accident that you are inspired by traditions that have grown around memorializing the recently departed, as a means of sending them on their way and strengthening your connection to them.

Closest proximity is achieved in the period just following the physical death of the entity prior to their pull into the vortex or "tunnel of light" that is achieved by the consolidation of the person's Energetic or Etheric body. However, it should be remembered that there is no real time obligation for the departed to move forward because time, as you measure it, is non-existent at the Astral level. Therefore an entity can linger in this particular state for as long as it takes to withdraw all Soul energy from the physical body. The consolidation of the Etheric body brings the realization that physical life is no longer possible, and this provides favorable energetics for further momentum into the Astral Sublevels.

Again, we caution against any understanding that there is an obligatory standard or time period needed for a Soul or its fragments to complete these mechanics as it regards Reincarnation, Transmigration or Ascension. However, we would suggest that there is in fact a general time and a specific process that takes place, particularly as it regards all lifetimes in a Wheel of Creation created by the Soul. Similarly, there is a process for the entry and removal of the Soul's energy into and out of the physical body and physical reality, just as there is a specific process related to a fragment's journey through every Astral Sublevel in anticipation of its reunion with its Soul.

It is not until an entity has adapted to the new Astral environment and is proficient not only with their co-creative abilities but particularly with the ability to recall and observe life memories that they are ready to proceed into the Fifth Sublevel of the Third Universal Dimension. The Fifth Sublevel begins the entity's journey through the higher Astral planes, and as the individual proceeds they gain more and more clarity with respect to their singularity as well as their purpose in the physical lifetime they have just lived.

In a certain sense, entry into the Fifth Astral plane is akin to what could be called a second death of the entity, although this passage is far less dramatic in terms of consciousness and remembrance. The clarity and "light" that forms around an entity as their vibration and resonance increases in the Fourth Sublevel begins to create a new vortex or energetic spin that is ultimately destined to propel the entity and their consciousness to the next Astral plane.

It should be remembered that the trilogy structure of dimensional overlap provides that the Fourth through Sixth Sublevels are closely related and connected. Because of this, even though all the Astral Sublevels have close connection, the transition between the Fourth and Fifth Sublevel is not nearly as drastic as the one between the Third and Fourth Sublevels.

At the point where the entity is ready to proceed by virtue of their rise in vibrational and consciousness integrity, the vortex that is generated through the individual's Free Will desire to explore the environment further and their naturally higher energetic output creates a new electromagnetic pull. This pull increases exponentially until such time as it becomes irresistible to the entity. Then, at its highest energetic point, the entity is once again pulled into a "tunnel of light" or vortex quite similar to the one that heralded the original entry from physical life into the Fourth Dimensional Sublevel and Astral state.

To a greater or lesser extent, such energetic pull from a dimensional overlap to the next is quite normal and these energy openings could be considered dimensional portals. In fact, at some point it will be widely acknowledged by your science and technology that the secret to inter-dimensional travel and the keys to the dimensional timeline itself lie in generating the right amount of energy at the proper vibrational frequency in the correct place to open electromagnetic openings, or portals, between Dimensions. Such technology is already secretly known and experimented with, derived in primitive format via treaties between the covert branches of several world governments and inter-dimensional extraterrestrial entities that made contact with Third Dimensional Earth decades ago on your timeline.

This is so for both the Sublevels and the Universal Dimensions as well, with each dimensional level having its own signature and vibrational or resonant key. These portals are easiest to engage and traverse between dimensional levels that are in close proximity, which is why entries from the Third to the Fourth, the Sixth to the Seventh and the Ninth to the Tenth are more difficult, dramatic and remarkable to achieve. This axiom also applies to the Dimensional Sublevels and the Universal Dimensions themselves.

This is why visibility is more problematic outside of a dimensional trilogy. It is also the reason your reality is comprised visibly of the First through Third Universal Dimensions, and why there is what we would consider a "giant step" between the next Universal Dimension trilogies. Transmigration of a Soul through the First, Second and Third Universal Dimensions is readily accomplished and the Sublevels are easily navigated, whereas transmigration from that dimensional trilogy to the next (Fourth, Fifth and Sixth Universal Dimensions) requires far greater levels of consciousness and much more energetic stamina in order to open the energetic portals on demand. Transmigration from higher to lower Dimensional levels is always easier, whereas lower to higher transmigration requires higher energy fields, light and augmented consciousness as per Universal Law.

As mentioned before, this is similar to the experiences often noted by those who have returned from what are termed near-death events. The sensation of a tunnel of light is the energetic vortex opening brought forth by vibrational and electro magnetic change that pulls the Etheric spirit forth once it has exited the physical body. It is, in fact, the very force intended to carry the Etheric body through the created portal and into the Astral Sublevel. The same or similar occurrence takes place with respect to movement between all Dimensional Sublevels.

With respect to near-death experiences however, the full Etheric body is not present and because the full gathering of Mental and Emotional bodies into the Etheric body has not been completed, the Etheric body is pulled back into the physical body. Essentially, this is what creates a near-death experience as opposed to actual death. Because the physical body is still functioning, the Etheric body returns to it and retakes its position.

In such cases, if the physical body no longer is viable or available the Etheric body remains in the limbo state between the Third and Fourth Dimensional Sublevels that we have already described until such time as it is reunited with the wandering Mental and Emotional bodies. Once consolidation of the energetic bodies has occurred and all Soul energy has been pulled from the physical structure, the vortex of energy or "tunnel," as it is known, will again be manifested so that the individual's complete consciousness and energetic body can be drawn definitively into the lower Astral experience.

In cases where the physical body is still viable and functioning, even if it had stopped functioning for a period of time, the individual regains consciousness and is then able to describe the journey that was begun but terminated. Generally most who have these experiences will have remembrance of the tunnel experience only, but a few who progressed further will have tales to tell of "heaven" or of meeting their favorite religious figure or family member when they return. Basically, they are providing a description of what occurs in the early stages of entry into the Fourth Dimensional Sublevel, in actuality the Dreamscape or lower Astral plane, before they are drawn back into the physical body due to the lack of energetic or Etheric body consolidation.

Though rare, such experiences are unique and will generally have a marked impact on the consciousness of the individual. This impact will usually raise their level of awareness in such a way that there is an increased vibrational resonance in the individual's consciousness. Higher vibrational resonance almost always translates into augmented intuitive or other psychic abilities for the individual, whether derived from a "near-death" experience or actively sought through the pursuit of enlightenment and higher consciousness during the physical lifetime.

Having fully explored the process of birth, death, entry and passage of an individual's consciousness and energetic body through the Fourth Dimensional Sublevel or lower Astral plane, let us now turn to an exploration of the Fifth and Sixth Dimensional Sublevels or Astral planes. It is within these realms that an entity's afterlife self-analysis is accomplished, and once adequate healing is generated and an energetic balance is reestablished, the individual continues their march through the higher Astral planes, towards reintegration with their Soul.

Stories from a Soul's Wheel of Creation
The Story of Joseph

At a young age, Joe made a vow to himself: He would dedicate his life to working with people to help them achieve emotional healing and spiritual wellbeing, particularly as it concerned the pain, suffering and mysteries surrounding death and the end of life. Through the circumstances that followed he worked hard to earn a Bachelor of Science Degree in Psychology, then a Master's Degree and finally a Ph.D. in the field. He entered the professional world already fairly well known among colleagues as a nationally acclaimed author, a talented Researcher and a licensed Clinical Therapist specializing in grief, death and dying.

Although friends and family considered his work depressing and his fascination with the process of death and dying some-what morbid, Joe seemed to have a natural talent for understanding the process a person goes through psychologically when facing the end of their life. In fact, his instincts and research were focused not only on the process up to death, but the period after death as well.

He became well versed in clinical research that explored the possibility of an after-life, researching and documenting individual near-death experiences, a phenomenon where patients who had clinically died returned to life bringing with them tales of what occurred after leaving their bodies. In conjunction with that research, he delved into the concept of reincarnation and also became an expert on the approach and practices that ancient cultures had towards death.

Joe became particularly well known for postulating several un-orthodox theories, correlating passages in the Tibetan and Egyptian Books of the Dead as well as the Hindu Mahab-harata. In those theories, he proposed that these works were derived from far more ancient cultural texts, possibly even orig-inating from Atlantis, and they detailed inter-dimensional pas-sage and Alien participation with Earth. He became fascinated by the idea the body was animated by a Soul that was eternal, and ancient cultures may have discovered ways to consciously link the Soul and the body in a way that allowed Humans to astral travel or "Ascend" when out of their bodies into higher dimensional frequencies.

Joe was happy and had established a small following but he was impatient with his progress and lack of worldly success. His theories were slow to catch on or largely ignored, and some even snickered at him behind his back. Then at a conference he was attending one day, Joe was approached by a young man who had rapidly gained widespread notoriety in the New Age community as a motivational speaker and Guru. The Guru told Joe he knew about his work researching the afterlife, and asked Joe if he would like to join forces in order to bring others into the "fold," as he put it.

Though Joe had doubts about the Guru's sincerity at first, he found him mesmerizing and quickly fell under his complete influence. Hoping that the Guru could deliver his message and work to a wider audience, Joe went along with things becoming an outspoken advocate of the Guru as they collaborated together. As the Guru's success unfolded, money and fame seemed to became part of Joe's everyday life almost overnight.

Then, just as suddenly as the success had come, all Hell broke loose. The Guru was accused of massive fraud and cult-like practices. Articles likened him to the most notorious cult leaders of the time and, in particular, accused him of unethical practices and misleading followers in the sole interest of making a profit and taking advantage of them. Joe had no direct knowledge or hand in any of this, but he was identified in the articles as the Guru's righthand man and fixer, perpetuating the frauds being committed from behind the scenes. He became guilty by association.

Soon, journalists and others began investigating and circling around Joe himself. His reputation in tatters based on his association with the Guru, Joe began to realize that the battles to defend his innocence would not only leave him professionally isolated, they most likely would leave him personally bankrupt and alone as well.

Reeling from the stress of the situation and facing a ruined reputation and financial disaster, Joe began to feel the effects of a heart defect that he had since he was a young man. Finally, it all became too overwhelming, and Joe suffered a massive heart attack and was taken to the hospital unconscious. In the Hospital Emergency Room, at the threshold of death, he actually died for nearly five minutes only to be revived after aggressive CPR and medical resuscitation.

That event led Joe to the greatest epiphany of his life. He had now experienced first-hand the near-death phenomenon he had researched and studied for decades. He vividly recalled exactly what had happened to him, despite the fact that he was unconscious and, for all intent and purposes, dead. As soon as his rehabilitation was complete, he began to piece together the revelations that he had been given as a result of the entire experience.

Although he was told his clinical "death" only lasted nearly five minutes, to him the whole experience was a journey that seemed to last for several days. As he left his body, he experienced rising to the ceiling and witnessing the doctors in the Emergency Room working to revive him. Then he remembered a swirling tunnel of light that seemed to pull him in forcefully, similar to the tunnels of light recounted to him by patients in his extensive research.

Most importantly, after passing through the tunnel into an astoundingly beautiful garden, he recalled being met by a group of deceased friends and relatives that included his father, his grandparents and a childhood friend who had died in his early twenties. *After speaking with these familiar faces for what seemed like hours, he recalled being brought before several figures, one that looked like the Buddha and one that appeared to be Jesus of Nazareth.*

These figures welcomed him lovingly but, surprisingly, told him he would need to return to his current life because his mission was not accomplished. Prior to going back however, they told him all would be revealed by an important group that knew his Soul's journey. With that they appeared quietly out of nowhere.

This group included several priests that he recognized from his research into ancient Egypt as being from approximately 3500 BCE. As the Egyptian priests receded to the sides, they made way for several other high priests and priestesses that he did not recognize culturally. They told him that they were his peers from the most important reincarnation he had lived that was connected to his Soul's mission in the current lifetime.

That life took place during pre-history times in Atlantis, and it was this important lifetime that they wished to discuss with him now. Solemnly, the Atlantean priests and priestesses told him that his current lifetime was linked karmically on his Soul's Wheel of Creation to a lifetime that had enormous impact on the fate of many individuals, even Atlantis itself. During that life, he was a High Priest in charge of what was known as the Temple of Beautification.

Originally, he had worked to heal individuals by perfecting their vibrational quality at a cellular level. This process, known as Divine Alchemy, allowed Atlanteans to experience both Third and Fourth Dimensional realities and properties simultaneously.

However, greed and the lust for power and control of others had brought the High Priest under the influence of a group that did not believe that all individuals should be allowed alchemical perfection of their physical bodies. Their view was that there was a hierarchy of deserving Souls of which they were part, and Divine Alchemy should be used to curtail or prevent Ascension between the Dimensions. As a result of their interference in the Universal Process of Ascension, the High Priest began to intentionally subvert the process, and because of it the Fourth Universal Dimension failed to reach critical vibrational mass and did not Ascend during the appropriate Ascension cycle. For a short time, the Universal process of evolution known as Ascension was halted and the Fourth Dimension fused with the Third Universal Dimension.

As a consequence, the period known as the Divine Fall occurred and to make matters worse, Souls that the High Priest was supposed to be helping became trapped in between the Dimensions, unable to Ascend. Some Souls were actually lost and returned to Source prior to their designated time while others lingered in "limbo," as the Fourth Dimension lost its vibrational quality and descended. This "fall" of the Dimension became known as the biblical Rebellion or the Fall of Lucifer and the

Angels, and the worldwide geo-physical upheaval that resulted from the Dimensional trauma caused the second major and near final physical destruction of Atlantis in the middle-At-lantean period.

The Atlantean lifetime of Joe's Soul, they explained, was forever associated in the Akashic Records with these resulting catastrophes. Joe, together with other lifetimes on his Souls Wheels of Creation as well as other Souls from the same group such as the Guru, would now need to work to balance the enormous karmic energies generated by their misdeeds perpetrated in that ancient lifetime. The weight of this karmic imbalance had already prevented his Soul from naturally Ascending for over two Galactic Ascension periods.

But there was more, as they continued to explain. An additional lifetime on the Wheel of Creation of Joe's Soul that was intended to help rectify and balance this situation, had also been subverted by the Free Will choices made by that entity during its lifetime. In that life, he was told he was a High Priest in one of the lost colonies of Atlantis following its final destruction in approximately 13,000 BCE. As High Priest, his Soul had intended for him to balance the karmic energies that existed by assisting people in their passage into the Astral world after physical death.

Instead, he hid the true process of death and journey into the Astral realms from the populace, and oversaw the fabricating of a mythological tale of half-truths and spells that eventually were passed down and ultimately became the basis for the Egyptian Book of the Dead. The priest also hid the true mysteries of the Soul's journey and Ascension, and made attempts to recreate the Divine Alchemy process of the Atlanteans, which was known mythologically but had become lost by that time.

The process he promoted utilized the ancient pre-existing pyramid structures to open energetic portals and force astral projection, tearing the Etheric energies from the physical body prior to actual death in an attempt to induce Ascension into other Dimensions. In effect, the attempt was to create a new Ascension machine, and it not only failed miserably; it caused a number of individual entities to again become lost in a state of limbo.

The High Priest in that lifetime had been given the opportunity to right the wrongs of the prior lifetime while assisting those previously harmed during the Atlantean period. This would have helped balance the extreme karma generated from interfering with the Souls of various entities. Instead, the Priest had for a second time allowed greed, power and the desire to control and manipulate others to overcome him. He had once again used his Free Will to override the intention of his Soul's mission, and in the process had generated even more karma in need of energetic balancing.

Joe's current lifetime, which had the mission of learning lessons around domination of others and patience, turned to the neg-

ative expression when his "impatience" (the negative polarity of his life mission) for success, and with not being heard or acknowledged, made him susceptible to the Guru's control. As a result of that doomed association, not only was he feeling the full force of the karmic energies of the past lifetimes, it was now up to him to deal directly with the difficulties around balancing all these energies on behalf of his Soul.

On hearing all this Joe was overwhelmed with emotion and regret as well as understanding, but he was grateful to the group speaking to him in death for providing this extraordinary knowledge. After they had finished connecting all the dots in Joe's current lifetime with those from several other past and future lifetimes of his Soul, they told him he would now be returned to his current physical life, despite having "died" momentarily. The hope was that he would now use the remainder of this life working towards helping humankind to understand the process of death and dying, while also helping balance these karmic energies through patience and without the need to dominate or control others..

In essence, Joe was being given an additional chance to use his Free Will to rectify as much of the situation as he was able to this time. The next thing he recalled was waking up startled in his hospital bed, feeling a whooshing sensation that greatly diminished his after-death sense of proportion followed by an enormous thud, as if he had fallen into his physical body from a very great distance.

After recovering his health and fully assessing his near-death experience, Joe was a new man. Like others that had experienced near death experiences, he now lived every day with a joy and immediacy that he had previously not known. He denounced the Guru and rather than defiantly defend himself set about sincerely apologizing to everyone for any involvement he had in the affairs or in any attempt to dominate, control or influence another's free will expression.

Joe publicly denounced abuse by all religious groups, cult leaders or any high-profile organizations that enabled or harbored mind control or abuse of others. Next, he wrote and published a book about his personal near-death experiences, as well as the process of death and dying, which he was now well acquainted with first hand. He worked tirelessly and sincerely to dissuade anyone from ever falling under the spell of religious fanaticism, cults or other cult-like organizations everywhere, while also creating several groups to explore other near-death experiences and explore the concept of life after death, from ancient cultures to modern day.

Joe was eventually exonerated both publicly and professionally from his association with the Guru, and as time went by he became known for his various books and seminars on reincarnation and experiences of the afterlife. Today, whenever he is asked he tells people that it took (near) death for him to discover his true life's purpose.

 CHAPTER 6

THE FIFTH AND SIXTH DIMENSIONAL SUBLEVELS OF THE THIRD UNIVERSAL DIMENSION: THE ASTRAL REALM OF HEALING AND THE ASTRAL REALM OF PERCEIVED HEAVEN

For the most part, the lower Astral plane where you find yourself after the Etheric body has completed its withdrawal from the physical body, is very similar to what you experience in the current physical reality but without physical attributes or density. That is to say, with the consolidation of your Mental and Emotional bodies into the Etheric body, your personality, awareness and consciousness remain fairly intact, albeit adjusting to a new state of being. In fact, we would suggest that the only added attribute of your consciousness is the fact that you come to realize that you have passed from a physical body and are now experiencing what could be called a lucid dream state. In that state your power increases as you become responsible for your thoughts and begin to understand the true impact of your manifestation abilities.

Perhaps the greatest knowledge you can have in the Fourth Dimensional Sublevel is the particular awareness of how to control your environment, and it is a necessary one that will become of utmost importance to allowing you entry into the Fifth Dimensional Sublevel and beyond. Without an understanding and awareness of how your environment and reality, whatever that reality might be, is created, you are stationary in the Astral reality you find yourself in at the time.

For most, the Fourth Dimensional Sublevel is an easy plane to ad-vance through, and once this awareness is mastered most individuals move quickly into the Fifth Dimensional Sublevel. Some however, can experience more difficulty than others and when this occurs the pe-riod just following physical death and entry into the lower Astral plane can be somewhat problematic. This is particularly true if the entity has been taught or is holding onto religious or other dogmas that negate self-awareness or have been used during the lifetime to control and trump personal power.

This is problematic because owing to its close proximity to the First, Second and Third Dimensional Sublevels and because these individ-uals believe reality is created for them and not by them, their envi-ronment can take on some challenging forms, to say the least. First of all, without understanding how to take personal responsibility and control the thought forms that create the surrounding reality, these individuals are subject to disjointed and disappointing experi-ences. We hesitate to make the analogy since many will automati-cally think of it as a validation of the concept of "Hell," which does not exist, but nevertheless the analogy is probably the best one in terms of relevance.

These individuals can be subject to what you might consider bad dreams or even, for some, ongoing and somewhat out-of-control nightmares. Coupled with this is the fact that the "Underworld" of thought forms found in the First and Second Dimensional Sublevels can poke their heads unrestrained into the Dreamscape and Astral reality. They do not cross over into the Astral realm, to be sure, but in keeping with the ability of Beings at higher Dimensions can see lower Dimensions, these thought forms can be seen by those in the lower Astral planes in much the same way they are visible at times to those who are very sensitive or trained in the Third Dimensional Sublevel. Naturally, this causes individuals in the Fourth Dimensional Sublevel that do not have an awareness of their responsibility and power in creating the environment no end of fright, confusion and regret.

Based on that, some will have the impression that all this implies they have arrived in a place of punishment, a personal proverbial Hell. To be sure, Guides will come to the rescue of these individuals in an attempt to increase their understanding and awareness that the reality is now completely governed by their own thought forms and co-creative abilities. We would add to this that many of the myths, especially ancient ones, about "rescuing" loved ones from the underworld have this at their core and are directly related to just such a phenomenon. The phantom thought forms are often enough to trigger some entities, with a bit of subtle guidance, into realization of their own power and abilities in the matter. The result is usually not much different than what you experience when you suddenly become lucid while dreaming and hear yourself saying, "Wait a minute, I think what is happening here is only a dream, so I don't have to let it affect me and maybe I can even control it." It is a rare individual that has not had an experience such as this at some point in the dream state.

Surprisingly however, some entities will ignore this guidance preferring to believe instead, based on their past life actions, that they are now subject to the same punishments they were made to fear by society, dogma and ignorant religious leaders. Free Will, as always, is a two way street and these individuals will experience their trials for however long they remain unwilling to take responsibility for what they have created in their reality. Ironically awareness is achieved when they take responsibility for their actions during the former lifetime. While it is this fact that eventually frees them by demonstrating the power they have over themselves, this has been translated in popular thinking as what you would consider to be the punishments experienced as "Hell."

That said, you should recognize by now that the belief in fire and brimstone meted out by an intolerant and demanding God figure, a device long used in equal measure by zealots and scoundrels to control others, is a real detriment to the Human Angelic psyche. It is ironic that many who think of themselves as the most noble and godly among you are often those with the most difficult karma and energy to balance. These individuals usually require the longest periods in the Fourth and Fifth Dimensional Sublevels, generally tortured by their high "ideals" as well as what those ideals have wrought in fabricating reality. Most are unable to move forward after death or transmigrate to higher Astral realms for quite some time.

If we are detailing this for you at all, it is to impress upon you the importance of your belief structures towards the end of physical life as well as your consciousness and a remembrance of your Universe-given co-creative abilities. This awareness can be carried through by the Etheric body into the Fourth Dimensional Sublevel following death and is inevitably available to you in order to speed your progress. It behooves you to banish any belief in the power of demons, devils or whatever you fear can harm you. If these negative thought forms do appear in your reality, now or after physical death within the Astral realm, exercise your dominion over them and inform them of the fact. Your power is always based on your vibrational integrity and level of consciousness, and at a certain point these lower vibrational thought forms cannot even see you.

Your power in this should not be underestimated and is perhaps best demonstrated by a popular children's story in which the beautiful, seemingly "good" witch chuckles at the ugly, seemingly "wicked" witch, and informs her, "…you have no power here. Be gone, before somebody drops a house on you too." Until you are able to fully understand this concept, not only do you remain stationary in the Fourth Astral realm, you subject yourself to whatever the Astral Dreamscape has to offer. That offer is limited and controlled only by your personal ability to conjure thought forms whether they are the things you love or the things you loathe and fear most.

The Fifth Dimensional Sublevel and Astral realm is known as the plane of karmic balancing and healing. Most will experience this in whatever manner is related to their particular belief system, as well as their personal awareness and consciousness level. The true experience of this plane following the stability achieved in the Fourth Sublevel allows an analysis of the purpose of the entity's lifetime and an in-depth look at major life events from the perspective of the Soul as it applies to the individual's success in accomplishing their life mission. Following that analysis, energetic karmic balancing and healing of outstanding events, which created and caused trauma or regrets, takes place. This is done out of necessity in full cooperation with the Soul since the karmic balancing and healing is accomplished both within the individual and also externally via various other lifetimes within the entity's Wheel of Creation.

Remembering that each lifetime is a spoke in the Soul's moving Wheel of Creation, it is clear to see that the Wheel distributes force and energy through its spokes, and the force, as well as stress of the Wheel is distributed through and balanced by all the spokes (or lifetimes) in the wheel. When the force exerted on any given spoke is extraordinary, or when that spoke is weak, damaged or unable to keep up with the load, the other spokes in the Wheel will compensate and shoulder much of the force the stressed spoke is unable to manage.

Now substitute the spokes in our metaphor for lifetimes. In the Soul's Wheels of Creation, the extraordinary force or pressure experienced by one lifetime is relieved through distribution of the "energy" to its counterparts within the same wheel. In this way energetic balancing, or karmic balancing as the more appropriate terminology, is achieved. In a manner of speaking, this rare definition of karma is perhaps one with the truest meaning. It is also the best analogy available as to how karma within a lifetime works by being balanced energetically (karmically) by others associated with it within the Wheel or cycle.

This process allows momentum within the Wheel to continue, and the "spin" or energy that is created by this motion, originated by the Soul, is the basis of each lifetime within the wheel. We call this momentum "spin" and some define it as a Merkaba or energy vehicle. Other philosophies refer to Chi. Whatever you prefer to call it, this process remains constant from one Dimension to another regardless of the degree of stress for one of the spokes within the wheel. In a Universal Dimension, every Wheel of Creation is linked to and affected by the energy distribution of its spokes, regardless of where that spoke or lifetime exists on the dimensional timeline, or in whichever Sublevel it happens to be manifesting.

Envisioning a Wheel with spokes that are all interconnected but operating at different time-space coordinates and at different Sublevels of a Dimension gives you a fairly accurate glimpse into how the Wheels of Creation work. When you add to this image the understanding that there are literally hundreds of Wheels being manifest within a single Universal Dimension, each with as many as 12 lifetimes or more and all of which are generated by a single Soul simultaneously, you are at the threshold of seeing just how magnificent and unique your Soul's energy truly is.

Many mythologies concerning death and the afterlife hint at bits and pieces of either the Fourth or the Fifth Astral plane experience, or combination thereof. These descriptions however are over simplified, not at all consistent with the actual experience and almost always focused on judgment, reward or punishment as the means to further passage through whatever that environment is to you. However incorrect or short on content these are with regard to the real experience however, what cannot be denied is that each individual creates an environment that surrounds these events based on their personality, as well as their cultural, spiritual and religious predilections.

This is natural, since each entity's life personality is responsible for co-creating the Astral environment at these levels. Thus, even though the scenes an entity witnesses are dressed up in particular cultural or religious garb, the method and process being experienced is universal and available to all. So as an example, ancient Egyptians experienced the Fifth Astral realm as the place they arrived following a long journey (the Fourth Dimensional Sublevel) at which point they were subjected to a trial before the Gods where their deeds were analyzed and weighed against a feather (the Fifth Dimensional Sublevel experience). Ancient Mesopotamians experienced death as a long and arduous journey (Fourth Dimensional Sublevel experience) followed by entry to a place where judgment (Fifth Dimensional Sublevel) was granted, not based on deeds but simply one to determine placement and position in an envisioned underworld City of the

Dead (the Sixth Dimensional Sublevel experience).

Somewhat similarly but with variations, the Ancient Greeks envisioned crossing a difficult river (another journey metaphor for traveling through the Fourth Sublevel), after which access to a somewhat dingy underworld was made in exchange for payment (karmic balancing and healing in the Fifth Dimensional Sublevel). After that, your position and environment were based on your personal relationship with the Gods (your Soul), which placed the greatest value on your contributions to them during life (a metaphor for what you have or have not brought back to your Soul based on your lifetime's experiences).

Pre Christian Norse and Celts believed that the body was animated by a composite of "energies," some of which closely resemble the Etheric, Mental and Emotional Bodies. Interestingly, some stayed in the world when the person left physical life while a portion of these energies unified with the entity after death, essentially serving as the vehicle for an individual to continue their journey into the afterlife. Similarly, as with other mythologies concerning the afterlife journey, there are various locations the spirit passes through and may ultimately reside (combining the Fourth and Fifth Dimensional Sublevel experience) depending upon life position and achievements.

Most Christians believe that following a long and arduous climb into the sky or up a mythical stairway they either arrive in Purgatory where they are held in that limbo until they are deemed "worthy" (a metaphor for the Fourth Dimensional Sublevel and being held there until they learn their co-creative powers), or they enter the Pearly Gates straight away (a metaphor for entry into the Fifth Dimensional Sublevel). Once there they receive judgment from Jesus who qualifies them as either suitable or not for resurrection, and approves their entrance into the Kingdom of God (Entrance into the Sixth Dimensional Sublevel or Perceived Heaven, which we will discuss shortly).

Similarly, Muslim mythology depicts a journey after death following a test to verify if the individual is a true and worthy believer (a metaphor for the entity's awareness and consciousness integrity as they enter the Fourth Dimensional Sublevel). This is generally followed by judgment (the Fifth Dimensional Sublevel experience) to determine if they will go to Purgatory (a longer stay in the Fourth Dimensional Sublevel necessitated by a lack of co-creative consciousness) or will have direct access to Paradise (the Perceived Heaven of the Sixth Dimensional Sublevel).

Perhaps the closest of these religious and spiritual mythologies to actual Universal Truth are those of the Buddhists and Hindus who, at a minimum, have a belief in Reincarnation. However, even these philosophies fall woefully short in understanding true Reincarnation cycles. They are also particularly void when it comes to Transmigration of the Soul through the various Dimensions, or the personality's relationship to the Soul.

First of all, the Buddhist and Hindu reincarnation philosophies count on a linear process where karma dictates the quality of the next lifetime in quick succession until Nirvana has been reached. It is noteworthy that Buddhists refer to a "wheel" of existence or rebirth, but unfortunately the concept is not well defined and is limiting and self-centric. Although the concept of a Soul reincarnating in physical form is present in the belief, it does not include the idea of one Soul casting off many fragments through Reincarnation cycles or wheels. Nor does it contain the idea that numerous lifetimes can be related to each other karmically with all of them happening simultaneously.

It also does not include the idea that each lifetime may balance its karma through other lifetimes related to it on the Soul's Wheel of Creation. Secondarily, it does not allow for the Astral journey of a fragment entity independent of its Soul after physical death, with the fragment retaining personality and consciousness until it is reintegrated into the Soul after a substantial journey and continued evolution of consciousness until it reaches the highest Astral planes.

The typical current view of Reincarnation is of a Soul bouncing from physical lifetime to lifetime in linear procession in an effort to obtain "Nirvana." While there is a modicum of relevance found within that view, it is incorrect in sum and is also a gross simplification of the true multidimensional aspect of the process. Finally, we have already addressed the incorrect idea that Human Angelic Souls will incarnate as non-human species as a form of punishment for prior lives not lived well, an erroneous idea that is prevalent in some mythologies.

Truth be told, most afterlife stories are vague and incorrectly combine the Fourth and Fifth Dimensional Sublevels into one realm or metaphor. Some similarities are shared between the two Sublevel experiences, but the Fourth Sublevel is really more of a "waiting room" where consciousness learns the ropes of how to manifest a new reality and that mastery is what provides access into the Fifth Astral Sublevel. In addition, the Fifth Sublevel requires transmigration from the Fourth Astral Sublevel via the dimensional portals we discussed, and it is for this reason that we refer to it as a kind of "second" death passage, albeit one not as intense or complicated as the transition from physical life.

Once accessed, the Fifth Sublevel does perhaps have certain hallmarks of a "Trial," which is why the process is depicted in many mythologies that way. "Trial" however, is by no means an accurate description and any belief that there is some kind of tribunal or judgment by a God-like or other figure at any point following physical death is a gross misrepresentation of the Fifth Astral Sublevel, or of any Astral Sublevel generally. We assure you that if judgment, reward and punishment were prerequisites for an entity's advancement from Dimension to Dimension, you would be hard pressed to find much transmigration at all between the realms of existence.

Analysis of a life lived by the fragment itself in order to better understand the purpose, lessons and relationships it chose to undertake is a far cry from the genre of harsh judgment many are taught to expect. And that analysis of the lifetime, which is not a judgment, is the purpose of the Fifth Dimensional Sublevel and the reason this Astral Sublevel is designated as the Healing Astral plane.

Although the surroundings and superfluous circumstances created by the entity are generally based on their particular cultural or social beliefs, the Fifth Astral plane is always experienced as a formal, institutional environment where all the aspects of the lifetime just lived can be explored. Memories, relationships, events and karmic interactions are re-played and re-experienced to reveal greater understanding with regard to the entity's personal motives particularly as it regards the life mission and purpose.

In a certain sense, the Fifth Astral Level could be called the Cathartic Astral plane. It is here that many entities resolve conflicts that have just occurred, and also here where each individual obtains a new perspective through enlightenment concerning life experiences. This naturally adds to the individual's vibrational consciousness, and as this occurs the understanding and awareness is also passed on to the

Soul, as well as communicated through the Soul's guidance to other lifetimes within the Wheel of Creation. This allows the Soul to refine its needs and desires for growth, karmic and otherwise, and also determines whether additional lifetimes are warranted within a particular Wheel cycle, in order to balance out the energetic formation. It also allows the Soul to determine if additional events should be added within Third Dimensional lifetimes on the same Wheel still transpiring at the lower Sublevels.

The degree to which this occurs can get quite complicated and confusing, especially since it may involve several other lifetimes in a single Wheel or even several other Wheels of Creation not directly related to the current entity, some possibly on different dimensional timelines and even in lower Universal Dimensions. For our purpose, suffice to say that the individuals experiencing the Fifth Dimensional Sublevel become balanced during this process, and as a result true healing begins.

Healing at this level is said to be cathartic, and in most cases energy blockages that prevailed during the lifetime are surmounted or otherwise permanently released. The understanding of why things occurred as they did during the lifetime is made apparent and this is a major catalyst in the healing and balancing process as well. Energetic imbalances caused by resentments and other pre-chosen attributes, including pride, envy, greed and anger, among other things, are exposed as misguided side effects in the entity's effort to experience a specific mission or purpose on behalf of the Soul.

Some of these things may be recognizable to you as so called "sins," such as those described in Christian philosophy or in other cultural or spiritual teachings. It is in the Fifth Dimensional Sublevel that these issues, "sins" if you prefer the term, are not only brought to light and explored for their relevance to you, but are forgiven in yourself when seen with the understanding of the higher purpose they served as viewed from your Soul's perspective. Again, this can only be accomplished by revelation of the Soul's true purpose and intention as achieved in conjunction with your lifetime. This understanding brings with it healing and higher consciousness to any entity experiencing the Fifth Dimensional Sublevel of the Third Universal Dimension, which is the Astral realm of healing.

Entities experiencing the Fifth Sublevel have contact, if they desire, with those known to them that either are already in the Astral state or are still focused in bodies within the physical realm of the Third Dimensional Sublevel. It is usually at this particular point that when communicating with these loved ones, especially those still focused in physical reality, entities are especially concerned with acknowledging their lifetime misgivings, and they will inevitably attempt to provide insight into their life and obtain forgiveness by expressing unconditional love.

These entities do so as a direct result of what they are experiencing in the Fifth Astral realm, reliving and analyzing their lifetime and its true purpose. This can accurately be seen as a matter of the healing that is taking place within them. In fact, their newfound awareness can even have an impact on those who were connected to them that are still in physical life without having direct contact. This is usually done via the Dreamscape or specific messaging through the subconscious connection maintained with the living.

It is for this reason that those still experiencing physical life will tend to have more tolerant and relaxed views of any person that has passed over, whatever the circumstances that may have occurred between the entities while the person was still physically alive. The admonition to not speak ill of the dead is essentially an inner awareness that the entity has or will ultimately reach a point where Fifth Sublevel healing is accomplished by virtue of an understanding of the impact and importance of their deeds. Healing for all parties involved is retroactively possible.

For the most part as we have said, individuals in the Fifth Astral Sublevel experience the realm as a visit to a large institute of learning, a healing complex or whatever has significance for them and impresses them with the symbolism of trust, importance and wisdom. As an example, many from the Western world will envision the experience as a visit to an institute of higher education, such as a University campus. Others will see it as a clinical experience and visit to a vast hospital complex. Those steeped in doctrine and religious belief will envision it as a visit to a massive Cathedral or religious complex, while those whose entire life revolved around business might find themselves exploring a vast corporate campus.

Those of Eastern persuasions tend to experience a visit to a magnificent or particularly holy Temple complex, historic monuments, gardens or places of high learning, meditation and spiritual enlightenment. Individuals with deep roots in the arts and culture will find themselves within the greatest Museum or Artistic Center they have ever imagined, while those whose lives revolved around animals, wildlife, the outdoors or nature will find themselves in the most beautiful natural settings they have ever known. The possibilities are endless, however they should not be confused with the Astral plane of Perceived Heaven, which is the experience to follow in the Sixth Astral Dimension. These details are simply to impress upon you that in every case the Fifth Astral environment is envisioned as a place the viewer considers will contain the highest ideals of the lifetime, embodied in an environment that is supremely attractive to the participant and where the entity is not only comfortable but also where the entity can above all else trust whatever process transpires there.

Each entity experiences the surroundings according to their own belief structure, as we have already detailed, and the experience is fairly unique since it is entirely self focused with respect to the individual as well as all the life events and relationships they formed along the way on the physical plane. Spirit Guides and other entities from higher Astral levels or even from other Universal Dimensions work within the Fifth Astral realm across the Universe, and their ability to do so is a specific specialty that provides them with substantial growth assisting Human Angelics. Many of these guides originate from the Seventh and above Universal Dimensions, and one of their roles, among others, is to help entities master these experiences and utilize the healing energies available to them. These Guides role-play and become the Teachers, Professors, Technicians, Doctors, Angels and Priests, or whatever else is appropriate to be present, assisting with the proceedings and revelations contained therein on behalf of the entities.

This is not to say that every individual assisting the entity now in the Fifth Astral Sublevel is in fact a Spirit Guide or Avatar, but they do generally have some deep connection with the entity experiencing the healing. However, during deep and intense dream sequences those still in physical bodies and living in the Third Dimensional reality do participate in the process, despite the fact that they are removed from the actual Astral Sublevel. This is particularly true if there is a need for the individuals to explain their own reasons for acting in such a way. Exploring emotions, intense feelings and the unseen mission in the relationship is an important part of this experience.

For the most part, those still in physical bodies forget these experiences or have only vague recollections as they do in the dream state. However, sometimes these are carried over and remembered, particularly if they revolve around those who are deceased and have close bonds with the entity, such as a parent, child, sibling or loved one. Often those still within the Third Dimensional Sublevel in a physical body will consider dreams where they are speaking with or interacting with loved ones that have passed on as coincidental remembrances when in fact they are experiencing actual contact with the individual that is no longer physically focused.

These experiences can become deeply buried within the psyche and their intensity usually precludes them from being remembered or brought forth into daily waking consciousness. However, we would suggest that those living are often actively participating with these entities that are reviewing their life experiences and relationships with others while journeying through the higher Astral planes. We explain this in order to demonstrate that to an extent healing can be effectuated for all involved, despite the fact that the entity is no longer focused in physical reality.

Moreover, this highlights for you the fact that it is never too late to continue to understand the real meaning of your experiences, or reach a state of forgiveness, grace and healing even after being separated by dimensional veils. In fact, in some cases relationships you have with those who have passed from physical existence can be stronger than when the entity was living beside you, since this can provide a significant altering of perspective and outlook. This is especially true if there was emotional or physical trauma associated with the individual who is no longer in a physical body.

Not only does this make it easier for the individual still in physical incarnation, it also allows the entity experiencing the Fifth Dimensional Sublevel to heal, something potentially not possible when the individuals were living side by side and role playing for purposes of the Soul's mission or to obtain Soul growth. Accomplishing healing through the Dreamscape between an individual still focused in a physical body and one that has moved on in Etheric form potentially allows both parties to shorten the period they may need for healing within the Fifth Astral plane.

Achieving neutrality and karmic balancing provides the entity with a true reflection of the life just lived and allows the individual to see their actions from a higher perspective with a focus on their higher purpose or mission. Therefore, standards that might be applicable in physical reality are not warranted nor are they used. With no good, bad, right or wrong judgments made, the individual is free to determine which choices were productive and which were not. It is based on this that the individual ascertains what they learned, positive or negative, from the experiences. As these experiences are viewed against the backdrop of other lifetimes within the Soul's Wheel of Creation, it also becomes possible to see what additional factors concerning the particular situation could be explored further, if desired. In keeping with the karmic balancing, any additional factors are "inherited" by other lifetimes within the Wheel, and these will balance with the entity passing through the Fifth Dimensional Sublevel.

Because the entity is now able to view situations from other perspectives, in particular the perspective of anyone who was subjected to experiences derived from involvement with the entity, these events and issues are especially ripe for exploration. They are also projected out to other lifetimes in the Wheel, and from there the balancing can occur. This is orchestrated by the Soul, in conjunction with the entity, incorporating new events in other lifetimes on a particular Wheel of Creation that will balance the karma going forward.

More often than not, even though they are vastly different and occurring at different points on the dimensional Timeline, lifetimes associated on the same Wheel of Creation have a good many similarities, which can range from Soul mates interacting with each other in one lifetime to planning several different lifetimes on the Wheel together. In every case, the lifetimes are interconnected and usually the roles switch from life to life within a particular Wheel. This adds a whole new multidimensional aspect to the Soul's Wheel of Creation. An analogy that might be familiar to you here is the continual linking and breaking of chemical bonds in a never ending chain reaction where molecules form, bond, reproduce, disengage and move-on in a seemingly endless cycle.

The opening of consciousness to reveal the deeper purpose and meaning behind life events or situations, however, is not always a simple matter. Nor is it one as obvious as you might think. As an example, one might consider the fact that they were abandoned or adopted as a child a major life event, which of course it is. On further analysis, however, one might discover that this challenging event was strategically and purposely agreed upon by all Souls involved prior to the lifetime in order to give the entity lifelong lessons around the issue of acceptance and rejection.

Suddenly a major life event creates specific sensitivities around an issue, which is carried by the individual throughout the lifetime. At the core, large and small life events then might all seem to bring up the same issue, and whenever this individual deals with feelings around being accepted or rejected, their life purpose is being explored. However, in this way, one lifetime event in need of energetic healing becomes hundreds of large and smaller life events, each with its own aspects, each needing its own analysis and understanding and each requiring enlightenment to bring about peace and healing for the entity.

Healing is a hallmark of consciousness growth at every dimensional level. Through the ages many have thought suffering is the means to growth when in truth healing is the key to consciousness. For this reason the particular focus of the Fifth Dimensional Sublevel is on healing within what could be termed the Healing Temples of the Fifth Astral plane. Opening consciousness to the reasons behind the events and situations or suffering that has befallen an entity allows them to achieve healing and this in turn allows the rise in vibrational energy and consciousness as a result. Higher consciousness contributes to an entity's vibrational signature and when consolidated becomes incorporated as part of the Soul's growth.

In particular, any traumatic or lingering residue or energetic blockages that accompanies the Etheric consciousness after the physical lifetime will be explored. As we have said, the Fifth Dimensional Astral Healing Temples, using this designation as more of a metaphor than an actual location, and the process of healing is formalized according to each individual's particular needs, desires and belief structures. It is formalized in the sense that while there is no primary attendant or Angelic Being in charge, the process is quickly apparent to each entity. Spirit Guardians and other entities are always ready to assist, and these Guides make themselves available for their own purpose of Soul growth by assisting the healing endeavors.

As we have described in the past, many of these Guardians and highly evolved beings are System Lords from the Seventh through Ninth Universal Dimensions who return and inhabit the lower Universal Dimensions, including the Astral levels, in order to work with entities and help guide them through their own process. They do so by assisting each entity to harmonize with their experiences by discovering a greater understanding of why life events occurred. Additionally, they assist entities to see and retrieve their power over these events in order to neutralize the energetic blockages that may have formed along the way.

Interestingly enough as an entity reviews life events they can be played backwards and forwards, and from various perspectives, from the entity's point of view as well as from the perspective of the participants. In this way, the entity is able to relive and see all aspects and every side of the events that occurred. In particular, the emotions, feelings and thoughts of the entity are explored, and this becomes an important part of the energetic release and healing.

Sometimes Guardians and Guides assisting an individual entity will take on the role of a participant and allow the entity to replay the event in a different light or through a different choice than was made during the lifetime. In some cases, this allows the entity to even change the event by understanding the event's purpose, correcting any misgivings and allowing different choices to affect the outcome of the situation in an entirely new way.

This is important since it is not always necessary to address these self-karmic issues in conjunction with the Soul through altering or modifications in the Soul's Wheel of Creation. Naturally, there are situations where the energetic blockage or karmic imbalance is so profound it must be addressed at the Soul level through events played out and balanced in other lifetimes on the Wheel of which the entity's lifetime is part. Self-karma, or energetic imbalances that are highly individual in nature and do not require other input or relationships to balance are sometimes more readily addressed through redress and higher understanding in the Healing Temples of the Fifth Dimensional Sublevel.

The fact is, the Fifth Astral plane has significantly greater lightness available to it, in terms of actual light frequency, and as a result tends to be a realm more luminous and therefore a place with more clarity than what is familiar in the Fourth Astral plane, or Dreamscape. This luminosity is related to higher vibrational frequencies and it is a reality that is far less dense and easier to manifest than what is experienced at lower dimensional levels.

It needs to be understood that even though the Fifth Astral Sublevel is more luminous and less dense physically than anything familiar to you in the physical density of the Third Dimensional Sublevel, this does not mean that the elements comprising the realm are completely foreign to the entity sojourning through it. As we have explained, when the entity proceeds through the "Tunnel of Light," or Dimensional Portal, the experience is distinctly different from Dimension to Dimension, even if the attributes and surroundings are similar and still recognizable to the entity.

This is because an entity emerging from one Dimension to the next sees what it expects to see. In other words, reality is composed of what is familiar, even if its construction or origins are vastly different. In addition to this, depending upon the person's expectation even Guides working with the entity will appear familiar to the individual based on their lifetime, their personality and their cultural or other experiences.

As we explained, it is possible that an individual's family, friends and loved ones who have passed on already may appear at the Fifth Dimensional Sublevel within the Healing Temples. Most often however, these family, friends and loved ones are actually Spirit and Higher Guides who are assuming the roles of those loved ones in order to comfort the individuals and facilitate their readiness to trust the process and understand what is happening to them. This is usually the first step to bringing about healing.

Contrary to popular belief, while no retribution or judgment is ever heaped on an entity with respect to anything they have chosen or done during the lifetime, the Fifth Dimensional Sublevel could be seen as the place where an entity is able to experience the consequences of its actions during life. As this occurs, the individual has a highly empathetic viewpoint, offering an immediate understanding of any harm that was caused to the entity or to others. Inversely, the individual experiences the benefit and joy it brought to others during the lifetime based on its choices, actions and reactions.

It is important to note that no entity is required to experience the Fifth Dimensional Astral realm, and some may linger in the Fourth Astral plane for quite some time. An entity is free to remain in any particular Astral level for whatever period it wishes. In fact, although not ideal, an individual can take up housekeeping in any Astral state and remain there indefinitely, if it so chooses.

Most are attracted to this possibility preliminarily since once they master the concept of manifesting their reality at the Fourth Astral plane or Dreamscape, they can find themselves in ideal realities that were not necessarily available to them in physical reality in the Third Dimensional Sublevel. Such a prolonged stay could be considered akin to the concept of purgatory as found in various religions. Then again, if asked those entities remaining indefinitely might consider this to be their "heavenly" abode. That said however, most lose their attraction to remaining in lower physical density at some point even with its attractive trappings. Eventually all will long for peace, at which point the process of advancing to higher Astral planes occurs.

Returning to the large and small-scale life events we were discussing, it should be kept in mind that every intense emotion, thought or experience lived through during the physical life incarnation is electromagnetically imprinted on the entity and, in a certain sense, stored. These impressions are imprinted in what has been termed the Hall of Records, or the Akashic realm.

What you know as the Akashic is in fact an entire Universal Dimension, the Eighth Universal Dimension to be specific. Bear in mind also that the Sublevels of a Universal Dimension correspond to the essence of their Universal Counterpart. Therefore, the Eighth Sublevel of every Universal Dimension is in effect related to the Eighth Universal Dimension, or to the Akashic plane.

Many of you recognize the Akashic Records as the metaphoric Halls of Remembrance, the Book of Life or the Mind of God. What may be less well known however, is the fact that the electromagnetic impulses related to your life within the Third Universal Dimension are encoded and accessed through the Eighth Sublevel of the Third Universal Dimension. As such, the Records are also accessible within the

Universal Dimension, and it is precisely this bank that is accessed by mystics, psychics and intuitives from the Third Dimensional Sublevel.

The records are similarly accessed by each entity that is in the Fifth Dimensional Sublevel undergoing the healing process that plane offers. Lifetime occurrences become part and parcel of the vibrational signature that identifies you and your Soul, and it is these electromagnetic impulses that you access, in conjunction with your Guides, in the Fifth Astral realm. Because time as you know it is not a factor of Universal time, these experiences are always accessible to you no matter when they occurred.

Similarly, each entity can access the lifetimes related to it on the Soul's Wheel of Creation, and in this manner the individual is able to see how their choices and experiences move backwards and forward through the other life incarnations connected to them. In a sense, you have access to them even during physical life in the Third Dimensional Sublevel of the Third Dimension, and although you attribute your memories to biological functioning in the brain, your memories would not exist the way you know them if those portions of the brain did not have a vibrational link accessible to the Records themselves. It is for this reason that some are able to access other incarnations or reincarnated selves, and can even detail, usually through hypnosis, other lifetimes related to them on the Soul's Wheel of Creation of which they are part.

But what is more important is that although your current focus of reality only allows you to access your experiences from one perspective, because they are electromagnetic in nature they are actually encoded from a number of different perspectives. In fact, these events are also encoded as part of the energetic experiences of other individuals - some with a Soul relationship to you and some without any connection.

Ultimately though, this means you have access to all these other perspectives, especially those that are more empathetic. Not only are you able to relive, experience and feel these situations again from your perspective, in the Fifth Astral realm, you can witness them from the perspective of every individual that was involved. A particular experience that you had, traumatic or otherwise, that was only available to you from one perspective is seen and reviewed by you from a myriad of viewpoints and angles, through the eyes of others as it were.

It is difficult to hide, fool oneself or lie about any event relived from various viewpoints and numerous perspectives, and this method allows for true reflection and rectification, whether it is achieved through an internal look from the individual's experience or karmically as it applies to others involved in the events. As you can see, this serves as a valuable tool of enlightenment for any individual still in denial or who had refused empathy, understanding and forgiveness during the lifetime.

Access to this information can truly change the way a life lesson or purpose is understood and opens each entity up to a wider view of how an event was experienced and its real purpose. It also has important impact in allowing an understanding of exactly why the individual or any other participant in the event behaved as they did. If as an example, the individual was someone that inflicted trauma or emotional damage on someone else, the situation is viewed not only from that individual's perspective but also through the eyes of those who endured the trauma. If another entity was responsible for causing the pain or difficulty you endured, you are now able to understand their inner most reasons for doing so and the purpose it had with respect to your participation and its importance in your own life mission.

Such revelations lead you to understand the hidden growth opportunities that are always present and being played out in every event and by every individual concerned. Since no event in reality should be considered accidental, reliving the experience from all sides provides the hidden understanding of why the event transpired, as well as insight into the subconscious invitations sent all around to the participants. With a newfound understanding of life events, from a higher perspective and as it regards the life purpose and EssencePath of all involved, healing can be achieved.

All of this, in one way or another, adjusts the karmic imbalances that through their energetic intensity have been electromagnetically imprinted in the Hall of Records on behalf of each participant. Some undergoing the Fifth Astral plane healing experience will have more to contend with, while others will have less. But what is key here is the fact that with the balancing of these imbalances by reliving and sometimes altering the electromagnetic imprints stored in the Akashic, healing in the Fifth Astral Sublevel has begun.

Each entity is different in how they process and handle what has befallen them during the physical lifetime at the Third Dimensional Sublevel of the Third Universal Dimension. Some have traumatic emotional experiences and some have actual physical trauma that is carried by them energetically and must be addressed at some point.

Each of these issues, emotional or physical in nature, are addressed in the Healing Temples of the Fifth Astral plane.

Sometimes the trauma is too intense for self-correction, and in that case it must be carried forward and worked out within other lifetimes as we discussed. Those life events and situations that are so highly charged they are carried by the individual into non-corporeal life and cannot be self mitigated in the Fifth Astral Healing Temples will ultimately be lifted from the individual by the Soul for rectification elsewhere.

If possible, this karma will be placed into a lifetime on the Wheel of Creation that is still being experienced in the Third Dimensional Sublevel. If this is not possible, the Soul may plan an additional lifetime within the current Wheel that is organized around the karma. Sometimes the karma or event is so traumatic and important to the consciousness and growth of the Soul that it will originate an entirely new Wheel of Creation built entirely around various issues and consequences of one single physical life event.

If the Soul is able to balance the karmic energy by placing it back into the Wheel of which the individual is part, the proximity of the Fifth Astral plane to the Fourth allows the participants access to the energetic exchange via the Dreamscape. In this way, other lifetimes still experiencing incarnation in the physical reality can participate by experimenting with the possibilities and probabilities of incorporating a completely new balancing event into their own lifetime. In essence, the entity taking on the balancing karma participates via Free Will in conjunction with the Soul.

This is experienced as what you could call new "Life Chapters," or times when there is a complete and dramatic change of personality and life. Some describe this phenomenon as "Walk Ins." The idea that a new Soul takes over an existing physical body when it has finished its mission is so rare as not to be a matter of consideration here. What is actually happening in most such circumstances is that it is likely a related lifetime from your Soul's Wheel of Creation is pushing through a new life mission to you that is needed to karmically or otherwise balance the Wheel. Though what you may feel happening to you is "karmic," it could actually be karma generated by another entity on the Wheel of which you are part that you are balancing through your own life events, without actually having created the karmic event in the first place.

This highlights another reason conscious awareness of your actions is so important, and this is the true meaning of the Biblical advice, "Do unto others, as you would have them do unto you." In conjunction with your Soul and related Souls and Soul Mates, the handicaps you develop during life, the new people who enter your life, the relationship dynamics that form or fall apart, all of which can seem quite dramatic, may be part of the "cure" for karma created elsewhere on your Soul's Wheel of Creation, or, more importantly, can actually bleed through and shift events in the other lifetimes on the Wheel.

Often this also heralds a new life mission for the individual, and it is not uncommon for an individual to have two principal life missions or purposes. On rare occasions, an individual can even have three distinct life missions or purposes during the course of the lifetime, particularly if significant growth is sought by the individual or Soul. Generally, all very dramatic or unexpected life changes that can alter personality and personal trajectory are related to this system of karmic balance within the Wheel, as a means of consciousness growth for the entity, and ultimately, growth for the Soul of which the entity is part.

In some cases dreams that you have that seem not at all related to you, as if you were someone else in the dream state, can also indicate experimenting with this. Additionally, sometimes dreams you have while still in physical incarnation of those who have passed away where forgiveness is being sought or where the individual seems familiar but like someone entirely new, is an example of an entity that is most likely in the midst of experiencing the Fifth Astral Healing Sublevel. Often, these individuals will visit you in the Dreamscape in order to seek forgiveness. Usually, this is an attempt to alter actual events on the timeline, which the individual is reliving concurrently in the Healing Temples of the Fifth Astral plane.

It is a mistake to think that what happens to the physical or emotional body while in physical incarnation remains static and is not imprinted on the Etheric or Energetic body overall. Physical vulnerabilities, especially those caused by physical or emotional trauma, remain with the Etheric and are not only carried forward after physical life, if they are felt intensely enough they can bleed through and affect other lifetimes connected to you on the Wheel of Creation. This is also the reason why physical and emotional trauma stemming from other lifetimes that seems unconnected to you can energetically and otherwise pass through to you. In addition, physical vulnerabilities and sensitivities, including talents, attributes and proficiencies that are not necessarily genetic but are originated in other lifetimes on the Wheel can also easily bleed through and become part of who you are.

It should be remembered that although it is true the physical body can be damaged, the reality is, as we have said before, there is almost no occurrence, physical or otherwise, that is not first lived by the Etheric body before manifesting in physical life. In fact, healing the physical body, while all fine and good, is not possible without healing the Etheric body, and those in need of physical healing should remember to address the Etheric, Emotional and Mental Bodies in addition to the Physical Structure, should healing be necessary. Based on this, what is imprinted on the Etheric remains until it is addressed, whether addressing that energy is accomplished in what you know as the physical world or at any point in the Astral realm.

If we are explaining this it is to demonstrate that in order to truly heal anything in the physical environment, it must also be simultaneously healed in the Etheric. The things not healed in the Etheric environment during the lifetime, such as emotional trauma or physical trauma from accident or disease, will linger in the Etheric body. This is so even when the physical body is no longer present, and the trauma or energetic imprint must then be addressed after the entity leaves the plane of physical existence. This is the primary function of the Fifth Astral plane, and as we have explained, the issues remaining that are imprinted upon the Etheric body after leaving the physical body, as well as the various karmic and energetic imbalances, will be explored and addressed therein.

Again, this is said with the understanding that right, wrong, good, bad or judgment with respect to these issues is never the case in the higher Astral realms. Although it may be true that the duality existing on the physical plane of reality creates an electromagnetic dynamic that can be seen as positive and negative, the particular worldview that sees positive elements as angelic/good and negative elements as demonic/bad is misguided. In truth, this is a point of view that for the most part is dependent on cultural or religious standards, as well as your Soul age, and has little to do with the reality of things.

The Fourth and especially the Fifth Astral plane, and all the higher Astral realms for that matter, are places of extreme love, peace and understanding where every entity in conjunction with their Spirit Guides and their Soul family are able to explore past adventures in greater detail, discover new horizons and continue their journey of growth. If the process undergone in the Fifth Dimensional Sublevel sounds a bit institutional or institutionalized, it is merely the description and the metaphors used to describe it to you. In fact, the experience is user friendly to the highest degree, created by and for the entity to correspond to their comfort level, understanding and consciousness.

Those who believe that the passage through the Astral planes is unimportant, uninteresting and not rewarding, or is a leisurely time where no real activity takes place, would be surprised to know that the journey offers the entity continual growth and new awareness throughout the sojourn. As you have discovered, this is especially true on the Fourth Astral plane and in the Fifth Astral realm while experiencing the Astral Healing Temples.

Once free of the physical body, the Etheric body is not subject to the same rules of physics as the physical body was in the Third Dimensional Sublevel. However, the Higher Astral planes do have to an extent specific physics to contend with. As an example, without a body to nourish or maintain physically, the concepts of nourishment, rest and sustaining livelihood are far different for the Etheric body than you need to survive in physical reality. We mention this only to demonstrate that there is a greater range of possibilities within the Higher Astral planes that are not available to you in lower, denser physical environments. These possibilities provide new and significant opportunities to you that are more flexible and available for achieving awareness and growth than you have in your current physical reality.

In conjunction with the healing that is performed, or rather, which is made available through grace to the Etheric body, instructions are provided to entities on the Fifth Astral plane to assist their continued learning. In a sense, excusing the pun, it truly could be called a place of higher education. Principal among these instructions is the fact that the entity needs to understand how thought energy is made manifest or how in the Astral realms thought forms can materialize instantaneously or be a means of propulsion transporting you to the place you envision.

The entities connected to younger Souls, who are naturally con- nected to the dense physical reality from which they just came, will create environments that are more or less similar to the earthly en- vironments from whence they came. Entities derived from older Souls will be more experimental in their environments and creations.

Though we caution once again against believing that there is a Heaven or a Hell in the afterlife or as some facet of an Astral plane, the Sixth Astral plane does in fact reflect back to you your truest Essence, and thus the environment created reflects your inner self base on the life just lived. In general, this is also consistent with how, in your view, your experiences and life efforts impacted others while in physical existence.

If your view of yourself based on your efforts to raise your conscious- ness and consequently your actions with regard to others is favorable, the environment reflected to you is one that is rewarding. However, if your view of yourself following the analysis that takes place in the Fifth Astral Sublevel has misgivings or if you deem your life mission and the opportunities for growth to have been sidestepped through

Free Will or unsuccessful in some way, the environment you perceive in the Sixth Astral realm can be less than optimum.

It is precisely from here that a concept of Heaven and Hell originates. Although these do not actually exist, if they exist for you in the Sixth Astral plane it is based on your belief structure with the understanding that who you truly are is reflected back to you based on your vibrational integrity and your consciousness. In this way, the Sixth Astral plane, or the realm of Perceived Heaven, is an abode based on the Truth of who you are. In a metaphoric sense it could also be considered the result of the judgment you pass upon yourself based on your own qualifications and analysis of the lifetime you have just lived after passing through the Healing Temples of the Fifth Astral Sublevel.

If the grand healing process of the Fifth Dimensional Sublevel is one that assures the dispelling of residual energies, the balancing of karma created in the physical lifetime and a definitive understanding of the entity's true EssencePath, then the Sixth Astral plane could actually be seen as the restful reward your life has brought you. It is important to understand however, that this is not a final resting place but only a stopping point on the continuing journey through the Astral realms towards reintegration with your Soul.

The Sixth Astral plane, Perceived Heaven, relies almost entirely on the individual's true self, and the environment is manifested for the entity in this Astral realm as a reflection of the entity's own perception of their merit and worth as seen from the newly discovered perspective uncovered through the healing experiences of the Fifth Astral Sublevel. The key variant here is that in the Sixth Dimensional Sublevel, the axiom that reality is based on the individual's desires and thought projections, which is present in the Fourth Dimensional Sublevel or Dreamscape and, to a point, the Fifth Dimensional Sublevel, is no longer valid.

In the Sixth Dimensional Sublevel the environment is not produced *by you* but is produced *on your behalf* as a reflection, and the basis for that reality is not thought form or intention but rather the core vibrational perception mirrored back to each entity. In other words, reality at this Sixth Dimensional Sublevel is a reflection of the entity's Essence and Truth, not a cascade of thoughts, desires and intentions based on random intentions or structural beliefs external to the entity.

Such a distinction is only possible following the healing experiences of the Fifth Astral plane aimed at unveiling the entity's Truth, or Essence. The easiest way to envision this difference is using an analogy based on your current physical reality. Your current reality is manifested by you through a combination of energetic factors that include the parameters created by childhood environment, you life mission, your Soul-based contracts and relationships with others and the energy of your thoughts, emotions and conscious intentions. You navigate the events, positive and negative, that are attracted and ultimately magnetized to you, for better or for worse, and through this process consciousness and Soul growth is achieved.

Physical life in the Third Dimension would be quite different if the quality of the person you are was solely what determined the reality that came your way. In such a world, pure, innocent, "good" conscious people would have nothing but pure, innocent, honest, good things happen to them from dawn until dusk. Similarly, deceitful, dishonest, tainted, "bad," egotistical people would only experience those kinds of things, since this would be the world reflected back to them.

Clearly, this is not how reality is manifested in the current Third Dimensional Sublevel of reality or there would be no need to ponder the question, "…why do "bad" things happen to "good" people?" and vice versa.

Although we have used the subjective standards of good, bad, right or wrong for demonstration purposes here, even though events may come from either the positive polarity or the negative polarity, both offer the same consciousness growth, and all consciousness growth is positive and beneficial. Therefore, your Soul is unconcerned with whether you experience your growth from a chain of positive events and relationships, or a chain of negative ones. However, both physical and Etheric life could be said to be far easier and more fluid if your experiences were always positive and never negative. This is precisely the difference that is reflected in one's reality in the Sixth Astral plane, or Perceived Heaven.

This is also why it might behoove you to do your utmost to discover and follow your EssencePath in the current physical reality. The key to that lies in knowing yourself, experiencing your life lessons through the positive polarity, finding worth by living your Truth, being compassionate with yourself and others and following your higher guidance. This combination helps streamline and ease the Third Dimensional experience, both in physical reality and when moving through the Astral realms. Then, in the Sixth Astral Dimension, the reward, if you will, is a reality manifested for you that is wholly based on the value of your true Essence.

We have used the term Perceived Heaven to describe the Sixth Astral plane for two reasons. First, this realm is the one that most resembles contemporary mythologies, in particular Christian philosophy, as the vision of "Heaven" or paradise expected in the afterlife. Many will perceive the experience as "heavenly," assuming their intentions and the view they have of their physical lifetime is productive and positive.

Secondly, in a sense the realm can be said to "perceive" the inner Truth of each entity, which is a reflection of their True Self. In turn, the entity "perceives" the environment reflected back to them as a deserving environment based on their impression of who they are and the merit they place on their physical lifetime. In other words, those who feel they are deserving of "Heaven" after discovering Truth (following the Fifth Astral plane experience) will find just that, while those who feel they are deserving of a lesser state, or even "Hell," based on their findings uncovered in the Healing Temples of the Fifth Astral plane will find what they feel they merit.

As we have explained through our analogy of how reality is manifested in the current state of physical reality, the distinction between an environment created by you based on your thought projections, core beliefs and desires and one that is a reflection created on your behalf and mirrored back to you based on your true Essence is a subtle but important one to understand. Unlike the Astral experiences of the Fourth and Fifth Dimensional Sublevels, the Sixth Astral reality is a realm of higher consciousness where the quality of your personal vibrational signature is recognized, matched and reflected back to you as your reality. Such a world is not conjured by you, but is presented to you as a kind of universal reward for whom you truly are found to be as an entity following healing in the Fifth Dimensional Sublevel and Astral healing realm. It is a reality that is reflective of your complete inner Truth, and is therefore highly compatible with you, as well as consistent with who you are at your core.

Because such an environment is so highly matched to your own vibrational quality, it is as if everything you find in it is compatible with you and in perfect harmony with your resonance. Unlike the realities of the Third Dimensional Sublevel, and even the Fourth and Fifth Astral Sublevels where a myriad of dualistic thought forms, core beliefs and personality features combine to create a reality comprised of situations desirable for purposes of growth, the Sixth Astral Plan provides a high degree of peace and respite for the entity. This is because nothing that is present or occurs in that environment is challenging to the entity since everything experienced will match the entity's resonance and, as a reflection of absolute Truth, will be completely neutral to the entity perceiving that reality.

Inevitably, a reality that is based on thoughts, core beliefs and personality is symptomatic of growth, while a reality that reflects back who you truly are is symptomatic of one where growth has already been obtained. In truth, the Fourth and Fifth Astral levels are instrumental in bringing each entity to a place where having analyzed their purpose and the growth achieved in the lifetime, they are healed.

Healing, and the state of grace that follows, makes it possible to experience the fruits of one's labors, so to speak, in the Sixth Astral level. This should by no means imply that the Sixth Astral plane is an end point, for it is not. However, as the realm of Perceived Heaven, this plane can be thought of as a place of fulfillment, rest and recuperation within an environment that completely matches the inner reflection or Essence of the entity.

Similar to the Fourth and Fifth Astral environments, the Sixth Astral plane is different for each and every entity. However, the Sixth Astral plane has a much higher vibrational frequency, and it is removed vibrationally from the Third Dimensional Sublevel in such a way that also has less familiarity or direct contact with lower dimensional levels. Once entities have reached this plane of existence, it is rare indeed for them to visit lower Astral Dimensions. It is usually at this point that the relatively frequent contact possible between an entity and loved ones still in physical incarnation, which took place within the Fourth Astral realm and Dreamscape or the Fifth Astral plane, is greatly curtailed if not halted entirely.

Though our designation for the realm is "Perceived Heaven," this should not be misconstrued as some kind of Paradise "Carte Blanche." This is especially true in that it is not derived based on your desires, choices or intentions, and rather is composed of the natural reflection of your true self-awareness, worth and Essence. This means that an individual's true merit or lack of merit is reflected back to them through the reality that unfolds in this environment. Because of this fact, sojourns through the Sixth Astral realm can either be, as defined by your current standards, an experience of paradise or an experience that is problematic.

This is especially so if the entity's inner vision of itself following the Healing plane of the Fifth Astral Level is lacking based on how it perceived its true merit during the lifetime. Thus, the "reward" you receive in the Sixth Astral plane, in terms of the environment you experience there, will be whatever you believe to be your true worth and value, as perceived by you following the extensive analysis and healing accomplished at the prior Astral level.

The energetic portal that separates the Fifth Astral realm and the Sixth Astral realm, both Dimensional Sublevels, is far less distinctive than other such portals. The vortex that portends entry is created as revelation occurs in the Fifth Dimensional Sublevel Healing Temples, and the transition that starts at the beginning of the Healing Temples and is finalized during the ending process is a gradual one that leads to a higher vibrational frequency when the healing has been accomplished.

One could say that the Healing Temple itself is the vibrational transitory "tunnel" except for the fact that what actually accomplishes the energetic transference is achieving the State of Grace that the Healing Temples perfect within you. The vibrational impact of this state cannot be underestimated, as it increases your energetic profile and spin exponentially, and this acts as a key to entry into the Sixth Astral realm.

It is not far off to state that an appropriate analogy would be working diligently on a project, completing it satisfactorily and feeling an enormous sense of accomplishment, peace and fulfillment at accomplishing it successfully. The Sixth Astral plane is arrived at the moment fulfillment and satisfaction at a job well done is reached. The experience of the Sixth Astral plane, or Perceived Heaven, is the period of relaxation and contentedness that follows, and this, metaphorically speaking, is your reward, whatever that reward may be as reflected back to you.

Although the Sixth Astral plane is peaceful and pleasant for the majority based on the reflection they see, this is not always the case. For most, the environment is completely consistent with their personal feelings of respect and merit as it relates to their ability to love and the amount of genuine affection or love that was returned to them by their fellow entities and Soul associates while in physical incarnation. For others, again cautioning against the notion of a Hell, if an individual's true reflection is related to a lifetime where they feel they were "rightfully" cruel or "righteously" abusive, hateful, disinterested or violent, an environment is created where they are provided with experiences based on these same sentiments.

It should be remembered that in many instances those who have done what you consider to be tremendous evil and harm in your world are sometimes participating in a grander scheme to provide opportunities for growth in mass consciousness and for larger populations. Although you may consider their deeds and actions to be particularly horrific and even evil, which in fact they might be, many times propagating or inspiring these destructive or negative situations on the physical plane was completely intentional on the part of the Soul. Often, the actions of the incarnations of the Physical System Lords can take on such appearances, if you recall that the Physical System Lords create physical life incarnations intended to alter the geo-political position of the world structure at specific points on the timeline.

For this reason, although an entity may be in need of healing in the Healing Temples of the Fifth Astral plane, it should be understood that often the Sixth Astral plane environment created for them is not as challenging or negative as you might expect. It is because of this that we again caution against belief in a "Hell," which is a construct of religious and ruling organizations to intimidate and oblige wider adherence to societal rules and fabricated dogma.

That said, despite the healing energy employed in the Fifth Astral Realm and the balance of karma being met, based on the deeds they explore, some entities will still consider themselves unworthy or not yet worthy of a positive state of being. These entities will have a projected reality that can be anything from a self imposed prison to an isolation based on the notions of their merit because of their past experiences. Many will remain for extended periods of time in isolation or in projected situations that are less than desirable. This especially tends to be the case for those who have had challenging existences where they caused great harm to other entities in the physical life. In certain cases, it can also be the experience of those who take their own physical life, once they discover that the challenges they faced in physical reality were intended as part of their Soul growth.

This may seem karmic in nature or even appropriate. However, it is usually merely an environment being projected for the entity in order for them to be alone with their thoughts in order to come to terms and balance out, or in some instances escape, the intense feelings derived from a lifetime where they harmed others or themselves

The role of the Healing Temples is not to change an individual's true self, but assist them to see all facets of their behavior through varying perspectives, thereby allowing neutrality and achieving healing and growth. Once that awareness and healing is accomplished, most entities achieve a state of grace. It is incorrect to assume that "grace" is automatically associated with your current standards of something "good." Rather, its hallmark is a state of neutrality and detachment.

Because there is no judgment or punishment, even in such cases, these individuals achieve neutrality through grace regardless, and this enables them to graduate from the Fifth Astral realm. When they do however, they are subject to a reality in the Sixth Astral plane that reflects back to them the inner view of exactly who they are, and this is not always as pleasant as you might think if you consider the true meaning of the term "Perceived Heaven."

For the most part, this is rare and usually occurs only in extreme situations where, having witnessed events from every perspective, the individual still believes their actions were necessary. This situation is usually present most often in the lifetimes of Souls who are oriented towards Service-to-Self, and as we have discussed, the majority of Human Angelic Souls tend to be oriented towards Service-to-Others. It might be observed that the point in these cases is that since the entity's True Self is the basis of its standards, each is entitled to whatever perspective they find following examination of their Truth.

This is where the realm of Perceived Heaven can also sometimes be considered a realm of healing similar to the Fifth Astral planes, since overtime even these Service-to-Self or disoriented individuals come to a more rounded understanding of why they do what they do, and are who they are. In fact, this revelation is usually brought about by the constant reflection of the environment they see, which as a reflection of their true inner self is void of unconditional love, presents them with every manner of challenge and results in the nagging inability to find real fulfillment or joy. In a sense, no matter how long it takes, once the individual becomes tired of experiencing a reality based on lack being played out for them constantly they almost always arrive at the realization that their Truth may be a limiting one in need of an expanded perspective. Once again, and even under difficult circumstances, Soul growth is achieved.

As their view of themselves slowly transforms based on this, the reality that is reflected back to them changes as well in accord with their evolving viewpoint. This is an important factor of the Sixth Astral realm. Bit by bit, a completely new reality is reflected back to them, and they become aware of the difference in their own Truth based on a newly reflected environment that the Sixth Astral plane or landscape of Perceived Heaven is offering them. That said, it is true that these entities generally spend much longer periods in the Sixth Astral environment than most in order to arrive at the neutrality, peace and joy that must be achieved by all before advancement to higher Astral planes is possible. We will leave it to you to decide if there is a measure of divine justice to be found therein that is reminiscent of some of your spiritual or religious teachings.

Once again, this brings up the question of how much time is required in each Astral Dimension or how long an entity is required to remain in any particular Astral division. There is no single answer to this since an entity is not required to progress at any particular speed or pace. Secondarily, because the notion of linear time is an abstract concept reserved principally for lower dimensional physics as we have stated, advancement times are not relevant to Higher Astral planes. For this reason, we reaffirm that there is no particular answer or time period required in any one Astral Dimensional Sublevel.

Having said this, there are certain generalities that can be made. As an example, other than entities that become lost due to the inability of the Etheric body to join with the Mental and Emotional bodies at the time of death, passing from the Third Dimensional Sublevel into the Fourth Astral plane or Dreamscape is fairly rapid in its progression. In addition, entities will pass relatively quickly from the Fourth to the Fifth Astral plane, although again this depends on their awareness and consciousness with respect to understanding that reality is being controlled and created by them, for them.

At times, this can also depend upon those that have been left behind in physical reality. Some entities, out of concern and love or if they are mourned and missed too severely, will wait for their loved ones in the Fourth Astral plane, visiting with them often through the Dreamscape. Others will move on quickly, depending on their consciousness and talents, and will prefer to visit loved ones from the Fifth or higher Astral planes.

Some immensely enjoy reality in the Fourth, Fifth or Sixth Astral plane, especially after the fundamentals of the plane are mastered, and many will linger in specific planes even if they are ready to progress to higher dimensional levels. There are also those individuals who have less complicated ties to either loved ones they have left behind or to Soul Mates or a particular Soul cadre known to them in the lifetime, and these entities tend to quickly progress to the level known as Perceived Heaven.

Speaking of this with regard to a Soul's methodology in creating Wheels of Creation, some Souls prefer to plan more lifetimes on the Wheel that are quicker, shorter lives. These entities tend to pass quickly through the Astral states to the Sixth Astral level as well. Other Souls plan Wheels with longer lifetimes that include a myriad of wide ranging adventures, karmic and otherwise.

As we have explained, with the help of other lifetimes on the Wheel these may be subject to balancing karma or to having two or even three life missions compressed into one lifetime. Since such lifetimes are generally more complicated and full of substance, these entities can tend to remain for greater periods in every Astral plane, especially in the Fifth or Sixth Dimensional Sublevels. All of this is very much individual and up to each entity to originate and plan in conjunction with their Soul.

It is with this in mind that you understand an entity that has progressed to the Fifth or Sixth Astral realm can utilize the higher vibration of these Sublevels, in conjunction with their consciousness, to sense, feel and in some cases return to lower Astral levels. In this way they participate and often communicate with individuals known to them who are still focused in physical bodies in the Third Dimensional Sublevel.

It is also for this reason that individuals in the more dense, lower vibrational physical reality cannot immediately sense or see higher Astral levels or entities focused there. Similarly, those that have just passed from physical reality do not have immediate access to the Sixth or Seventh Astral planes and must progress as customary through the Astral levels in order to achieve the needed consciousness and vibrational signature that permits them entry to higher Astral spheres.

The level at which an entity finds itself at any given time is a good indication of its vibrational rate. Relative consciousness remains unchanged until momentum is provided by virtue of their frequency and the effect this has on creating the vortex (tunnel) that will allow transmigration to a higher Astral state. An entity cannot move freely to higher realms without this occurrence, and it can only move back and forth between the Astral plane in which they are currently focused and lower Astral realms or planes of reality.

It is important to know that beginning with the Fourth Astral plane, there is not a specific mass consciousness backdrop, nor is there a structure, location or environment in these realms as you are familiar with in your Third Dimensional physical reality. In the lower Astral realms, each environment is created either by or for the entity, and there are as many realities as there are entities and Souls.

There are however shared realities, or realities held in common, in the higher Astral realms, especially realities that are created by or for entities from the same Soul group, and these are accessible by individuals at will, assuming their vibrational integrity is compatible.

In a manner of speaking, vibrational signature also becomes a key that unlocks various realities in the higher Dimensions, and in this way there are no intruders in any given individual reality especially at the Sixth Astral Dimensional Sublevel, or Perceived Heaven.

Based on this, one can assume that entities create or, in the Sixth Astral Plane, have created for them environments that they prefer, whatever that may be. Many revel in palaces or grand edifices and similar environments, but just as many prefer to re-create their exact home and neighborhood from the prior physical lifetime, or whatever their preferred surroundings from that lifetime were. This includes structures, landscapes, gardens, wilderness, cityscapes and whatever else was pleasant and comforting for them during the physical life. It is not uncommon for loved ones, neighbors and other individuals known to each within the Astral plane to cohabit or become neighbors within these creative environments. However, for the most part this usually occurs only when individuals are intrinsically related to each other as part of either the same Soul group or as Soul mates.

These environments are not static or lonely, and not only are individuals that are Soul related able to visit, Spirit Guides, Guardians and other entities known to the individual visit freely and even inhabit these environments in much the same way you might live in a large city, aware of other presences around you but without interacting unless desired by one or both parties.

In almost all Astral planes, the environments tend to be ones that are pleasant, relaxing and rewarding, where pursuits and interests of the entity, whether from the lifetime lived or based on Soul associations, are pursued. Often, entities become highly proficient at things only touched on during the physical lifetime whereas those already proficient may pursue higher levels of learning in that field, teach others or explore different talents and areas of interest.

The Sixth Astral level is far from a plane of isolation despite the fact that each individual is placed in the environment that is reflected back to them based on their True Self. In fact, it is here that specialties are explored, some of which are particular to the personality of the entity and others that are entirely Soul derived. As an example, a talented musician may continue to pursue their talents as a musician or might choose to begin to explore other talents that interested them personally during the lifetime. Additionally, if the Soul itself is leaning towards a certain specialty at higher Astral levels, such as serving others at lower Dimensions as Spirit Guides for example, the entity might begin to explore what this entails and may actually experiment with guiding other creatures and beings created within its current environment. The possibilities are as endless as the number of Souls seeking growth and a return to the Twelfth Universal Dimension and All That Is.

All Astral planes offer a high degree of communication overlap that is for the most part ignored in the Third Dimensional Sublevel of physical reality. Individuals are constantly communicating with each other within the same Dimensional Sublevel, and this is happening interdimensionally between different dimensional realms as well. Though it is possible for an individual to refrain from communication and happily isolate itself at will, it is also possible to communicate with others much as you do in physical reality. Only the means is different depending upon what Astral plane you find yourself on and what plane of reality the entity with whom you wish to communicate is at.

At higher Astral levels communication is telepathic in nature. If an individual senses that someone in a lower Astral plane is thinking of them or if in turn the individual in the Sixth Astral realm happens to think of or remember someone at a lower Astral level, visits can be almost instantaneous even if the visit is not apparent to all participating entities. Were you to become more sensitive and aware of these talents and undiscovered senses in your current physical reality, you would find that when someone not currently focused in physical life pops into your head it is not a matter of whimsy but rather that they are most likely visiting or thinking of you, or that you are doing the same to them.

Individuals who have reached the Sixth Astral level can also travel in a sense, although travel in that realm is not by mechanical means but by virtual means instantaneously. We would suggest that emerging technologies that allow you to interface across great distances visually as well as virtually are in fact a precursor and physical trial for the telepathic virtual experiences you will one day have. This will become your experience not only at higher Astral levels, but when you ascend to the Fifth Universal Dimension and incarnations on Terra, Earth's counterpart in the Fifth Dimension. Physical teleportation, which is being experimented with now in your reality and will in the not distant future revolutionize your world, is another mode of experience available in the higher Astral realms as well as in higher Universal Dimensions. This is covered for you more extensively in Part Two of our book, *Timeline Collapse and Universal Ascension*.

In a certain sense you are constantly being visited not only by Spirit Guides that have Soul contracts to assist you but also by closely related entities that are no longer in physical incarnation. Though there is no physical means of communication available, were you to foster your intuitive abilities rather than fear them or believe them to be fiction, you would discover a constant link to any and all individuals that are known to you, whether they are living, dead or directly in front of you at any given moment.

It is often possible for entities in the Sixth Astral realm to also communicate with those in physical life with whom they would seem to
not have direct connection. In many cases, those individuals with
whom you have had extremely difficult relationships in physical life
are actually connected to you as Guides or Soul Mates. Often that
Soul mate may have had an agreement with you to assist your Soul
growth by presenting you with challenging or even negative situations. It is even possible that your worst enemy during the physical
lifetime is one of your principal Soul Mates.

Once the veil of physical life is removed and the life experience has
allowed for growth to be achieved, as part of the healing process in
the Fifth Astral realm that same enemy may work with you through
the Dream state to discover and understand their role in assisting
your growth. It is an extremely intense experience to understand
the emotions and hurt another has felt at your hands, or that you
have perpetrated on another being. It is an even more intense experience to see, from inside out, the higher good that Soul Mate may
have been pursuing by causing you hurt and challenges in the first
place. Both parties benefit from such "unveilings," as they are referred
to in the Fifth Astral Healing realm.

This is important to understand because the notion that the Astral
planes are places where you lounge the daylong and where no accomplishment or growth is achieved is totally incorrect. Through their
pursuits and communications of this nature with various dimensional
levels, all entities are constantly at work perfecting their consciousness growth and, as a result, their vibrational resonance.

The notion that there is a "Heaven" that is a place of idle fancy where one lounges and nothing transpires or "Hell" as a place where punishments are doled out endlessly is one that is untrue and needs to be banished forever from Human Angelic belief systems. Whatever the reality, the Dimensional Sublevel, the Astral realm or the form that physical being takes, you and your Soul are constantly in a state of renewal, change and growth. This is a fundamental Universal precept.

In general, the Sixth Astral plane is considered a place of happiness and unconditional love, since the individual revels in the fruits of their experience via whatever joy rings true for that personality. Since Human Angelics mainly have a Service-to-Others orientation, their life experiences are usually of a giving nature, and as we said, when they are not, it is almost always as part of a prior agreement at a Soul level.

This is not the case with Alien Soul races incarnating as physical human beings in the Third Universal Dimension, and these incarnations can be quite challenging. However, they are also more conducive to Soul growth, which is the reason an Alien Soul might choose to experience incarnations as a Human Angelic Being on Earth.

There are also Alien Soul races incarnated within the Third Universal Dimension, who are incarnating within cycles that are not in the Earth sector. Thus, there are a multitude of Soul races and types incarnating throughout the Third Universal Dimension but in different sectors of the Universe designated for that particular Soul group. We mention this only as a means of letting you know that the Third Universal Dimension, or any Universal Dimension for that matter, is not the exclusive domain of Human Angelics even if Earth is considered the predominant home of Human Angelics. Similarly, there are Human Angelic Souls that incarnate in different sectors designated predominantly for other Soul races, in much the same way as an Alien

Soul might plan certain Wheels of Creation on Earth.

This happens much more in the Fifth Universal Dimensional. It is there that inter-stellar and inter-planetary contact, and interaction with Alien Souls, is far more prevalent. That said, the process of physical life, death, reincarnation, transmigration and passage through the Astral realms is similar from Universal Dimension to Universal Dimension, Galaxy to Galaxy, sector to sector and Soul race to Soul race. The difference however is only with regards to how the process and the Dimensional Sublevels are experienced or perceived, since the actual journey is always based on the belief structures, cultures and norms of the particular Soul group.

In that regard, Souls could be said to experience Higher Astral realities that are related to their sector of Universal space-time. This highlights another interesting topic. Because each Astral level has a connection to its corresponding Universal Dimension as we have explained, the Sixth Astral plane naturally corresponds to the Sixth Universal Dimension. Since the Sixth Universal Dimension has the widest range of connection between inter-planetary races, when Beings are in this Astral level there tends to be thematic overlap, which means participation and cooperation between inter-planetary species is available to all entities therein.

This offers those who believe, discover or wish to be part of what could be called "alien" perspectives when in Perceived Heaven to have the possibility of those kind of new commitments and connections. In other words, if you have in some way had extraterrestrial contact or connection while in physical life on Earth, these connections are augmented and possible if desired in the Sixth Astral plane. As a matter of course, such connections with Alien Beings and extraterrestrials becomes the norm for most individuals and Souls incarnating in the Fifth, Sixth and Seventh Universal Dimensions. In order to facilitate our current explanation however, we have limited our discussion to the process as it is primarily experienced by the Human Angelic Soul species, using the Earth locale as a backdrop. Suffice to say that it is important to understand that Wheels of Creation are not exclusive to Earth or Human Angelics, and this system is the experience of numerous Soul races throughout your Galaxy and beyond.

Once established within the Sixth Astral plane, individuals are spontaneously encouraged through the projection of their own likes, joys and loves, to pursue any and all activities they wish to pursue. Sometimes these activities are related to the previous lifetime, and sometimes they are new and unique.

Using our previous example, if you were a great musician with extraordinary talent who had chosen, because of karma and other subconscious or Soul life goals, to experience an inability to express your musical talents during the lifetime, the Sixth Astral plane would allow you to explore the depths and joy of expressing that talent unimpeded. You might explore those musical talents as a musician, or you might just as easily explore them as a composer, or a conductor or a concert manager, despite the fact that you may never have done any of these other things during the physical lifetime.

Such adventures lead to great cooperation, camaraderie and associations with Soul mates as well as other entities and Guides known to you from the lifetime. Then again, some take on experiences here with completely different and newly forged relationships made within the Astral realm. Regardless, such possibilities exist as a result of understanding why you were forced to ignore your talents or unable to attain the success you sought in the first place during the lifetime. More importantly however, it is also a result of the grace you obtain through forgiveness of Self and a fuller understanding of unconditional love as well as real experiences of true gratitude, generosity and appreciation of yourself and of others.

With respect to our example, the musician whose life seemed thwarted for whatever reason and was blocked from any success in expressing their talents could potentially be found providing concerts on a regular basis to others in the Astral realm, with their talents and efforts truly appreciated by all. This in turn would generate an experience of extreme gratitude and unconditional love for all concerned. Again, this points to the reason the Sixth Astral plane is considered the realm of Perceived Heaven.

The Sixth Astral environment is a realm where relationships, particularly relationships that we would designate Soul relationships, are cultivated, acknowledged, continued and pursued. Please understand however, that such experiences are unconditional in nature, and do not have the same objectives they might in physical life where the life mission, biology or ego might come into play. In effect, these relationships are not in any way sexual in nature. Unlike the Fourth and even the Fifth Astral realms, the Sixth Astral plane is fairly far removed from physical existence and therefore physical love is not an objective and relationships tend to be highly evolved and unconditional owing to the non-corporeal nature of life in the higher Astral planes.

Frankly, most relationships in physical incarnation are either based on prior Soul agreements, karma or your ego and biologics. Sexual objectives are not sought in the non-corporeal realm, and they are not needed or desired when in the Etheric body, nor are they of any consequence to your Soul. This is not to say that sexual relationships on the Third Dimensional Sublevel where you currently exist are inconsequential since many of these can have important impact on life lessons, karmic endeavors or your Soul's energetic expression in duality and physical reality.

Physical sexuality and drive have much to do with procreation to ensure continuation of the species, as you are well aware. What you might not realize however is that although not an absolute, procreation is also based on the need to have physical bodies available for the purposes of Reincarnation and incarnations related to particular Wheels of Creation.

In that respect, Souls sometimes prefer to incarnate over the course of large segments of the timeline within the same genetic lines. This is because genetic cellular memory that is passed down from generation to generation can facilitate both the creation of personality and genetic attributes, reinforce certain desired environmental catalysts and allow important karma and karmic balancing criteria for lifetimes that are connected within gene-based familial lines.

In this way, lifetimes on the Wheel of Creation can interconnect for several generations or through the centuries, and many members of the same family can not only be related at a Soul level, such as with Soul Mates, they can actually be derived from the same originating Soul. It is therefore quite possible that you *were* your great-great grandfather (derived from the same originating Soul) or that your mother was your sibling generations ago, or will be your son or daughter in some future lifetime. Procreation facilitates this and in certain cases is also what makes it possible.

In fact, those who do not have occasion to physically procreate during their lifetime generally have no need to do so knowing at a Soul level that genetically connected lifetimes are no longer necessary for the purposes of Reincarnation. Sometimes it is caused by the fact that the Soul will be cycling off Third Dimensional incarnations completely sometime soon, or that, in a manner of speaking, the Wheels are full. Based on this subconscious knowing, which can be experienced in numerous ways including infertility or the inability to find a permanent partner to produce offspring with among other things, procreation and genetic continuance for the purposes of Reincarnation becomes unnecessary. This can be cited as the most common reason ancient genetic familial lineages are said to "die out."

Relationships on the higher Astral planes are closer, more caring, more fulfilling and infinitely more rewarding. Carnal desires and other similar physical needs of your reality, whether you consider them worthwhile and valuable or, as some religions and cultures do, as transgressions and "sins," are of little importance either way and are removed from the equation at the Sixth Dimensional Sublevel. This includes things (sometimes highlighted by religious and cultural doctrines) such as lust, gluttony, envy, pride, greed and anger, to name a few, most of which are actually biologic, hormonal or neurological physical functions.

In the Astral worlds these are non-issues primarily by virtue of the absence of a corporeal or biological body (with the accompanying hormones and brain activation centers) as well as a result of the unification after physical death of the Emotional and Mental bodies into the Etheric body to form one Energetic Being. It is also a product of the vibrational distance these Astral realms have to the Third Dimensional physical reality. In fact, physical desires of this nature are so exceedingly unnecessary and remote by the time an entity has transmigrated to the Sixth Astral realm that they are usually no longer recalled or thought of at all.

In general, most entities tend to remain in the Sixth Astral plane for substantial periods of time enjoying old and new connections with others and pursuing the desire to accomplish many things that they did not or were not able to accomplish formerly in the physical lifetime. As they do so, they become accustom to and talented at mastering their abilities, creative and otherwise, and this is important with regard to honing an individual's skills and areas of interest. In fact the skills honed in the Sixth Astral realm can sometimes be more important to your Soul overall than those explored in Third Dimensional physical reality.

These "skills" however may not be related to what you think in that they are not necessarily related to the mechanics of doing anything but rather to using the mechanics to perfect unconditional love, patience, cooperation and service. The concept formed in some religious groups that bases the person's connection to God and Spirit with work and effort they put into what they work at or create tends to derive from this Truth. There is much to be said for the belief that in a sense you achieve Godliness through the pursuit of perfection in whatever work you perform.

In other words, again using our example of the musician, in Higher Angelic realms (the Seventh Astral realm and beyond) one might choose to use one's musical talents as a Spirit Guide to assist a budding musician and young Soul just entering Third Dimensional physical reality. Thus it is the perfection of the inherent musical talents that makes this possible when it is combined with the necessary traits to be a Spirit Guide such as unconditional love, patience and inspiration. Those talents and skills are always initially explored on the Sixth Astral plane.

Inevitably, developing such talents that are part of the entity's true nature and the "skills" that will make these things useful in Higher Astral realms is facilitated by the ability to achieve success as well as the fact that the entity no longer has to consider either merit through success or "survival," as it does in the physical reality. The need for survival can create life missions and energy blockages that are valuable for consciousness growth but may not be as useful to developing the actual skills used by entities in much higher Astral or dimensional levels.

Almost all entities eventually discover and will pursue such a "specialty" for lack of a better word. These specialties are related to the work the entity will take on when it reaches the Higher Angelic Realms beginning in the Seventh Astral plane, and can include a wide and diverse range of things, including Spiritual Guidance, providing inspiration to younger Souls in lower dimensional incarnations and assisting entities using their talents to navigate the Fourth, Fifth or Sixth Astral realms.

In the meantime within the Sixth Astral realm, the deeds and accomplishments conducted there can have greater relevance on who you will become as you move forward into the higher Dimensional Sublevels than your many deeds and accomplishments in Third Dimensional physical reality. Although we are aware that you consider physical life missions and successes to be most important and aligned with avocations, societal standards and your important life advancements, the truth is that these things serve generally as mere backdrops. True lifetime missions in physical reality are much more related to emotional and spiritual growth through interactions, karma and learning the aspects of conscious intention as well as the expression of unconditional love.

As an example, a physical life mission is more apt to be learning the aspects of controlling one's expression of Willpower than becoming a famous doctor or lawyer. In such a case, an individual who through a lifetime of oversight and conscious intention discovered when it was appropriate to state their needs to others and when it was appropriate to allow others to control their needs might be enormously successful from the perspective of their Soul even if they never graduated High School or held a job. On the other hand, an individual who had this same life mission who was highly academic, received every earthly honor and became a successful doctor or lawyer, but never learned to control the expression of their Willpower or how to listen to others, could easily be considered a great disappointment in the eyes of their Soul.

The real point here is that even in a supremely restful and satisfying environment such as Perceived Heaven, the individual is accomplishing the things that will ultimately be shared with all the reincarnations on its Wheel of Creation and with its Soul. Growth and expansion is unending, and that is a universal precept. Inherent talents, skills or predispositions for how those talents are universally used are more accessible in the higher Astral Dimensions. In the physical reality that you know, we would suggest your focus should center less on professions, worldly achievements or societal merits and more on individual compassion, empathy, charity, unconditional love and growth earned through awareness, the pursuit of enlightenment and the mastering of conscious intention.

It is a great irony that in physical reality many entities will make an extraordinary effort to have as many worldly accomplishments and experiences as they can during the lifetime believing that life is a one-time occurrence and that any aspect of physical life not explored is lost forever and forfeited by that individual. This is far from the case.

In fact, it should be noted that this is usually something that Baby and Younger Soul incarnations are learning. Such incarnations can appear to frantically explore every possible aspect of accomplishment or domination in the physical environment. Learning to distinguish what is important to life from what is not can be related to a younger Soul's lesson as they chase seemingly endless quests with no real objective or goal.

Such quests can appear pointless or reckless to older Souls, but this is primarily because younger Souls often jump blindly into action and go out of their way to find opportunities for karma and quick Soul growth. This may include physical harm to themselves or others. We would even suggest that on the current timeline the great preoccupation with undertaking as many physical "experiences" as quickly as possible is symptomatic of the proliferation of younger Souls incarnated in physical reality at this time.

Contrary to this, not only is an entity able to investigate and achieve many if not all of the things they desire when in the Higher Astral planes, particularly the Sixth Astral realm, a good many additional experiences are accessible by virtue of the connections they have to other lifetimes on their Soul's Wheel of Creation. Granted, experiencing these events through the eyes of other lifetimes on the same Wheel may seem vicarious from your current perspective. However, in the Astral world this is not necessarily true based on the immediate and close connectedness you have to your Soul and the other reincarnations on your Wheel of Creation, all of which are essentially linked to you. Suffice to say that no one is precluded from pursuing, to their heart's content, any and all experiences they desire once they arrive on the Sixth Astral plane and have reached the realm of Perceived Heaven.

Stories from a Soul's Wheel of Creation
The Story of Lucinda

Lucinda loved children. From the time she was a child herself, she would follow her younger siblings around and care for them as if they were her own children. She told her family that her only ambition when she grew up was to have as many children as she could.

She was so good with children in fact that she became an elementary school teacher, and as soon as she married in her mid-twenties, she tried to become pregnant right away. Try as she did however, she and her husband could not become pregnant.

Lucinda was aware that she had always had very painful menstrual cycles and experienced gynecological issues but now her doctors told her that she had a rare condition that caused her uterus to detach and the vaginal canal to collapse. It would have to be surgically corrected, after which she was informed that having children would be difficult if not impossible. Even if she did by some rare chance become pregnant, the odds were that it could become life threatening for both mother and child. Reluctantly, she had no choice but to correct the condition.

Following the surgery however, Lucinda seemed changed. She still wanted children desperately, but now there was an extreme fear associated with the possibility. The fear that she might be-

come pregnant immobilized her, and the inner conflict of wanting children but fearing what could happen if she did become pregnant pushed her into a deep depression.

That intangible fear, which quickly turned into an outright phobia, now created dramatic intimacy issues between Lucinda and her husband. She was distant, uncommunicative and pushed him away without really understanding why. Rejected and demoralized, he secretly looked for affection outside of the marriage.

Lucinda was now cutting herself off from everything she had ever wanted or loved in life, and she could no longer bring herself to confront any of the things that once brought her joy and happiness. Unable to bring herself to see her young students day-to-day, something that reminded her even more of her situation, she quit her job. Then one day her husband announced that he had fathered a child with another woman. Now he was leaving Lucinda to start the family he had always wanted; the family he always thought Lucinda and he would create before the dramatic events of the past year. Lucinda was crushed.

Exasperated to see what was happening, a close friend convinced Lucinda to go see a Therapist that was also an intuitive specializing in past life regression. The friend felt that there was something "other worldly" and out of the ordinary going on in Lucinda's life, especially considering her past ambitions and how quickly the love of children had morphed into a phobia around child birth, taking over her entire life.

Lucinda made the appointment without expecting any real revelations but feeling she had nothing to lose. At least, she
thought, perhaps the Therapist could assist her in dealing with
the realities of her pending divorce.

The Therapist wasted no time regressing Lucinda to a lifetime
in England in the mid 1400's. Born in a convent, she was the il-
legitimate child of one of the Nuns in residence there. No ordinary convent, this particular one also ran an orphanage next
door, and although the Nuns were devout for the most part,
there were several instances of Nuns and some wayward
women living amongst them becoming pregnant. When abortion using herbs and other natural means failed, the women
found to be with child were confined and hidden in the convent
until they delivered their babies behind closed doors. Low and
behold, a new orphan baby would then mysteriously appear in
the orphanage next door.

As a young child in that life, Lucinda was placed in charge of
the new babies, and she loved her job. The young children
thought of her as their mother, and the Nuns encouraged the
relationship. Not really knowing motherly love of her own, she
reciprocated the young orphans' affection ten-fold.

At the age of 13 however, attempting to defend one of her
young wards from being beaten by a group of high-ranking

travelers who had sought shelter for the night on the grounds of the convent, she was violently raped. Damaged emotionally and physically from the attack, despite notable past indiscretions by the Nuns themselves the order turned on her and blamed her for the terrible fate she had suffered. Afraid of alienating the convent's benefactors, she was told by the sanctimonious Mother Superior that such a thing could only happen to someone if that person was somehow wanton and rejected by God.

Relieved of her duties she was turned out of the convent and orphanage, the only home she had ever known, and forced to beg on the streets. Barely fourteen years old, shortly afterwards she realized that she had actually become pregnant from the rape. Eight months later, still living on the streets and shaken more at being discarded by the only family she had ever known than even from the violent attack, she and her baby died in childbirth.

The Therapist explained that Lucinda's mission in that lifetime was to learn the lesson of "acceptance." Experienced in the negative polarity, she was learning the lesson not only by being an outcast orphan but through rejection, the polar opposite of acceptance, which she received after the intense and unsettling experience. Moreover, because that lifetime had actually been successful (realizing that the Soul does not distinguish between good, bad, right or wrong experiences, which are subjective viewpoints) it was always intended to finish prematurely.

However, the intense and traumatic attack had left Lucinda's Soul with an energetic blockage that bled through into Lucinda's current lifetime and severely affected her root chakra. Since karma is essentially an imbalance of energy that a Soul needs to balance from one lifetime to another, the current lifetime of Lucinda was being used to balance the traumas that lingered in the lifetime where she had died homeless and starving at such a young age.

Balancing this energy would entail not being able to physically bear or have children in this lifetime. In this way the extreme energy blockage associated with the traumatic events that had led to her death in the past life would be countered and would provide her with opportunities that forced her to deal with such an eventuality here and now. It would also allow her to face and utilize her experiences around abandoned and orphaned children, which would further serve to assist her to walk through and overcome the traumas of the past lifetime.

In this lifetime therefore, not having the ability to bear children was not a punishment but a badge of honor, and dealing with the energy blockage created by being barren and dealing with the intense emotions this brought up for her was her final conquering of these circumstances. She was further told she had agreed to the karmic balancing in this manner prior to the lifetime, and that is why she had experienced the rare circumstances and illness that affected her uterus in the first place. Instead of having her own children, she would triumph by being *given fulfilling options intended to diminish and help overcome the past trauma, which had left a blockage due to the fact that it caused physical death in Medieval lifetime of her Soul.*

These options included loving and working with children not her own through teaching, social work, fostering and adoption. By being able to be with children in a way that was not life threatening, her Soul would experience service to others doing what she loved in a gentle and positive way that cleared the blockage and also brought good to the world and to others.

In the process, the Therapist assured Lucinda that her life would be even more fulfilling, successful and beneficial in the future than if she were able to have her own children. Her Soul would balance the hurt generated in the prior lifetime by using her current life's mission and choices to do good for abandoned children, while also overcoming the blockage in her root chakra around the subject of childbirth.

Shortly after hearing this, Lucinda happily went back to teaching, and soon found herself led in the direction of advocacy and social work on behalf of children in need. She met an extraordinarily caring and empathetic man who was a professional legal advocate for children, and remarried. Her husband and she discussed the situation in detail and agreed that with so many abandoned and orphaned children in need of stable parents and a family, they would foster and adopt.

Today they have successfully fostered a dozen children together, four of whom they have formally adopted. Their family
continues to grow and evolve joyfully, and Lucinda has never
looked back.

(A final note: After several years of marriage, Lucinda learned
from a different Intuitive that the baby she had failed to deliver
in that past life was a lifetime of the same Soul as her new
husband. As a Task Mate of Lucinda's Soul, they had agreed at
a Soul level that he would come into Lucinda's life later in order
to ensure opportunities where she could continue her work
overcoming the trauma and karmic imbalances generated in
the tumultuous past life experience they had shared.)

 CHAPTER 7

THE SEVENTH, EIGHTH AND NINTH ASTRAL SUBLEVELS OF THE THIRD UNIVERSAL DIMENSION: THE ASTRAL REALM OF CELESTIAL GUIDANCE, THE AKASHIC REALM AND THE REALM OF THE SYSTEM LORDS

In the Sixth Astral plane entities carry on with their efforts as they meet desires in an ageless and timeless environment, continuing to grow from the experiences for as long as they want and at whatever pace they wish in any way that is most comfortable and suited to them. Using our prior example, if one is exploring various endeavors that utilize musical talents, they will move through those undertakings and arrive at whatever depth of learning and understanding they choose. It is for each individual to decide along the way at what point they feel they have reached completion based on satisfaction and fulfillment after having pursued their endeavors completely.

Although there is no limit on how much effort each puts into their exploits or how long they pursue them, at some point continuation becomes monotonous and the entity reaches a point of contentedness that has no real parallel in your physical reality. This point is best described as transcendence for an entity that has reached the ideal fulfillment of their innermost desires.

Such fulfillment can be compared to achieving a state of mystical "ecstasy," and we would go as far as to say that it is precisely this state that is the subject of the ecstasy you are told is experienced at physical death by religious saints and other such figures, usually meant to indicate that they are being transported directly into the hands of God. However, this condition actually is the result of reaching a state of true and final completion in the Sixth Astral Sublevel, and it is available to all through the inner peace, joy and contentment they feel having reached every possible fulfillment available to them in their Perceived Heaven.

It is generally at this point that thoughts of transcendence, change and excitement begin to stir within the entity. In your terms, this stirring could be compared to deep contentedness and the most profound longing for centering, peace, home and family that anyone has ever had. The ecstatic presence heightens an entity's vibrational resonance and ability to absorb light (light being consciousness and awareness), allowing an almost translucent luminous glow within and around the entity. This announces that a period of preparation has begun, and the process of transmigration to the Seventh Astral plane or Realm of Higher Celestial Guidance and Awareness has now arrived.

Achieving this energetic luminous glow with its newfound metaphysical transparency is noticeable to everyone in contact with the entity, and it is considered a true blessing that signals to all entities and to the Self that the entity is beginning passage into the Higher Astral realms. However, the portal that allows for the energetic transference and transmigration into the Seventh Astral Realm is quite different from the previous portals found between Dimensional Sublevels.

Previously, it is the individual's rise in consciousness combined with mastery of intention expressing one's manifesting abilities that generates the energetic spin necessary to form a vortex-portal to transport and usher the Etheric body into the next Sub-dimensional realm. But entry into the Seventh Astral realm is made possible through what we will call "ecstatic divine cooperation." Transmigration through this portal requires not only a lighter density and higher consciousness, but also the express help of one's own Guides and especially Guides from the Seventh Universal Dimension, or the Celestial Beings who inhabit this realm and specialize in assisting transmigration of entities to higher dimensional realities.

For most, these are the Light Beings of Angelic encounter usually talked about in mythology or expected by most individuals as their primary assistance throughout the physical lifetime. Although direct assistance from Angelic Beings and Ascended Masters does happen sometimes at lower dimensional levels, these are rare and usually are prearranged Soul occurrences. Generally, Angelic assistance is mostly available to entities either directly before or directly following actual physical life. Their assistance however, is especially available and relevant as an entity passes from the Sixth Dimensional Astral realm into the Higher Astral or Angelic realms.

Entry into the Lower Astral planes requires you to possess, at varying levels and stages, conscious intention, healing and ultimate mastery of your consciousness. The key to entering the higher dimensional realms however, is the ecstasy that identifies you as a true Light Being and signifies your graduation to a lighter density having achieved enlightenment through healing and the pursuit of your innermost Truths in the Sixth Astral realm. Ecstasy literally alters your vibrational density and structure making you more "light" filled, and this provides you with a new vibrational spin that can only be described as Celestial in nature. This state makes you ready for transmigration into the Seventh Astral Realm, and also makes you recognizable to higher Celestial Angels and Beings as you now prepare to become one of them.

In a certain sense, departure from the Sixth Astral Realm can be considered "another death" that is not unlike the distinctive departure one experiences when leaving the physical body and transmigrates using the Etheric body to the Fourth Astral plane. This is because, as we have explained, Dimensions and Sublevels tend to be grouped into trilogies with close associations being between one to three, four to six, seven to nine, and so forth.

Just as transmigration from the Third to the Fourth Dimensional Sublevel can seem traumatic and very different, so too transmigration from the Sixth to the Seventh is equally new and unique. To say the least, there is quite a difference in the energetic qualities and reality experiences from the Sixth Astral plane to the Seventh, Eighth and Ninth Astral planes, and the transition from the Sixth to the Seventh plane is so dramatic as to make it similar to your departure from Third Dimensional Sublevel physical reality at death.

In that way, this second death is very much like what is experienced when the physical body has become outmoded or unusable to you, when as a result the entity passes from the physical vehicle into its Etheric or Energetic form. Similarly, transition from the Sixth to the Seventh Astral level requires the transition from one body form to another, from the Etheric body to a body of Light. The new Light Body is less dense than any previous body, including the Etheric body, and it is more luminous and closer to pure consciousness and awareness than has been experienced by you at any point prior.

In fact, this transformation is quite substantial. During the journey through the lower Astral planes, despite the fact that an entity is in

The Seventh, Eighth and Ninth Astral Sublevels of the Third
Universal Dimension: The Astral Realm of Celestial Guidance,
The Akashic Realm and the Realm of the System Lords

their Etheric body, the entity maintains their physical appearance just as they were seen in physical life. That appearance can be based on either a point on the timeline that they feel most resonates with them or their appearance at the time of death. The latter appearance is usually dropped by the entity as soon as they become proficient, aware and master the lower Astral environment.

The point however, is that an entity continues to maintain their past physical appearance, even though this is done in varying stages of density. In the lower Astral planes an entity might appear as they were at the moment of death, as they were during a happy young adult or middle age period or even as they were as a child or teen. Sometimes, an entity will alter their appearance through the period, although it is always consistent with the true physical appearance they had during some period from their former physical lifetime.

As an example, it would not be uncommon for your grandmother to choose to appear to you as a teenage girl in either the Dreamscape or the lower Astral planes. Regardless of this you would recognize her immediately through her vibration even if you had never met her in life or seen an image of how she looked at that time. In the same way, a child lost early in life, even prior to birth, could choose to appear to a parent or sibling as they would appear as an adult. The choice is highly individual but it is always based on the entity's own Truth.

In the Seventh Astral plane physical appearance of almost any kind is abandoned in favor of pure consciousness rendered as light. The body taken on from this point can be referred to as your "Light" body, which is birthed by you out of the Etheric body at the appropriate time. Again, though your vibration continues to identify you and is recognizable to all, appearance no longer has consequence here, and therefore it is muted and contained within a Light body that does not carry the physical traits you are accustom to in your current reality. This is why this plane is known as the realm of Celestial Beings, since this is the true Angelic realm. If you prefer, this is the Celestial Heaven where angels as spheres of light reside, as depicted widely in your religious mythology or in fiction as "heaven."

This transformation is also why entrance into the Seventh Astral realm and metamorphosis of the Etheric body is considered a second death. Leaving behind one's Energetic body, as well as the ability to maintain the physical appearance based on the former lifetime, is not unlike leaving behind the dense Physical body in favor of the Energetic or Etheric body following physical death. Suddenly, your vibrational resonance is far more impactful and much more of a truthful indication of the Spiritual Being you are than any physical look you have had thus far.

Make no mistake, this transformation is one of the most important you will ever make, and in many ways it is more consequential than even your entry into physical reality or, later on, your transition out of a physical body and into an Etheric body. It is vital to understand that upon reaching the Seventh Astral realm the individual begins an entirely new process related to its reintegration with the Soul. This occurs starting with the entity's shedding of the Etheric body in the Sixth Astral realm and accelerates as it passes into the Seventh Astral realm with creation of the Light, or Celestial body. This transformation continues through the Seventh Astral level, and is finalized when the entity reaches reintegration with its Soul in the Tenth, Eleventh and Twelfth Astral Subdivisions of the Universal Dimension.

In a certain sense, although you may feel your life is only relevant

during the period in which you are in the physical body you now
know, the truth is your "lifetime" as a measure of who you are in
personality, consciousness, activity and identity-wise actually consists
of a much broader range. This range includes physical life at the Third
Sublevel of the Third Universal Dimension through your life in the
Etheric body from the Fourth through the Sixth Dimensional Sublevels. It is during and up until this point that growth in terms of consciousness, awareness and intention predominates and continues.
Therefore your real existence as a "physical" entity, albeit in different
vibrational densities, could be considered the range or period from
incarnation in the Third Dimensional Sublevel to entry into the Seventh Dimensional Sublevel. After that, you take on a dramatically new
form and unique celestial existence.

Entry into the Seventh Dimensional Sublevel of the Third Universal
Dimension brings one closer to their original state of Being as a spiritual entity and part of the Soul itself. And for this reason, the Seventh
Astral plane is the starting point for the reunification of consciousness with aspects of the Soul. This process occurs slowly as one progresses through the higher Astral realms until, having reached the
highest Astral realm, complete reintegration and fusion of the entity
into its Soul is accomplished. When all the lifetimes of a Soul have
done so, the Soul is ready for Ascension to the next Universal Dimension, where the Soul's grand cycles of reincarnation and the
Wheels of Creation begin anew.

It is here that a side note might be useful. We understand that it
may be difficult to understand how individualized personality can
ultimately become incorporated into the Soul without being lost.
The aspect of exactly who you have been and are however, is never
lost but forms union with your Soul. A good analogy is seen when

looking at it on a cellular level.

It is clear that every cell in your body is part of you and is also individual. Furthermore, it is clear that every cell functions independently, has its own predispositions however slight, and functions within the body that is you. These individual cells are always forming, and in a sense they create who you are in much the same way your life and personality, together with many other lifetimes (reincarnations) on your Wheel of Creation, and beyond, form the basis of your Soul.

There are numerous cells in your body, each with a specialty, in exactly the same way there are numerous lifetimes, each with a specialty, that form your Soul. Ultimately and in the same manner, the many Souls created and cast out from the Twelfth Universal Dimension by the originating force also form All That Is, the Universe and the composite that is known as the Being of God (if you prefer the traditional narrative).

Reintegration does not mean annihilation in much the same way cells continue to exist independently within you but, for the most part, make up who you are. The whole cannot exist without its parts, and each piece, though independent, cannot exist without the other. Entry into the Seventh Astral realm is the end of your continuous state of "formation," if you will, and with that formation completed it marks the beginning of your functioning within the actual body of your Soul.

In fact, this is a joyous occasion similar to graduation from a higher level of schooling, signaling that the entity is now ready by virtue of its consciousness to realize its place within the structure of its Soul. In a way, it can be likened in your physical reality to entrance into society

The Seventh, Eighth and Ninth Astral Sublevels of the Third
Universal Dimension: The Astral Realm of Celestial Guidance,
The Akashic Realm and the Realm of the System Lords

and adulthood following your youth and schooling. In this case however, it is achieved through reintegration with your Soul, a process that begins as you enter the Seventh Astral plane and the Celestial realm.

Accomplishing all this is no easy task, nor does entry into the Celestial realm signal the end of an individual entity's travails. In fact, we would suggest it is actually the real beginning of serious cosmic and universal endeavors for every entity, particularly considering the more self-expressive experiences of the Sixth Astral Realm. Though this might sound challenging, Seventh Astral plane endeavors are far from difficult or tedious and instead are considered some of the most rewarding and fulfilling experiences that can be had in any Universal Dimension or on any Dimensional Sublevel.

This is because the Seventh Universal Dimension is a Dimension dedicated to higher spiritual guidance. In other words, it is from here that Celestial Angelic Beings exist, function and in a sense are trained as Spirit Guides to all Souls experiencing life at varying stages in diverse forms within lower Universal Dimensions. Consistent with our universal model then, the Seventh Universal Dimension corresponds to the Seventh Dimensional Sublevel of every Universal Dimension.

In the Third Universal Dimension therefore, the Seventh Astral plane is the staging realm where Angelic Celestial Guides and Ascended Masters interface with entities in the lower Dimensional Sublevels in their role as Spirit Guides. Additionally, this realm interfaces with the higher Dimensional Sublevels, particularly the Eighth and Ninth Dimensional Sublevels, in its role as intermediary between the Soul and its many reincarnations expressed through the Soul's Wheels of Creation.

The roles and activities of this realm can become quite complex, but we will attempt to outline some generalities for you. All entities moving towards reintegration with their Soul pass through the Seventh Astral Realm and ALL will serve some aspect of guidance to other entities still incarnated at lower Dimensional Sublevels, usually in the lower Astral planes such as the Fourth, Fifth or Sixth Astral planes. Close associations, such as incarnations on the same Wheel of Creation, or incarnations of the same Soul or Soul group are always highlighted and favored. Therefore, in most cases guidance comes from someone who is at a higher plane of existence and was either known to the entity in their lifetime or comes from a lifetime that was connected in such a manner.

It is interesting to note that most Soul Mates do not actually participate with an entity from within their physical lifetime, but (assuming the Soul Mate has reached the Seventh Astral plane) does so in a capacity as a Guide to an entity still physically incarnated or traversing the lower Astral realms. Such arrangements are always planned through cooperation with the individual and the Soul, and coordinated by what we will call Masters who are Seventh Universal Dimensional Celestial Beings, as we shall explain.

This particular Astral realm is home to Seventh Universal Dimensional Celestial Beings and Masters who are essentially working across Dimensions to assist other entities by providing the knowledge, enlightenment and higher guidance needed for Soul development and growth. These Masters operate in groups, usually comprised of seven distinct Angelic personalities, to bring enlightenment, wisdom and assistance to all those who seek it. It is also these Masters that teach entities reintegrating with their Soul and passing through the Celestial

realms the significance of their responsibilities in mentoring and guiding other entities still existing within lower Dimensional Sublevels, especially those with whom they might have particular association.

To facilitate understanding of this, it is best to envision these groups
under two designations, the first being Ascended Master Celestial
Beings working from the Seventh Universal Dimension and secondly
the newly formed Angelic Beings that have taken on new Light Bodies
as they enter the Seventh Astral realm on their way to reintegrating
with their Soul. The former group imparts the highest guidance directly to the entities with whom they are associated and also provides instruction and teaching so that newly formed Light body
entities can learn how to take on roles as guides themselves to their
familiars. In turn, the latter group becomes the Angels and Guides
that are generally familiar to you in your daily existence and prayers,
entities watching over you and inspiring you in whatever Dimensional
Sublevel you are currently residing.

The Ascended Master Celestial Beings provide universal wisdom and
knowledge throughout the dimensional structure of the Universe,
and although no interference or direct action is ever undertaken by
these Guides, they are known for bringing enlightenment and inspiration, as well as creative inspiration sometimes recognized by you
as Muses, into many worlds. It is easy to distinguish higher guidance
from guidance of lower dimensional entities in as much as Seventh
Universal Dimensional Master Guides are always neutral and will
never require or oblige adherence or loyalty to them. They simply
inspire. Nor will you ever be instructed in or obliged to believe any
dogma, perform any ritual or adhere to any other obligations. Above
all else, your Free Will is respected and you will always be provided

with pure Truth without any effort to cajole, oblige or coerce.

If we may, we humbly hold ourselves as an example of this manner of Seventh Dimensional Angelic guidance. When we began this work, it was of great importance to many in your reality that we identify who we were, and rightfully so. We described ourselves as a group of seven Ascended Master Guides from the Seventh Universal Dimension that had come together to assist individuals in the Third Universal Dimension with respect to discovering their personal EssencePath and facilitate access to higher wisdom during a wondrous and important time known as Universal Ascension.

We collectively identified our group as "Samuel" based on our Soul connections and past incarnations on the Wheels of Creation of our own Souls. Our efforts are generally focused on providing wisdom and insight, sometimes prophetic in nature, during great changes of a Planetary Age. Although currently focused in the Seventh Universal Dimension, each of us has ascended through every Universal Dimension up to the Seventh Universal Dimension, including passage through the Third Universal Dimension where you find yourself now. Each of you will, in due course, ascend in much the same way as well.

Like you, we are from the Human Angelic Soul race, and universally assisting Human Angelics is our goal as well as the foundation of our own Soul growth. Those who have come across these materials, whether through desire, curiosity, synchronicity or what may appear to be coincidental, agreed to do so prior to the lifetime or agreed actively within the current Dreamscape. They explore this content in exchange for the potential growth of consciousness it might afford them during the course of this lifetime. We are honored with all such associations.

It has been our objective to do this work in many different ways, and each of the Seven Master Guides that comprise our Celestial group have had input into this important mission. You have since come to know that those meant to discover the information we impart are led to it when they are ready to receive and understand it. Those that have not uncovered it or for whom it has no resonance or comprehension have not reached the level of consciousness needed to allow its understanding or its acceptance to permeate their Being. This is completely justifiable and synchronicity ensures that each will discover what they need when the time is right for them. In that regard, there is no need to do anything with this information but express its content faithfully, ponder it and allow its presence in the world at this time without regard to consequence and without attaching dogma or obliging any belief structures around it. We joyfully continue to do so.

All this is to say that we hold our efforts, with which by now you are very familiar, as one example of Celestial Angelic guidance coming from the Seventh Universal Dimension and gifted to you through the Seventh Dimensional Sublevel of your current Universal Dimension. But there are also many other examples of this type of guidance coming from the Celestial realm, some of which we will explore with you now.

First and foremost is the guidance afforded to entities transitioning through various Astral realms. For many, this can be a harrowing experience because it is a largely unknown transition. Believe it or not, early cultures that you consider "primitive" were better equipped to deal with passing from one form to another and into the Astral

State by sheer virtue of the fact that their tales and stories concerning these encounters were so vivid, widely known and accepted. Modern culture has lost much of this, and many pass from physical reality without any understanding of the Astral passage, or what is transpiring and what is to come.

In addition, Shamans together with family, friends and even professional mourners, prayed and chanted at the side of the deceased for long periods to assist the transiting person and coax them on from their position in physical reality. Such methods are extremely comforting to a transitioning individual, and this can partially be seen in the fact that it is common for entities, once they are aware their physical death has occurred, to attend memorial or services provided for them even though they are not physically present. Though a generality, it is unfortunate that many individuals in your modern culture die alone or in unfamiliar surroundings like hospital.

After death, unlike in the past where the uninhabited physical body was kept in surroundings familiar to the deceased, nowadays it is immediately shuttled off to an unfamiliar morgue, funeral parlor or similar unit, where the entity's isolation and confusion is doubled. This is especially true since receding from the physical body during this time is usually not yet complete and entities can remain along side the physical body, if still in tact, for up to three days or longer at times. In any case, they are still highly aware of their surroundings and the other events still occurring around them in the physical world. Moreover, those who are newly passed out of body tend to be reluctant to quickly depart a physical presence that appears to them as a known quantity and a cherished loved one, until of course they have made their peace, gained their balance and are ready to transition.

Seventh Universal Dimensional Celestial Beings are always present at physical death in the Fourth and higher Astral levels to assist this transition, both by guiding individuals and by comforting them, particularly if the passing is traumatic. Sometimes this is done when these Angelic Beings take on the form of a figure that the entity that has passed will trust, which can be a family member, friend or even religious figures depending upon the individual's lifetime belief system.

Sometimes for older Souls and those more aware, they will simply appear as they are, as Light or Angelic Beings radiating light with only a general Angelic appearance and without specific physical traits. We would go as far as to say that the phenomenon of a "tunnel of light" has much to do with their illuminated presence as well. In all cases their goal is simply to assist the transitioning entity in any manner they can.

Over time, it is the guidance provided by Seventh Universal Dimensional Celestial Beings that will bring an entity to full understanding of where they are and why, as well as assist them to master their new reality at every stage of the Astral journey. This includes the Fifth Astral realm, where these Beings are instrumental in coordinating and orchestrating the healing endeavors meant to lead entities into the Sixth Astral or Perceived Heaven as we have discussed. This assistance and celestial guidance is no less important and becomes even more pronounced once the entity has reached the Seventh Astral realm, where the guidance becomes mentoring with respect to the role expected of them in their new phase as Angelic Beings themselves.

It is important to distinguish here however, the difference between Ascended Master Angelic Beings from the Seventh Universal Dimension, who are participating in your Dimension through the Seventh Astral plane, and those entities that are passing through the Seventh Astral Sublevel in Light Bodies on their way to reintegration with their Soul. Ascended Master Guides are always from a higher Universal Dimension, in this case the Seventh Universal Dimension, in much the same way Souls incarnating as System Lords, which we will discuss, work through their incarnations at lower Universal Dimensions but originate from the Ninth Universal Dimension.

The difference here has to do with incarnation, since Seventh Universal Dimensional Ascended Masters do not reincarnate but only act as Angelic Master Guides, whereas Ascended Masters from the Ninth Universal Dimension actually descend to lower Universal Dimensions and incarnate physically in order to work within these realms. Regardless of this difference, all these Master Souls choose to participate in lower Universal Dimensions as a matter of their consciousness levels, the natural work of their Universal Dimension and as a factor of their own continued Soul growth.

Another form of guidance that comes from the Seventh Astral realm is what you would consider "inspiration." Though we are certain most of you feel all inspiration comes from deep within your own psyche, and although there is indeed a certain sensitivity you must have in addition to a necessary technical grasp of the field you pursue, most true inspiration originates from guidance and your connection to the divine. That is to say, in a sense you have been made to "*divine*" something greater than yourself or have been inspired through subconscious suggestions, inspirations or demonstrations given to you. Guidance comes to you through subconscious suggestions and in the Dreamscape offered by your Guides and Angelic Be-

The Seventh, Eighth and Ninth Astral Sublevels of the Third
Universal Dimension: The Astral Realm of Celestial Guidance,
The Akashic Realm and the Realm of the System Lords

ings working from the Seventh Astral plane, Celestial Heaven. Higher inspiration is also available to you at times, and thus guidance can also come from Master Guides or other Celestial Beings originating in the Seventh Universal Dimension and working with you through the Seventh Astral plane.

This in no way minimizes the talent, work or effort you put into any manifestation or creation in physical reality, whatever form it might take, but it should be noted that divine inspiration is usually at its basis and the results always have greater purpose. In fact, most Guides make arrangements with entities related to them prior to physical incarnation in order to assist them in the specifics of such matters either for the purposes of individual Soul growth or as a matter of assisting the collective in some manner creatively, scientifically, healing wise or in any way that contributes to mass consciousness in the world at large.

Of greatest importance in all this is the guidance a Soul receives in the preparation and the on going alterations made to the lifetimes in each Soul's Wheels of Creation. That guidance inevitably comes via the supremely valuable work of Seventh Universal Dimensional Celestial Beings working through the Seventh Astral Realm. This is possible since these Celestial Guides are closely associated with and operate in conjunction with the Eighth Dimensional Sublevel, which is the realm of the Akashic.

As we have already described, the Akashic realm, sometimes known as the Akashic Records or the Hall of Records, contain the electromagnetic imprint of every lifetime within a Universal Dimension. In many ways, the Akashic has aspects of what has been termed the "collective conscious," and it is literally from here that information, which many refer to as a collected consciousness relevant to the entire Universal Dimension, is accessed and derived. But the Akashic is more than just the storehouse of mass consciousness. Indeed, in addition to being a realm of collective consciousness, this Dimensional Sublevel stores the energetic imprint of each and every lifetime that takes place within the Universal Dimension. That includes the missions, associations, relationships, personality traits, energetic expressions, emotional content and life events of the Soul's numerous lifetimes in the Dimension. All these energetic imprints are contained and accessible in the Eighth Astral plane of every Universal Dimension.

In turn, the Eighth Sublevel of every Universal Dimension is directly linked with the Eighth Universal Dimension, the Universal Akashic, and all records available at the Eighth Dimensional Sublevel of every Universal Dimension also become part of the Eighth Universal Dimension. Thus, the imprinted record from every lifetime in the many Wheels of Creation of every Soul in every Universal Dimension is forever stored within the Akashic Record and this is found in the Eighth Universal Dimension.

The multidimensionality and complexity of Universal Structure can become confusing here, but suffice to say that a detailed record of all entities and lifetimes in the Third Universal Dimension is also available at the Eighth Dimensional Sublevel, which serves as the Akashic realm of the Third Universal Dimension. This is true for all groups, races and any other Beings found within the Third Universal Dimension, which includes solar, planetary, galactic and other bodies. For our purposes, we will limit our discussion to Human Angelic Souls and associated Soul groups.

The Seventh, Eighth and Ninth Astral Sublevels of the Third
Universal Dimension: The Astral Realm of Celestial Guidance,
The Akashic Realm and the Realm of the System Lords

By virtue of the high consciousness and experience they have attained, Seventh Dimensional Angelic Masters act as intermediaries
and assist in communicating these recorded imprints that are derived
from the Akashic realm. They do so by interfacing with Eighth Dimensional Angelic Masters and Light Beings, whom we will discuss
shortly, by bringing the information received from these Beings in
the Akashic to the newly transformed entities entering the Seventh
Astral plane. In effect they coordinate as bridges of information,
downloading the light information received from the Akashic so that
it becomes the basis of a vibrational signature found within every
entity's newly formed Light body. It is in this way that the entity's
Light body is truly formed.

Adding to the possible confusion here is the fact that beginning with
the Seventh Universal Dimension, although the Dimension may not
be completely experienced by those in lower dimensional forms,
Higher Dimensions within the dimensional trilogy, meaning here the
Eighth and Ninth Universal Dimensions, can be perceived and even
accessed by Seventh Dimensional Beings. A possible analogy to explain this would be pointing to the fact that in the Third Universal
Dimension you cannot yet perceive, as an example, the Fifth Universal Dimension. You cannot perceive it, and while you may surmise its
existence, there is no hard and true evidence since it is not truly part
of your reality. However, Seventh Universal Dimensional Beings are
well acquainted with the true existence and even the details of the
Eighth and Ninth Universal Dimensions (as well as even higher Universal Dimensions, but we will deal with that discussion later).

In fact, these Angelic Beings understand the higher Dimensions vibrationally even if they are not joined with it, do not visit it and are

not able to pass through as a part of it yet. This is similar to you knowing that Europe or some other distant continent exists -- you have seen pictures, meet visitors from there and even speak the languages -- despite the fact that you have never actually resided there. You might even be wearing or using some article everyday that originated from there, knowing full well where it came from even though you did not actually go there or visit personally to acquire it.

The same is true then for access of the Akashic in the Eighth Astral realm by Seventh Dimensional Beings. And this is important, since Seventh Dimensional Angelics are in fact the ones that coordinate and act as intermediaries between a Soul, positioned in the highest Dimensional Sublevels, and all its lifetimes not only in the Seventh Astral realm, but also in all lower dimensional Sublevels as well. The important consideration here is that this provides them with the ability to assist a Soul not only in planning its incarnations on its various Wheels of Creation in the Dimension, but also allows them to assist entities that are returning from lifetime experiences, whether they be physical or non-corporeal and reintegrating with their Soul.

They do so using the Akashic imprints and records found in the Eighth Astral realm as guidance. This underscores a main reason the Akashic records exist in the first place. Since the Soul's Wheels of Creation are dynamic and their manifestation is on-going, as we have already explained, it is through the Akashic lifetime imprints that it becomes clear if balancing, karmic or otherwise, is needed within the Wheel. This is accomplished through the addition of new karmic events in related lifetimes on the Wheel, through creating entirely new lifetimes on the Wheel or even through creating new Wheels if necessary. In doing so, these Master Guides from the Seventh Dimensional realm assist Souls to appropriately juggle and balance the lifetimes generated through all of their Wheels of Creation.

All this is accomplished within the realm of Celestial Heaven or the Seventh Astral level of the Universal Dimension. It could therefore, be considered a clearinghouse of some importance. To do so, Seventh Universal Dimensional Guides interface with all entities returning from lifetimes and moving through the Astral planes in almost all the Dimensional Sublevels. In this way as well, Seventh Dimensional Celestial Angelic Beings act as Guides not only to the entities themselves but also to the Souls that created them, directing their energies as needed from the highest dimensional levels into the process of creation and awareness.

By now it becomes clear just how vital the Seventh and Eighth Astral realms are. From the perspective of the Soul, one sees clearly how Seventh Dimensional Master Guides coordinate with Souls and Soul groups in the creation of their many reincarnations, balancing karmic endeavors, identifying the goals and missions of the entities involved and further guiding them to fulfillment. At the basis of this process lies the Eighth Dimensional Sublevel of the Akashic records, which essentially, through the photon imprints held by the Light Beings there, identify what is lacking, what needs balancing and what should be further pursued or improved by the Soul in its quest for continued growth and Universal Ascension.

From the perspective of the entities transmigrating from lower dimensional levels, these Master Guides mentor them as they pass through the Celestial realm and become Light Beings, inspiring them towards reintegration with their Souls. Once the entity's Light Body has been adopted in the Seventh Astral realm they now have full awareness of who they are, as well as their place on their Soul's Wheel of Creation.

Furthermore, an entity now has complete awareness and understanding of all the lifetimes or reincarnations connected to it that are also derived from their Soul. Finally, the entity has full knowledge of all its Soul affiliations, its Soul group and its Soul cadre (a Soul unit within the group), and it begins to understand its unique participation within the Soul's being as well as the universal process it is undergoing.

With full consciousness of its lifetime and all other associated lifetimes related to its Soul, the entity is able to understand and even meet with other individual entities within its Wheel. It is in this manner that the entity is made aware of its connection to not only the spiral time-wave that it participated in within the Third Universal Dimension, it becomes aware of all the lifetimes its Soul has lived, is living or will live on the timeline and throughout the various Dimensional Sublevels.

In this way, at any point on the timeline or at lower dimensional levels the entity can choose to participate and assist others known to it in a capacity as Spirit Guide, or it can assist other related lifetimes as they move and grow through the various lower Astral planes. All of this is done under the guidance of Seventh Dimensional Ascended Masters and it is for this reason that we call these Angelic Guides mentors to those who have newly taken on Light Bodies in the Seventh Astral realm and are now working as Angelic Guides themselves.

The Seventh, Eighth and Ninth Astral Sublevels of the Third
Universal Dimension: The Astral Realm of Celestial Guidance,
The Akashic Realm and the Realm of the System Lords

What is important to understand, as we have said previously many times, is that the time-wave which actually forms what you know as the Third Universal Dimension is non-linear and everything we are discussing here in any Dimensional Sublevel is happening simultaneously during the space-time wave continuum. This space-time wave defines the Universal Dimension until it raises its vibration as a whole and the Dimension itself ascends and becomes the next Universal Dimension. Thus, though you are currently fixed at a particular point on the spiral of that timeline, reincarnations related to the Soul's Wheels of Creation within the Universal Dimension, whether they be past, present or future, are all occurring in the dimensional "Now."

What one needs to consider however, is that the same applies to all Sublevels of the Universal Dimension, and despite the fact that physical lifetimes will seem to begin and end at different points on the timeline, which they do, in the grander scheme life is continuing at various Astral levels of the Dimension and everything is dynamically occurring simultaneously. This can be difficult to grasp if you include all the lifetimes on all the Wheels of Creation in all the time periods you are familiar with. All of this culminates in Ascension, the Universal Ascension of not only all the Souls (together with their lifetimes) in the Dimension but of the Dimension itself.

It is exactly for these reasons that creation is continuous within all spheres of the Dimension and while some may currently exist in physical bodies, others are traversing each and every Astral environment until the grand cycle of Ascension is complete. On another note, this is also why a lifetime taking place in your ancient past, say Atlantis or Ancient Mesopotamia, could easily be related to you in the current time period, or just as likely could be related to you through an incarnation in what appears to be your linear future. Similarly, when any of those lifetimes ends at the physical Sublevel of reality that you know, it actually continues on in higher Astral realms.

This is also how one entity connected to you via your Wheel of Creation that has taken on a Light body and transmigrated to the Seventh Astral plane might become an Angel or Spirit Guide to you in your current life and time. Furthermore, this makes it possible for an entity to come from a period before known history or from the future, up to and including the final Ascension passage that will transpire with the great reset of the current dimensional timeline expected on Earth in the 26th Century.

All of this is to underline how entry and passage into and through the Higher Astral realms can be far different from the natural progression one makes through the lower Astral environments. It is only in the Seventh Astral realm that an entity has the ability to appreciate and understand the multidimensional aspects of itself and its Soul, and in a manner of speaking the attachment to Self becomes minimized in a way that before it was not.

In addition, an entity begins to take a back seat when referencing its connection to other incarnations on its Wheel of Creation as well as to the Soul itself. This is an important asset in order for the entity to provide objective guidance to others and, in doing so, become an Angelic presence or Spirit Guide. It is also a vital component in the continuing reintegration of itself into its Soul, which evolves naturally at this level once an entity becomes focused on the other lifetimes it is assisting and is no longer self-oriented or centered.

The Seventh, Eighth and Ninth Astral Sublevels of the Third
Universal Dimension: The Astral Realm of Celestial Guidance,
The Akashic Realm and the Realm of the System Lords

It is important to remember that a Soul incarnating in any given Universal Dimension creates many Wheels of Creations, or reincarnations if you prefer. Each Wheel can have anywhere from seven to a dozen lifetimes or more on it, and since there is no number required or preset limit some younger Souls can have upwards of twenty or more lifetimes on a single Wheel. Younger Souls tend to generate more lifetimes on a Wheel since karma is a preferred means of growth for them and therefore karmic balancing necessitates more lifetimes. Older Souls plan smaller groupings of lifetimes on any given Wheel, since karma for Older Souls is more self-generated and thus the need for karmic balancing through other lifetimes on a Wheel is not as necessary.

Regardless of the number of lifetimes on a Wheel of Creation, an entity in the Fifth and Sixth Astral realm will always choose to examine and heal itself first. Stepping back from its focus on "Self" after adopting a Light body however, this focus changes as the entity enters the Seventh Dimensional Sublevel, or Celestial Heaven, where the first order of the day is to learn, understand and, in many cases, actually meet the other lifetimes directly related to it. Specifically, the entity is preoccupied by those lifetimes that are linked to it karmically on its Wheel of Creation or by way of close Soul associations and familial or other relationships.

In doing so, and through access to the information provided readily from the Eighth Dimensional Akashic Records, the entity discovers the true purpose of its Soul in creating the Wheel of which it is part, and also gains insight into why the life's mission and parameters were selected. It also discovers the higher reasoning behind the various connections found within each lifetime. After this the entity will review not only all the lifetimes on its particular Wheel of Creation but also any other significant or important Soul reincarnations including those found on other Wheels of Creation created by its Soul in the Third Dimension for purposes of growth and Ascension.

Thus, the first phase of existence in the Seventh Astral realm is an entity's understanding of all lifetimes and all life missions on its Wheel of Creation. This includes all karmic endeavors, associations and relationships, as well as the specific and ultimate purposes for growth originated for each lifetime. An entity spends a good deal of time in the early stages of existence in the Seventh Astral plane investigating these relationships and learning the karmic consequences, sorting out what was successful, what was not quite successful, what needed to be experienced from a different perspective and what was the end result of each. In effect, this becomes one of the most important aspects of the entity's reintegration process with its Soul, which begins as part of its effort to understand spiritual guidance and then ends with a profound understanding of its interconnectedness with its Soul.

What stands out however, is that the Seventh Astral level is a platform for the entity, in conjunction with its Soul and all the other reincarnations of the Soul, to discover what balancing is needed and what other aspects would improve the Soul's growth in the Dimension. This is no simple task considering that the Akashic records are dynamic imprints, in a constant state of revival and revision. However, it is in this manner that the Soul, as guided by the entity that is part of any given Wheel of Creation, will either create additional incarnations on that Wheel of Creation, create an entirely new Wheel of Creation or will imbue those entities still focused within physical reality (at different points on the timeline) with new attributes, associ-

The Seventh, Eighth and Ninth Astral Sublevels of the Third
Universal Dimension: The Astral Realm of Celestial Guidance,
The Akashic Realm and the Realm of the System Lords

ations and relationships needed to finalize karmic balancing and deliver consciousness growth.

We have informed you already that lifetimes within a particular Wheel are constantly communicating each with the other (albeit subconsciously or through the Dreamscape) and what transpires in one lifetime on a Wheel has an immediate impact on what may or may not happen in other lifetimes on that same Wheel. Anything undetermined, unaccomplished or requiring karmic balancing can affect what happens in other lifetimes on the same Wheel of incarnation by virtue of added karma, events or associations.

In addition, association with these events can be cellular in nature in as much as Soul information is communicated to you through your DNA. It is because of this that a physical ailment or trauma in another lifetime on your Wheel of Creation can have serious impact on you within your own life, and furthermore this can sometimes be the reason physical or psychological vulnerabilities arise in one's life that have no basis within current life events or circumstances.

In other words, being impaled in one lifetime, as an example, can affect the cellular balance of the same physical anatomy in the current life making you prone to ailments and weaknesses in this general area that do not correlate to any known genetic or other event that took place in the current lifetime. Similarly, again as an example, a death by fire or drowning in one lifetime can generate a real phobia of fire or drowning in another, and so on and so forth in a multitude of ways, even if there is no basis for the phobia in the current lifetime.

Hopefully, this assists you to understand that the events and particularly your actions in one lifetime are shared within the Wheel of Creation and are not limited experientially to just you. Rather, they may be experienced in a metaphysical manner by all other lifetimes on your Wheel. This is a consequence of the close association you have both in terms of your Soul and your distance to other incarnations on the dimensional timeline, not to mention the dynamic bonds generated by way of your Soul's overall investment in experience and growth seen from all sides and perspectives.

As we have said, the greatest difference between the Lower and Higher Astral planes is the fact that the Seventh, Eighth and Ninth Dimensional Sublevels are less separate in density and vibrational resonance. As a result they tend to be more unified and connected with far less vibrational division than is present between the Lower Astral planes. Whereas the Lower Astral planes are in fact separate levels with distinct division, the Seventh, Eighth, Ninth and indeed all levels through the Twelfth Astral realm exist virtually side-by-side due to the thinning of dimensional separation at higher ranges of the dimensional divide. Therefore the Higher Astral planes are less linear and far more lateral and conjunctive, with similar enough vibrational frequencies to allow for compatibility, regular bleed-through and connectivity between these realms.

We mentioned prior to this that Spirit Guides and other entities from the Higher Astral planes are able to descend to all lower Dimensional Sublevels in order to assist those therein with understanding their lifetimes and healing the karmic influences. This type of connection becomes much more concrete and substantial in the Higher Astral planes. Once an entity has increased their consciousness and awareness in the Seventh Astral realm, entities from the Eighth and Ninth

Astral planes will also assist these entities, as we shall see.

There may be some confusion concerning the Akashic Records of the Eighth Astral realm with regard to exactly how electromagnetic lifetime imprints are recorded, so to speak. In fact, Master Guides from the Eighth Universal Dimension work closely within the Eighth Dimensional Sublevel and with Seventh Dimensional Angelic Guides to make this so. In effect, Eighth Dimensional Masters "embody" these life "Truths," and the photonic imprints and patterns pertaining to every lifetime are carried within the stored consciousness of these Master Spiritual entities. While it is convenient to picture the Akashic as external "records" or a vast heavenly library of sorts, in actuality the records are embodied within the Light Bodies of Spiritual Beings who specialize in this.

Whimsically, you might consider these Guides to be Master Librarians always on call. However, they are quite literally Universal Seers, Sages and Speakers whose Souls originate out of particular energy expressions and they are destined to utilize their unique talents in this way on behalf of the Universe operating as they do from the Eighth Universal Dimension, the Akashic Halls of Remembrance.

The ultimate universal purpose of Eighth Universal Dimensional Masters is to electromagnetically house and embody all information related to their sector of the Universe from the many Wheels of incarnation that exist there. Thus, as an example, for Human Angelic Souls the Eighth Sublevel is manned by Human Angelic Ascended Master Sage and Speaker Guides who imprint and record within themselves the life and life events of all those related to their Soul groups. While not our subject presently, the mechanics of this are related to the fact that energy is merely transformed and never destroyed as it washes over the time-space reality.

As it does so it is transformed before being gravitationally pulled towards its ultimate recycling into various galactic and universal Black Holes. As this occurs, as photon energy all events are imprinted within the consciousness of these high Celestial Beings, in much the same way a camera is able to capture light as images and store them as information. What is important however, is the fact that this information, or "en-light-en-ment," is closely held and available universally to all Light body Angelic entities that have reached Celestial Heaven, that is to say, the Seventh Universal Dimension and the Seventh Astral realm of the Third Universal Dimension.

All information specific to a particular planetary or galactic sector, as well as the Soul groups incarnated within particular galactic fields is available in this way through the Eighth Dimensional Sublevel to Seventh Dimensional Masters and Angelic Guides residing within the Seventh Astral Sublevel. And that information is stored within the vibration of Eighth Universal Dimensional Master Angelic Beings responsible for particular Soul groups or specific galactic races. In this case, since we are taking Earth's planetary sphere and the Galaxy that you know as our model and example, the Eighth Universal Dimensional Sublevel or the Eighth Astral plane, is where the Akashic records for the Human Angelic Soul race and galactic sector are stored.

This includes all information related to karmic cycles of all Souls as well as individual Human Angelic reincarnations and lifetime imprints of those incarnations anywhere on the dimensional timeline. This information covers each lifetime's karmic endeavors, relationships, life missions and events, as well as the same information related to

The Seventh, Eighth and Ninth Astral Sublevels of the Third
Universal Dimension: The Astral Realm of Celestial Guidance,
The Akashic Realm and the Realm of the System Lords

any other Soul groups and Beings found to exist therein. This includes the animal, plant, mineral, Devic and all other kingdoms at any Dimensional Sublevel.

It should be realized also that this is a two way street. Thus, the information stored for all entities in the Third Universal Dimension passes through the Eighth Dimensional Sublevel and is further found universally within the Eighth Universal Dimension. Since we are limiting our discussion to Human Angelics we are simply focusing on that Soul group here. However, you should be aware that stored information from other Third Dimensional Soul groups in distant sectors of the Universe are also present in the Third Dimension's Eighth Astral Akashic records. In addition, there are Eighth Universal Dimensional Angelic Beings from those races carrying the imprints, in the form of light energy, for extraterrestrial Soul groups and their created lifetimes as well. All this is present and available within the Eighth Dimensional Astral Sublevel or the Akashic.

As you may assume, the Eighth Dimensional Master Guides and Guardians of the Akashic are well versed in the overall goals of their particular Soul group, as well as the missions, features and karmic issues of specific lifetimes within a Soul's Wheel of Creation as it connects to the incarnation processes. In most cases however, broader information regarding other entities connected to you on your Wheel of Creation, as well as information concerning the nature of the Dimension's space-time wave and particulars concerning the Ascension of your Soul are not generally explored until the entity has reached the Seventh Astral realm and fully embodies their Light body. This is because it is not until the entity has begun to grasp the many lifetimes that comprise it and its Soul that the information becomes relevant to the entity's own growth and process.

Certainly, the fact that there is only slight subdivision between the Higher Astral planes facilitates this. It is also for this reason that communication and interaction with higher knowledge is much easier once an entity has taken on their Light Body. As a result, interaction across Dimensions is better making the understanding of particulars for related lifetimes not only easier to uncover but easier to assimilate by the entity itself.

An interesting analogy would be to identify the Seventh Astral realm as an institution of higher learning in your current reality. If you like, you could see the Eighth Astral plane as a campus "library" and the professors, assistant professors and counselors as the Seventh Universal Dimensional Celestial Beings assisting you, the newly minted student, with your education. Finally, you could see the Eighth Dimensional Celestial Beings as Master Librarians working closely with your Seventh Universal Dimensional Celestial Guides (professors) to identify the research and literature that would best contain what you need to assist your mastery in understanding yourself and your Soul.

The Akashic contains an additional element of each individual lifetime that is dynamic and is also in a constant state of change during the lifetime of the entity. This includes records of the entity's life following physical death in the Astral planes. An important aspect of the record as well is the prior "contracts" and agreements organized by the Soul on behalf of the entity with Soul mates and even other Soul groups. Since these tend to be quite dynamic, the imprinted records store agreements that are met AND those not met as the lifetime unfolds. In understanding these, an entity becomes familiar with how and why meeting up with another entity during their lifetime was planned and for what specific purpose. In this way the entity now

The Seventh, Eighth and Ninth Astral Sublevels of the Third
Universal Dimension: The Astral Realm of Celestial Guidance,
The Akashic Realm and the Realm of the System Lords

made privy to the various backup agreements, whether fulfilled or not, that are stored in the Akashic and were made in order to obtain specific opportunities for growth. It also becomes aware of exactly when and why the entity exercised Free Will during the lifetime to preempt, postpone or prolong any such Soul agreements.

As a note here, sometimes during the actual physical lifetime these backup agreements can be such that the individual feels as if they are experiencing the same events, situations or style of relationships over and over again or in a loop. Truly these are the occurrences that present-day consciousness would do well to analyze as they happen, especially with respect to the lifetime and the Soul's possible intentions or purpose. Usually, individuals have several preplanned arrangements that the Soul has orchestrated in order to ensure that a specific life purpose is achieved, even if circumstances arise through Free Will that make it difficult to obtain.

Typically, as an example, a Soul will organize any number of pre-arranged possible meetings during an entity's lifetime with another Soul in order to accomplish a specific goal, mission or to balance karma. Should either entity, through Free Will, not appear at the designated point on the timeline, or having met, should the entity refuse to follow through, there is ample possibility for such a meeting to occur elsewhere. There is probably not anyone among you who has not met someone of great importance to you in your life and then discovered that they were in the same place as you or knew someone you knew at an earlier time. Or quite possibly, you were within a few miles of meeting earlier, despite the fact that you ultimately did not meet until much later in life.

An additional example of pre-planning stored in the Akashic that is dynamic is the entity and Soul's ability to identify several possible opportunities for leaving physical incarnation through death. Usually, the entity expresses an ultimate example of exercising Free Will by subconsciously choosing, based on several prearranged moments, the actual time and manner of physical death. Naturally, these things are not immutable and normally an entity has great discretion and Free Will with regard to them. However, they clearly represent examples of intensive Soul planning for each and every lifetime within a Wheel of Creation that is also logged in the Akashic.

All of these factors are finally sorted through and understood by the entity in conjunction with their Soul in the Seventh Astral realm using the information coming directly from the Akashic in the Eighth Dimensional Sublevel. It is at this point that the entity consciously uncovers an understanding of exactly what was missed or postponed, and based on this discovery, suggestions can be made to the Soul for other continuing lifetimes on the Wheel of Creation for that entity. All of this occurs through the auspices of the Masters of the Akashic records, in conjunction with the entity and its Soul, under the auspices of the Seventh Universal Dimensional Celestial Guides assisting them.

We realize it may be difficult to understand a process that includes finalization while also remaining dynamic, which is the case when the Akashic is used by the Soul to further plan additional lifetimes or events on its Wheels of Creation and incarnation, but such is the process as an entity takes on its Light Body and works with its own Soul to balance its energies from the higher Astral realms. Additionally, because the concept of karma has been erroneously diverted to mean a "Tit for a Tat," it is perhaps difficult to understand that for the Soul, balancing energy through all its lifetimes on every Wheel of Creation is perhaps

The Seventh, Eighth and Ninth Astral Sublevels of the Third
Universal Dimension: The Astral Realm of Celestial Guidance,
The Akashic Realm and the Realm of the System Lords

the most important part of the process of Ascension. At the very least,
it is the most important preparation the Soul can have in order to
achieve a consciousness level and vibrational integrity that will allow it
to transcend and ascend to a Higher Universal Dimension.

What is of most importance to remember however is that assistance
from higher Celestial Beings is always available at every level of the
process. Nowhere is this more noticeable than those coming from
the Ninth Astral plane, or the Realm of the System Lords. Great appreciation is expressed throughout the higher Dimensions for these
self-less Ninth Universal Dimensional Avatars, who having completed
all reincarnation cycles within lower Dimensions and voluntarily
choose to descend to lower Universal Dimensions where they reincarnate as physical Beings to specifically influence spiritual and geopolitical mass consciousness. Many of the best known historical figures
in your world that affected, each in their own way, vast portions of
world thought, society, culture, religion, science, war and peace are
actually lifetime incarnations of these important Master Souls.

We have discussed at great length the work and experiences, as
well as specific examples, of the Ninth Universal Dimensional Master Beings that we have termed "System Lords" in our previous
book, The System Lords and the Twelve Dimensions. Therefore, we refer
those interested in greater details on this subject to that work.
What we wish to discuss here for our current purpose is the Ninth
Dimensional Astral Sublevel, which, consistent with the previous Astral planes, is connected in a broader sense to the Ninth Universal
Dimension or what is known universally as the Dimension of the
System Lords.

It should be stressed at this point that use of certain terminology, such as "System Lords," is intended as a metaphor only, and we do not wish to imply that these entities are a ruling class, have any official dominion over a Dimension or have any extraordinary or mythical powers that can be used on Human Angelics, Humanity or Earth's Solar System generally. That said however, these Soul Masters do indeed incarnate in physical lifetimes at lower Dimensions in order to influence planetary, spiritual and geopolitical conditions and generate environments with mass consciousness backgrounds that offer the maximum number of opportunities for Soul growth on various segments of the timeline.

For that reason, the physical lifetimes or Avatars that they create tend to be historically consequential, or at least regionally notable. System Lord lifetimes can be born or raised in any economic or social environment but will inevitably rise up to positions of power, importance and privilege in the world. Dispelling the notion that they are good or bad, subjective designations that depend upon your perspective, these Avatars usually possess visionary sensitivities, unique abilities and extraordinary talents that they employ and exploit during the lifetime. Most often their efforts are accomplished through seemingly miraculous and lucky connections with others. Those other individuals may or may not be System Lords, but almost all of them will have some degree of Soul agreement with the System Lord in question.

Although not all notable or famous personages on the dimensional timeline are lifetimes related to these Ascended Master Souls, a great many are and the entities created within a Master System Lord Soul's Wheels of Creation are incarnated for the purpose of assisting all entities within the lower dimensional realms to grow. What is further interesting from your current perspective is that because the lifetimes generated through these incarnated System Lord Avatars are independent entities, much as every lifetime is, they each have life missions, specific attributes and Free Will. In other words, similar to most Human Angelics in physical incarnation, they are not necessarily conscious of their Soul origins or connection to a Ninth Universal Dimensional System Lord. Nor are they usually aware of their participation in the world as an Avatar lifetime.

Even so, since they are derived from the Souls of a Ninth Universal Dimensional Master, they generally have some sense of their destiny. This often makes them appear egotistical and narcissistic to others, especially with respect to feelings they may have of their importance in influencing local, regional or world events.

It is based on the inner knowing that all entities and Souls have pertaining to the existence of System Lords who are using their Avatar incarnations to assist humanity that various global concepts of rule based on "Divine Right" originated. However, the true meaning and understanding of this was corrupted long ago. In fact this concept has no real merit if you understand that System Lords only influence mass conscious environments, tend to be very specific in their range of interaction and are not as frequent or prominent as one would imagines.

Nonetheless, this basic idea was hijacked early on by one extraterrestrial Soul group in particular and has been used ever since to ensure that their lineage incarnated on Earth would be assured positions of wealth and power over your planet's major cultures and societies. You know this Soul group as the Draconian or Reptilian Soul group that we discussed at length in our book, *The System Lords and the Twelve Dimensions*. This Soul race has long believed Earth to be their dominion, wrongly taken from them with the elimination of their precursor races the reptilians and dinosaurs on Earth by Human Angelic Galactic Guardians more than 65 million years ago. Even so, to an extent this Soul group has continued to incarnate in physical human bodies ever since alongside Human Angelics.

Unfortunately, though they are certainly a minority in terms of all of Earth's Soul incarnations, the reincarnations of this Soul group have managed to predominate in the modern age by prearranging lifetimes on their Wheels of Creation that exist exclusively at certain levels and within higher castes of society, particularly amongst ruling blood lines or blood lines already connected to power and wealth. Naturally, this has provided the group with unfair advantages on the timeline, which, backed up by the concept of Divine Right, has been used to subjugate and control others, particularly the Human Angelic populations.

This continues to be of concern in lower Sublevels of the Third Universal Dimension and you should be aware that efforts to dominate the planet by this group are being stepped up by them at this time. Human Angelics are only now awakening to this awareness by virtue of the added sensitivities afforded them through the increasing energies in your Solar System. Those increased energies are the result of the current Galactic Ascension period you are living through now.

Our effort in describing this for you is not to identify any group as good or bad, which is never the case, but merely to distinguish a Soul group currently holding sway over large swatches of political and societal governance from the Ninth Universal Dimensional System Lords working to assist Human Angelics through participation within your reality. Thus, if you were to assume that any problematic leader of a large Western Republic displaying dictatorial tendencies was a

The Seventh, Eighth and Ninth Astral Sublevels of the Third
Universal Dimension: The Astral Realm of Celestial Guidance,
The Akashic Realm and the Realm of the System Lords

System Lord, you would be incorrect and we would suggest you become aware that such leaders might instead be driven by the influence of their extraterrestrial Souls to dominate and control the Human Angelic populace.

Extraterrestrial (non Human Angelic) Soul lifetimes on the current timeline have set out en masse at the present time to oblige, control and dominate the Human populace, not for the benefit of their Soul growth but in order to consolidate their Soul Group's control over Earth's future incarnations. This will never be the case, but the important thing here is to understand that right now on Earth and in your Solar System, Ascended Master System Lords from the Ninth Universal Dimension have no connection whatsoever to this particular extraterrestrial Soul group and should probably not be mistakenly associated with the erratic behavior of certain well known political and business leaders in your world today.

As we have described, the Ninth Astral Sublevel is directly linked to the Ninth Universal Dimension, as is the case with other Dimensional Sublevels, and Ascended Masters from this realm voluntarily participate in lower dimensional levels through the Ninth Dimensional Sublevel or Astral plane of that Universal Dimension. Ninth Universal Dimensional Masters operating through System Lord incarnations at lower dimensional Levels will ultimately ascend to the Tenth Universal Dimension following their work. Once they have ascended to the Tenth Universal Dimension they are designated as "Sons of Gods" or, as they are also called, "Arch Angels." Whatever their designation, once these high Angelic Beings have ascended to the Tenth Universal Dimension, they do in fact become linked with the God Force by virtue of the divine dimensional Trilogy comprised of the Tenth, Eleventh and Twelfth

Universal Dimensions, which is in fact the realm of All That Is.

Sons of God, that is to say Ascended Master Souls from the Tenth Universal Dimension, have the ability to return to lower dimensional levels but they do not incarnate lifetimes therein, whereas Master Souls or System Lords from the Ninth Universal Dimension incarnate at lower dimensional levels as part of their work and growth within the universal structure. Many Ninth Universal Dimensional Ascended Master Souls will not ascend to the Tenth Universal Dimension at times even if their vibrational integrity and Ascension permits. Instead they remain at the Ninth Universal Dimensional level in order to continue their important work as System Lords in lower dimensional levels. Because of this, these Beings are highly honored and their work is considered a great sacrifice that they make to all Souls in the Universe. As a result, substantial consciousness and Soul growth is available to these Masters, and it is for this reason that once they ascend to the Tenth Universal Dimension their high consciousness makes them universally honored and this in turn explains their designation as Universal Arch Angels or Sons of God.

Interestingly, the concept of divine personalities who are considered "sons" of God who return to lower Dimensions on occasion to assist humanity is well known in many of your world religions. Historically as an example, mythological figures such as Osiris or Apollo, among others, were always identified as sons of that culture's primordial Godhead. This example is further found in the historical figure Jesus of Nazareth. As a System Lord incarnation, the story of Jesus can be credited, at least partially, with widely transforming spiritual thought, cultural standards and philosophy for millennia. This System Lord incarnation remains the perfect representation of a life-

The Seventh, Eighth and Ninth Astral Sublevels of the Third
Universal Dimension: The Astral Realm of Celestial Guidance,
The Akashic Realm and the Realm of the System Lords

time derived from a Ninth Universal Dimensional Spiritual Master Soul incarnated on Earth as an Avatar to transform world spiritual thought and philosophy. It is no accident that he is also identified in these philosophies as a "son" of God.

Coming from the Ninth Universal Dimension, these Masters utilize the Ninth Astral Sublevel of a Dimension as a staging point for the System Lord Wheels of Creation they manifest. Because they are Ninth Dimensional Beings, they have the ability to access, see and use the imprinted light information available in the Eighth Akashic sublevel and in doing so they explore world dynamics as well as the specific needs and goals of all Souls and lifetimes within the Dimension.

This information becomes the basis of the lifetimes of System Lord Avatars that incarnate in physical form to work within the parameters of the timeline and strongly influence mass consciousness to bring about the catalysts that will trigger new spiritual and geopolitical thinking in the world. The cultural, religious, political, artistic, societal and other movements these incarnated Beings generate and put into motion allow mass consciousness to be guided to create a diverse and substantial number of life opportunities for the entities that take them to heart. Souls use the local, regional and world mass consciousness events, created by System Lords and situated at certain points on the timeline, to orchestrate the personal opportunities and events needed for growth within their own lifetimes.

These opportunities can be made available to humanity through peaceful cultural, artistic and religious movements but may also be made available to Human Angelics through large-scale dramatic changes and consequences, including but not limited to war, social unrest, cataclysmic events, or racial and cultural conflicts. Inevitably, the influences are world altering either spiritually, philosophically, culturally or geopolitically, and all entities that face these changing situations on the timeline are presented with real choices that they must undertake. A philosophic trend that sweeps the world at a certain point or a devastating war that draws vast numbers of people into its grasp is anything but coincidental. We consider the choices individuals make as a result of such occurrences to be the very substance of opportunities for growth available to everyone at whatever point they unfold on the timeline.

Like the Seventh and Eighth Dimensional Sublevels, the Ninth Dimensional Sublevel or Ninth Astral realm is not so much a place as it is a state of being. For this reason, it is not truly possible to describe it as one would an environment or a location, but rather it should be seen as a vibrational energy field where celestial Light Beings participate in whatever manner is preferred by them. It is precisely the resonant vibrational patterns that correspond to the Ascended Master Souls in these Astral realms that distinguish them from entities that are residing in lower Dimensional Sublevels or Astral planes.

As explained however, there is very little vibrational difference between the higher Astral fields owing to the high consciousness of those there, and this is particularly true in what we have described as the higher dimensional Trilogies (the Seventh through Ninth and Tenth through Twelfth Dimensions). Naturally, again owing to levels of consciousness, there is a marked delineation between those entities that are newly arrived on the Seventh Astral plane that have taken on Light Bodies as they proceed to reintegration with their Soul and the Seventh Universal Dimension Celestial Ascended Mas-

The Seventh, Eighth and Ninth Astral Sublevels of the Third
Universal Dimension: The Astral Realm of Celestial Guidance,
The Akashic Realm and the Realm of the System Lords

ters who assist them. Likewise, there is a substantial vibrational and
consciousness differences between a Soul's ascending fragments and
the Angelic Masters from the Seventh Universal Dimension, the Master Souls working with the Akashic fields and the Ascended System
Lord Masters. Differences of this sort are always recognizable based
on each Soul's level of consciousness, Soul age, vibrational resonance
and density. Additionally, each and every Soul, regardless of their position on the timeline, their placement in the universal hierarchy or
their consciousness status, carries a personal vibrational signature
that identifies it in every Dimension throughout the Universe.

As we have mentioned already, beginning in the Seventh Astral Sublevel, the Dimensions have closer proximity in terms of communication, crossover and alliance than do the lower Dimensional Sublevels.
Transmigration across platforms and Dimensions, whether they are
Universal Dimensions or Sublevels of a Universal Dimension, is facilitated and easily accomplished in the higher Dimensions and Astral
realms where movement is lateral, whereas in the lower Universal
Dimensions and Astral Sublevels the progression is more linear. The
denser and weightier physicality of lower Dimensional Sublevels gives
lower Sublevels far greater vibrational distinction, and therefore the
lower Dimensions and Sublevels have a higher degree of invisibility
one from the next. The opposite is true at higher Dimensions and
higher Dimensional Sublevels or Astral environments.

It should be easy to understand therefore, that the Ascended Master
Souls that have reached the Seventh, Eighth and Ninth Universal Dimensions, including those that reach out from the higher Universal

Dimensions into the corresponding Sublevels of other Universal Dimensions, are in some cases literally one Universal Dimension away from reintegration and inclusion into what is considered the true realm of the Universal God Force or "All That Is." Naturally, the consciousness required to reach these high Universal levels is profound, and Seventh, Eighth and Ninth Dimensional Celestial Guides and Ascended Masters are considered by most aware Souls to be the Angelic working hands of God itself; thus the appellation Arch Angels.

We remind you that ultimately every Soul, including the one that you yourself are part of, will progress to these high states eventually, rising through all Universal Dimensions by means of Reincarnation, Transmigration and Ascension, eventually reintegrating with the God Force itself from whence they were originally cast out. For the most part, Souls follow the pattern described, however there are rare circumstances when higher Universal Dimensions may be skipped by transmigrating Souls. An example of a Soul skipping a Universal Dimension is most often experienced at the level of the Seventh, Eighth and Ninth Universal Dimension. At that level, a Seventh Dimensional Celestial Guide might choose not to experience Master guardianship of the Akashic Records and will rise instead directly to the Ninth Universal Dimension in order to serve as a System Lord.

This is because at these particular high levels of consciousness, certain specialties of Soul expression have consequence, and as we mentioned previously most Souls serving as Master Guides working with the Akashic records are Souls derived from the Sage, Speaker or Teacher Soul energy expressions. This energetic expression has a preference for working with the Akashic fields in the Eighth Dimension. Other Soul energy expressions prefer Seventh or Ninth Dimensional fields,

The Seventh, Eighth and Ninth Astral Sublevels of the Third
Universal Dimension: The Astral Realm of Celestial Guidance,
The Akashic Realm and the Realm of the System Lords

working directly as Seventh Dimensional Master Guides and Ascended Masters from those Dimensions.

Progression through the higher Astral planes is not vertical or linear
as you are accustomed to, and beginning with the Seventh Astral realm,
entities with newly acquired Light Bodies do not necessarily progress
through the Eighth or the Ninth Dimensional Sublevels. This is another
distinction that must be understood with respect to progression from
one Astral level to another within the higher Astral realms. This fact is
particularly true in that the Eighth and Ninth Astral Sublevels are primarily the realm of the Akashic Records and the System Lords. However, these sublevel dimensional energy fields, or Astral realms if you
prefer, still have considerable cross contact in order to assist entities
in the Seventh Astral realm and facilitate reintegration and consolidation with their Souls in the higher Astral planes.

As we originally stated, the Soul's journey carried out through its many
lifetimes within a Dimension is principally lateral in nature even though
it may culminate with Ascension, which is essentially a vertical progression. However, the Soul itself could be said to "transmigrate"
rather than ascend from one Universal Dimension to the next since
it remains at the highest levels of the Dimension and it is the Soul's
lifetimes that journey through all the Sublevels of a Dimension. In other
words, whereas the lifetimes created by a Soul within a Dimension
rise through all lower Dimensional Sublevels until they are reunited
with the Soul, the Soul itself technically migrates from the Twelfth Astral
realm of one Dimension to the Twelfth Astral Realm of the next higher
Dimension. (See Page 454, Figure 8 of Diagrams in the Appendix.)

Both definitions, transmigration and Ascension, are valid since both occur for the Soul. The lateral migration of a Soul, Celestial Guide, Ascended Master and System Lord or Arch Angel from one Universal Dimension to the corresponding Sublevel of another Dimension is generally considered Transmigration whereas the vertical rise of a Soul's many lifetimes through the Astral planes or Dimensional Sublevels is generally what is meant by Reincarnation followed by Ascension. In this way, the Soul transmigrates across platforms but because of its many lifetimes in the Universal Dimension, it also evolves through Universal Ascension.

When an individual entity representing one lifetime of a Soul reaches the Seventh Astral Sublevel, that entity begins to reconsolidate and join its energy with its Soul's energy. The entity will first reunify with all of the lifetimes connected to it on its Wheel of Creation, and then it will explore and unify with all the lifetimes on all of the Wheels of Creation of its Soul within that Dimension. Finally, the entity will explore and incorporate an understanding of all associations, agreements and any other Soul considerations as guided by Seventh Dimensional Celestial Beings, the Akashic Masters and finally the Ascended Masters familiar with or connected to its particular Soul group.

Technically speaking, the transfer of energy that follows this and begins on the Seventh Astral plane is not unlike the photon transfer that originally occurs as life events and agreements are imprinted into the Akashic Records in real time. The only difference here is that whereas previously this information is downloaded to the entity itself in the lower Astral realms to assist with its birth agreements, help in major life-event planning or as guidance used by the entity in accordance with its level of consciousness, once the entity has taken on its Light body in the higher Astral realms the opposite occurs. New information from the entity pertaining to life dynamics, alterations, karmic balance or other information and events gathered while in the lower Astral planes is now "uploaded," so to speak, via the Akashic directly to the Soul.

That work takes place in conjunction with the Soul at higher energetic levels under the auspices of Ascended Master Guides within the Tenth Dimensional Sublevel. In a manner of speaking, except for the fact that this is an ongoing and dynamic process, one might say that the entity's growth culminates in the Seventh Astral realm but the Soul's growth starts when the entity takes on its Light body in the Seventh Astral realm and reconsolidation with the Soul begins. The work of the Soul towards reintegrating its lifetimes is thus undertaken starting in the Tenth Astral Realm, and it is in that Astral plane that the entity and its Soul are electromagnetically and, we would add, irresistibly drawn together.

The process of reintegration with the Soul is sometimes called the "Resealing" of the Soul. From the Soul's perspective in the Twelfth Astral realm of the Dimension, this "Resealing" is done with the assistance of the Eighth Dimensional Akashic Masters working closely in conjunction with the Tenth Dimensional Arch Angels or Sons of God. The miraculous work of Resealing prepares and readies the Soul for Ascension and renewed Transmigration to the next Universal Dimension once the energy of all its lifetimes and reincarnations within the Dimension have fully reintegrated with it. Reintegration and the reconsolidation of the Soul's energy with all lifetimes on its Wheels of Creation are definitively accomplished in the Tenth, Eleventh and Twelfth Astral planes, as we shall now explore.

Stories from a Soul's Wheel of Creation
The Story of Christian

From a young age, Christian was well aware that he had three distinct eccentricities. First, he tended to seek out very small, enclosed spaces, and even normal sized rooms made him feel uneasy, disoriented and anxious. Secondly, he had a very strong interest and admiration for Catholicism, the Catholic Clergy and the Pope, even though he was raised a Lutheran and as a child his family frowned upon his fascination with Catholic precepts they considered to be anti-Lutheran and unnatural to them. Finally, and perhaps most importantly, his fear of crowds and of speaking in front of more than a few people at a time seemed more a phobia than a fear, one that held him back in school, in his chosen career and in almost every other facet of his life.

Smarter than the majority of his peers and more talented than most, this last peculiarity was the one that caused Christian's family the most concern. They tried to brush it off as shyness that would one day recede, but ultimately it became the difficulty that caused him the highest degree of consternation, regret and sorrow in life.

His agoraphobia and inability to be part of any group without feeling extreme anxiety, and especially his inability to speak with more than one or two people at a time, blocked him from succeeding at almost everything worthwhile. To compensate for his phobia, he operated invisibly and in a secretive manner. In

The Seventh, Eighth and Ninth Astral Sublevels of the Third
Universal Dimension: The Astral Realm of Celestial Guidance,
The Akashic Realm and the Realm of the System Lords

*fact, as an adult he worked overtime to make sure he did not
have to be part of any group activities or be placed in any situation where he needed to communicate in front of more than
one or two people at a time.*

*Often, a smart manager or working colleague who realized this
would become his pseudo-spokesperson, taking over projects
or manipulating events so that Christian did all the work but
the manipulator in question took all the credit. Christian's career, as well as his finances, floundered as he was passed over
for promotion after promotion, if not let go by insensitive em-
ployers convinced he was just not up to their standards, or
somehow unworthy based on the fact he never spoke up and
always seemed to be missing in action.*

*As he reached middle-age, he found he could only work incog-
nito from behind the scenes, and he did whatever was necessary to keep himself hidden and invisible. The slightest
recognition or praise, anything that required him to be acknowledged or singled out in front of others, was hopelessly traumatic, leaving him anxious and pushing him into overdrive
trying to avoid being identified or called upon to speak or be
part of some group activity. Inevitably, this would lead to severe
depression as his condition deteriorated and his agoraphobia
became too much to handle over time. Still, it was easier for
him to stay at home isolated and alone than to even contemplate the slightest interaction with others in any way.*

This vicious cycle continued to dominate his life, with Christian unable to work or live in any situation where he was not completely removed and invisible. The same isolation that allowed him to be able to cope with life however, also caused him severe loneliness and despair. Able to only be with one person at a time by now and unable to work, his life was in a tailspin. Feeling hopeless, Christian began to contemplate taking his own life in order to end not only the extreme anxiety that the smallest interaction with the world would cause him, but also the sadness and lack of fulfillment his life had become.

Finally acknowledging to himself that he was in trouble, Christian reached out to a Jungian therapist who began to dive into the root of his phobia. As they made progress, the therapist told Christian that she had once worked with a well-known Intuitive who was renowned for helping people look into the deeper hidden aspects of exactly where their anxieties originated.

She said that although there are certainly deep-rooted early life circumstances leading to his situation, often her experience was that these things had a component buried deep inside the psyche that was Soul related. Bringing both the conscious and subconscious aspects into view, in her opinion, would help shed more light on the situation giving them both a better picture to help navigate his state fully. The therapist suggested Christian call the Intuitive so the three might work together, albeit independently, in order to get to the heart of what was happening to him.

Having felt some shifting of his fears from working with the Jungian therapist, Christian agreed and called the Intuitive for a phone consultation. The Intuitive wasted no time focusing on the Soul aspects of Christian's fears, and provided him with a close look at a particular past life that she said was being re-flected and balanced by his Soul through Christian's current lifetime.

In that lifetime, which occurred in the mid 18th Century in France under the reign of Louis XV, Christian was the youngest son of a reasonably well-to-do and established family in a neighboring hamlet of Paris. Weavers and merchants by trade, his family boasted indirect royal connections in as much as they were weavers of fine cloth and linens that had been established by and placed under the patronage of the French Kings begin-ning during the reign of Louis XIV. Their position in the com-munity and their ongoing royal patronage made them extremely conservative and fierce royalists.

Handsome and eloquent, in keeping with family tradition as the youngest son he was pushed into the priesthood in his late teens, and by his mid-twenties he was ordained as a priest. Based on his family's connections he became associated with a prestigious Cathedral.

Well-liked and highly educated, the young priest was also ex-tremely idealistic and his views of life, society and class struc-

ture soon became shaped by the emerging views and advanced perspectives of the Enlightenment Age. These ideologies and philosophies were being discussed openly around Paris, and the young priest took an active and vocal interest publicly in promoting the equal rights of all men, discussing social injustice openly and advocating the need for social reforms.

Before long, the young priest's sermons were being interpreted as a call to revolution, and he began to gain notoriety for his opinions and views that called for limits to monarchy, a constitution and equality and justice for all men obtained by whatever means necessary. A highly visible Cathedral close to Paris and connected to the Kings of France, as his audiences grew the young priest soon found himself under political scrutiny. This scrutiny only emboldened him further however, and his sermons and speeches in which he now advocated complete social and governmental policy change became more and more attended by larger and larger populace audiences.

One day the size of his audience became so large that a violent skirmish started when those wishing to attend a "sermon" were forcibly turned away. This was as much as the authorities were willing to take. They seized on the incident and promptly arrested the young priest charging him with inciting riots and fomenting conspiracy against the Regime.

Known just well enough to peak the citizenry's interest but not

The Seventh, Eighth and Ninth Astral Sublevels of the Third
Universal Dimension: The Astral Realm of Celestial Guidance,
The Akashic Realm and the Realm of the System Lords

well enough to cause any major scandal as a result of his arrest, the priest was tortured for a confession, convicted and sentenced to be imprisoned in a small, dank prison cell for a minimum of ten years.

Fearing retribution from their Royal patrons, his family quietly disowned him and he was left languishing as a political prisoner. To make matters worse, because of his intelligence, his eloquence and the fear that he might incite other prisoners to riot, he was kept chained and isolated from the general population, and was not allowed to communicate with anyone.

Abandoned by friends and family, ignored by the people he had once championed and excommunicated by the Church for heresy, he faded from existence in a tiny dark cell where he had difficulty procuring even the most basic sustenance (during that time the families of prisoners, prisoners themselves or certain charities were expected to provide the bulk of a prisoner's food and needs while in prison). Having no one to count on and with no real hope of being released, the young priest existed on scraps of stale bread and water given to him occasionally out of charity by the few jailers who still remembered he was chained up there. Over time however, he was completely forgotten and finally died of starvation and neglect still chained in the same tiny prison cell where he had been originally incarcerated.

The Intuitive explained to him further that in this life the young priest's intelligence, talent and willingness to fight for what he believed in were all readily available to Christian. The bad news however, was that the imprisonment, torture and circumstances that led to the priest's death were associated with his public addresses and his association with groups and crowds. This association, with the trauma and sad death it had created for the priest, was so deep that it reverberated into Christian's lifetime. As a result, Christian's Soul was seeking to balance the energy by creating the fears of the priest in Christian's life.

The Soul mission for Christian's life was subtle but complex, and it revolved around issues the Intuitive called the learning of the expression of his "Will." This had also been the life mission of the young priest, and for both connected lifetimes it involved lessons around knowing when and how to be discriminating about expressing one's opinions or Will and when to hold back and give others the power to express themselves.

The young priest had not been discriminating in the expression of his views to others and had not carefully considered the consequences of doing so, which led to his ultimate demise. On the other hand, Christian discriminated and edited his personal expression down to a fault, curtailing his Will and, at times, not allowing an expression of his beliefs or views at all. Each lifetime on their Soul's Wheel of Creation was being directly balanced by the other, and all aspects of the mission, pro and con,

The Seventh, Eighth and Ninth Astral Sublevels of the Third
Universal Dimension: The Astral Realm of Celestial Guidance,
The Akashic Realm and the Realm of the System Lords

were ultimately being experienced by the Soul.

Unfortunately for Christian, he was experiencing this life lesson through the negative and more challenging polarity. If Christian were able to fight his fears and contain his tendency to hide, avoid people or public situations and not express his Will, the karmic imbalance would be lessened and would recede (although still being present in him). However, when he succumbed to those fears and he cleverly avoided expressing himself, the fear would grow to the point where not only would it impede him, it could potentially ruin his life.

In essence, Christian's abnormal fear of people and public scrutiny and expressing his views was meant to create opportunities that would oblige him to overcome the fear of speaking out by walking through his fears. This would cure outstanding karmic imbalances on his Soul's Wheel of Creation. By not doing so for the greater part of life however, he had created his own psychological and emotional prison, retreating to his tiny apartment where he could never learn to discriminate or measure the expression of his Will to others. Christian's prison was self-imposed because he would not express himself, whereas the young priest's prison was forced upon him for by external forces because, in a manner of speaking, he was practicing "over" expression.

At a minimum now, he could begin to mitigate the imbalance, by reemerging, to an extent, into the world. With the help of the Therapist he was able to reenter life somewhat and live a fairly normal existence, including the ability to go out in public, operate in large groups and express himself, to a certain extent, without fear. However, Christian was not truly able to completely overcome the dread he felt speaking or participating in front of any group. Despite this, according to the Intuitive this was not considered a failure since the energetic blockage was also being worked out by his Soul through similar issues generated in a future lifetime connected to both Christian and the priest on their Soul's Wheel of Creation.

The Tenth, Eleventh and Twelfth Dimensional Sublevels of the
Third Universal Dimension: The Astral Realms of Reintegration
with the Soul, Realm of the Sons of God and the Soul's
Preparation for Transmigration to the next Universal Dimension

Chapter 8

The Tenth, Eleventh and Twelfth Dimensional Sublevels of the Third Universal Dimension: The Astral Realms of Reintegration with the Soul, Realm of the Sons of God and the Soul's Preparation for Transmigration to the next Universal Dimension

As we explained earlier, until now the pattern of Soul Reincarnation, Transmigration and Ascension we have described is in keeping with what you might expect, from your perspective, in terms of a general tendency to see things as linear and vertical in progression. This tendency is reflected in most of your hierarchies such as levels of society and social standing, climbing a career "ladder" or the graduating levels of education you face as you rise to the top of familiar institutions, structures and enterprises. Clearly, this linear hierarchical vision facilitates your ability to envision and understand how things progress, grow and culminate.

However, it is important to understand that in the higher Astral environments, beginning with the Seventh through Twelfth Dimensional planes, both in the Astral realms and in the Universal Dimensions, a linear, vertical approach or pattern is no longer valid. In those higher environments crossover experiences between various dimensional realms are what lead to Soul advancement and growth. We would therefore consider the experiences in the higher Astral planes to follow a horizontal or lateral pattern of method, approach and success. Based on this important difference, we need to briefly summarize what we have discussed so far regarding Ascension cycles as well as the manner in which we are using certain terminology.

As you know, Ascension can be broken down into evolutionary cycles that occur approximately every 25,000 to 26,000 years, every 250,000 to 260,000 years, and every 250 to 260 million years. Ascension cycles are periods where universal photonic energies are magnified around specific Souls, Beings, Timelines, Planets, Galaxies and other Universal Bodies in extraordinary ways to facilitate and allow access to higher levels of consciousness and, as a result, multidimensional transformation that affects the entire Universe.

The increase in consciousness and vibrational frequency allows for evolution of the entire system, depending upon the Ascension cycle being experienced. Keep in mind the multidimensional aspects of this, since, for example, the 26,000 and the 260,000-year Ascension periods are Galaxy specific and may change depending upon the Solar System and Galaxy in question and its location in the Universe. For our purposes here, we are discussing your Galaxy and your Solar System, and the length and time periods used reflect that. Notably however, the 260 million year Ascension cycle is universally timed and experienced.

Approximately every 26,000 years, your Solar System enters what has been called the Solar Ascension Cycle. Many miraculous things occur during Solar Ascension periods, some of which we have discussed elsewhere, but for the purpose of our current discussion we will approach this cycle from the Soul's position within your Universal Dimension.

When a Soul is forged and cast out by Source, it enters a specific Universal Dimension and incarnates in various ways within the many sublevels of that Universal Dimension. Some sub-levels of the Universal Dimension pertain to physical being and some are Astral or non-corporeal in nature. As we have seen, the Soul incarnates various lifetimes through what we term a "Wheel of Creation," and there are many Wheels of Creation that a Soul manifests within any given Universal Dimension. Again, as we have discussed, each Wheel can have different numbers of lifetimes within it, and the lifetimes on any particular Wheel are generally interconnected karmically and otherwise.

You call the lifetimes on your particular Wheel of Creation a "reincarnation," and this term is true but only to an extent. Contrary to popular belief, reincarnations are not linear in nature and do not originate with you. Equally true is the fact that each entity on a Wheel of Creation, including your life, is a unique and independent lifetime created by the Soul. That unique lifetime, entity or self if you prefer, travels, even after physical death, through various sub-levels of your Universal Dimension, climbing through the Astral planes of the Universal Dimension until such time as it is reintegrated with its Creator Soul at the highest sub-levels of a Universal Dimension.

When all the lifetimes or "reincarnations" from every Wheel of Creation of a Soul have completed their independent journey through the Universal Dimension, including all of its Astral planes, and have reintegrated with the Soul, the Soul is said to be ready for "Ascension." In that case, the energetic opportunity for a Soul itself to "ascend" to the next Universal Dimension is rendered possible at any 26,000 year interval during the period known as the Solar Ascension Cycle.

In addition to this, approximately every 260,000 years there is what can be termed the Galactic Ascension Cycle. It is during this cycle that the Universal Dimension itself evolves if the vibrational frequency and consciousness within the Universal Dimension have augmented to the point that Ascension is possible. As this occurs, the Universal Dimension evolves and merges into the next Universal Dimension, taking its place in a manner of speaking, and this happens from Universal Dimension to Universal Dimension. In this way as an example, during the Galactic Ascension period the Second Universal Dimension actually transforms itself vibrationally into the Third Universal Dimension, the Fifth Universal Dimension into the Sixth, and so on and so forth.

This Galactic, or Grand Ascension period as it is also sometimes known, is a smooth transition that represents the evolution of the Universe's dimensional Time-Waves. In a sense it can be seen as a kind of reset of each dimensional timeline or Time-Wave. This is so because basically a Universal Dimension is a product of its Space-time wave, or, said in another way, the Space-time wave spiral is what ultimately creates a Universal Dimension.

At the 260,000 year Ascension mark not only does the Universal Dimension Time-Wave evolve, it is also the period where the greatest number of Souls within that Timeline have the ability to ascend vibrationally in unison with the Universal Dimension. Therefore, even though Souls may ascend to a new Universal Dimension if they

The Tenth, Eleventh and Twelfth Dimensional Sublevels of the
Third Universal Dimension: The Astral Realms of Reintegration
with the Soul, Realm of the Sons of God and the Soul's
Preparation for Transmigration to the next Universal Dimension

are ready and wish to do so about every 26,000 years during the Solar Ascension Cycle, they are not obliged to do so and may ascend in unison with their current Universal Dimension during the greater Galactic or Grand Ascension. In truth, most Souls prefer to remain within a Universal Dimension experiencing incarnations an entire Galactic Ascension period of approximately 260,000 years, at which point they ascend in an almost piggy-back manner with the Ascension momentum created by the Ascension of the entire Universal Dimension itself.

Because of this, most Souls create Wheels of Creation and lives, within a Universal Dimension that span the entire 260,000-year period. It is for this reason as an example, a lifetime such as your own might easily have connections on your own Wheel of Creation to a lifetime taking place during any other point on the timeline within a 260,000-year period. Therefore, a reincarnated self could be related to you from the time period of the Empire of Atlantis, or even from some future point on the timeline as well as anywhere in between.

Even a Soul that is ready to ascend has the option of creating additional Wheels of Creation within the existing Universal Dimension if it chooses to have new experiences related to its growth. For that purpose the Soul has the ability to "hold itself back" from Ascension at any point, and might instead choose to ascend during any 26,000 year Solar Ascension period thereafter.

For Souls that may not have reached the required consciousness or vibrational resonance required to ascend, this allows an opportunity to ascend with the Solar Cycle every 26,000 years instead of waiting the additional 260,000 years when the Galactic Ascension cycle completes. Similarly, it provides those Souls that are ready to ascend and have reached their desired consciousness growth or vibration, including those with other universal goals or priorities, the possibility of ascending prior to a 260,000 year Galactic Ascension period.

Finally, approximately every 250 to 260 Million years there is what we shall term the Cosmic Ascension period. This cycle is relatively difficult to explain as it relates to discoveries yet to be made by your science, particularly with regard to what lies in between and beyond the Galaxies you have mapped that are part of the Universe's composition. Suffice to say however, that it is the Ascension period associated with the phenomenon sometimes known as the Grand Attractor, and represents the Ascension of all universal planetary bodies and all galaxies. In a manner of speaking, this great mystery could be considered Ascension of the God Source itself, expressed through redesign and Ascension of all planetary, galactic and other bodies within the known Universe by a Cosmic force that encompasses all and remains a universal mystery, even within the Twelve Universal Dimensions.

Great planetary and galactic changes occur throughout the Universe during the Cosmic Ascension period. In addition, it represents the particular cycle when the highest Angelic Beings, the "Sons of God" or Arch Angels, as we have called them, from the Tenth and Eleventh Universal Dimensions reach final reintegration with the God Source in the Twelfth Universal Dimension. In effect, the reintegration of these Arch Angel Souls allows the God Source, or All That Is, to experience Ascension (and thus evolution) itself.

As a result, the Cosmic Ascension Cycle could be said to herald an increase in the very consciousness of God and Universal Source energy itself, and this is the reason it is a period of dynamic planetary, galactic and universal change. It is also the reason the Universe appears to always be "expanding." That expansion is indicative of not only an increase in the universal psyche achieved through reintegration into the God Source of the Arch Angelic Souls cast out by Source long before, it is the literal expansion of the Universe that comes from an increase in the consciousness of All That Is -- God, if you will.

Within your Solar System all of these Ascension cycles are taking place now and happening almost simultaneously. This is extremely rare and it greatly increases the energetic intensity for all involved within every sector in question.

With the Ascension cycles explained let's now discuss the terminology we use to describe the journey of the Soul within and between the Dimensions. We take Reincarnation to mean a Soul's incarnation into various entity-lifetimes within a Wheel of Creation generated for that purpose. Soul growth comes from an entity's incarnation by the Soul and the subsequent journey it takes through a particular Universal Dimension (both the physical and all the Astral aspects of that Universal Dimension). Although you may have been taught that reincarnation, or reincarnated selves, is defined as extensions of yourself in a linear fashion, even if this may have minor relevance based on the interconnectedness of a Soul's many lifetimes, reincarnation is actually the many independent lifetimes or entities generated by a Soul on a specific Wheel of Creation within a given Universal Dimension.

Next, we use the term Transmigration to mean traveling through dimensional levels. This applies to the Soul travelling from Universal Dimension to Universal Dimension and is also applicable to an independent reincarnation or lifetime journeying through the many Astral or other Sublevels of a Universal Dimension, including the journey through physicality as well as all non-corporeal forms. As an entity traverses the various Sublevels of a Dimension it is said to transmigrate from Sublevel to Sublevel. The use of the term transmigrate here is to prevent any misunderstanding, since Ascension is generally reserved to describe the Soul's ability to evolve to the next Universal Dimension during the appropriate Ascension period.

At the lower Sublevels of a Universal Dimension, Transmigration appears to be linear and vertical in nature, and thus an entity, corporeal or not, moves through the dimensional system in essentially a hierarchical or vertical progression. However, in higher Universal Dimensions and at higher Sublevels of a Universal Dimension, the higher consciousness and close vibrational resonance of these planes of existence allows for Transmigration to occur horizontally across platforms, or in other words, to be lateral in nature.

As a result and based on this, a Soul cast out from the Twelfth Universal Dimension easily "Transmigrates" to the Twelfth Dimensional Sublevel or Astral plane of any Universal Dimension. Similarly, Ascended Masters, Angelic Celestial Beings, Akashic Guides, System Lords, Arch Angels and Sons of God, originating as they do in the Seventh, Eighth, Ninth, Tenth and Eleventh Universal Dimensions respectively, readily "Transmigrate" from their prospective Universal

Dimension laterally and across Universal Dimensions to the corresponding Dimensional Sublevel of another Universal Dimension, if they desire to be present or participate there.

Thus, as an example, beginning with the Seventh Universal Dimension, Celestial Beings from that Universal Dimension are able to transmigrate vertically within the dimensional "Trinity" (consisting of the Seventh, Eighth and Ninth Universal Dimension), but they are also able to transmigrate laterally to the Seventh Dimensional Sublevel or Astral plane of any other Universal Dimension. More importantly, this means that Angelic and Celestial Beings from higher Universal Dimensions, like the Seventh Universal Dimension, are able to cooperate and participate with other Ascended Masters within these three higher realms, irrespective of the Universal Dimension from which they originate.

They are also able to observe and guide those in lower Universal Dimensions by accessing the Dimensional Sublevel or Astral plane that corresponds to their own Universal Dimension. Similarly, Tenth, Eleventh and Twelfth Universal Dimension Beings are able to do the same within their Trinity or dimensional structure. Additionally they have the added feature of being able to participate vertically with lower Universal Dimensions, through the Dimensional Sublevels.

It should be understood that while such participation is possible, for the most part universal laws strictly prevent direct intercession or interference by Higher Dimensional Beings into the realms of lower Dimensions. They may guide, inspire, suggest and assist entities in lower Dimensions but will almost never interfere or take direct action therein. There are however, two noticeable exceptions to this, if they can be called exceptions.

The first exception is related to the interface of Ninth Dimensional Beings and their creation of Physical or Spiritual System Lords in lower dimensional realities. Notably however, as independent entities these System Lords are actually physical incarnations of the Ninth Dimensional Master Souls, and thus the System Lords themselves, who are not fully conscious of their role or connection, reside within the lower levels of the Universal Dimension. Because these incarnations have Free Will and are subject to the same physics of all lower dimensional entities, they cannot truthfully be said to directly "interfere" with lower dimensional reality planes. They are however, able to influence it in ways that alter the mass consciousness environment of lower density realities for the purpose of providing opportunities for growth of all Souls with lifetimes incarnated therein.

The second exception is with respect to the guidance and acceptance of the highest dimensional Souls known as the Sons of God, or the Arch Angels. In fact these entities do have the consciousness and ability to alter certain lower reality outcomes and occasionally reach into lower Universal Dimensions to assist individuals, communities, races, species and even planets. In fact, there are times when what you might consider extraordinary, paranormal or divine intervention is indeed intercession from one or other Angelic Beings. However, not only is such assistance extremely rare, when it occurs it is usually never a direct interaction and very seldom manifests as intervention on behalf of one particular individual. Such assistance by these Beings, when warranted, tends to generally be of a more galactic or universal nature, whereas assistance directed towards personal entities is usually derived from the individual's Soul itself.

The Tenth, Eleventh and Twelfth Dimensional Sublevels of the
Third Universal Dimension: The Astral Realms of Reintegration
with the Soul, Realm of the Sons of God and the Soul's
Preparation for Transmigration to the next Universal Dimension

An example of the divine intervention we are describing might be, as we have mentioned before, the attempt by a Soul species working interdimensionally from another Universal Dimension to usurp the galactic, Solar System or planetary endowment of another Soul species. References you may have heard in passing to a "Galactic Council" exemplify this and although there are alliances that are extraterrestrial in nature, for the most part this is a metaphor describing that in fact Tenth and Eleventh Dimensional Arch Angels are vested with the ability to intercede when necessary to prevent galactic interdimensional domination of one Soul species by another.

They can sometimes also serve as arbiters of pending situations, particularly if it concerns unnecessary outcomes, planetary bodies or energetic field creations amongst various different Soul groups or cadres. This is not to be confused, however, with the interdimensional and interplanetary alliances described as the "Galactic Federation," which tend to be alliances formed to carry out assistance to aligned planetary systems, usually at the behest of the Higher Dimensional Arch Angelic Beings we are describing herein.

Soul species dominance does occur, but usually it is only with the cooperation and agreement of all involved Soul groups for the purposes of Soul growth in that Universal Dimension. An example of such cooperation might be a Soul group (usually a hive Soul group) that agrees to serve another Soul group as biological sustenance. The animal kingdom is full of such examples, and within your own species the use of livestock for food is a well-known example.

This does not however, provide any group with a license to abuse such an agreement or those Soul groups that make themselves available as part of a greater plan for such purposes. It is for this reason that honoring biological inter-species cooperation such as this and acknowledging the bond each time you partake of it is very important. When those Soul agreements are not honored, karmic consequences relative to the entire Soul group exploiting the gift are possible, and we would suggest to you that the focus on food sources you are currently experiencing and the shortages that will become more pronounced very soon are a prime example of karmic awakening to this. Mistreatment of a particular Soul group, hive Soul or not, can only last so long before karmic balancing is required, and the current manner in which the ground and water are poisoned and animal food sources are abused, treated and, in some cases, tortured will come home to roost.

This is also true in cases where a Soul species exploits others within the same Soul group, as is most often the case of slavery, bondage or human trafficking. In general, such practices create challenging karmic imbalances and difficult learning experiences that can require many additional lifetimes to balance for all participants on either side of the equation. However, because such interchange is within the same Soul group and usually chosen by all participants, usually younger Souls for the purposes of growth, karmic balancing is derived as the result. Higher Celestial entities do not intercede in such cases other than to provide guidance intended to help the individuals in each group move beyond these imbalances and, hopefully, eliminate the need for such life experiences to be created in the first place.

It is a different story with inter-Soul species, and particularly with any attempt by one Soul species to dominate another, especially in any galactic quadrant designated the homeland of another Soul species. The ability of Arch Angelic groups to intercede is precisely the reason the current bio-invasion of Earth by an extraterrestrial Soul species, the Draconian-Zeta Soul group, via incarnations of hybrid humans, as we have already discussed, will never actually be completed on Third Universal Dimension Earth. Working in conjunction with the Planetary Being itself, the great reset we have described that is intended to take place on Earth in the 26th Century is a prime example of Galactic and Arch Angel intercession.

To be sure, none of this should imply any universal hierarchy or legislative body, but should be seen instead as indirect assistance and guidance offered to all entities from the highest realms and Dimensions. As we have always reminded you, in general higher can see lower (or at least is aware of its existence) but lower is not able to participate with higher when it comes to vibrational resonance or Dimensions. However, this is also the reason Beings of relatively higher consciousness can offer assistance to lower Dimensions and less conscious Beings. For purposes of explanation here it can be seen as another reason Beings of higher consciousness are provided the option of transmigrating across dimensional platforms laterally, as well as up and down vertically.

Naturally, this example of transmigration is used primarily as it relates to being of service to lower Universal Dimensions and lower Dimensional Sublevels. It should be understood that Celestial Guides are primarily concerned with assisting those in lower Dimensions as part of their mission to further their own consciousness growth within the higher Universal Dimension where they are focused. Efforts made by these Exalted Celestial Guides to assist Souls by providing opportunities for growth within lower Dimensions to all the entities on a Soul's Wheels of Creation simultaneously helps these Celestial Guides to achieve their own personal Soul growth.

What should start to be clear to you by now is that these Arch Angel or "Son of God" Souls, advanced Souls from the Tenth and Eleventh Universal Dimension that transmigrate through to the Tenth and Eleventh Dimensional Sublevel of other Universal Dimensions, are also Souls that themselves were originally cast out from the Twelfth Universal Dimension. Cast into lower Universal Dimensions in much the same manner your Soul was once cast out from All That Is with a mission to grow and evolve through the Process of Reincarnation, Transmigration and Ascension, these Master Souls are completing their Universal experience. That experience culminates, for all Souls, in reunification with Source.

In other words, having ascended through all the Universal Dimensions these Souls are finally reuniting with their primordial Source, now ready to reintegrate with it. This process of reunification with All That Is, or the originating God energy, is not unlike the process you and every entity goes through in reuniting with their Soul having completed their journey through a Universal Dimension. In fact, reintegration of all lifetimes on all Wheels of Creation with the Soul is a prerequisite of the Soul's evolution and Ascension to the next Universal Dimension. One day that same Soul, having traversed all Universal Dimensions and earned the status of Arch Angel, will reintegrate with its Creator having reached the pinnacle of consciousness, awareness and growth.

Seen from another perspective, one day the Soul returning and reuniting with the God Source carrying the consciousness of every

The Tenth, Eleventh and Twelfth Dimensional Sublevels of the
Third Universal Dimension: The Astral Realms of Reintegration
with the Soul, Realm of the Sons of God and the Soul's
Preparation for Transmigration to the next Universal Dimension

lifetime on every Wheel of Creation it has created in every Dimension might be your own Soul carrying with it your own life's consciousness. Thus, you and your Soul will one day ascend to the status of Arch Angel and be considered a Son of God Being. Following that reasoning one step further, you can see that all Souls and Universal Beings together with all the lifetimes they create in whatever Dimension can actually be considered the grandchildren, if not the actual sons and daughters, of God. In a manner of speaking then, every sentient entity not only has connection to its own Soul, it has a direct connection and relationship with the God Source through their Soul. This is precisely why throughout time the idea that everyone is ultimately a "child" of God has been the basis of nearly every religious, spiritual or metaphysical philosophy known to man.

Nowhere is such awareness more relevant than in the Tenth Astral Realm or Tenth Sublevel of a Universal Dimension. This is where the true nature of every entity as a child of its Soul and, therefore, as a child of the God Source is revealed to them following their Universal Dimension experience. It is here that all prepare for the final return and reunification of their energy with the Soul that first created them.

Again, we emphasize that reunification does not obliterate your or your independent "Being-ness," but instead integrates who you are into a living system that is ever expanding and augmented by virtue of the integration of your unique vibrational energy and consciousness. In a manner of speaking, you and many others like you actually represent the growth in consciousness of your Soul. Though transformed, who you are is always present as part of your Soul, and the Tenth Dimensional Sublevel is where that transformation truly begins.

Many higher Celestial Beings that reach levels of consciousness compatible with higher vibrational resonance and awareness commensurate with their Universal Dimension have the distinct ability to assist the lower Dimensions. We have already discussed the Ascended Master Beings from the Ninth Universal Dimension that we have called System Lords who return to lower Dimensions and generate Wheels of Creation for the purpose of assisting the geo political and spiritual aspects and growth of those realms. In addition however, you should know that a good many Tenth Dimensional Beings, Arch Angels or Sons of God, also return to lower Dimensions and generate Wheels of Creation for this same purpose as well.

Though technically they are considered System Lords, the life entities generated by these highest Souls tend to be more aware and enlightened. This is particularly true of the Spiritual System Lords, those entities that influence spiritual and philosophical mass consciousness through the Avatar lifetimes they create. In such cases, though a local political leader might be a System Lord entity generated on a Wheel of Creation of a Ninth Dimensional Being to influence changes in geopolitical mass consciousness on a regional basis, a System Lord such as the figure known as Akhenaten, Jesus of Nazareth or the Buddha, among many others, might be an entity generated by a Tenth Universal Dimensional Arch Angel that has transmigrated to lower Dimensions for very specific purposes. It is not by accident that these figures are often called the "Son of God" in the religious and spiritual materials generated about them. Their purpose might include, as an example, the complete altering of the philosophical and

spiritual direction for an entire timeline or the era in question, regionally or, in some cases, globally.

This is simply to let you know that there may be different degrees
of guidance and assistance. Moreover, it reflects the fact that not all
System Lord physical incarnations should be considered equal in nature or scope. This also leads to the fact that while a good many
choose to assist and grow in this manner, once a Soul has ascended
to the Tenth Universal Dimension there is no requirement for them
to transmigrate to lower Dimensions if they do not choose to do
so. In fact, many choose to focus on their advancement in other ways,
not necessarily as guides to lower Dimensions. Thus it is important
to make the distinction that not all System Lords are Ascended Masters or Sons of God from the Tenth or Eleventh Universal Dimension, and additionally, not all Ascended Masters from those
Dimensions act as System Lords.

Once a Soul begins reunification starting in the Seventh Universal
Dimension and then transmigrates to the Tenth Astral plane for final
reintegration together with all the Soul's lifetimes in that Dimension,
the Soul has a unique ability to follow its own course. This includes
several things, such as whether to prepare for Ascension, create new
or add lifetimes to its existing Wheels of Creation or linger at lower
Sublevels of the Dimension, in service to other Souls and the entities
on that other Soul's Wheels of Creation.

This is because as we stated already, passage through the Seventh
Astral plane allows close communication with the Eighth and Ninth
Dimensional Sublevels, but does not necessitate working or existing
within those Astral Sublevels exclusively. As a result, the entity has

direct access to its Soul in the higher Astral Trinity, that is, the Tenth, Eleventh and Twelfth Dimensional Sublevels, and many will transmigrate directly from being of service in the Seventh Astral plane to the Tenth Astral plane.

However, it should be noted that Souls, and each entity that comprises it, tend to have areas of interest that are specific to them and sometimes related to either an energetic expression or the various interests cultivated and developed through its lifetimes experienced on the Wheels of Creation. Because of this, a Soul will usually pursue an energetic specialty when reunified, and will inevitably endeavor to become proficient at skills related to that specialty, especially if they are applicable to the manner in which lower dimensional Beings are assisted and guided by higher dimensional Beings.

Thus, a Soul reintegrating in the Tenth Astral realm that desires, as an example, to continue to work with the Akashic energy fields will choose to linger in the Eight Astral Sublevel until such time as all lifetimes are completed, reintegrated and the Ascension cycle is present. Much as in the lower Dimensional Sublevels, Souls will in a sense apprentice, exploring the electromagnetic impulses registered in the Akashic and working to fully understand the full breadth of the many unique and miraculous experiences that other Souls obtain through their creations.

Many Souls will do the same at still lower Dimensional Sublevels depending on their areas of expertise and interest, participating in the Healing Centers of the Fifth Astral plane, as an example, or in the Perceived Heaven environments of the Sixth Astral plane. These Souls do so simultaneously as their many lifetimes reintegrate with them in the Tenth and Eleventh Astral environment, and continue to do so until such time as they have reached full integration and a vibrational resonance where Ascension is possible, assuming an Ascension period is on hand.

Souls that have not fully reintegrated the lifetimes from their Wheels of Creation will continually make themselves available throughout the Universal Dimension according to intention, interest and the specific specialization and consciousness of that Soul. These specializations are varied in nature and range from assisting lower Dimensions in capacities such as helping to influence decisions of those it is guiding in the Dreamscape to taking on the form of a loved one or religious figure known to an entity to greet them as they pass from corporeal existence.

Often, a Soul will be the principal guide to all the lifetimes or entities it has created, or at other times will assist all entities known to it by virtue of its own Soul group or cadre. This is not to say that every individual entity that has reached the Seventh Astral plane is not also doing important work. However, it should be recognized that there are degrees of experience and mastery, just as there are different levels and kinds of spiritual or consciousness guidance. The assistance of a Soul that is working as a Spirit Guide in lower Dimensional Sublevels while it is reintegrating its reincarnations is far different from an individual entity or lifetime of that Soul that is reaching through the Astral worlds but is not yet fully reintegrated with its Soul.

In addition, the specialties of a Soul can span the realm of those who provide guidance as we have just described to physical beings in the Third Sublevel of the Universal Dimension and those that assist in the physicality of lower reality planes, including the First and Second Sublevels of the Universal Dimension. Souls working in the realms of the First and Second Dimensional Sublevel will often participate in natural phenomenon, such as planetary weather patterns or other natural, environmental or planetary phenomena. Similarly, they might work with what we term Hive Soul Being groups, such as some aspects of the insect or animal kingdom. Rarely, they may also assist with inter species spiritual guidance working with individualized, sentient, high consciousness, non-Human Angelic Soul groups, such as those found among some Earth primates, mammals and cetaceans.

Much of the mythology present in your world that is related to stories of Nymphs, Sprites or other personified Nature or Animal Spirits, including hybrid Beings such as the famed teacher, Chiron the Centaur, are related to Human Angelic Souls assisting lower Dimensions in this way reaching out from the Tenth Dimensional Sublevel, or another High Astral plane. A large portion of Souls that have reintegrated the many lifetimes found on their Wheels of Creation that are awaiting Ascension will comprise this group of Spirit Guides.

Despite this, most Souls that are reintegrating all their lifetimes within a particular Universal Dimension, other than those that have a specific interest working in these realms, do not necessarily participate at lower dimensional levels and will bypass the Eighth and Ninth Astral levels completely. In truth the majority of Souls, and their created life entities, proceed directly to the Tenth Astral Sublevel to continue reintegration and reconsolidation of the Soul's energetic Being.

It is for this reason that the Tenth, Eleventh and Twelfth Astral realms of a Universal Dimension, when linked together, are sometimes referred to as "True Paradise." This is so because these unified Astral realms are as close to the metaphoric Heaven some expect as one can come within a particular Universal Dimension. We would add that if this can be said to be true in the higher Astral realms of a Universal Dimension, it stands to reason that the unified Tenth, Eleventh and Twelfth Universal Dimensions themselves are a place of particular perfection, an experience as close to supreme harmony, peace and unity as one can get.

You begin to see in the higher Astral realms a pattern that suggests overlap of these higher Dimensions as well as the valid connection each Astral or Sublevel of a Universal Dimension has to its Universal Dimension counterpart. You can also further understand that as an entity within a specific Universal Dimension rises to the highest levels of the Astral divisions of the Dimension, an entity is highly motivated and even compelled to seek wholeness, which is achievable only through reintegration with its Soul. It thus becomes clear that Ascension can only occur at the highest levels of a Universal Dimension.

This is important to understand because many are currently being taught that Ascension can take place at lower Sublevels of a Universal Dimension, or even that Ascension can occur spontaneously during a physical incarnation. This is not the case. All Ascension occurs at the reunification of the individual entity with its Soul at the highest dimensional levels, and then only when the Soul's consciousness, through consolidation of its many reincarnations in that Universal Dimension, is able to generate and navigate the higher vibrational energy fields necessary to ascend.

This alone is the factor that permits Ascension of the Soul itself once its individual lifetimes have reintegrated with it at the Tenth, Eleventh and Twelfth Sublevel of the Universal Dimension. The often repeated idea that one day a mysterious culling event will take place described by some as a "Rapture," that disincarnate bodies of this or that religious persuasion will rise from tombs at the behest of a specific deity, or that each and every individual will miraculously be hurled wide awake into another world in a higher Dimension will, at best, bring disappointment to anyone awaiting such fabled events.

Returning to our exploration of the Tenth, Eleventh and Twelfth Astral or Dimensional Sublevels, a substantial number of entities generally will not necessarily have an interest in working with either the Akashic records in the Eighth Astral plane or the Eighth Universal Dimension, or assisting as System Lord Guides in the Ninth Astral plane or in the Ninth Universal Dimension. In such cases, following a certain degree of reintegration and reconsolidation with the Soul as well as the many other lifetimes that are part and parcel of the Soul, these entities usually transmigrate from the Seventh Astral plane directly to the Tenth, Eleventh and Twelfth Astral planes of the Universal Dimension. This demonstrates a further example of how, at the highest Astral levels, linear or vertical progression is far from the norm.

Once reaching the Tenth, Eleventh and Twelfth higher Astral realms, it is somewhat difficult to distinguish the entity from its Soul, although individual distinction does remain fully intact. This is better explained by the fact that in these higher Astral planes it becomes somewhat difficult to discern where the individual entity leaves off and the Soul begins, or vice versa. This is the point at which the concept "you are your Soul and your Soul is you" becomes the most clear as well as most relevant.

Additionally, the highest Astral Sublevels all have specific intended purposes although in these realms it is not really possible to designate one as better or more exalted than the last. The highest Astral planes share almost complete equality and uniformity in terms of importance and they also have an extremely close vibrational structure. Once an entity has reached this point, that is to say a point at which there is no longer a true separation from its Soul, a place where the hierarchy and structure is more permeable and the overlapping veil between planes is so thin as to be virtually imperceptible, depending upon its orientation, its higher purpose, its destiny and its Soul cadre or grouping each Soul then decides where it wishes to linger. Once this point is reached, these realms become the place a Soul spends the duration of its time in the Universal Dimension, pursuing whatever it wishes, until such time as Ascension becomes possible.

If one were to insist upon a designation for each of these high realms, for the purpose of better understanding them in metaphoric terms, such distinction might be presented to you thusly: The Realm of the Sons of God is in the Tenth Universal Dimension, as well as in the Tenth Astral plane of each Universal Dimension; The Realm of the Spiritual Psyche of all Beings is found in the Eleventh Universal Dimension, as well as on the Eleventh Astral plane of each Universal Dimension, and; The Realm of "All That Is," sometimes called Nirvana, the Kingdom of God or the Ultimate Paradise, is found in the Twelfth Universal Dimension as well as on the Twelfth Astral plane of each Universal Dimension. Souls that have reintegrated and reconsolidated with the many entities they have created in the Dimension tend to wait for their opportunity to ascend to higher Universal Dimensions within one of these three high Astral planes and Dimensional Sublevels.

We already mentioned that at these higher dimensional levels, the Tenth, Eleventh and Twelfth Sublevels of the Universal Dimension, entities have access through the Akashic records to an understanding of all the lifetimes their Soul has lived both in lower and higher Astral levels of the Universal Dimension. In addition to this, they begin to understand their universal purpose and "Raison d'Etre" from the perspective of their Soul. In fact, most of the effort and experience of Souls waiting to ascend in these particular Astral levels is related to pursuing this understanding as well as the planning of other lifetimes or Wheels of Creation in conjunction with their Soul. This is done within the higher Astral plane of the Universal Dimension that the Soul most identifies with or feels the most compatibility.

For this reason these areas as a whole can be considered Nirvana, Ultimate Heaven or True Heaven since they are co-created by each Soul in close unity with All That Is, the God Source itself. Many spend a great deal of their existence in the Universal Dimension here planning higher aspirations for themselves and the many entities that now comprise who and what they are. Not only do they plan such experiences in the current Universal Dimension but in Universal Dimensions to come following their Ascension. This is why these planes are sometimes referred to as Paradise, since the vibrational energy Souls experience in the Tenth, Eleventh and Twelfth Astral planes of a Universal Dimension is akin to being at one with the ultimate God Source. Those Astral levels, linked as they are with the universal tril-

ogy of the Tenth, Eleventh and Twelfth Universal Dimensions, allow a
Soul to bathe in the highest spiritual and blessed energies that exist
in the Universe.

Parallel Universes

This brings us to an important point as to the reason why Ascension
as an evolutionary progression is so universally important. When Ascension is not possible or is not achieved for a Universal Dimension
during the 260,000 Grand or Galactic Ascension cycle, many of the
Souls within the Universal Dimension will tend to linger and remain
fixated in those realities. When trapped within a particular Universal
Dimension during an Ascension period, these Souls will tend to reincarnate again and again at lower physical levels of the Universal Dimension even if there is no real reason or need to do so, assuming
they have reintegrated in the highest levels of the Astral planes with
the lifetimes they have already created.

To be clear, when this occurs it does not impede the entire evolutionary process of all Universal Dimensions, but it can have direct
impact on the former Universal Dimension that does not reach the
momentum to ascend. In other words, the vibrational transformation
of all Universal Dimensions will still occur, but the Universal Dimension that does not reach Ascension at that time becomes trapped in
its own time-wave, almost like a bubble of air trapped within torrents
of water that continue their motion regardless.

The isolation and trapping of a Universal Dimension, if not corrected through a return to the proper vibrational Ascension process, will ultimately result in the collapse of that particular time-wave, and therefore of that Universal Dimension's timeline. While such a Dimension, Solar system or Galaxy, as the case may be, within that Universal Dimension may become the bubble or pocket of air we reference as our example, in a sense this heralds a fate removed from that reflected by the true journey of a Soul, which is our primary concern here. Nevertheless, it is not difficult to see such occurrences as bubbles originating at the bottom of the sea that rise independent of the ocean's natural motion, and because of that they will almost certainly burst at some particular point before succeeding in their rise to the surface of the water.

Naturally these are generally not ideal situations. The timeline in such a case will deteriorate to a point where its separation from the universal process will also be its demise, as a new Universal Dimension takes its place vibrationally. This becomes a complex scenario for the Souls that find themselves within an errant and un-ascended space-time wave.

While a Universal Dimension in which this takes place might seem a formidable trap for the Souls within it, it is only truly a trap for those Souls that have decided to remain within it based on their own desires or for their own purpose that originates from a refusal to accept higher guidance, or should they prefer to pursue creative strategies that compete with the universal process and are therefore misguided. Just as you find entities in your life that are on seemingly destructive paths, the same is possible at the level of the Soul.

In a way, a lost generation of Souls can be said to go hand in hand with a lost Universal Dimension. You know such occurrences as parallel Universes, and it is not by accident that your science fiction sees such worlds as inherently degenerate, the polar opposite or as the antithesis of any on going timeline. In reality, they are simply Dimensions that have splintered off from the evolutionary path of Ascension, and eventually this is reflected in the lost Dimension's overall makeup at all levels of reality within it, physical and Astral realms. These realities tend to parallel the newly emerging Universal Dimension and timeline that takes its place, until the time they are no longer cohesive or resonant and their structures cease to be universally energized or powered.

To be precise, most Souls that find themselves in such a circumstance will inevitably cycle off a wayward, disconnected Parallel Universal Dimension on their own and proceed to higher Universal Dimensions as prescribed by the law of Universal Ascension. But the truth is that some Souls will remain by choice. The problem here is that these remaining Souls quickly veer off the trail of their original purpose or the expressed life missions they wanted to create within the Universal Dimension. In fact, having stepped beyond the coordinated Wheels of Creation where lifetimes balance each other karmically based on the Akashic plane and other celestial influences, some of these Souls can become involved in the physical world of the errant Universal Dimension in isolated and even corrupted ways. More importantly, they become universally unlinked from the universal life force not to mention their own Soul groups, guides and cadres.

Once this occurs, repeated reincarnations created through the Wheels of Creation in the errant timeline have less and less purpose, and the lives they are living become uniquely superficial and mainly an addiction to quickly repeated physical incarnations that delve into and experiment exclusively with the manias, fascinations, trappings and intense situations of physical life experiences. These Souls become obsessed with their physical Wheels of Creation and, specifically, their lifetime creations, and in doing so begin to see themselves as rivals to the universal God Source as well as the guidance from higher Universal Dimensions. In a sense, they set themselves up as a unique and alternate God force within the former Universal Dimension, which is now in effect merely an errant space-time wave rapidly deteriorating and losing vibrational continuity as it hurls itself into the void.

The abandoning of divine universal principles and the sacred geometric spin that propels the entire Universe and all the Universal Dimensions into Ascension has unforeseen consequence. Those Souls who, through their own choice, remain within such systems have in effect created their own kingdoms through the loss of the Universal Dimension's placement.

You know such occurrences, described vaguely in your religious mythology, as celestial rebellions or the "Fall" of Angels. In reality, the inability of a Universal Dimension to ascend is a departure from the intended divine process of Ascension. It can often become a disengagement from the process of Ascension, and as such is sometimes considered a "competition" with the God Source or a fall from the grace of All That Is.

Once before in a dimensional time-wave prior to your own, Galactic Ascension was lost by Souls incarnated during the height of the Atlantean Empire. Vibrational resonance was not achieved, and a gen-

The Tenth, Eleventh and Twelfth Dimensional Sublevels of the
Third Universal Dimension: The Astral Realms of Reintegration
with the Soul, Realm of the Sons of God and the Soul's
Preparation for Transmigration to the next Universal Dimension

eration of Souls was lost. Many of those who were able to ascend on their own at that time are watching carefully and guiding you in the current Ascension period. Others who were nearly lost may even be karmically involved through physical Wheels of Creation in the current Galactic Ascension period in an attempt to balance and right the karma caused by that occurrence formerly. Those Souls who chose to remain within the deteriorating space-time wave and set themselves above the Galactic Ascension process without ultimately ascending, are known as a Lost Generation of Souls.

If we mention this, it is simply to demonstrate the importance of consciousness, vibrational resonance and integrity during important Ascension periods such as the current one. It is wrong however, to assume that collective consciousness and vibrational resonance supersedes these qualities in an individual Soul in order to allow for Ascension. On the contrary, an individual Soul always has the ability to ascend independent of the Universal Dimension by virtue of its own resonance, merit and intention whether the Universal Dimension's space-time wave is collapsing or in ascension, whatever the case may be.

Ideally, a Universal Dimension transforms itself into a higher vibrational resonance and consequently a higher Universal Dimension naturally during the designated time periods. Ascension, seen this way, is similar to the same entity growing into different life periods, the child becoming an adult and the adult growing into maturity and finally old age. This reflects the same process that occurs with Ascension as one Universal Dimension evolves into the next, or a higher version of the same Being.

The process facilitates Ascension for all Dimensions, as well as all Souls that in a sense piggyback the Dimension. What is problematic however, is when, through low resonance or the use of artificial technologies or blockades, the curtailing of the Ascension promise is attempted by a Soul group. There are in fact, as we have discussed, extraterrestrial groups attempting to curtail the current Galactic Ascension of the Third Universal Dimension on Earth. As we have already explained, this will not be successful, and those Souls intending to ascend during this cycle will be able to do so. Those attempting to bio-engineer a blockade of the Universal Dimension will not be allowed to do so, and many higher Astral Guides, Arch Angels and the planet itself are able to prevent such meddling, which will ultimately be accomplished by a reset of the planet itself during the 26th Century on your current timeline.

This struggle is at the heart of what is known to you as the dualistic struggle of good and evil, God and the (perceived) Devil. In fact the real message here is that every Soul has, through choice, the ability to find resurrection (another way of expressing Ascension), to use your religious vernacular. Those not choosing to ascend are actually choosing to experience the resulting "fall from grace." This means that those Souls pursue a direction within a deteriorating timeline that dismisses the universal process and consequently negates their own salvation through Ascension.

The Universe sees this as a rebuttal of natural and divine process. This is why you are presented with various myths and allegories related to exercising Free Will by choosing between the sides of good and evil, a gross simplification of the real struggle at hand. Those Souls that choose to ascend will ascend and, in a certain sense, continue

The Tenth, Eleventh and Twelfth Dimensional Sublevels of the
Third Universal Dimension: The Astral Realms of Reintegration
with the Soul, Realm of the Sons of God and the Soul's
Preparation for Transmigration to the next Universal Dimension

their journey towards All That Is, the God Source.

Those who choose to remain trapped within a fallen timeline turn their back on the universal process, which dictates a continual expansion of consciousness in order to raise the vibration of the entire realm and experience Ascension. These Souls will ultimately find that such a choice leads to their probable demise, and it is in this manner that they become part of a Lost Generation of Souls, as we have described.

Be assured that such a failure does not take place easily nor does it take place even after one, two or sometimes more universal Galactic Ascension cycles have been reached. It can take close to an infinite amount of linear time for such actions to actually lead to the total disintegration of a particular wayward Universal Dimension. As it spirals out of the universal Ascension process it becomes a parallel Dimension until its final collapse, which we will discuss shortly. The scenario we are discussing may or may not be relevant to the situation of your Third Universal Dimension at this time. However, what we are attempting to demonstrate here is the process itself and the scenarios that it may create universally with regard to Reincarnation, Transmigration and the Ascension of Souls within a Universal Dimension.

It is important to remind you at this juncture that your Soul is not necessarily you in the sense that "YOU," with your particular belief systems and talents, are not necessarily the limit of your Soul. Therefore, while currently you are focused within your own personality and reality, and may witness things that you believe will impede your own growth or your own Ascension, remember that you are just an

aspect of your Soul, which has unlimited expanded talents and resources at its disposal. Therefore, even if you are not able to resist
or counter the inequities you see in your physical reality that may
be imposed upon you, do not assume that your Soul does not have
the bigger picture completely under control. This is particularly true
regarding any attempted electromagnetic or other Ascension boundaries or blockages that any group might try to erect, attempt or place
upon you during your current lifetime.

Most, if not all of these issues, are easily and readily surmounted by
your Soul, which as you recall operates from the highest Astral
realms. More importantly, it helps to also keep in mind that your Soul
created your current lifetime in an effort to achieve higher consciousness and Soul growth. The situations you face therefore may
be directly related to that consciousness growth, and in this way it
becomes important to see every challenge or obstacle as a possible
opportunity for Soul growth.

If you are faced with others dominating you or attempting to do so,
even with respect to coordinating challenges that you feel opposed
to or that will attempt to block your consciousness and subsequently
your Ascension, these may well be opportunities for you to exercise
your awareness and connection to your Soul, and you have an opportunity to grow by facing them. Your fears, how you react to the
situations presented in life and your subsequent choices based on
these opportunities are never coincidental and are almost always related to your Soul growth.

This is not only for those things experienced in physical reality, at
the Third Sublevel of the Third Universal Dimension, but as your jour-

ney through all the Dimensional Sublevels. Moreover, while there is significant bleed through from all the lifetimes that are lived, the unification of those lifetimes with the Soul in the higher Astral realms creates what is unique and independent to the Soul. Reunification tends to incorporate rather than individualize what you have learned.

At the highest levels of the Universal Dimension, you become a greater composite than you would be if you were only your current personality, or individualized self. So for entities in the higher Astral planes, it becomes invalid to discuss a particular life's journey without relating it back to the other lifetimes lived or being lived by the Soul in that Universal Dimension.

Thus the Tenth, Eleventh and Twelfth Astral planes serve as a significant departure from what you would expect in the idolized heaven scenarios that are expressed in your mythology where your personality and lifetime are predominant. For example, it is not you personally bathing in the light of the Divine when you reach these higher Astral planes but rather you in conjunction with your Soul. It is for this reason that the Tenth, Eleventh and Twelfth Astral planes are by their very nature levels of higher awareness and consciousness. It is because of this that you are truly able to reach forward from these realms and begin, with your Soul, the process of Transmigration and Ascension.

As we have said in the past, beginning in the Seventh, and particularly from the Eighth through the Twelfth Astral planes, there is considerable Transmigration of Souls. This cross communication is important and could be considered, if you will, divine in nature based on the fact it allows all Soul therein, once reintegrated with their Wheels of Creation, to harbor greater consciousness, especially as it concerns the Soul's higher purpose, which may not be fully visible to all parts of the Soul until reintegration has occurred.

In the higher Astral planes, the highest guidance to a Soul becomes significant in that it permits peer understanding and a Soul that has been reintegrated has exponential communication and awareness of not only its purpose but also of its Soul group and Soul cadres. Within the higher Astral planes, the Soul has direct access and understanding of the many Avatars, System Lords and other Celestial personages able to bring the Soul to completion in the Universal Dimension. This knowledge greatly facilitates the Soul's Transmigration from one Astral plane to another as well as its ultimate Ascension to a higher Universal Dimension.

An interesting aspect of this is that whereas you might have believed that a Soul cast out from the highest Universal Dimension originally would enter a lower Universal Dimension through the bottom tiers of its Sublevels, the truth is that Transmigration and Wheels of Creation (Reincarnation) allow the Soul to remain in the Twelfth Astral plane of any Universal Dimension. In a sense, this generates a metaphorical two-way highway that exists between the realms of Universal creation and the highest Astral levels of every Universal Dimension. This two-way path allows Souls to transmigrate and ascend as well as reincarnate within a particular Universal Dimension.

It is from the Twelfth Universal Dimension that Souls are cast out originally and then transmigrate to lower Universal Dimensions.

From the related Twelfth Astral Sublevel of any Universal Dimension Souls then cast Wheels of Creation, or reincarnations, within the Dimension. In this way, the Twelfth Astral Sublevel of every Universal Dimension acts as a bridge through which all Souls transmigrate. Here they reside while imagining, analyzing and creating the many lifetimes within the Universal Dimension until such time as they integrate those lifetimes back into themselves and are ready to ascend to a new Universal Dimension.

As we have mentioned before all of this hinges on particular sacred geometric configurations in coordination with universal energetic spin that creates the necessary vortexes, portals and impetus that allows not only a Soul to ascend but also ascension of entire Universal Dimensions. These energetic alignments are related to planetary and universal alignment as well, and they are electromagnetically charged to attract and repel, creating the spin necessary to open the dimensional portals. Specific alignments are always required to permit a Universal Dimension to begin its transformation into the next Universal Dimension and these energies are activated through the energetic messaging received by way of higher consciousness and resonance that is achieved. When these elements are unified, Ascension is possible.

While much of this might sound magical and while we cannot deny that it is a mystical and divine event, most of these energy transfers, whether Ascension, Transmigration or even Reincarnation, are the product in some way of specific elements of sacred geometry juxtaposed to vortexes created through universal spin. The magnitude of these elements and specific configurations reached during specified times are required in order for these events to take place. In mythology, religious and otherwise, these elements have been called the "Keys of the Kingdom." However, in order for the keys to actually open the doors at any given point, all configurations must be correct to permit transcendence and Ascension, which is accomplished through a trans-configuration of individual Souls and the Universal Dimension.

It is difficult to describe the actual condition or life of Souls at these high levels of existence. This is because Souls at this level of reality have particular vibrational resonances that are vastly different from your experience. As an example, Souls at these higher states of Being do not have relatable social structures, hierarchies, prejudices or other sociological and physiological belief systems. In truth, those who are within these particular areas maintain a transcendence that is sometimes difficult to imagine or understand. In many cases, it is for this reason that the Soul can sometimes be confused with the concept of God, since the qualities of Being and existence are in many ways similar.

It is interesting to note however, that Souls can, on a limited basis, take on specific features and attributes from the lifetimes that are of principal importance to it in terms of its growth. Yet even here, it is difficult to discern if the important lifetime is actually exhibiting traits of the Soul or if the Soul is picking up traits from the lifetime. We would tend to say that every lifetime manifest by a Soul has some connection to its creator, and therefore many of the person-ality attributes, specific traits, interests, skills or other features you find that make up who you think you are actually form a link directly back to your Soul.

Another item of interest here is that although there is generally no specific or required appearance or physical trait that a Soul has or bequest it makes to its many different lifetimes, lifetimes of the Soul, particularly those that are found on the same Wheel of Creation, can sometimes exhibit similar physical features and personal preferences. Physical resemblances of the Soul's various reincarnations tend to bleed through from one lifetime to another, and a particular group of entities manifest by a Soul can carry many resemblances. This is why reincarnated lives, as documented in your reality, seem to have a high degree of what could be considered similar traits, skills, interests and desires.

Souls that have reintegrated at the highest Sublevels of the Universal Dimension are in fact communicating with higher Beings who will work together with them to determine their Ascension potential, particularly as it pertains to the Ascension potential of the entire Universal Dimension. The trans-configuration of a Universal Dimension is a complex process that culminates in the transformation of the space-time wave that defines it into the next space-time wave, and it is this universal energetic act that seems like the breathing in and out of the Universe. It is the motion created in this process that actually transforms one space-time wave into the next, and consequently transforms one Universal Dimension into another. Most know this as the Universal Reflex, and it has even been measured by your current science.

As we have mentioned in the past, particularly in our book, *Timeline Collapse and Universal Ascension*, Human Angelic Souls that have reconsolidated in your sector of the Universe at the highest Sublevels of your Universal Dimension are now poised to begin Wheels of

Creation on Fifth Universal Dimension Terra, the Fifth Universal Dimension denomination for Earth, which is a Third Universal Dimension identification. We would go as far as to say that a good many of these Souls have already begun the process of ascending, cycling off and out of the higher Astral planes of the Third Universal Dimension, and many have already begun lifetimes in the Fifth Universal Dimension.

Many of those currently still focused in the Third Universal Dimension, whether in the Third Dimensional Sublevel of physical reality or journeying through the Astral planes, have a distinct sense that they are finishing something and ultimately leaving something behind forever. This is related to the fact that many of these lifetimes, despite the fact that they may remain physically focused in the Third Dimensional Sublevel, will soon find themselves journeying through the Astral planes and rejoining their Souls through the process we have described. Once they have done so, following the end of any current physical lifetime, they will reintegrate with their Soul as it prepares to cycle off reincarnations in the Third Universal Dimension and begin lifetimes on Terra in the Fifth Universal Dimension.

It should be remembered, however, that not all Souls are prepared for Ascension, nor will they be ascending during this particular Galactic Ascension cycle. In fact, the recent proliferation of Baby and Young Souls into physical life incarnations that began approximately two centuries ago in terms of your linear time period are Souls who have already ascended from incarnations in the First and Second Universal Dimensions. Just as many Souls from the Third Universal Dimension are beginning incarnations in the Fifth Universal Dimension, so too these younger Souls have begun incarnations in the Third Universal

Dimension as it also transforms the space-time wave.

It is for this reason that more and more you will find, assuming you are of a certain consciousness and resonance, that even though you are discussing matters with those that appear your same linear age, their reasoning seems nonsensical to you in terms of their approach and their outlook on the world. We have said many times before that younger Souls see the world as me and other me's, just as children do, and they will attempt to conform others to their particular way of thinking. In fact, these Souls tend to push aside and ignore anything or anyone that does not think and act the same as they do. Usually Baby and some Young Souls are fearful of any thought process or beliefs that break with uniformity or the prevailing standards and norms. Many even see those things different from them as being "evil."

These Souls, and their corresponding lifetimes, tend to prefer institutions, governmental and otherwise, that are authoritarian in nature, much as young children respond to strong parental figures. Older Souls, however, particularly those ready to ascend, form their experiences through lifetimes that are far less karmic or judgmental, and they understand intrinsically that each individual should be permitted to have their own vision and that all perspectives have value.

They tend to move forward without attachment to any specific dogmas, belief structures or perspectives. Almost in every case, an older Soul and its life incarnations will never attempt to force specific views or dogma on anyone else, nor will they ever oblige another to think or act like them. This in fact is a sign of higher consciousness and awareness, whereas those obliging certain thoughts and beliefs at all cost are almost always Young Soul entities looking for karmic adventures and other experiences, as we have often explained.

What you are possibly seeing currently in your world is an indication of what we are discussing with respect to those Souls that are ascending and those other Souls just beginning incarnations and Wheels of Creation within the newly forming Third Universal Dimension. Should you happen to find the world around you to your liking, you may well be a life incarnation of a Soul beginning its journey in the Universal Dimension. If on the other hand your surroundings suddenly seem unfamiliar, nonsensical or errant, after you have accomplished your current physical life as planned your Soul may well be on its way to cycling off life incarnations in the Third Universal Dimension, and ascending with you to Wheels of Creation in the Fifth Universal Dimension.

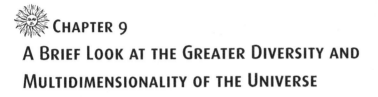

Chapter 9
A Brief Look at the Greater Diversity and Multidimensionality of the Universe

The Universe is constructed in a diverse and highly complex multi-dimensional way. An orderly process of expansion, growth and evolution prevails in each of the Twelve Universal Dimensions, and each Universal Dimension, together with its twelve Astral or Dimensional Sublevels, is superimposed within the same space with one Dimension overlapping the next. They are separated only by virtue of the space-time wave they represent, as defined by a difference in the vibration and frequency that the space-time wave creates.

This should not be confused with the popular notion of the existence of Parallel Universes, which is in reality a "fallen" Dimension, as we have already discussed. In a sense, the concept that most have of Parallel Universe is actually a misunderstood or fictionalized attempt to describe the Dimensional Sublevels of a Universal Dimension, which are superimposed one upon the next.

As an example, Dimensional Sublevels we have described for you like the Fourth Astral plane, or Dreamscape, and the Fifth Astral Healing Realm appear parallel because the entities journeying through them are creating those realities based on their belief systems and the thought forms they retain from lower vibrational physical existences. Thus just as when you dream, together with your Soul you use the symbolism and fabric of what you know in physical reality to generate

378

the dream reality, and all entities (making the journey through any of the Dimensional Sublevels or Astral realms in order to rejoin their Souls) use their established belief structures in creating the realities found within these dimensional overlays and Astral realms.

In this way the Astral Sublevels can appear to be "parallel" Universes from your perspective, but they are not actually different Universes per se. They are instead planes of existence with unique frequencies existing within the structure of the same Universal Dimension you are in, albeit simultaneously exhibiting different and sometimes strange (to you) attributes.

Within the Universal Dimension, the multidimensional order is particularly well defined with respect to Soul Reincarnation, Transmigration and Ascension. When Souls are first cast out from the highest dimensional level, from the "God" Source as we have called it, they are cast according to specific attributes and, you might say, sacred geometric principles that relate directly to that Soul species, and the Soul groups contained within that species. These sacred specifics generally determine exactly where the Soul species being cast out will emerge in the Universe. In other words, these sacred forms determine where they will locate themselves galactically, and there are unique magnetic attractions based on the fractals generated by their spin that compels them to this or that space within the space-time wave or Universal Dimension that they are being magnetically drawn into.

The vastness of the Universe is never an impediment to its creation. In fact, this vastness makes creative diversity even more abundant as Source seeks to fill its emptiness. In that regard, the postulate that "Nature abhors a vacuum" is completely valid when used in attempting to understand universal structure and the enormity of all creation.

As a result, whereas a Human Angelic Soul will be cast out into the First Universal Dimension in the Solar System familiar to you, other Soul species may be cast out in the same Universal Dimension (space-time wave) but into their own particular Solar Systems, at great distance from you. This is always the case when Baby Souls are first cast out from Source, but it should be remembered that a Soul species is able to transmigrate and universally "relocate," if you will, when a Soul has reached higher Universal Dimensions and higher dimensional Wheels of Creation and reincarnations.

Though rare, as we have discussed, beginning in the Third Universal Dimension Soul species are able to incarnate in forms and bodies that are not necessarily native to them. In this way, an extraterrestrial Soul species is sometimes able to incarnate on Third Dimensional Earth, just as Human Angelic Souls are able to do the same in areas of the Universe that are not necessarily designated a homeland for Human Angelic Souls.

Furthermore, beginning in the Fifth Universal Dimension, Soul species are able to incarnate in their defining or original physical form in any area of the Universe where crossover of living species has occurred, assuming they can identify other related Souls already incarnated there to act as genetic "parents." This includes Fifth Dimensional Terra (Earth in the Fifth Universal Dimension) as well as other Fifth Dimensional planetary and galactic systems, as we have discussed in *Timeline Collapse and Universal Ascension*.

A Soul's Wheels of Creation can become extremely complex at that point, with a Human Angelic Soul able to have a lifetime as a Human Being on Terra (Earth) juxtaposed and balanced by a lifetime incarnated and living as a Pleiadian Being inhabiting the Pleiades Star System, as an example. The opposite arrangement is also quite possible, as would be any number of other combinations.

Though this is very rare within the Third Universal Dimension and more common starting in the Fifth Universal Dimension, it is not impossible and it is not uncommon for some among you, by virtue of your Soul, to already be experiencing this and to have bleed-through memories of lifetimes as an alien Being on another planet or in another world. In fact, not all but some "alien abduction" memories are actually related to this fact.

This is also the reason extraterrestrial Soul races are currently able to incarnate among you in human physical bodies, and it is the fact that they are alien Soul races incarnated in human physical form that allows them to be identified as hybrids (as opposed to a mixture of a Soul species into a newly engineered physical body, which is being attempted by some). For our purposes here, we wish only to bring forward yet another example of the multidimensionality of the Universe as it regards the processes of Reincarnation, Transmigration and Ascension.

Universal Soul species and subgroups are quite numerous, and although they can be closely linked, they are usually not related to each other in ways you think. If you were to expand your thinking universally, you might compare such diversity seen on a much wider scale to what you witness within your current physical world, where there are links, similarities and recognizable factors, but literally thousands of variations even within related genres. As an example, you may be closely linked to other mammals but you are not they, just as they are not you. And as you know, there are literally millions of species of plants, insects and animals on Earth alone, even several races of humanity, not to mention the genetic variations found within the races as well as in all human beings in your world today.

Based on this you can see that universal Soul species and Soul groups
are an almost unlimited number and their diversity is equally abundant. In fact, multiply the number of species and subgroups in your
world by whatever number of worlds you imagine there to be in the
Universe, and you still would not correctly count all the Soul races
or Soul groups in all the galaxies in the entire Universe.

Moreover, multiply this number of Souls again by the number of Universal Dimensions there are, including the Dimensional Sublevels
contained within each Universal Dimension, and you begin to see
the magnitude of universal structure as it relates to consciousness
and creation. Rest assured that you and your Soul, as you make you
way through the Twelve Universal Dimensions, will be permitted the
chance, if you choose, to partake in as many or as few of these universal realities as desired.

It should also be understood as well that there are distinct and numerous Soul variations found within each Soul group. As an example,
the Human Angelic Soul race or group is further dissected into various cadres, orientations, purposes and no less than seven major archetypal energy expressions, as we have discussed in the past.
Although these archetypal energetic expressions are usually cast out
from Source simultaneously together, when they are cast out they
are also linked together into cadres with Souls that may carry different energetic expressions or spiritual orientations (Service to Self,
Service to Others).

This is a reason why you will find that Task Mates, or Soul Mates as
they are more commonly known by you, usually form between Souls
of differing energetic expressions or missions, sometimes complimentary and sometimes not. These differences, when combined with
differences in Soul missions, among other things, not only create di-

versity they form the balances and polarities that are intrinsic in almost all important life (as well as Soul) relationships.

Despite the fact that most consider a Soul Mate to be the person with whom they have the most in common, we would disagree with that assessment and state that a Soul Mate is the individual who offers you the greatest counter balance. Lessons derived from these relationships are generally the most beneficial to Soul growth. This is why we prefer the term "Task" Mate in speaking of such agreements rather than Soul Mate, which has become a somewhat misleading designation. Task Mates to whom you are inevitably drawn are always the ones working with you by Soul agreement to manifest and generate the most growth during the course of an individual lifetime. Often, these participations in life can seem as overwhelming and challenging as they are inevitable, relentless and, at times, difficult to discharge or leave.

What is important to understand however is that throughout the Universal Dimensions there is enormous variety as well as vast difference not only in terms of Soul groups, energetic orientations and individual archetypal energetic expression but also in terms of physical life, form, composition and universal purpose. This extends to the diversity of Souls as well as the unique, splendid and diverse environments found throughout the Universe within different galaxies and star systems. This also includes all the Astral environments (the non-physical Sublevels of a Universal Dimension) of every Universal Dimension, which adds another layer of multidimensionality and creative uniqueness to the equation.

As we have said, for the most part a Universal Dimension is defined by its particular space-time wave and this wave contains various vast galactic spatial regions, most of which contain specific life forms living according to their own realities. In this way, a Solar System such as your own, which is designated as the home location for predominantly Human Angelic Souls, can exist side-by-side with other Soul races and groups, albeit separated galactically or inter-galactically by great distance and relativity. Although the positioning and locations are vastly different, all life within a Universal Dimension exists simultaneously within the same space-time wave, meaning within the same Third Universal Dimension.

As we have already determined with you, all the Universal Dimensions, together with their Sublevels, occupy the same universal space in general. Despite the fact that each Universal Dimension is expansive and not measurable in a real sense due to its on-going growth, it should be noted that there are some universal structures that exists outside of the usual universal structures. While we do not wish to severely divert our current discussion, we would like to identify two such anomalies.

The first we have already identified previously as what we term the "Cosmic" structure. This is the space (or void, depending upon your perspective) that lies in between the Galaxies and in between each Universal Dimension. Though these areas remain a mystery to most who exist within the structure of the Universal Dimensions, and despite the fact that we have identified the Twelfth Universal Dimension as the realm of the "God" force, it is here that we must become more specific concerning such designations.

In truth, what we have designated the God force in the Twelfth Universal Dimension is for convenience and the sake of comprehension. However, this force should perhaps more aptly be called the "Creator" force. Make no mistake, this Creator force is the origins of all creation in the Universe, and all Souls and other Beings are originally cast from here.

Yet this is only part of what can be truly known of the unknowable energy that is a Universal God Force or All That Is, if you will. To be clear, the God force, momentum, spark or whatever you wish to call it that is responsible for all creation exists at the level of the Twelfth Universal Dimension, housed within the Trinity of Existence we have discussed, the Tenth, Eleventh and Twelfth Universal Dimensions. This creative force predominates within the structure of all Twelve Universal Dimensions and these highest Universal Dimensions are the origination of the process we know as Reincarnation, Transmigration and Ascension of all Souls.

However, there is more to this force than meets the eye, as we will now attempt to demonstrate to you. Between the formed galaxies as well as between the Twelve Universal Dimensions, there exists an even greater Universal force than any we have thus far discussed. For lack of better terminology, we will describe this as the Universal Cosmic force. Although the Creator force of the Twelfth Universal Dimension is certainly part of this greater universal force, this is the realm of what we have already termed earlier as The Grand Attractor.

The Grand Attractor is deemed to be the one **true** universal God force and, if you will, the Twelve Universal Dimensions exist or are held *within* the body of the Grand Attractor. In a way, this cosmic force is the "glue" that binds the entire Universe, including all Galaxies and the space-time waves of the Universal Dimensions, together. The Grand Attractor then is the fabric and substance existing in, through and around all galaxies and planetary bodies. Although its ultimate reality remains a mystery to all universal Beings and creatures even now, including those at the highest Universal Dimensions, it is nonetheless recognized as the overriding central force of the Universe.

We make this statement in as much as it is the motion of the Grand Attractor that makes Ascension and the very process of spin, electromagnetic vibrational frequency and energetic force possible throughout the known Universe. The Universe is said to breathe in and out by the will of the Grand Attractor, and in doing so, the Grand Attractor, which is the ultimate Cosmic God force, ensures the Universe's continual movement, existence and growth.

Secondarily, in addition to the creative forces it exerts the Grand Attractor is also the purveyor of what you commonly refer to as Black Holes and Dark Matter. Black Holes serve to pull galactic energy forth and through the system and reformulate it in the process. This phenomenon is responsible not only for the recycling of energy universally, as energy is drawn into the Cosmic force that first created it, it is the pull of this mechanism that makes space-time waves (by definition, the Universal Dimensions) possible. (See Pages 455 & 456, Figure 9 and 10 of Diagrams in the Appendix.)

In a sense, the expansion and contraction (the heart beat or breathing) of the Grand Attractor creates the scalar energy that forms reality, and then pulls that energy through the system creating Universal Dimensions, the space-time waves and the possibility of a formed reality in its wake. The divine energy and molecular structures that compose reality in all its various formats are continually moving and changing as they pass through the system creating this or that form as they go. It is the most present and relevant composition of molecular structures within the reality where you find yourself that creates the experience you know as "Now." That "Now" quickly transforms itself yet again as the molecular structures reformat and disengage, continuing their journey and pulled through the space-time wave by the universal energetic recycling forces.

Ultimately, this used energy, the former "Now" of each reality, is transformed definitively as it is pulled into galactic Black Holes, where it rejoins the Cosmic force and is rebirthed on the other side of the phenomenon. It is for this reason that the process is considered a form of Cosmic Ascension, as we called it previously, since the energy that creates all Universal Dimensions, planets and Beings is ultimately drawn back into itself, and as a result the Cosmic Creator, All That Is or the Universe itself (whatever name you prefer) ascends, expands and grows. In simple terms, the continuous expansion of the Universe, as postulated by your own science discoveries, is made possible through this continual process.

We do not wish to stray too far from our current subject, and proper explanation of the Cosmic Force or Grand Attractor as the overseer of all Universal Dimensions and the Cosmic Ascension process would probably take an entire book itself. However, we do wish to demonstrate the whereabouts and provide at least an introduction to the existence of such an overriding, omnipotent divine force for those interested in universal structure and the bigger picture.

Moreover, it is our goal to shed some additional light on the sheer enormity of the universal structure. Although we have provided you with more than is currently known in your reality concerning cosmic and divine mysteries, please be aware that the wonder, magnificence and infinite reality that is the Universe should be continually pondered for it is far more complex, mysterious and beautiful than anyone, including us, can potentially tell you and no Being should ever become overly complacent or confident that it knows all there is to know.

Returning to our discussion of the diversity and multidimensionality of the Soul itself, for the most part physical reality is a projection onto the atomic structure related to the particular belief systems, expectations and desires ingrained in a Soul group. Because of this, the reality experiences of any particular Soul groups, such as the Human Angelic Soul group for example, share commonality. Thought forms projected energetically onto passing atomic particles, seen and unseen, inform structural shape, mass and, in a sense, a predisposed and agreed upon perspective as to how certain forms shall appear in certain ways. This principle remains consistent and true throughout Galactic regions within a specific Universal Dimensions, such as the Third Universal Dimension in which you are currently focused.

Make no mistake that these agreed upon predispositions regarding thought form projections and mass consciousness are real and substantive once formed. However, it is equally important to bear in mind that each Soul group, particularly within that group's designated sector of a galactic region, experiences reality based on certain pre-generated norms and standards together with the physical parameters that are consistent with their sector and the principles of the current space-time wave or Universal Dimension.

Commonality does exist in a sense, as you discover each time it becomes known that elements abundant in your world are also expressed in worlds throughout your Galaxy and beyond. This commonality is specific to each Universal Dimension and will exist everywhere, galactically speaking, within that Universal Dimension. We would add to this however, that there is naturally great variance in terms of the structural intentions and projected outcomes within a Universal Dimension, many of which you have yet to discover, and these physical outcomes or structures are tempered and altered further by vibration, resonance and consciousness quality in any particular Galactic sector. Thus, the physical compositions found in your Solar System may be completely different from those found elsewhere in the Galaxy or Universe, despite the fact that the composing materials and the Universal Dimension are the same.

As you are well aware by now, lower Universal Dimensions tend to have more dense physical and material substance, and are able to absorb or retain less light (light carries consciousness and knowledge as we have already explained). As one proceeds up the chain of either the Astral planes (meaning the Sublevels of a Universal Dimension) or up the Ascension steps from one Universal Dimension to the next, all Beings therein will have gradually less density, and therefore their appearance will seem more translucent and ethereal the higher one ascends. Your conception of ghosts, spirits and divine Beings from higher Astral states are indicative of this. These Beings are indeed more translucent, a factor related to a higher vibrational resonance and a greater ability to absorb light (en-light-en-ment) when in higher Astral realms and these depictions can be quite accurate as a reference point.

Another important difference with respect to both a Universal Dimension and its Sublevels can be said to be the Dimension's actual purpose. Whereas lower Universal Dimensions tend to relate to, in general, density and therefore are focused on the actual materialization and substance of physical reality, as one rises through Universal Dimensions and the Sublevels, the purpose of all Beings within that Universal Dimension becomes far more esoteric in nature. In a general sense, the purpose of a Universal Dimension is related to the

overall purpose of the Souls within it, and consciousness within a
Universal Dimension is relative to the consciousness of the Souls
that are experiencing lifetimes therein.

Thus, as an example, the First and Second Universal Dimensions will
be principally the realm of Baby Souls experiencing lifetimes in complete union with others (literally as unified substances and Beings),
such as the dense physical Beings of the planet or a Solar System,
which includes such things as Mountain ranges or the Oceans of
Earth, as we discussed earlier. The Third Universal Dimension for
Human Angelic Souls, however, would primarily be the home of Young
Souls that are immersed in independent life experiences, usually in
humanoid form, to foster an understanding of co-creation, physical
reality manifestation and the impact of thought forms and mass consciousness on physical reality.

Higher Universal Dimensions become attuned to specific purposes,
as the Souls therein are of a higher consciousness and Soul age, if you
will. In addition, as the Soul ascends through the Universal Dimensions, the quality and resonance of consciousness also means an evolution and higher consciousness of the life forms created in those
realities. This is another Universal maxim, namely that higher consciousness Souls never go backwards in this process, nor will they
reincarnate as a lower physical life form, with the exception being the
Ninth Dimensional System Lords, who return to lower Universal Dimensions in physical bodies as a matter of their purpose and choice.
Their ability to do so is representative of their higher consciousness.

This being true, definitively in the Seventh Universal Dimension, and
in some cases depending on the individual Soul in the Fifth or Sixth
Universal Dimension, Souls do not necessarily need to follow the
pattern of Ascension followed until then, which is usually sequential

in nature. In fact, higher Universal Dimensions can act as a staging ground for accessing and assisting lower Universal Dimension through the process of Transmigration using various portals related to the Dimensional Sublevels, as we have also discussed already. However, these Souls do not generally reincarnate or create Wheels of Creation at lower dimensional levels, again with the exception of Ninth Universal Dimension Souls.

Lifetimes in higher Universal Dimensions always demonstrate a higher universal purpose, and Souls, as well as the lifetimes they foster on Wheels of Creation within higher Universal Dimensions, can reach across dimensional platforms metaphysically to accomplish their missions. Thus there is no real need to generate physical incarnations in lower Universal Dimensions. Transmigration used thusly is based on the Soul's specialization, and higher Universal Dimension populations have distinct specialties, purposes and related goals that they pursue, foster and share when assisting Souls (via guidance or metaphysically) in the lower Dimensions.

As an example, Souls in the Sixth Universal Dimension will focus on developing their own telepathy, clairvoyance and a comprehensive understanding of their innate talents, abilities and desires. Then, once they have ascended to the Seventh Universal Dimension, these Souls will create lifetimes on various Wheels of Creation where those entities use their talents as Guides (in any number of capacities) to lower Universal Dimensions and Beings.

Seventh Universal Dimension Beings are specialists in helping Souls to plan, conduct and reintegrate the lifetimes they create universally, and we have already identified our own Soul group and our own Soul entities in this regard. These Souls do so in conjunction with Master Guides from the Eighth Universal Dimension who maintain the

Akashic Records where electromagnetic impulses and feedback from entities and Souls everywhere in the Universe are stored.

We have discussed with you already the fact that Souls in higher Universal Dimensions are able to transmigrate from one Universal Dimension to another using the corresponding Astral plane of any given Universal Dimension. This means, as an example, that a Seventh Universal Dimension Being has the ability to access any Universal Dimension it desires through the Seventh Astral Sublevel of that Universal Dimension. As an example, when one who is termed a Medium or Psychic accesses communication with higher Astral planes, they do so by the special intuitive ability they have to vibrationally tune into that Astral plane within their own Universal Dimension.

Thus, an Intuitive in a specific Universal Dimension who accesses certain types of higher spiritual information usually does so by virtue of their access to the Seventh Astral plane or an entity communicating from that plane in the Universal Dimension. The source of the information they receive comes from the Seventh Universal Dimension by way of that Seventh Astral plane. This information or guidance is delivered by Seventh Universal Dimensional Beings transmigrating to a Universal Dimension through the corresponding Seventh Astral plane of that lower Universal Dimension.

What is important to note here, particularly in discussing the multidimensionality of the Universe, is that a Soul does not "float" or travel through space and time, in the way you might expect one to travel. In fact, there is no "traveling" involved at all. Rather, vibrational frequency and resonance is what allows a Soul to transmigrate in this manner and it does so through its own frequency and vibrational patterns. When combined with that Soul's intention, the corresponding Astral realm of any lower Universal Dimension allows the Soul or entity to spontaneously bi-locate and be present there.

Such bi-location is not permanent, but allows Souls or entities from higher dimensional realms access to lower Universal Dimensions, as well as to any individual in those Dimensions that is able to raise their vibrational output and receive the information. This occurs in much the same way a radio broadcaster might send out a broadcast signal from afar, and a listener might tune into that station on their radio if the radio is operational and equipped to receive the signal being broadcast.

Almost all universal guidance as well as access into dimensional realms not native to a Soul is accomplished in such a manner. So, as an example, as a Soul is cast out from the Twelfth Universal Dimension, it accesses the Universal Dimension it will now generate Wheels of Creation within through transmigration to the Twelfth Astral plane of whichever Universal Dimension it is incarnating within. So in the case of the Third Universal Dimension, the Dimension your Soul is currently focused in, the Soul will access the Universal Dimension via the Twelfth Astral plane of the Third Universal Dimension.

From that higher dimensional position, the Soul will orchestrate all of its Wheels of Creation within that specific Universal Dimension. Surely this informs you of the extreme multidimensionality and divinity inherent in each Soul, as it not only transmigrates to the Twelfth Astral level from its origination in the Twelfth Universal Dimension, but also sends out parts of itself into multi-location incarnations within the lower Universal Dimension.

It is for this reason that we have often said the concept of "God" in your world is more or less a representation of the actual function of your Soul, and many of the traits and power you project on your divinities are more reflective of how your own Soul operates, even if it represents a microcosm of how the Creator God force actually works in conjunction with your Soul, which is that force's true creation. Not only are you a part of your Soul (as some feel they are a part of God), much of the planning of your lifetime, your missions, your goals and your overall journey, are all part of the intention your Soul has and is experiencing by virtue of its creation of You.

These parts of itself that the Soul creates through its various life incarnations do not at any time cease to exist, and lifetimes could also be seen as emissaries sent out to gather the stuff of life and return to incorporate it back into the collective that is your Soul. In many cases, the guidance you receive actually comes directly from your Soul, even if you feel it comes from "God," which in a manner of speaking, it actually does – since for you, your Soul is the creator of your life experience.

We have spoken already of the possibility that a Universal Dimension becomes wayward or loses its connection to the Ascension process. This is an important consideration, to be sure, however we would like to again reiterate that Souls do not necessarily become trapped within particular Universal Dimensions due in great part to the availability of the Transmigration process, which we have just discussed. There are cases where, through lack of understanding, self absorption and an attraction to incarnate existences, some Souls will resist or refuse the natural evolution via Ascension into a higher Universal Dimension even when they are ready to ascend following the reintegration of all lifetimes in that Universal Dimension. These are the Souls that are sometimes called "Fallen," and together with these Fallen Angels (to use a term from your own mythologies) the Universal Dimensions that become alienated because of an inability to achieve the needed vibrational resonance to ascend can take on a life of their own, at least temporarily.

However, a fallen Universal Dimension does not necessarily render all Souls within it unable to ascend, and for the most part, the greater number of Souls still existing therein will, at some point, have the ability to either ascend to the next Universal Dimension or Transmigrate out of the fallen Dimension, depending upon the case. It should also be understood that a fallen Universal Dimension will be replaced by another space-time wave that replaces it in short order due primarily to the necessity of the Ascension process itself. In this manner, the universal structure remains stable and constant, and it can regenerate itself. More importantly, this provides the necessary release for any Souls trapped therein that wish to depart, and that departure is accomplished through multidimensional Transmigration.

Hopefully, you are beginning to have a picture of the multidimensional connections enjoyed universally by you, your Soul and the Universe at large, even if from your current position in physical reality this seems unimportant or not a point of view necessary for living your day-to-day life. However, we continue to assure you that in every case, the multidimensional aspects of the Universal Dimension, its Astral environments and all the Souls within it remain intricately tied to your own life. It could even be said to be paramount to the very reason your own lifetime is currently taking place.

Understanding and accessing the various frequencies that enable what we have termed Transmigration, which we define as the ability to migrate across dimensional platforms, will one day be the greatest discovery your future scientists will make. When it is recognized that certain energetic portals and vortexes exist that permit access to corresponding Dimensions and a basic understanding of the principles of Transmigration can allow for swift relocation and bi-location of matter, your world will become very different. Naturally, these advancements are generally reserved for entities from higher Dimensions (well know on Fifth Dimensional Terra) and sadly they will be made by your civilization just prior to its loss during the Great Reset of your civilization that will take place in the 26th Century on Earth.

Now, to be clear, Universal Law cannot be overridden and a main one pertaining to all this is that higher dimensional levels are aware (even if they ignore them) of lower dimensional levels but lower dimensional levels are not necessarily aware of higher dimensional levels, other than in a metaphysical sense. Likewise, higher Dimensions are more attuned and able to access the means or portals of transmigration whereas lower Dimensions are not able to access these portals from their vibrational state unless artificial means is generated and used. Even then, such access is problematic, and is usually reserved for higher vibrational states than Third Universal Dimension Beings can attain. In general therefore, transmigration remains a factor of higher dimensional proclivity, higher consciousness and (usually, but not absolutely) higher vibrational integrity.

We have discussed many times the fact that many of the unidentified extraterrestrial occurrences (UFOs, UAPs and the like) in your world are in fact most often entities from higher Universal Dimensions that have gained access to these portals, through technology or otherwise, and are accessing your reality in that way. We would say that for the most part these beings are Fifth and Sixth Dimensional. Beings in higher Universal Dimensions have no need to use technology to do so, and can readily access the Dimension if not physically, spiritually through Transmigration.

The Transmigration we are discussing that utilizes portals artificially opened through technology are the ones of notice here, since many of these Beings do not have the Seventh Universal Dimension consciousness necessary to not interfere with your world. Moreover, their contact can be physical whereas higher Celestial Beings will never bi-locate physically.

Any discussion concerning these physical incursions must also make it clear that these are the "aliens" that have concluded treaties and agreements with various world governments, most notably, the United States, Russia and China. Sadly, based on the technologies they have received these governments believe the extraterrestrial visitors to be their "friends" and protectors. They are not aware of the dire consequences they may face based on these interactions, such as the ones we have already discussed with regard to one Soul race currently attempting to usurp the Third Dimensional Earth realm through bio-invasion by their Soul species.

Seeing this attempt, other alien races have now tried to create new races in the Third Universal Dimension by mixing their genetic structure with that of humans, which is far different than attempting to re-engineer human DNA from the inside out in order to make humanoid forms or the human environment suitable for their Soul species. Much of the Zeta experimentation you have seen with respect to abduction and the taking of human embryos is actually based on the creation of a mixed-race Being rather than the usurping, from the inside out, of an already established species via their Soul race.

As we mentioned, Transmigration of Seventh Universal Dimensional Beings is a kind of teleportation of their consciousness through the power of intention and energy alone, as applied to the Universal structure and interface of Dimensions and Dimensional Sublevels.

Any guidance or interaction with these Beings is not interfering in lower dimensional realms. However, physical appearances and incursions into your world that come from dimensional levels such as the Fourth, Fifth or Sixth Universal Dimensions are mechanically engineered, and great caution and care should be used when interfacing with these extraterrestrial, interdimensional entities.

Frankly, such interdimensional interface is not as common as you might think, although it is currently on the rise based on the Solar and Galactic Ascension energies now occurring throughout the Universe. Our purpose is simply to highlight the difference between natural, multidimensional phenomena such as Transmigration and technology-driven access to portals that allow for interdimensional interaction. The difference, though subtle, is highly important and you should be aware of it.

As we have pointed out to you already, the focus of physical reality where lifetimes are first generated by a Soul, to a greater or lesser extent, is always found at the Dimensional Sublevel corresponding to the Universal Dimension in question. Thus, in the Third Universal Dimension, independent physical reality lifetimes (as opposed to the larger-scale incarnations we identified that start in lower Dimensional Sublevels) take place beginning at the Third Sublevel of the Universal Dimension. Following this pattern, Fifth Universal Dimension physical incarnations of independent Beings begin at the Fifth Dimensional Sublevel, and so on.

As a result, lifetimes cast into that Sublevel will be linked to the overall theme of that Universal Dimension. Thus as an example, life in the Third Sublevel of the Third Universal Dimension has, as a general theme, experiences of co-creation, physical manifestation and independent form. In the Fifth Universal Dimension, where physical life occurs in the Fifth Sublevel of that Universal Dimension, life has, as a general theme, experiences of healing through understanding, telepathy and higher empathy. Similarly, Souls in the Seventh Universal Dimension take on physical forms in the Seventh Sublevel of that Universal Dimension, and the experiences for them are related to offering guidance and higher awareness universally.

So in the First Universal Dimension, the Soul incarnates its lifetimes beginning at the First Sub-level of the Dimension, and this is the area where lifetimes in a physical sense are expressed. Once "death" of the physical form occurs, the entity continues on through all the Sub-levels of the Universal Dimension, until it rejoins its Soul at the Twelfth Sublevel. When all lifetimes within the Universal Dimension are reunited with the Soul, the Soul ascends to the Second Universal Dimension, and the process begins again starting with physical life in the Second Sublevel of the Dimension. The same occurs after the Soul ascends to the Third Universal Dimension, with physical life beginning at the Third Sublevel, and so one and so forth. (See Page 454, Figure 8 of Diagrams in the Appendix.)

The progression continues through all the Universal Dimensions and all the Universal Dimension Sublevels until such time as the Soul has completed its many Wheels of Creation in each Universal Dimension. At that point it is made whole again at a point of origination in the Twelfth Universal Dimension. Once there, the Soul's consolidated energy, consisting of every lifetime generated in every Universal Dimension, is reunified with the force that created it. This occurs in much the same manner in every Universal Dimension and through this process of continual reunification, the consciousness of the entire Universe is continually expanded.

Timeline Continuums

It is difficult to fully understand the multidimensionality of the Universe without understanding how lifetimes on a Soul's Wheels of Creation can exist simultaneously within different perceived time intervals on one dynamic timeline. This is possible based on the fact that the space-time wave that defines a Universal Dimension is essentially spiral in nature, and as a result most points on the timeline have, in a sense, proximity or relationship without direct interaction. (See Page 449, Figure 3 of Diagrams in the Appendix.)

We have often addressed the concept we call "spin." Spin is a fundamental motivating energy that propels Souls, Galaxies, Timelines and the entire Universe forward. It may help if you envision the Universal Dimension as a cone of energy, a spiral if you will. (See Page 455, Figure 9 of Diagrams in the Appendix.) At different points on that spiral all time coordinates exist simultaneously. From there, it is clear that as a Soul casts out parts of itself into various lifetimes it can easily do so at any given point on the timeline.

This is not to say that a Soul cannot create lifetimes together in the same or almost same time sequence. In fact, many Souls do just that and some even prefer numerous lifetimes closely situated on the timeline or overlapping so that these lifetimes can interact and participate in each other's growth, karmic and otherwise. This is an acceptable substitute to having another Soul from a different Soul Group participate in specific agreements with the Soul planning the lifetimes in question. Indeed, there are instances where family members, couples or those met during the course of an entity's lifetime, all living in the same time periods, are actually lifetimes of the same Soul and the same Wheel of Creation. These entities and relationships are literally "Soul Mates," and this would be the most accurate description of a Soul Mate that can exist.

To be sure, Souls plan lifetimes to correspond to precise historic and event points on the timeline, since all these events are happening simultaneously and therefore can be identified by the Soul as to their relevance to the entity's life mission, and consequently the benefit to the Soul. Recall that the concept of linear time management as you know it is more a matter of convenience than accuracy, and all time transpires concurrently.

This is an important point, since a Soul generally coordinates lifetimes on the timeline to correspond to particular timeline events and the mass consciousness environment that is taking place. These energetic moments provide a lucrative and plentiful backdrop that gives the Soul, through the lifetime being created, maximum experiences and opportunities. These opportunities revolve around the prevalent attributes and attitudes that the entity will face and navigate, based on its choices. This includes explorations of such things as belief systems, emotional and other personality features and personal or social traits relevant to that lifetime's path and conducive to the Soul's overall growth.

A Soul's lifetime entities found on a Wheel of Creation, even if living at different timeline intervals, can in many cases have similar traits, skills and desires, and there are instances where strong physical resemblances of all the lifetimes on a Wheel of Creation are noticeable. In fact, similar energetic or personality features can sometimes prevail from incarnation to incarnation. Reincarnations on any point of the timeline can have strong connections, memory bleed-through and shared predispositions, and this tends to be the main reason your current research into reincarnation focuses on shared personality traits and bringing forth reincarnation memories.

It should be remembered as well that another component to lifetimes planned by Souls on various Wheels of Creation in a Universal
Dimension are the genetic associations and parameters. Individuals
who are known to each other at the Soul level will tend to incarnate
together to form families, groups, organizations, regions, countries
and even nations. Due to this, they will generally carry many recognizable genetic traits. For those born into family and related groups,
DNA connections are discernible and some of these genetic connections are assumed to be forged over the course of hundreds or
thousands of years despite the fact that they are actually developed
on a timeline that is dynamic and transpiring all at once.

DNA, as we have informed you, is an important component in the
communication each living Being has with its Soul, not to mention
that Being's day-to-day cellular structure. This allows constant access
and communication between the Soul and the individual lifetime and
DNA acts as an intermediary resonating antenna receiving not only
guidance from the Soul, but also input with respect to the entity's
status, mission and life parameters.

In addition, DNA is a vibrational signature that is able to subconsciously communicate with other Beings and entities known to it or
to the Soul, or anyone that may have some purpose in the entity's
lifetime. There is deep mystery and reward inherent in finding this
kind of resonant kinship, which we define as the feeling that you are
participating with someone who has deep connection to you, no
matter if that connection is based on familial ties or a stranger you
have just met. It is important to understand that the resonating frequency (signature) of your DNA carries with it your Soul's vibrational frequency and it is always recognizable to both you and others
on a metaphysical level. This is perhaps the single most significant factor that attracts you to individuals, groups, organizations or cultures,

as well as attracting them to you.

Whether you consider this attraction to ultimately be positive or negative, which a great many might prove to be from your perspective, be assured that they are related to the resonance and vibration frequency that you yourself are emitting. This electromagnetic signaling is always what invites participation on both sides, for better or for worse, as the case may be.

A Word About Interplanetary and Interdimensional Incarnations

Having explained reincarnation cycles, Wheels of Creation as we term them, and the Soul's journey through all Sublevels of the Universal Dimension, it is perhaps time to speak briefly about the kind of Souls that incarnate in Universal Dimensions galactically as well as universally.

First of all, we have touched on the fact that Souls cast out from the Twelfth Universal Dimension generally have one of two Soul orientations: Groups whose focus is chiefly on serving their own needs or the exclusive needs of a specific group, hive or cadre, known as Service-to-Self Souls; and those Souls whose focus is on serving all Beings, which we designate as a Service-to-Others orientation.

We have also discussed that Human Angelic Souls are principally a Soul group cast out with the orientation of Service-to-Others. Although there can be some minor variations within this designation depending upon a group's specific universal mission or purpose, for the most part this orientation indicates a Soul species that incarnates for the purpose of assisting others, both those inside and outside of its own Soul group, to achieve Soul growth within their Solar System and beyond.

For the most part, Service-to-Others Soul species, such as Human Angelic Souls, prefer to incarnate together, and they overwhelmingly incarnate within their designated home Solar System. This is natural, since these Souls will naturally work to assist the growth and well-being of other Souls and Soul groups, and are at a disadvantage when amongst Service-to-Self Soul species and groups.

As we have already indicated, this does not mean however that the Human Angelic Soul species is the only Soul species incarnating in your Solar System today, and we have amply covered the fact that there are instances in your world currently where Soul species other than Human Angelics are incarnating on Earth in human bodies. Despite this however, and despite the fact that the current example of this is out of a perceived necessity by the alien Soul species, in general most Soul species will almost always prefer to remain embodied in the physical form intended for their Soul species. Furthermore, they incarnate within the designated home planetary system of that Soul race.

Since the human physical biological structure intended to receive Human Angelic Souls has evolved through many genetic generations and variations, in a sense the physical form created is tested and true for incarnation by Human Angelics. As we said already, this means it is highly conducive to not only the Soul's incarnations in physical Third Dimensional reality, but also conducive to the entity's continued journey after physical death through the Astral planes in that particular locale.

Alien Souls incarnated in solar or galactic locations and within physical biological structures not originally suited to them presents the incarnating Soul with numerous difficulties, particularly as it relates to the biologic functioning of the body. This includes hormonal and emotional factors. Some Soul species do not possess such interfaces,

THE WHEELS OF CREATION

as well as other features, as an inherent mechanism in the biological structures suited to them. As a result, there can be fundamental flaws in their ability to manage or cope when placed into physical environments where these physical and emotional body mechanics are the norm, not to mention constantly in play.

In addition, the Soul's connection to its own lifetimes in such cases is lopsided and diminished making direct guidance difficult. Think of this as a translation problem. Since, as you now know, DNA is the communications link through which guidance is received and the emotional and physical state of the physical body is communicated back to the Soul, these individuals can have an impaired electromagnetic line of communication. It is for this reason that they can have a sense they are abandoned, exist without any higher connection or are completely on their own in the world. Sometimes that can feel emotionally stunted and their actions within the reality often take shape accordingly.

On one hand, this can tend to make them egocentric or seem not engaged to any large degree with others in the world. But in other cases, they can suffer from alienation, depression, delusions and other emotional disorders. Left unguided, some will develop severe psychoses. Although these can be cleverly hidden within a world that generally considers aggressive behavior, callousness and bravado to be an indication of superiority, most Human Angelic Beings will find these individuals to be cruel and seem "Soul-less," and will consequently disengage from interaction with them as much as possible. This can further foment consequences.

In addition to all this, these Souls have great difficulty guiding their lifetime entities through the Astral planes after they have passed from physical bodies. Since all created entities have "Will," an entity's refusal to move through the Astral planes, or rather, their inability to perceive the benefit of doing so, can stall them in different Astral environments indefinitely, if not forever. Ultimately, this will prolong the Soul's ability to reintegrate and, as we have discussed, their ability to evolve through Ascension to higher Universal Dimensions, as well as their ability to assist the Universal Dimension to reach the frequency rates it needs to ascend as well.

As we said, the consciousness levels and abilities required to successfully accomplish lifetimes that are not native to a Soul on a Wheel of Creation is usually Fifth Dimensional in nature. Most Third Universal Dimension Souls (whether they be Human Angelic or extraterrestrial in nature) will have distinct difficulty orchestrating Wheels of Creation that take place in either different universal locations or in biological forms they are not adept at manifesting in dimensional reality. These entities will inevitably "stand out," so to speak.

This said, be aware that the physical nature of Reincarnation does in fact change and differ from one Universal Dimension to another. Frequency, vibrational resonance, time sequences, dimensional physics, sacred geometry, fundamental principles, density, color and luminosity, not to mention genetics and physical properties, as well as many other factors, are very different from one Universal Dimension to the next.

So although you might be able to vaguely recognize the physical incarnation of a Human Angelic Being from let's say the Fifth or even the Seventh Universal Dimension, their physical appearance, attributes, density, ability to absorb light and particularly their personal abilities, talents, features and senses would be so distinctive and foreign as to make you feel they were aliens or extraterrestrials. Bear in mind that the appearance, attributes and innate senses entities possess always correspond to the Universal Dimension in which they are created, as well as the Sublevel of the Universal Dimension in question.

Although we have mainly discussed instances where inter-Soul species incarnation can be possible, albeit problematic, under certain circumstances, there is one additional point that should be addressed concerning the subject. Certainly, there are many religious traditions in your world today that hold forth the concept of Reincarnation. Some of these profess a belief in Reincarnation across species in your world today. In that regard, it is thought that a human being can be incarnated as an insect in a kind of karmic retribution, or that a beloved pet will one day incarnate along side you as a human being.

As we have already said, inter-Soul species incarnation is not a norm, even for those beings that take on humanoid-like forms, wherever they may be located in the Galaxy or Universe. Interspecies incarnation of the kind expressed by some ancient religions found on Earth is essentially nonexistent, if possible at all.

A distinction must always be made amongst Soul groups. Some are from what is considered a Hive Soul group, and the majority of plants, animals and insects in your world share one Soul as a group. Although each entity or lifetime within such a hive Soul group is distinctive and unique, much as you are a distinct entity originating from your own Soul, nevertheless these species share one Soul as opposed to the many Souls casting incarnations on Wheels of Creations for Human Angelics, as an example. That is to say that while there might be distinction and can have unique personalities, for each Being originating from a Hive Soul group a single Soul is shared by all.

This is particularly true in the plant and insect kingdoms, and these Beings will never incarnate in human form, nor will humans ever incarnate as one of them. Hive Soul groups can have various missions, and the most important is growth for a Soul group of this kind through service to others, by providing some biologic or other function. This is also the case when a certain group or plants, insects or animals is somehow related to the food chain of other Soul groups, those independent and not.

Yet there do exist independent Souls for some species of animals. Distinct among these are Cetaceans (Whales and Dolphins) and some Mammals, in particular Primates, which can be related genetically and as a consequence can have direct relationships with Human Angelic or other independent Soul groups. Some, like Cetaceans, are Soul groups and entities unto themselves (even if some among these could be considered in their childhood of genetic development and evolution) and these will never cross-incarnate as humans or vice versa, while others are genetically related to Human Angelics.

Just as Dinosaurs and some Reptilians on Earth now may be considered genetic predecessors of, for example, Draconian and Zeta Soul groups who may someday incarnate using the physical bodies of these Beings, similarly, some Mammals are genetic evolutionary ancestors of Human Angelic Souls. For instance, certain primate groups may well be serving as biologic vehicles for Human Angelic Soul incarnation in the Third Universal Dimension now.

It is necessary to understand that development of the genetic physical structures required to potentially house individual Souls from any Soul group is not something that occurs simply or easily, and is something that occurs through the process of genetic evolution running hand in hand with degrees and levels of consciousness as well as Soul age. In some cases, very young baby Souls beginning Third Universal Dimension incarnations will choose to incarnate as simple beings in physical bodies that have a relationship with the Soul group, such as Primates for Human Angelic Souls. Inevitably, these Souls evolve quickly during the Ascension cycle in question, and ultimately they will take on incarnations in humanoid form. It is perhaps from this fact, however, that the concept of Human Souls incarnating as animals arose originally as a mythology in ancient culture. But aside from this example, let us assure you this is not the rule and for Human Angelic Souls incarnation in any form other than human, as divine punishment or retribution of any kind is never really the case.

With this in mind it is clear that as a Soul species rises in consciousness and age, these Souls are physically housed in advanced genetic physical bodies conditioned and evolved for them through the process of natural evolution as described by your sciences and the evolutionary Darwinian viewpoints that you know. Again, we reiterate that in general Souls from higher Universal Dimensions never incarnate in lower physical life forms.

This is also true within the same Universal Dimension, and Souls that are of an older Soul age and greater experience will never "stepdown" and incarnate in earlier genetic physical variations, even if those variations are related to their species. This same process and concept applies for nearly all Souls in all the various Galaxies throughout the Universe, including the example we have already given with respect to primitive Reptilians being the genetic ancestors of many advanced Galactic Reptilian Soul races such as the Zeta Draconians.

Our main point here is to not only help you understand how much of this can be related to Soul age, the Soul group and specific Galactic or Universal sectors, but also to help you understand that it is possible for Baby and very Young Souls to be incarnated next to you. This is despite the fact that they may not be members of your human species and may only be emerging into Third Dimensional incarnations for the first time using the physical bodies of species that are genetically related to you.

This also provides an example of how various Soul ages can incarnate along side each other, and this is not limited to different species but applies to different Soul ages incarnated within the same species. In this way, a younger Soul might be your neighbor, your teacher, your friend or even a sibling. Nothing precludes various Soul ages from existing in the same Universal Dimension together, but what may separate these Souls is whether or not they are ready for Ascension, or remaining within a Universal Dimension even if older Souls are in the process of cycling out of physical lifetimes in that Dimension.

Sadly, often Soul age can be a determining factor, and many an older Soul is appalled at the intense karmic endeavors younger Souls will strive to generate in physical reality for purposes of Soul growth. This is especially true at times like the current period, where Ascension energies highlight and augment the fundamental differences in Soul ages, as we discussed earlier in this book.

Whatever the Soul age, knowing this fact makes it imperative that respect, understanding and compassion always be considered towards all species, particularly one's own as well as those species even remotely related to Human Angelics genetically through the evolutionary process. Younger Souls that have graduated to physical bodies incur karma when they subject those genetically related to the Soul group with challenges and difficulties or death and destruction.

As an example, those who are hunters who hunt not out of necessity for sustenance but for "sport," particularly those hunting primates, such as those found in the Ape kingdoms, have a strong kinship with these genetically related species. Baby and younger Souls incarnated as human beings can possibly have just cycled into humanoid form lifetimes, and may have Soul group (family) members still living in physical bodies of a different (from your perspective) species as we are discussing. Karma is always generated when a young Soul hunter pursues and kills, as an example, an Ape thinking it is a member of another species with no earthly connection to it only to discover in the higher Astral realms that prior to their own human incarnation this was a sibling or a Soul Task Mate. Naturally, even balancing this energy field leads to growth, but we would suggest that less challenging means of Soul growth are always available, even to younger Souls, if a degree of compassion and empathy is fostered in society for all beings.

In that regard, much can be said for developing early on compassion, understanding and caring for all one's fellow living Beings, Soul related or not. This is applicable particularly to those Beings that are not similar in nature or genetic structure remembering that these may be incarnations of younger Human Angelic Souls. Of course, this is not to pass judgment upon anyone and once again there is no right or wrong, as any karmic energy generated will always be balanced. But hopefully it allows you to understand that there is in fact a distinct karmic exchange inherent in such encounters with other living Beings, or with the abuse and mistreatment of any life form, whatever kind it might happen to be.

Thus you can see that the manner of incarnation within various Universal Dimensions are not all similar and are not all at the same age quality or level of consciousness vibration. Understanding this is important in seeing that evolutionary process is intertwined with not only the Universal Dimension but Ascension as well. Moreover, genetic evolution within a Universal Dimension can transcend Ascension in order to provide physical bodies of higher and higher quality in which Soul groups may incarnate.

This is true whether speaking of Souls beginning physical incarnations or Souls coming into physical forms and bodies that are of premier physical status and the epitome of the highest physical biological structure available for life incarnations of a Soul within the Universal Dimension. The structure of the Universe allows Souls of varying Soul age and consciousness to be able, through the many variety of physical bodies and types available, to incarnate as needed and as desired according to the Soul's age during the particular Ascension cycle being experienced.

You now see that Souls, particularly those that are younger, have the ability to sample and become familiar with physical life through incarnations in evolutionary simpler physical forms that are less complex in terms of their life interactions and responsibilities. These Souls quickly graduate into creating Wheels of Creation and incarnations in physical form that are more advanced, such as the human body that you are aware of and accustom to.

This is the case in all Universal Dimensions, and one lifetime on a Wheel of Creation of your Soul could indeed include an existence in a simpler form, humanoid or otherwise. However, if you have assumed that you will automatically incarnate into various species including those not at all related to the primate or humanoid genetic lineage in this Universal Dimension you would be mistaken. Ultimately, a Soul will always incarnate within the highest physical structure related to its Soul species that is available in a Universal Dimension. This is despite the fact that the Soul has the option of beginning early incarnations within a Universal Dimension, and particularly at the beginning points of the timeline, in physical bodies that are simpler to manifest for the purposes of growth.

This principle does not always need to apply to a different (but genetically related) species either. As an example, a Soul can start incarnations in physical bodies that are sometimes considered impaired or damaged, physically, psychologically or emotionally, as the case might be. Inevitably, these incarnations will kick start incarnations that will lead to higher consciousness and evolutionary patterns.

It is important to remember however that not all lifetimes that your society might consider "impaired" are so because of young Soul age. A good many of these are actually much older Souls manifesting such lifetimes for the benefit of parents, families, friends and society at large in an effort to bring these participants growth or in order to bring awareness to mass consciousness concerning the intrinsic value of any specific group.

We would site lifetimes such as that of Helen Keller or of Temple Grandin as examples here. Each of these individuals are old Souls bringing society at large and the world understanding and enlightenment with respect to particular issues that these Souls successfully brought to light, despite lifetime obstacles and seeming impairments (which ultimately proved not to be impairments at all). Lifetimes of this sort demonstrate the potential for success, brilliance and leadership hidden beneath insurmountable odds or physical and mental disabilities.

It is important, however, to understand that karma can be generated between Soul groups of any age, any species or within any physical world reality. As an example, having a seriously ill child is almost always an older Soul (the child) creating opportunities for growth for another Soul (the parent). Yet there is also the possibility that the child is a younger Soul being cared for and taught by a Soul Task Mate. In general, as we have always stated, young children who are seriously ill or who pass from physical life during childhood are older Souls providing their parents with opportunities to grow from the tragic loss they experience. These entities are always special lifetimes created by Souls that are to be commended for their high Service-to-Others act, whereby they provide the highest sacrifice through the early departure from their own physical life.

It is precisely in this manner that, as we have said, karma can be generated between various levels of Soul age and consciousness for the Human Angelic Soul species. This includes, as we have just discussed, compassion and caring for every Group of Humans, as well as any other animal species, whether genetically related or not.

There are very few exceptions universally with regard to the cycles of incarnation and the Ascension progression made by a Soul as it journeys through the Universal Dimensions. While this is a general Truth, there are some variations related to specific Beings and physical worlds, and this applies even in Galaxies that are housed within the same Universal Dimension.

For the most part, Beings within a specific Universal Dimension can have similar physical properties, attributes and senses since these all tend to relate to the vibrational spin and the consciousness frequencies available to Beings within that particular Universal Dimension. In addition, there is little variation, other than particulars of the environmental superstructure based on entities' expectations and manifestations of the Sublevels or Astral planes of a Universal Dimension. While you may have assumed that the Astral Sublevels of your Universal Dimension are solely populated by Human Angelic's Souls, it needs to be understood that the Sublevels, like the Dimension itself, are the same, albeit divided by spatial differences related to the specific sector of the Universe they interact with.

However, there tends to be little crossover in any Sublevel of a Universal Dimension, other than the crossovers we have already described. While it may be true that the Astral Sublevels of the Universal Dimension known to Human Angelics are for the most part segregated in terms of being specific to Human Angelic Souls, there is in fact additional overlap with respect to the Sublevels, and separation is only a product of the vastness of the Universe and the space-time wave or Dimension in question.

This is difficult to comprehend from your current perspective just as it may be difficult to understand the multidimensional aspects of the Universe. That includes how various dimensional space-time waves are able to superimpose themselves one upon the other in much the same way that an onion is layered and could be considered infinite in its own expression. This is the main reason your current society's push into exploring the Universe confirms for you its enormity and tends to make most draw the conclusion that you are alone in the Universe.

We would suggest this is so because of your Earth-centric perspective that originates within the principles and properties of life in the Third Universal Dimension. When you look at Saturn, for example, you are looking at Saturn as it is found in the Third Universal Dimension, from the perspective of the Third Sublevel of that Universal Dimension, which is where you are focused. However, superimposed on this, above and beneath it so to speak, Saturn exists in every Universal Dimension we have discussed. While you cannot necessarily see Saturn in those various other Universal Dimensions, particularly those above the Third Universal Dimension, they nevertheless exist.

Following this to its logical conclusion, it is quite possible then that an extraterrestrial colony is present on Saturn in the Fifth or higher Universal Dimension. Yet you would be convinced that based on your observations of Saturn – the one you see in the Third Universal Dimension – no such colony is possible.

Thus, there may be life on Saturn that is non-Human Angelic in the Fourth, Fifth, Sixth, Seventh or a higher Universal Dimension. Similarly, Earth or some other planet in another Solar System might appear completely void of life to another extraterrestrial Soul group when seen from the First, Second or even Third Universal Dimension. Again, understanding this disparity is important to understanding how diverse the Universe can be and also how any rules or systems intended to formalize where physical life is or isn't can not be standardized unless you are using a multidimensional perspective.

One last thought we would like to bring to you with respect to the multidimensionality of the Universe is related to the universal rule that higher can see lower, but lower cannot see higher with respect to full dimensional awareness. As you know, this maxim generally permits Beings from higher Universal Dimensions to in effect see the substance of lower Dimensions, even if they do not directly comprehend or have interaction with them. As a result, in your world you see First and Second Dimensional Beings all the time but are not aware of their life cycles or sentient existence. This includes things that to you seem fairly inanimate or non sentient, such as rocks, clouds, mountain ranges and rivers.

In this same vein certain Beings in higher Universal Dimensions, particularly those Dimensions just beyond your own like the Fourth, Fifth or Sixth Dimension, are aware of you even if you are not aware of them, despite the fact that they may have little or nothing to do with you. Most of those Beings are content to live their lives without becoming concerned or even aware of you, in much the same way that you probably would not interact in the life of a mountain range, a grain of beach sand or a river. In addition to this, we already discussed extensively that true celestial guidance comes from the Seventh Universal Dimension, and Beings in that Universal Dimension provide guidance to lower Dimensions as a matter of that Dimension's mission and purpose.

However, you need to be aware that information coming from higher Dimensions, other than from the Seventh Universal Dimension and higher, can sometimes be incomplete, misleading or erroneous. This is an important aspect to consider, since there is in fact potential for misguidance and influences from other-dimensional Beings who are not necessarily oriented towards Service-to-Others, as Human Angelics are.

Such interaction creates responsibility in those that are being guided or receiving information in a multidimensional or intuitive way. Higher dimensional Beings know that if a lower dimensional Being acknowledges and then accepts their guidance, doing so is generally considered an expression of their Will, and therefore no karma is attributed to the higher dimensional Being. In other words, if you are told something or shown in plain sight what is transpiring, and accept it without question or thoughtful consideration, you have chosen to follow that path voluntarily. Although there may be consequences, some of which could be challenging, they are not karmic in nature for the perpetrator.

The fact that such misguidance is so widely available today, as a result of new digital technologies and global 24/7 media outlets, is intended as a primal lesson in shaping your ability to recognize Truth and distinguish it from guidance that is questionable, erroneous or self-serving. It is an important lesson that is necessary to your Soul growth, particularly as you increase your consciousness and raise your vibration during this time of Ascension.

We would further suggest to you that the monumental questions currently being faced in your world with respect to what is True and what is not, such as the phenomenon of "Fake News" is not accidental or coincidental. The need to question what is Truth and what is interference and manipulation is important to understanding how primal knowing what is True can be to making life choices and expressing your own power in reality through the use of your own "Will." These are vital lessons the Human Angelic Soul community is currently undergoing in preparation for Ascension, especially as it concerns those headed for Human Angelic Soul incarnations in the Fifth Universal Dimension on Terra (Earth's Fifth Dimensional equivalent).

In this respect, it is important to be able to decipher when you are being manipulated by an untruth and when you are being guided by higher consciousness. Independent thinking and honing your intuitive abilities to decipher what is True from what is false will well serve those ascending to Fifth Dimensional incarnations, and the current world situation is in a sense a lesson for doing so.

Moreover, recognizing that influence can be positive or negative and that guidance, no matter how real or True it seems, should be explored and questioned thoroughly before using your Free Will to make choices. This is paramount not only to being in the position of receiving proper (higher) guidance but also an important preparation for those Souls who in higher dimensional realms will one day actively guide others.

Human Angelic Souls by nature are oriented to assist other universal creatures and Souls wherever possible and it is important for each Human Angelic entity reincarnated on a Soul's Wheel of Creation to realize and recognize the power to guide and influence others, as well as the potential for this ability to be corrupted and used against a Soul species or race. What you see transpiring in your world today where Truth changes from group to group, is not as clearly dualistic as it has been in the past or is completely false and being used to manipulate others is precisely the lesson needed. This is being explored through mass consciousness as many Human Angelics prepare for Ascension into higher dimensional realms.

Those of you familiar with our prior work, *Timeline Collapse and Universal Ascension*, understand that Human Angelic Souls from Fifth Dimensional Terra have implemented several particular tests, or more appropriately lessons, in order to prepare disoriented groups of Third Universal Dimension Human Angelic Souls for possible Ascension. Bringing lessons such as this that obliges entities to distinguish or at least consider Truth from falsehood in expressing their Will is one such important lesson. This is intended to allow higher vibrational consciousness and awareness in those Human Angelic Souls that will one day be cycling off lifetimes in the Third Universal Dimensional on Earth and ascending to incarnations on Fifth Universal Dimension Terra.

 **CHAPTER 10**
CONCLUSION: THE UNIVERSAL ASPECTS OF SOUL GROWTH THROUGH REINCARNATION, TRANSMIGRATION AND ASCENSION

The question of Reincarnation, Transmigration and Ascension of the Soul is not fully addressed until there is a brief discussion concerning the evolution of physical matter and the life forms in which Souls incarnate within a Universal Dimension. Evolution, environmental physics and the genetic development of physical vehicles that provide the temporary housing for Soul incarnations within specific Dimensional Sublevels of reality are important concepts to understand as they are universally known and accepted in the majority of higher Universal Dimensions.

For the most part, with the exception of the very highest Universal Dimensions, all Universal Dimensions have some form of a physical vehicle or carrier for the Soul. That body is subject to physical change and evolution on certain dimensional planes in much the same way the Soul is subject to metaphysical evolution from Dimension to Dimension through Ascension. There are distinct properties and principles related to this evolution that are applicable within each Universal Dimension. In order to describe this further, let us take a look at the Third Universal Dimension and the properties that are inherent in the structure that you call the physical body, which the Soul uses at the Third Dimensional Sublevel as a vehicle and depository for its energy and growth.

First and foremost, it is important to understand that there are distinct evolutionary factors related to the ideal physical structure or body intended to house a Soul's incarnations on its journey through a Universal Dimension. Certain aspects of this evolution can be accomplished over the course of a single Galactic Ascension period (260,000 years) if necessary but the ideal form is more commonly evolved during the course of many, many Ascension periods.

In fact, the evolution of the Human Angelic body physical structure has been in constant alteration and refinement within the Third Universal Dimension for tens of millions of years. Many reading this probably believe we are discussing here the evolution of mammals and primates into Humanoid forms over the course of that time period, as you are told by your current sciences. However, you will be surprised to discover that this is not necessarily accurate and there have been many human physical form renditions that were neither primate related or primitive prior to what is the current physical human body. Most of these existed well before the current understanding of history and prehistory.

Furthermore, it is wrong to assume that your particular physical genetic and cellular structure has evolved in a linear manner as you currently surmise based on available remains and archeology. It is equally erroneous to believe that there have not been numerous human physical renditions, cultures and civilizations prior to your current modern civilization. Some of these renditions have failed or been lost genetically, and others evolved and continue to be incorporated into your genetic makeup.

You might be surprised to know that some of the most ancient of these were mixtures of humanoid and animal forms. The mythologies that tell of animal and man physical mixtures are cellular remembrance of these original beings as Souls and Celestial Beings attempted to perfect a physical form for Human Angelic incarnations and physical experiences. There were several different physical renditions such as this as well. Some were what would be considered giants while some were entire civilizations of people of short stature.

In most cases, over time these bodies were considered unsuitable for Third Dimensional Earth incarnations and these races either died out or were absorbed into other groups. The current races are generally an evolved mixture of the most successful genetic features, both physical and spiritual (as contained within the DNA variations) needed for life in the Third Dimensional Sublevel of the physical planet, Earth.

Each time a genetic reset occurred, this evolutionary process generally began over, retaining and incorporating what was viable while discarding what would not be ideal for Human Angelic Souls. The present physical structure, though not perfect and still in a state of evolution, has evolved in such a way as to facilitate Human Angelic lives in Third Dimensional reality, ensure continuation of genetic lineages in order to allow for continued reincarnations on the timeline and foster familial and cultural Soul group relationships wherever possible.

This understanding includes a variety of prehistory human races and civilizations from hundreds of thousands and even millions of years ago measured in linear fashion prior to your current time. In many respects not only were there cultures and civilizations that existed on the current dimensional timeline (the Galactic Ascension period of 260,000 years) that were far superior to your own in both technology and knowledge, there were also Earth cultures and civilizations that existed before the current Ascension period, stretching back into the millions of years.

Many will find this difficult to rectify with their current understanding of prehistory, however just as we have spoken of a coming great "Reset" of Third Dimensional Earth, you should understand that there have been numerous "resets" in the distant past. Some could even be considered minor resets where most but not all was lost, such as the great catastrophes and subsequent floods that reset civilization by bringing a close to the Atlantean civilization between 13,000 and 12,000 BCE.

The Atlantean civilization, which itself had different incarnations over the course of approximately one hundred and fifty thousand years, had many precursor civilizations that existed before it, some prior to the current Galactic Ascension. Remnants of this great world empire are seen in ancient pyramids and other structures yet undiscovered, and hints of it are intertwined and hidden within some Egyptian, Mayan, Hindu and Buddhist traditions, mythologies and culture. All of these, and others yet to be found, were outpost regions of Atlantis that developed from scratch after the demise of Atlantis and the great reset of that time.

An analogy would be if the most rural and remote areas of your world continued on after the complete collapse of civilization in your metro and urban areas, with those distant places indirectly and vaguely recalling concepts that were prominent in the cities until over time even those concepts were completely lost. Similarly, after the final fall of Atlantis, over time certain rural regions of the world recovered from complete social, cultural and technological collapse. As they did so they incorporated small remnants of the prior Empire's knowledge and wisdom from before its disappearance into their culture and mythologies, until eventually the understanding and origins of even those bits and pieces were completely forgotten and disassociated.

The point is that there have been advanced civilizations on Third Dimensional Earth since before the high point of the Atlantean civilization and the course of the current Galactic Ascension period, and these cultures and civilizations were quite technologically advanced. Many were not only accustom to air travel, they were well acquainted with Galactic travel and interdimensional technologies and capabilities you are not familiar with even now. Early epics like the Hindu Mahabharata are not mythologies about the exploits of Gods but rather stories adjusted through time for their audiences based on tales that were already ancient when written during your prehistory about the struggles of these many former advanced civilizations.

Some Earth-based civilizations from several Galactic and even several Cosmic Ascension Periods before the current age actually had bases and were connected to other advanced civilizations located on various planets and moons within your Solar System, including on Earth's Moon, the planet Mars, the planet Venus and an additional planet in your Solar System that was destroyed and is no longer in existence known to you now as the Asteroid Belt. In addition, there have been colonies, bases and civilizations that communicated freely with the Earth planet in the Third Universal Dimension on several Moons of Jupiter and Saturn, of which Titan was the largest and most notable colony.

There was also wide spread interdimensional travel during the Ascension period prior to the current one that was quite prominent and freely utilized the many interdimensional portals found throughout Earth's electromagnetic grid system and in various locations throughout the Solar System. These portals permit actual physical travel between Universal Dimensions to locations in close proximity to the current ones. There was a good deal of interdimensional travel from closely related higher Dimensions with physical properties that could be easily adjusted to the Third Universal Dimension, particularly from the Fourth, Fifth and, at times, the Sixth Universal Dimensions.

Returning to our discussion of the evolution of physical bodies for Soul use during incarnations, the concept of perfecting the physical vehicles used in such a manner is an important factor for all species in most Ascension cycles. It should be noted that the pros and cons of your world's current genetic manipulation of the physical body is soon to become one of the most important discussions of your age. Generally, civilizations that reach such capability are unconsciously acting in order to evolve and perfect the human genetic structure in which coming generations of Human Angelic Souls will incarnate in during the next Galactic Ascension period.

Usually, the perfections achieved will be carried on, even after civilization and culture have collapsed and begun over from very primitive beginnings. Yet the genetically improved versions of the human physical body will continue on into the next chapter of Ascension. We call the continual perfection of physical form for incarnation purposes of coming Soul generations Genetic Evolutionary Ascension, and it is for this reason that, more or less, the human form is in continual state of re-generation and perfection regardless of the Ascension period.

The same is of course true for almost all Soul species, particularly in the First through Sixth Universal Dimensions where some form of physical reality at one or more Dimensional Sublevels is normally encountered. Beginning in the Seventh Universal Dimension, how-ever, Soul incarnations are carried out in more ethereal forms at all Dimensional Sublevels. These higher dimensional forms lack the densities lower Dimensions are accustomed to, and the bodies Souls incarnate in there are far more luminescent, etheric and ce-lestial in nature in keeping with the higher vibrational quality of those Dimensions.

Though we do not wish to enter the debate that still rages in your world over first creation, other than to identify Adam and Eve as mythology fairly far removed from truth, we do wish to point out that there are numerous factors that have effected humanity's evo-lution over time. In fact, human creation does not have one origi-nating point and has been diversely approached and continuously altered, improved and reformulated both within an Ascension cycle as well as from Ascension period to Ascension period.

In some cases, different creations or seedings of man have been ef-fectuated in different regions of Earth, and we suggest this has much to do with minor feature differences, physical and physiological, that you may find in human races on Earth. There have also been many human creations originated by off-world relatives as well as creations orchestrated by non-related extraterrestrials, such as in the case of the Annunaki in the ancient Mesopotamian regions, as an example.

Seedings are generally built one upon the other, with variations fostered by the originating extraterrestrial or based on the goals of higher dimensional Celestial Beings involved in physical creation. There have also been creations that were left on their own to naturally evolve over time, some of which include the primates we discussed earlier, although to be clear somewhere along the way there is usually some measure of outside assistance originating from either off planet or from higher dimensional Beings.

In fact, the Lemurian and Atlantean races were originally seeded and created by higher dimensional Celestial Beings working in cooperation with Human Angelic Souls from the Fourth Universal Dimension. We would consider these to be among the first and earliest successful attempts at creating a viable physical human form ideal for Human Angelic Soul incarnations in the Third Universal Dimension.

In that regard, there were at least three different early seedings of humanity derived from those Beings during the period. The initial seeding featured physical structures that were smaller, lighter and more ethereal or Fourth Dimensional in nature. The second seeding tried to integrate hybrid Beings that were denser by adding physicality through the incorporation of some successful animal features into the human physical structure. Those first and second seedings failed in the long-term, despite heroic early Atlantean efforts to perfect them through the Temples of Beautification that were created for that purpose.

It was, however, the third seeding derived with the additional assistance and genetic participation of the Pleiadians that was most successful offering the perfect blend of mind, body and etheric energies. Much later, other humanoid species such as those from the Sirius

Star System also contributed genetic substance to create an off-shoot of these original human races that took hold predominantly in the world's Southern Hemispheres. Current physical human bodies hold close resemblance to various elements of such inputs, especially as regards to outer appearance, physical traits and stature, even though consensus is that the current global human physiology, particularly biochemical function, represents more devolution than progression since those early seedings.

It should be understood that in the initial stages of some of these prehistory pre-Ascension period civilizations, the physical Beings were as much Fourth Dimensional in nature as Third Dimensional, and there were close connections maintained between these two Universal Dimensions. Thus, the very earliest Lemurian and Atlantean worlds could almost be considered Fourth Dimensional civilizations. It was after a disastrous "fall" during one Ascension period when Third Universal Dimension Ascension was not fully achieved that the Fourth Universal Dimension actually fell and merged with components of the Third Universal Dimension. After that period physical incarnations were mostly lower in consciousness, denser and closer to what you are familiar with today as being Third Dimensional in nature. However, some Fourth Dimensional characteristics were retained, such as your nightly reach into the Dreamscape or the Dream reality.

If we do not often mention Fourth Dimensional Human Angelic Beings, or a Fourth Universal Dimension version of Earth, it is not necessarily that those space time-waves did not exist but rather that within your sector of the Universe the challenges related to that Ascension fall, which occurred many Ascension cycles ago, are still being felt and balanced out. Due to this, there are currently no

Human Angelic Soul Beings incarnated in the Fourth Universal Dimension, and life within it is in effect void other than limited minor etheric remnants of those past civilizations superimposed at times on the structure of Third Dimensional Earth.

As a continuing result of the "fall," those remnants, most of which are located under ice in present day Antarctica, materialize from time to time as real matter in your Universal Dimension when conditions are right. For the most part however, these manifestations are only echoes reverberating into your dimensional reality occasionally. However, you should be aware that the "fall" remains the main reason Third Universal Dimension Human Angelic Souls can spend more than one Ascension period perfecting incarnations on Third Dimensional Earth and now ascend directly to Fifth Universal Dimension lifetimes on Terra when incarnations on Earth in the Third Universal Dimension are completed.

While Earth is designated the home world of Human Angelic Souls, as we have said, you have many humanoid cousins in this Universal Dimension, as well as in others. Among them are Beings from the Sirius Star System, who have a close relationship with the Annunaki, as well as humanoid Beings from the Solar System of Proxima Centauri. In addition, there are the Pleiadians, which as we mentioned are perhaps closest to you in genetic formulation particularly since some of your current genetic structure was borrowed from them and incorporated into your own current physiology.

Astronomical, architectural and other ancient references to these various Star Systems all reflect these connections and are based on an ancient understanding of that fact. Still, none of these Beings are one hundred percent related to you, and though some of these Soul groups may work at higher dimensional levels with Human Angelic Soul groups (especially the Fifth Universal Dimension and higher), each represents a unique Soul race that is not Human Angelic.

As you have learned, a Soul's evolution can occur at different rates than the physical forms used by them for incarnation, and this is so during specific periods on the current dimensional timeline as well as during different Ascension periods. In the early days of the Lemurian civilization, and afterwards at the onset of the Atlantean civilization, interconnection and communication with Beings from higher Universal Dimensions allowed great knowledge and technology to be available in the Third and Fourth Universal Dimensions. This communication however, was not limited to technology but also enabled a degree of cross-Soul species integration, interaction and, in some cases, Soul incarnations. This is precisely where the current extraterrestrial bio-invaders of Third Dimensional Earth conceived their idea to incarnate as alien Souls into Human Angelic or hybrid Human Angelic physical bodies. For the purpose of our discussion here, it is enough to understand that various physical evolutions of the human structure used for reincarnation on Earth is a standard of process that occurs within specific dimensional time-waves and many Ascension periods.

In fact we might suggest that the current physical form represents a relatively primitive rendition with respect to intuitive senses developed by humans. The coming reset and the emergence of a new Galactic Ascension period will bring with it on a later timeline a superior human physical form where the electromagnetic properties of the DNA will be highly attuned. This will have the effect of creating individuals that have a far superior connection to Earth and the electromagnetic structure of Earth, as well as to their Souls, their life purposes and their Source energy.

Naturally, this comes as an evolutionary result following the highly blunted senses that the physical body exhibits today. This is intended as an evolutionary step of the physical body to overcome the DNA deadening, the electromagnetic blockages and the technological fencing imposed on humans via current technologies, especially technologies that will emerge in the coming decades and centuries. Such DNA improvements will not only assist life on future Third Universal Dimension Earth, they will improve human intuitive abilities and facilitate transition to higher Dimensions for all Human Angelic Beings during the next Ascension cycle. Much of what you hear promoted in prophecies concerning the evolution of human senses and intuitive abilities in the future as a result of Ascension refer to this factor.

The most important conclusion to arrive at based on this is that physical evolution of the bodies used for reincarnation in physical reality is an important aspect related to the growth and learning processes of the Soul. This is the reason physical forms in higher Universal Dimensions typically demonstrate higher physical evolutionary properties, and in particular augmented sensory perceptions are almost always seen in conjunction with higher levels of consciousness.

Yet higher levels of consciousness are not relegated to higher Universal Dimensions exclusively, and they are always available at any stage within every Universal Dimension assuming the Soul group incarnating there has achieved the growth and age needed for awareness and understanding. Physical bodies tend to parallel the Soul's level of consciousness available in the Universal Dimension. In other words, the physical forms you encounter in your world reflect the level of consciousness and vibrational resonance that is standard at that point on the timeline for your Universal Dimension. If the forms are not to your liking on the timeline where you are focused, it is almost always because you are a lifetime of an older Soul that is preparing to cycle off further incarnations or lifetimes therein.

During prior Ascension periods, Soul consciousness at particular points early in the historic theater of the Earth had high consciousness, vibrational resonance and, in some cases, much older Soul age. Yet because these were experimental civilizations, some of which were hopelessly diverted from connection to their missions, Souls and life purposes, quite a few of them derailed spectacularly. This was indeed the case with the Lemurians, and again came into play with the later Atlantean civilizations. No doubt, you see similar experiences taking place around you at the present time and it is for this reason that we would caution against making the assumption that higher is always better, or that older Soul age and consciousness necessarily portends wisdom and integrity.

As we mentioned already, despite the intervention of higher Celestial and dimensional Beings, the early use of hybrid (animal and human forms mixed) physical bodies in the first and second seedings of physical humans for Human Angelic Soul incarnations did not succeed. In a second example, genetic modifications of the physical body for purposes of forced Soul Ascension and migration to higher Dimensions by one group of highly conscious Service-to-Self Human Angelic Soul Atlanteans was the kernel and beginning of that empire's decent into chaos. The subsequent conflicts and divergent purposes ultimately led to that civilization's demise as well as the destruction of its landmasses. This is regardless of the fact that the Atlantean civilization's demise occurred after no less than three spectacular periods of destruction that took place over the course of over one hundred thousand years of time.

These prehistory civilizations and cultures are particularly interesting as they relate to the subject of Reincarnation. By now you are aware that physical civilizations and cultures, like individuals, carry specific missions and goals. You are also aware that the missions generated by civilizations, cultures and nations facilitate the advancement of spiritual consciousness and awareness by all incarnating Souls that use the developing physical body vehicles to utilize and grow from the experiences generated.

The early cultures we are discussing, in particular the land of Mu or Lemuria and the Atlantean civilizations, are of interest in that when these civilizations began more than a million years prior to your own, one of the primary purposes behind them was the healing and improvement of genetic composition and structuring related to perfection of the human body or vehicle. For the most part, purification of the human form was complete by the third human seeding just prior to the current Galactic Ascension period over 260,000 years ago. Those interested in further insight into the efforts to purify and improve the human physical body for Soul reincarnation within the Atlantean Temples of Beautification will find this subject amply covered in various sessions provided to you by Edgar Cayce, referred to by many as the Sleeping Prophet.

In conjunction with the aspects of purifying the human appearance however, what is perhaps less well known is the Atlantean effort to augment and streamline the communicatory ability inherent in the DNA and cellular structure, as well as an effort to redesign the body's chakra orientation and energetic systems to be in better harmony with the electromagnetic grid of Earth.

Many misunderstood ancient structures still standing in your world today (although these actually originate as copies created in the very late periods of these civilizations) were based on the designs of Atlantean amplifiers that incorporated extraterrestrial as well as Fourth Dimensional understanding and were intended to augment Earth's portals and electromagnetic chakra structure. These were meant to facilitate and increase numerous natural phenomena allowing such things as weather enhancement, the sharing of electromagnetic energies, balancing of environmental and natural Earth occurrences, interdimensional travel and communications, as well as an enhancement of the human DNA's natural communications abilities with higher dimensional Beings and the Soul itself.

The perfection of mankind or, more appropriately, the human physical body intended for the experiences of the Human Angelic Soul group were primarily achieved through evolution of the various seedings that permitted ever-increasing consciousness through the development of reality choices and improved sensory perceptions, which augment as physical structure evolves. This is true in every Universal Dimension and Dimensional Sublevel, and it is the reason Souls tend to discard denser physical bodies continually as they move higher in either the Astral realms or in higher Universal Dimensions.

The Universe is always in a state of restructuring and growth through the evolutionary expansion of Ascension, and this is highly applicable to the physical structures found within a Dimension as well. Evolution of the physical body and its inherent sensitivities of perception are an important consideration for all Soul groups as they incarnate and transmigrate across Dimensional divides. Improvement in consciousness levels that translate into higher energetic reception and the ability to absorb light more efficiently are important considerations since these evolutionary traits foster higher resonance and frequency, the hallmark of progression towards Ascension. Constant evolution of the physical body in this way prepares all Souls for the new incarnations that await them in higher dimensional levels as they journey from Sublevel or Sublevel, and Universal Dimension to Universal Dimension.

What we are attempting to demonstrate here is that a Soul's growth through physical existence can depend largely on the type of physical body employed for incarnation. The quality of choices presented in physical reality and the nature of the experiences rendered when in physical reality can be directly related to the way in which the body functions and the quality of its structure. Therefore the physical body's evolution can be just as important to the Soul as the process of Ascension, since the Soul's growth depends on higher vibrational resonance and the more evolved the physical body the more evolved the experiences that foster high vibrational frequency.

We have described for you in the past how during the current Ascension cycle a majority of Human Angelic Souls will cycle off incarnations in the Third Universal Dimension and will begin incarnations on Fifth Dimensional Terra. Physical bodies on Fifth Dimensional Terra are far less dense than the ones you currently know in the current Third Universal Dimension. Physical senses are highly augmented in terms of perception, and there is an innate ability to use thought and energetic perception in understanding themselves, their Soul's mission for the lifetime, as well as the Soul mission of those around them. This is understandable considering that physical life in the Fifth Universal Dimension is focused in the Fifth Dimensional Sublevel or Fifth Astral plane of that Dimension. (See Chapter Six: The Fifth and Sixth Dimensional Sublevels of the Third Universal Dimension: The Astral Realm of Healing and the Astral Realm of Perceived Heaven)

Perception such as that available to Fifth Dimensional Human Angelic Beings is actually quite helpful in the accelerated understanding that takes place through the physical senses in that Universal Dimension. It would be the equivalent of you having strong ESP and intuitive abilities regularly available to you in your own current physical reality. Naturally, life would be easier if you had an innate understanding of what each and every person you met wanted from you, an understanding of what you life purpose was and an immediate understanding of what everyone else's Soul purpose was as well. At the least you will agree that survival might be far less taxing if you knew in advance the daily direction of the Stock Market, which sports team would win or lose or the inner most needs of your boss without it being directly expressed to you.

While this is not to imply that these are actual things on Fifth Dimensional Terra at all, it is simply to explain that physical senses facilitate growth. Having the proper vehicle with the ideal sensory and other traits needed for experiencing physical life is an important consideration, one that evolves as consciousness itself evolves. Similarly, individuals not prepared for such advantages, such as might be the case with younger Souls, would not know what to do with such advanced senses, other than to perhaps use them for occasional party tricks.

The most important aspect to understand with respect to this is the fact that societal, cultural and even physical norms related to the

Human Angelic physical body on Third Universal Dimension Earth will always be subject to and in keeping with the consciousness and growth that is prevalent at the time a Soul is incarnating. Incarnation into a physical body within a specific time, place and, subsequently, form has much to do with the goals a Soul sets out to achieve for that lifetime. Learning the management and innovations of a particular space-time physical body can be as much part of the experience as the Soul's actual intentions and mission for the lifetime.

With respect to the specific seedings related to the creation of physical bodies that we have mentioned, we would be remiss if we did not mention that much of this can also be related to Soul group development, and many cultural standards and norms can be based on the physical body or vehicle used at the time. Slight genetic differences in various populations are sometimes involved in mass consciousness and the types of events that are manifested by specific groups of human beings in physical reality. Naturally, these are related to Soul group choices for purposes of growth, and to create opportunities for potential growth amongst all Souls as a result of the slight biological or other differences.

It should be noted that even among Human Angelic Souls, there are a variety of diverse groups and cadres, as we have identified already. Usually, these cadres, no matter how diverse or feuding they may appear to be during the physical lifetimes, are related Soul groups that are cooperating together even in their diversity for the purpose of creating opportunities for social, cultural and racial change in the Soul species overall.

In a certain manner, all forms of discrimination are the result of Soul manifested situations to assist the groups concerned to grow through such experiences and ultimately understand the unity of humanity. Failure to do so generates the need for karmic balancing, and through such balancing it is hoped that diversity and unity are achieved once and for all. Those who refuse such guidance, or who resist these opportunities for growth are young Souls indeed, and they will generate the need for further karmic balancing that will be met at one point on the timeline or another. Usually, this includes challenging lifetimes on the Soul's Wheel of Creation where they are in fact the very kind of person, ethnic or cultural group they resist or fear.

Distinct differences in terms of nationality and culture within your historical timelines and races are mostly based on this. Similarly, it is why it may appear as though lifetimes reincarnate together over and over again in a variety of close familial relationships, or in a larger sense, in terms of ethnicity, religious affiliation or culture. To be clear, these differences, whether they are societal, cultural or race related are usually linked to specific points on the timeline as well as periods when there is a specific shift in the development or prominence of one or another type of physical body. Once again, the reason for this is to achieve situations and opportunities for maximum growth of the Soul through the lifetimes being experienced.

With regard to this, younger Souls do tend to congregate and incarnate within specific social and cultural structures in physical reality at particular points on the current timeline. This is because older Souls are less in need of these types of experiences. Older Souls and higher consciousness Beings are more adept and comfortable with living independent lifetimes where thought and intention replace the focus on physical traits. As a result, experiences based on an over emphasis of the physical body, its genetic components or its cultural

438

and racial affiliations are not as important. Having a degree of high personal independence and separation from social and cultural norms tends to be a prerequisite and sign that the Soul is preparing to cycle off incarnations in that particular Universal Dimension.

Ironically, Human Angelic Souls in the Third Universal Dimension will soon find many more opportunities for growth related to new co-operation rather than disharmony based on cultural, racial or societal associations and considerations. As we have mentioned in the past, the physical bodies of Fifth Universal Dimension incarnates do not have racial distinctions and all Human Angelic Soul lifetimes in physical incarnation on Terra appear to be multi-racial or multi-cultural. A trend towards one unified race through mixed ethnicity and a singular global culture is in fact a precursor on Third Universal Dimension Earth of what will be experienced in life on Fifth Universal Dimension Terra.

In fact, we would emphasize that the current disharmony and racial tensions on Third Universal Dimension Earth are in fact meant to create opportunities for Soul groups still incarnating on Earth to overcome such division in preparation for lifetimes in the Fifth Universal Dimension. Having said that however, there will be baby and young Souls remaining in incarnations on Third Dimensional Earth whose mottos will remain, "Me, and others like me." Any turmoil being generated is directly linked to these younger Soul groups, who are generating karma that will be met over the course of their journey through the coming Ascension cycle and after the great reset, where the bulk of their incarnations will play out.

One additional thought with respect to physical body genetic variations and the continuation of the physical body relates to the familial ties you enjoy. Although cultural and national groups may have a close connection in a broader sense to large Cadres of Souls, familial groups also exist and a smaller finite number of Souls who may be twin Souls or Soul Task Mates tend to incarnate lifetimes and Wheels of Creation in conjunction with each other regularly. Surprisingly, these Souls incarnate together by using the physical bodies that are procreated inside specific genetic and familial ancestry lines.

While this is not uniquely the case, up to fifty percent of a Soul's Wheel of Creation incarnations in any given Ascension period can be through physical Beings that are somehow genetically related with direct familial or ancestral ties. It is for this precise reason that pro-creation is the focus of so many religious organizations, and this could even be said to be an underlying basis for the struggles around abortion. We would suggest that without understanding the true reasons for such strongly held beliefs, these individuals and organizations are unconsciously attempting to protect the idea of lineage and procreation, which turns out to be an important aspect of Soul reincarnation for younger Souls.

You may in fact not only be related but actually share your Soul with your mother, father, grandfather, grandmother or even you great, great grandfather or grandmother. Similarly, a Soul Task Mate might share the Soul that incarnates as your spouse, your sibling, your grandson, your granddaughter or your great, great grandson or daughter. This aspect of incarnation and reincarnation is actually intended to not only better the physical body over time but is also intended to assist with the availability of physical vehicles for incarnation by specific Souls at various points on the timeline.

It is for this reason that as you may have heard, the genetic composition of your ancestors carry not only the genetic components but actual cellular memories, which include the actual emotions and impact of what is experienced, imprints if you will of experiences carried from generation to generation. In this way, for the purpose of growth specific Human Angelic Soul groups are regularly updating, reinvestigating, refueling and reworking the many actual events that have taken place in the past or similarly that take place in the timeline's future.

Furthermore, this facilitates karmic balancing on the Soul's Wheels of Creation and continues the growth experience from generation to generation. Additionally, a Soul's specific growth can be aligned with opportunities to expand consciousness and vibrational fields not just through one lifetime, but through numerous lifetimes gathered together as a whole.

Continuity of experience and Soul growth, whether it comes from a genetic component or through cellular memory, in a sense accelerates the Soul's overall progress. Passing learned information on genetically means that subsequent generations are always reliving and re-experiencing the growth achieved over sometimes hundreds and even thousands of years. It is no small irony that the phrase "Sins of the Father" has been coined since this is one direct manner by which a Soul grows and a lifetime's experiences can be shared, reinforced or re-experienced in the event new adventures are necessary along the same line of growth.

Conclusion

The biological connection between the Soul's physical vehicle and the Soul itself is one that is profound and links at the cellular level the physical body and the metaphysical planes of reality for the Soul. Because of that, there is perhaps a much more important connection between the physical body and the Soul than what is really understood. Happily, many in your physical reality believe in the concept of higher guidance, and we confirm that guidance is in fact an important aspect of every incarnation and each physical existence.

What might not be clear however, is the distinction between higher guidance from your Soul, which commonly communicates with you daily through your DNA and is cellular in nature, and the guidance that comes directly from higher dimensional guides and related Beings. Then there is the guidance that comes from those related to you in the Astral realms that are not incarnated with you in physical life currently. There are also those Guides such as us, who communicate with you through available avenues and attempt to provide higher levels of consciousness and awareness. We do so in the hope you will utilize discernment in making your life choices in order to lessen your challenges and burdens. Indeed, guidance in each Universal Dimension abounds if one knows where to look for it.

Aspects of cellular guidance should not be diminished in importance and this is perhaps the smoothest and most proficient form of guidance you receive on a daily basis in physical reality. DNA acts as a vital communications link with your Soul, providing not only cellular information exchange, but also exchange with respect to your Soul's purpose and mission for you within the physical environment, against the backdrop of parameters created around you for the purpose of Soul growth and enlightenment.

We have explored with you an in depth look at how lifetimes formulated by your Soul act as vehicles for Soul growth and Ascension. Ultimately, these lifetimes correlate to create an identity for the Soul as it journeys through each Universal Dimension. As it does so, it casts out reincarnations of itself organized independently on Wheels of Creation that interact, balance and work each with the other until such time as the Soul reintegrates with them at the highest levels of the Universal Dimension. The union of the Soul and all the lifetimes it represents brings about the levels of consciousness and vibrational resonance that enables Ascension, the evolutionary process that allows the Soul to ascend to the next Universal Dimension.

If you were to look at this from an outside perspective, you would see the Soul orchestrating cycles of lifetimes, organized on Wheels that spin in unison within the time-space continuum that defines the Universal Dimension you are in. From that broad perspective you would see Wheels within Wheels within Wheels, all interconnected and rotating in continual fashion and evolving as they proceed, pushing the entire arrangement higher and higher. (See Page 448, Figure 2 of Diagrams in the Appendix.) Through the continual motion and universal spin of Wheels of Creation within Wheels of Creation, the multidimensional Universe propels each individual, every Soul, each Universal Dimension, each Soul race and species, every Soul group and Soul cadre, every planetary body and each Galaxy forward into a never ending Ascension and evolutionary expansion that culminates in the concept of All That Is.

However you envision or define it, the expedition of your Soul through Reincarnation, Transmigration and Ascension is a glorious

443

and magnificent journey. And as a part of the extraordinary story of your Soul, you and all the lifetimes that are also you, by virtue of your Soul, are carried across vast stretches of time and space, through a multitude of diverse experiences in many different dimensional realities. This is the multidimensional miracle of your Soul's journey as it charts the marvelous evolutionary process of which you are part in an ever-expanding Universe that has no beginning and no end.

Appendix

Diagrams

Figure 1

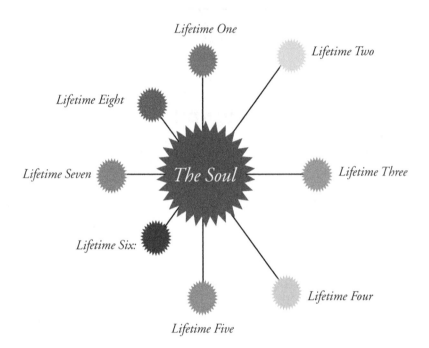

A Soul's Typical Wheel of Creation or Reincarnation Cycle Created within a Universal Dimension
(Using Earth, Human Angelic Souls and the Third Universal Dimension as a Model)

Figure 2

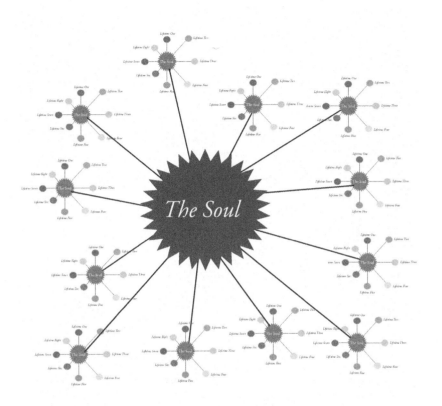

A Soul's Many Wheels of Creation and Reincarnation Experiences within a Universal Dimension*

*A Soul can have many Wheels of Creation, each with numerous lifetimes contained within it. Lifetimes within a Wheel of Creation are connected dynamically, and what happens in one reverberates in others connected to it; Karmic balancing and bleed-through can occur. Each lifetime progresses naturally and will include the journey through all Sub-levels of a Universal Dimension, including the Astral realms. Note: For demonstration purposes. Even though consistent numbers of lifetimes and Wheels of Creation are pictured, there is no set number of lifetimes a Soul can create on a Wheel of Creation, and no limit as to how many Wheels a Soul may create within any particular Universal Dimension.

Figure 3

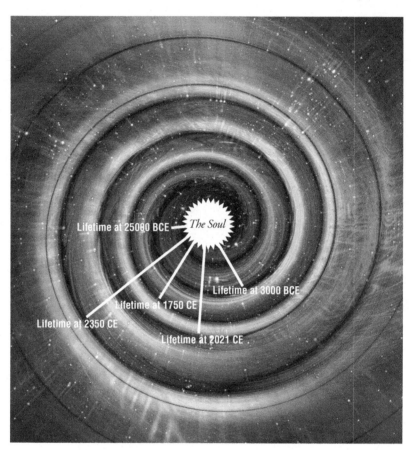

A partially reconstructed Wheel of Creation on the Universal Dimension's Space-time Wave demonstrating, as an example, that a Soul's life incarnation (reincarnation) in 25,000 BCE in Atlantis can have close proximity and a relationship to lifetimes on the Soul's Wheel in 3000 BCE in Egypt, 1750 CE during the Age of Enlightenment, in the current time period of 2021, or in the linear future in 2350. (Note: For demonstration purposes and not drawn to scale.)

Figure 4

The Twelve Greater Universal Dimensions

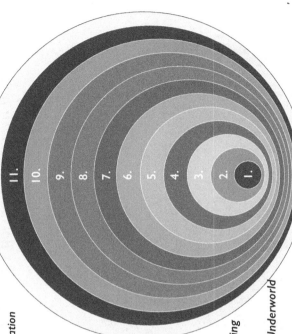

12. The Divine Dimension, Primordial Source of Souls & all Creation

11. The Dimension of Spiritual Reunification with All That Is

10. The Dimension of the Arch Angels & Sons of God

9. The Dimension of Universal Avatars & System Lords

8. The Dimension of the Akashic Universal Records

7. The Dimension of Celestial Guides & Guidance

6. The Dimension of Perfection & Peace

5. The Dimension of Healing Consciousness

4. The Dimension of Etheric Being

3. The Dimension of Emerging Consciousness & Sentient Being

2. The Dimension of Devic & Elemental Being

1. The Dimension of Planetary Being, Solar Systems & the Underworld

"The Ultimate Purpose of the Universe (the God Force or All That Is) and everything in it, is to achieve greater states of perfection through a continual expansion of Consciousness derived through the process of Ascension, forever and without end."

Figure 5

The Third Universal Dimension's Twelve Dimensional Sublevels and Astral Realms

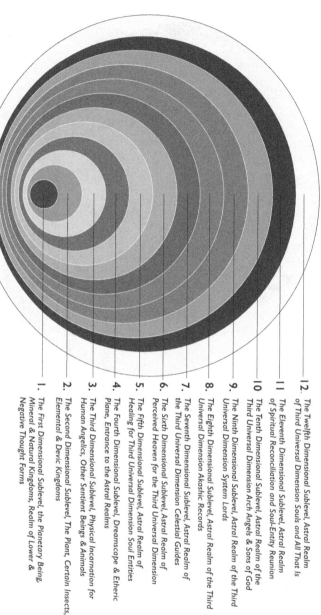

12. The Twelfth Dimensional Sublevel, Astral Realm of Third Universal Dimension Souls and All That Is

11. The Eleventh Dimensional Sublevel, Astral Realm of Spiritual Reconciliation and Soul-Entity Reunion

10 The Tenth Dimensional Sublevel, Astral Realm of the Third Universal Dimension Arch Angels & Sons of God

9. The Ninth Dimensional Sublevel, Astral Realm of the Third Universal Dimension System Lords

8. The Eighth Dimensional Sublevel, Astral Realm of the Third Universal Dimension Akashic Records

7. The Seventh Dimensional Sublevel, Astral Realm of the Third Universal Dimension Celestial Guides

6. The Sixth Dimensional Sublevel, Astral Realm of Perceived Heaven for the Third Universal Dimension

5. The Fifth Dimensional Sublevel, Astral Realm of Healing for Third Universal Dimension Soul Entities

4. The Fourth Dimensional Sublevel, Dreamscape & Etheric Plane, Entrance to the Astral Realms

3. The Third Dimensional Sublevel, Physical Incarnation for Human Angelics, Other Sentient Beings & Animals

2. The Second Dimensional Sublevel, The Plant, Certain Insects, Elemental & Devic Kingdoms

1. The First Dimensional Sublevel, the Planetary Being, Mineral & Natural Kingdoms, Realm of Lower & Negative Thought Forms

Figure 6

The Twelve Dimensional Sublevels and Astral Planes of The Third Universal Dimension
(Based on Human Angelic Soul Incarnations Originating at the Third Sublevel of the Third Universal Dimension)

12. The Realm of Divine Unification: Final Soul reintegration & preparation for the Soul's Ascension to the Next Universal Dimension

11. The Realm of Reconciliation: Reintegration of a Soul with all its lifetimes experienced within the Universal Dimension

10. Realm of the Arch Angels & Sons of God: Guidance for the reconciliation of a Soul with all its lifetimes during a Universal Cycle

9. Realm of the System Lords: Spiritual Plane Associated with the Ninth Universal Dimension Avatars and System Lords

8. The Akashic Realm or Akashic Records: Karmic Balancing and Understanding of your connection to your Soul's Wheels of Creations

7. Realm of Celestial Guidance and True "Celestial Heaven": Adopting the Light Body and awareness of your connection to the Soul

6. The Astral Realm of "Perceived Heaven": Plane of heavenly reflection providing you with your highest ideals based on life achievements

5. The Astral Realm of Healing: The plane of healing for entities after achieving awareness and orientation following Physical Death

4. The Etheric Plane: Entry to the Astral State following Physical Death; Associated with Dreamscape and the Subconscious

3. Physical Incarnations of Human Angelics, Animal Species and other Sentient Beings in the Third Universal Dimension

2. The Plant, Elemental & Devic Kingdoms

1. The Earth, Mineral & Underworld Kingdoms

EARTH IN THE THIRD UNIVERSAL DIMENSION

The Universal Dimensions with their
12 Sublevels: Human Angelic Physical
Density & Celestial Incarnations through
the Ninth Universal Dimension

Figure 7

Twelfth Universal Dimension.

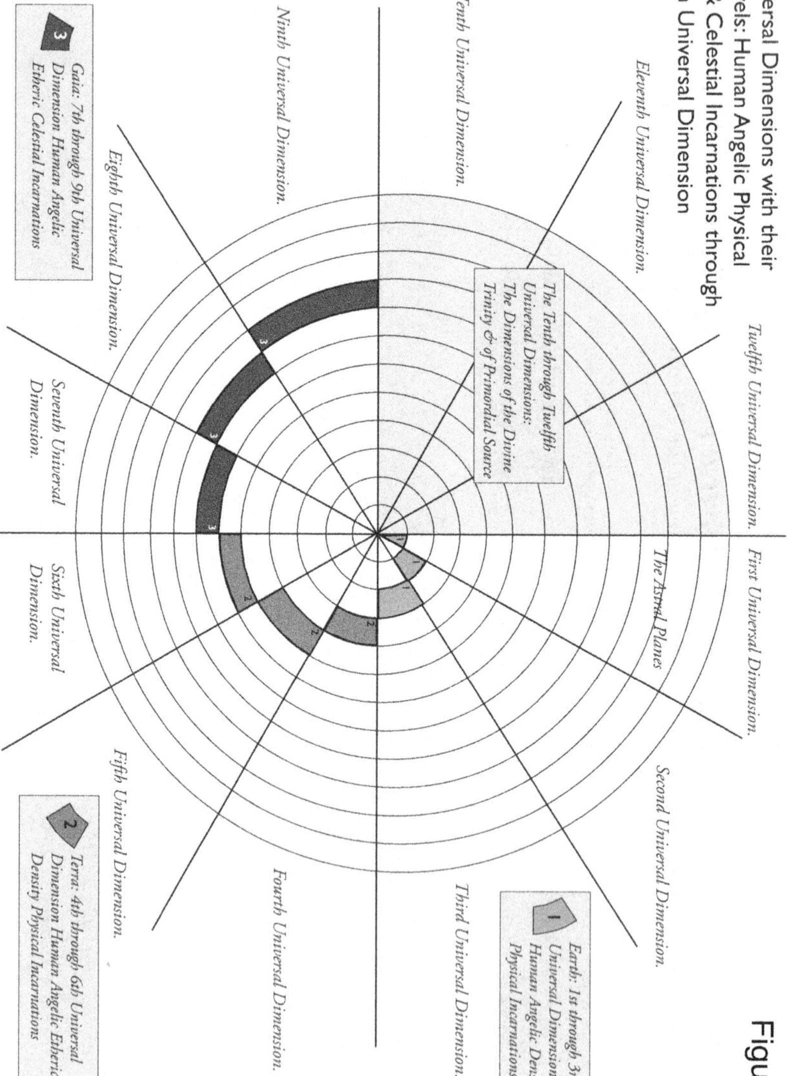

First Universal Dimension.

The Astral Planes

Second Universal Dimension.

Third Universal Dimension.

Eleventh Universal Dimension.

Tenth Universal Dimension.

The Tenth through Twelfth
Universal Dimensions:
The Dimensions of the Divine
Trinity & of Primordial Source

Ninth Universal Dimension.

Eighth Universal Dimension.

Seventh Universal
Dimension.

Sixth Universal
Dimension.

Fifth Universal Dimension.

Fourth Universal Dimension.

3 Gaia: 7th through 9th Universal
Dimension Human Angelic
Etheric Celestial Incarnations

2 Terra: 4th through 6th Universal
Dimension Human Angelic Etheric
Density Physical Incarnations

1 Earth: 1st through 3rd
Universal Dimension
Human Angelic Dense
Physical Incarnations

Figure 8

The Soul's Journey of Life Reincarnations through the Twelve Universal Dimensions and their Twelve Dimensional Sublevels and Astral Realms

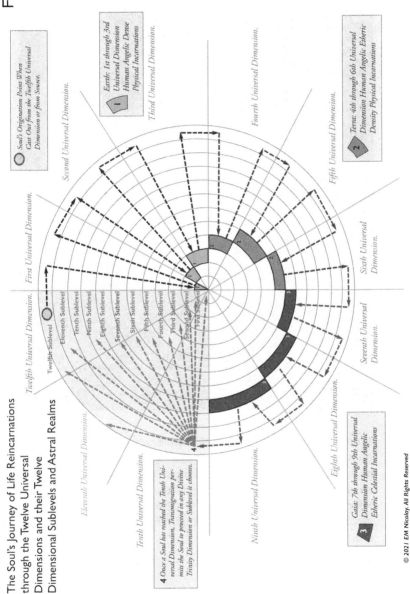

Soul's Origination Point When Cast Out from the Twelfth Universal Dimension or from Source.

1 — Earth: 1st through 3rd Universal Dimension Human Angelic Dense Physical Incarnations

2 — Terra: 4th through 6th Universal Dimension Human Angelic Etheric Density Physical Incarnations

3 — Gaia: 7th through 9th Universal Dimension Human Angelic Etheric Celestial Incarnations

4 Once a Soul has reached the Tenth Universal Dimension, Transmogrification permits the Soul to proceed in any Divine Trinity Dimension or Sublevel it chooses.

First Universal Dimension.
Second Universal Dimension.
Third Universal Dimension.
Fourth Universal Dimension.
Fifth Universal Dimension.
Sixth Universal Dimension.
Seventh Universal Dimension.
Eighth Universal Dimension.
Ninth Universal Dimension.
Tenth Universal Dimension.
Eleventh Universal Dimension.
Twelfth Universal Dimension.

Twelfth Sublevel
Eleventh Sublevel
Tenth Sublevel
Ninth Sublevel
Eighth Sublevel
Seventh Sublevel
Sixth Sublevel
Fifth Sublevel
Fourth Sublevel
Third Sublevel
Second Sublevel
First Sublevel

Figure 9

Universal Structure, including Universal Dimensions, the Dimensional Space-Time Wave, Galaxies, Solar Systems and an individual's personal energetic vehicle (or Merkaba), is based on electromagnetic "spin". Here the Fireworks Galaxy (NGC 6946), which bears close resemblance to the Milky Way Galaxy, demonstrates a spiral formation that generates spin, the essence of creation.

Image Credit: NASA/JPL-Caltech

Figure 10

Black Holes are Interdimensional Portals, drawing in used energy particles in a Universal Dimension and returning them to the Source of all creation, "All That Is" (the God Source), for renewal and regeneration. (Note the electromagnetic "spin" motion visible around the Black Hole.)

Image Credit: NASA/JPL-Caltech

APPENDIX

OTHER ESSENCEPATH BOOKS

The Samuel Sessions:

A Collection of Sessions, Essays, Transcripts and Revelations for achieving Higher Spiritual Guidance, understanding the nature of the Multi-Dimensional Universe and discovering your EssencePath

"You are principally spiritual beings having a physical experience. As such, you are also multi-dimensional, and the being you really are resides simultaneously in numerous dimensional frequencies or vibrations. It is unfortunate that because of your physical life focus and the subsequent necessity of physical limitation, you forget that your true origination is multi-dimensional in nature. However, because of the energy that is coming into the world at this time, you are once again able to sense, to realize and to discern the fact that you are in truth an extension of a spiritual being that has simultaneous projections of itself in many other universal realities."

This book, *The Samuel Sessions* brings unique insights to awaken us to our full potential and provide the keys needed to unlock vast mysteries, including a truer vision of the Universe, the real story behind a Soul's extraordinary journey through the Twelve Universal Dimensions and a look into your own relationship to your Higher Self and your guides. Join us as light is shed on the reasons we are currently facing upheaval and transition in a world that is passing through the current period of Ascension, an ancient evolutionary process natural to all Universal beings, time-space waves and celestial bodies. *The Samuel Sessions* offers a bold new perspective on the unwinding of the current timeline and will assist you to understand the truth about how entire Solar Systems and Galaxies evolve to higher dimensional fields. This book is a vital and timely travel guide for use by all Human Angelic Souls navigating the sweeping energies of Ascension.

a FORETHOUGHT PUBLISHING *book*

www. ESSENCE*path*.com

Timeline Collapse & Universal Ascension:
The Future of Third Dimensional Earth and Fifth Dimensional Terra

"What we have attempted to explain in this book is that although history carefully constructs historic conflicts and events so they can be placed within specific regions at certain time periods, seemingly without connection, the truth from a Soul and karmic perspective is that these things are far more universal, multidimensional, ongoing, interconnected, unending, ebbing and flowing than they may appear. In fact, they transpire over many hundred and even thousand-year intervals with the participation of Souls who keep coming, going and returning, again and again, for purposes related to continuing their own Soul growth and karmic balancing."

Over a decade of telepathic work has led to the astounding revelations compiled in the EssencePath series. Book Four in the Series, *Timeline Collapse & Universal Ascension: The Future of Third Dimensional Earth and Fifth Dimensional Terra*, continues an extraordinary journey into higher levels of spiritual guidance and awakening. Part One provides us with new detailed information concerning the collapse and regeneration of the current Third Dimensional timeline, predictions concerning major world events as they appear on that timeline from now through the 26th Century, and an explanation of why there is an ever widening rift between those destined to continue on within Third Dimensional incarnations and those destined, through Ascension, to incarnate on a higher vibrational version of Earth called Terra. Part Two opens an unprecedented window into the Ascension of Human Angelic Souls with details of life on Fifth Dimensional Terra, including its many extraordinary features, and an analysis of galactic events seen on the future timeline of the Fifth Dimension.

a FORETHOUGHT PUBLISHING *book*

www. ESSENCE*path*.com

The System Lords and the Twelve Dimensions:

New Revelations Concerning the Dimensional Shift of 2012-2250 and the Evolution of Human Angelics

"The 'End-Time' tales of woe and foreboding concerning 2012 that you have heard are only relevant in that they generate fear, which closes you off from the higher vibrational energies seeking to activate your DNA and cellular structure at this time. From our perspective this is far from the end, but rather a truly miraculous turning point for mankind, Earth and the entire Solar System. Your world finds itself in a state of transformation, a transition related to the collapse of your current time line and your emergence into a higher universal vibration and new dimensional reality. It is through this process, known as Ascension, that every individual Soul, Earth itself and all worlds in the universe evolve. In that regard, you are living at an extraordinary moment indeed."

This book, *The System Lords and the Twelve Dimensions:New Revelations Concerning the Dimensional Shift of 2012-2250 and the Evolution of Human Angelics* builds on themes began in "Discovering Your EssencePath," Book One and Book Two of the EssencePath series, providing us with a more complete analysis of coming Earth changes, the reasons an intensification of energy is coming from the Galactic core and altering our Solar System at this time, the collapse of our dimensional time line, the evolution of our DNA, the structure of the multi-dimensional universe and how the vibrational quality of our beliefs, emotions, thoughts and choices combine to raise our cellular resonance. Book Three also provides an in depth examination of Soul polarity, so-called "alien" exchanges, what to expect in the coming Golden Age and an overview of our dimension's interaction with Ninth Dimensional System Lords, Avatars who return periodically to our world and incarnate in human form to facilitate momentous leaps in consciousness like the one we are now experiencing-a time that promises to be one of the most monumental periods in the history of the planet.

a FORETHOUGHT PUBLISHING *book*

w w w. ESSENCE*path*.com

Fear, Faith and Physical Reality

"*...And what's all this talk about a new age of peace, harmony and happiness? It is insight, and, in many cases, guidance related to the understanding that within the current synchronicity, where physical materialization of reality is sped-up, a world based on Faith (not the religious kind, but the kind that accepts that life's events have a purpose orchestrated and understood by your soul if not by your conscious waking self) will attract events and situations of a like kind. But a world based on your Fear will attract into it, faster than ever before, exactly what is feared. More and more, your predisposition for a lifetime wrought with endless challenge, or a life filled with peace, harmony and happiness, is directly related to whether you are aligned vibrationally with the frequency of Fear or Faith.*"

This book, *Fear, Faith and Physical Reality*, Book Two from the "Discovering Your EssencePath" series, builds on the themes began in Book One providing a more complete analysis of the coming vibrational changes, description of the coming emergence of Fourth Dimension attributes within the Third Dimension, the nature of universal dimensional overlap, the polarity of belief, emotion and thought and your relationship to the manifestation of your personal reality. Book Two also examines further the reasons mastering Fear and maintaining Faith by understanding the purpose of your Higher Self during the lifetime is paramount to a successful life mission, and how your ability to carry light (en-"lighten"-ment) at the cellular level -- a component of the vibrational signature that identifies your Soul throughout the universe -- is being increased exponentially as we approach one of the most transforming periods in Earth's history.

a FORETHOUGHT PUBLISHING *book*

w w w. ESSENCE*path*.com

Your EssencePath and Other Quintessential Phenomena

"Life can truly be seen as a dance. It is your Higher Self that is leading this dance, holding you up as you guide across the ballroom floor. When you are in touch with and accepting of your Higher Self's lead, you enter into the flow of the dance and your life is smooth and seemingly effortless. But when you refuse the lead of your Higher Self, distracted by fear and your Ego, you stumble and fall out of sync...Continue to resist, and the pull will be so great as to knock you to the ground. In metaphysical or symbolic terms, this is the dance of life."

This book, *Your EssencePath and Other Quintessential Phenomena*, Book One from the "Discovering Your EssencePath" series, builds the foundation for a unique understanding of the interaction between your Higher Self and your physically-bound self. EssencePath provides the knowledge and techniques you need to begin the discovery of your Essence, or Soul, path. In addition, Book One explores the nature of our causal reality and its relationship to thought, feeling and the fabric of life, the multi-dimensional nature of your Soul and its journey, the truth about higher guidance in the Third Dimensional realm, the world altering energetic changes we are facing and relevance those changes will have to our lives, how dreams and the astral state contribute to your reality, and the reasons why increasing your energetic vibration through higher consciousness is particularly important as we fast approach the monumental 2012 time period..

a FORETHOUGHT PUBLISHING *book*

www. ESSENCE*path*.com

Made in the USA
Las Vegas, NV
12 March 2021

19458712R00272